MISTS OF REGRET

MISTS OF

REGRET

Culture and Sensibility

in Classic French Film

DUDLEY ANDREW

PRINCETON UNIVERSITY PRESS

PRINCETON, NEW JERSEY

Copyright © 1995 by
Princeton University Press
Published by Princeton
University Press,
41 William Street,
Princeton, New Jersey 08540
In the United Kingdom:
Princeton University Press,
Chichester, West Sussex

All Rights Reserved

Library of Congress Cataloging-in-Publication Data

Andrew, James Dudley, 1945–
Mists of regret : culture and sensibility in classic
French film / Dudley Andrew.
p.   cm.
Includes bibliographical references and indexes.

ISBN 0-691-05686-2
ISBN 0-691-00883-3 (pbk.)
1. Motion pictures—France—History.
2. Motion pictures—France—Aesthetics.
3. Motion pictures—Social aspects—France.
I. Title.
PN1993.5.F7A745   1995
791.43′0944—dc20   94-15486 CIP

This book has been composed in Dante

Princeton University Press books are printed
on acid-free paper and meet the guidelines
for permanence and durability of the Committee
on Production Guidelines for Book Longevity
of the Council on Library Resources

Printed in the United States of America

10 9 8 7 6 5 4 3 2 1

10 9 8 7 6 5 4 3 2 1

IN HONOR OF ————————————————

François Truffaut

Jean Mitry

Christian Metz

Contents

Preface

YOU ALWAYS DREAM of another cinema, one gathering like a summer storm, approaching majestically, and raining on your upturned face. Such a cinema would moisten your parched imagination and root your life in life itself. Maybe you dream further, of the real consequences such a cinema might bring beyond you: to the earth and the billions living on it or to your land and people. In any case the cinema you live with day to day will never do. It belongs to someone else, to a corporate nonentity. The mirage it tenders in its better moments only makes you dream further. And you dream not of some unimaginable holographic cinema, but of the past. You dream of films that have whispered to your imagination, films that somehow delivered a horizon surrounding their own delectable experience, the promise of a world of films, a chorus of voices speaking the world as it makes sense to speak it.

The names that surface as you delve into this past resonate with moments and feelings belonging to the other arts: "expressionist," "futurist," "impressionist," "realist," "Surrealist," "poetic," or "constructivist" films. Vague yet hopeful terms, these tie the cinema to grand cultural aspirations, leaving behind the clumsy economy of ordinary movies and daily life. Most often the treasured films cradled by these "art terms" come from a past and from a place so remote as to make them nearly as imaginary as a cinema of dreams. And so it is with the cinema I am dreaming, the one I plan to evoke now in this book, a cinema whose abundant source lies back in France more than a half century ago. My challenge is to conjure something of these films and of this France, thereby imagining what the cinema has been capable of meaning elsewhere, not just what it means in these our meager days. The measure of independence I accord these films by watching them behave in the social environment of their origin is meant to invite a mature rapport between this cinema and our present time, one we can learn from and enjoy.

Poetic realism is composed of two of the vaguest "art terms" critics have applied to the cinema in their pretense to precision. Nevertheless, within the myriad conjuries of this oxymoron there lies something true about the power of the cinema, about its abstract potential and about its realization in history. André Bazin affirmed that in the cinema "poetry" and "realism" were congenitally conjugated, that there was no way of speaking of realism without poetry and conversely that no film or technique could approach the poetic without a degree of realism.[1] The degree is what mattered to him, the ratio of poetry to realism, which in the course of history produces discriminable styles and genres. On the one side Bazin wrote of the oneiric and fabulous effect of scientific documentaries about plants and animals; on the other, he praised Albert Lamorisse's fairy tale, *Le Ballon rouge*, for its startlingly objective photography.[2]

Bazin liked to remind us of the parascientific origin of the *cinématographe* in the inventions of savants like Jules Marey, glad that the cinema from its outset confounded what otherwise our culture neatly separates into facts and fables, positive science and poetic value.[3] Not surprisingly he opposed with equal vehemence the advocates of "pure cinema" who claimed an alliance with music and painting, and those for whom the cinema was only an instrument to gather and organize information. Bazin indicated another, middle route, the direction traveled by films that would ultimately be termed "poetic realist." True to the peculiar parentage of the medium, this impulse would strive to be most radically cinematic by resisting the extremes of art and of science so as to combine them as only it was capable. Bazin is just one of many critics enticed by a kind of film that encourages far-reaching aesthetic speculation while remaining a cinema of broad consumption and hence of great social significance. Unlike the necessarily restricted, elite audiences addressed by "arty" films and by scientific or documentary products, "poetic realism" vaguely addresses what most audiences seek at the movies, something that is true to life, yet more concentrated and intense than life.

Although the name "poetic realism" is seldom pronounced outright in the conversations of theorists and intellectuals, its program has been on the table throughout the century. Bazin's theories seem most congenial to it, but only rarely did he address an unmistakably poetic realist film. Importantly, his major piece in this vein, on Marcel Carné's *Le Jour se lève* (1939), was designed as a pedagogical model for those directing *ciné-club* discussions.[4] Bazin could find no better example of cinema at work in its standard conditions. The greatness of *Le Jour se lève*, and thus of the cinema, stands out in the way it provokes its "poetry" by reference to the social conditions it directly sets forth, and at the same time by the way it inflates a social conception of life to a level Bazin was not hesitant to call "metaphysical."

While Bazin's theories certainly support films like *Le Jour se lève*, he relied on them more often to gain access to neorealism, the western, ethnographic films, theatrical adaptations, and so on: modes, styles, and genres deviating from the "poetic realist" middle path I have marked out here. Nevertheless, poetic realism can gather under its name, as under some gaudy flag, a set of questions so endemic to the medium that theorists will always grapple with them. But the term, or more certainly the impulse, exists for an audience wider than scholars. To study poetic realism is to watch an aesthetic be negotiated by myriad cultural forces only one of which, the loudest but by no means the most powerful, is the intellectual. Poetic realism identifies a range of films and, more important, a function for the cinema that go deep into culture. To understand its past and its possible future—and I do not shrink from this goal—is to observe it suspended in the web of historical situations.

Poetic realism may be thought of as a general impulse in the heart of cinema, but far more important to me is its coming into phase with a culture that at a certain moment relied upon it for vision and expression. One can also watch it move out of phase, as the culture grew in different directions during the Occupation and postwar period. The result of this exploration should be a history that pays tribute to a certain moment (the Popular Front) while it examines the development, exaltation, and decline of a particular way of making and using films.

Such a film history is simultaneously a film aesthetics, even a film theory, insofar as one holds that film aesthetics (what is possible in terms of signification and value in the movies) can be examined only on the basis of concrete cultural manifestations. There can never exist a hypothetically important film style, because signification (or art, for that matter) only exists for someone, indeed for a group of "someones" we call a culture. The history of cinema and of aesthetic theory is to my mind the competition of views and practices that in specific moments have produced films and reflections upon them.

Its historical embeddedness should keep us from understanding poetic realism as an airy impulse, attractive because logical. Its vagueness suggests that it be taken instead as a complex "quantum" or "identity" made up of the mass of aesthetic, technological, social, and psychological facets that must characterize any but imaginary cinematic categories. Beyond this, a comprehensive view of poetic realism explicitly seeks to know "what cinema has been" and "what cinema might be," contributing thereby to the more abstract questionings of theorists who ever ask in their own idiolects, "What is Cinema?"

Why poetic realism? Because it beckons with a look that is at once familiar and exotic, and because, in its quiet but alluring manner, it tempts us to turn to a different era, so as to explore the possibilities of this difference for our life and for our time. For whom were these movies made? For others, surely, others I will need to summon up, but also—and this is the point—for us and the kind of spectators we might become in watching these films.

Begun as a series of independent but coordinated forays into the films and period of the 1930s, this study soon took on a perspective and a focus, even an argument. Consequently, many topics that I read and thought about have been shoved to the background or into the notes and bibliography where I encourage the reader to rummage. Industry matters were a principal casualty of my restricted view, although I am relieved to have included in the bibliography numerous monographs that delve into these tangled issues.[5] As for my filmography, the chronological appendix reveals that this book puts in play less than 15 percent of the films made in the decade, and by no means all the films I screened during my research. Again the argument—plus my feel for the material—conquered my initial urge to write in encyclopedic fashion.[6] The Appendix supplies minimal requisite information (dates when films premiered, their English title equivalents, and their directors) that otherwise would have cluttered the body of the text. It can be scanned like a flowchart of the book's concerns.

Those concerns move toward their fulfillment in chapters 7 to 9 (on realism, on the poetic, and on the incomparably important Jean Renoir). For here I treat the films that gave poetic realism its reputation and its claim to an identity. To understand these films, to comprehend their function and what I am tempted to call their portent, I devote the first six chapters to a search for relevant predispositions in the type of history I write and in the culture I write about. The final chapters test the persistence of a kind of film or film culture across the barriers erected by the Nazis in 1940 and by the modernity that replaced them in 1945. What kind of identity can a national cinema claim? What sort of existence do films, and related groups of them, claim for later epochs? Can something of the sensibility of poetic realism live on in a culture markedly different from that which produced it? To treat these films and their period nostalgically or as a myth is to treat them as both present and absent to us. It is to see them the way we see movies, as insubstantial yet unmistakably affecting. It is to look through a mist of films we can feel even if we cannot quite touch.

As for the illustrations, their corporeality introduces some texture to the mist of films we have in many cases forgotten or scarcely heard of. Occasionally chosen to seal a point made in the text, they more often serve multiple functions and have been placed in the general vicinity of the most obvious of these. Whether frame enlargements or production stills (and I do not try, and would be in some cases unable, to distinguish these), they articulate a parallel discourse to my text, playing off one another and off my words in an only partially predictable manner.

And this again points to my method. I invite the reader to enter this book as I entered the subject it treats: with a sense of one's own concerns, but a willingness to adopt provisionally the concerns of another. The habit of circling from text to illustration and back to text promotes a historiographic strategy that leads from the films to the culture for which they were in some way consequential and back again to the films; this strategy in turn inscribes itself atop that greater, hermeneutic circle that whisks us from our embeddedness in the present back to the 1930s where we search not only for the significance that these artifacts—these strange and tantalizing films—portend, but where we may equally fabricate, under their guidance and that of the period, an import for our own lives and futures.

Acknowledgments

ALTHOUGH French cinema entranced me as an undergraduate at Notre Dame, it was only in 1978 while I was teaching at UCLA that I determined to study it to the limit. In the course of routine research, I noticed in the archives there a title that startled me, *La Tosca*. This was indeed a rare print of the film Jean Renoir had begun to make in Italy with Michel Simon just after *La Règle du jeu* and that his German assistant Karl Koch had completed when Mussolini asked the French to leave. Through Alexander Sesonske, I was able to screen this film for Jean Renoir, who had never seen it. I watched this man in the last year of his life, as he in turn watched for the first time images he had shot when he was at the top of his game and was surely among the greatest artists in any medium. I kept glancing from the screen to the man and then beyond to the wall on which hung *Jean at the Hunt*, the painting his famous father had made of him in the full vigor of boyhood. A good part of the century hovered in the room for him and for me that day, and with it an astounding spectrum of sensibilities that I wanted to sort through and genuinely learn from. It made me want to write a book on what the cinema has meant and might mean, a book not about Jean Renoir but about the life of cinema in France when he was crucial to it; it was clear to me then that I would need to assimilate what I could of French culture, not just of the thirties, but of the decades from the Belle Epoque of Pierre Auguste right up to this moment I shared with his son in Bel Air, California.

The University of Iowa allowed me to contemplate such a project when in 1981 it appointed me a Faculty Scholar with extended research leave. In 1985 the university renewed its support through an invitation to work at its Center for Advanced Studies. The ambience fostered by the center's director, Jay Semel, and his assistant, Lorna Olson, beyond the amenities found there, gave this book a warm nest to grow up in. I benefited from other institutional support as well: one memorable term was spent as a Fellow of the Camargo Foundation in Cassis, France; another entire year was freed up by the Guggenheim Foundation. Well-timed grants from the American Philosophical Association, the National Endowment for the Humanities, and the American Council of Learned Societies took me to collections of materials and gatherings of colleagues I needed to visit.

As the *La Tosca* anecdote indicates, screening rare films will always be the deepest pleasure as well as the most salient form of research in this field. And so I am particularly pleased to recall the welcome I received at the Cinémathèque royale de Bruxelles from Gabrielle Claes and the late Jacques Ledoux, at the Cinémathèque nationale de Luxembourg from Fred Junck, and at the Cinémathèque française from Vincent Pinel. Ed Buscombe arranged for me to work with the competent personnel at the British Film Institute. I was also given access to films at the Museum of Modern Art, the Library of Congress, and the French Consulates in Quebec and Ottawa. As for documentation, I relied most heavily on the Bibliothèque de l'Arsenal (Emmanuelle Toulet helping here), the library of the Institut des Hautes Etudes Cinématographiques, and the British Film Institute. On this continent I found material at the Margaret Herrick Library of the Academy of Motion Picture Arts and Sciences in Beverly Hills, the New York Public Library for the Performing Arts, the French Library in Boston, and the library of the Cinémathèque québecoise in Montreal.

Scholarship requires archives and libraries, but it comes alive in discussions with colleagues. Of the many comments and exchanges my ideas have occasioned, I must mention those from Nataša Ďurovičová and Richard Abel first of all and then those from Ed Turk, Francesco Casetti, Steven Ungar, Roger Odin, and Ginette Vincendeau. In the United States Angela Dalle Vacche, Kelly Conway, Dana Benelli, and Jeff Ruoff were sounding boards. In Paris I profited from conversations with Michèle Lagny, Geneviève Sellier, Lenny Borger, Glenn Myrent, Daniel Serceau, Eric Le Roy, Pierre Sorlin, Marc Vernet, and Marie-Claire Ropars. I was also privileged to interview several people associated with French film in the thirties: Jean Mitry, Pierre Chenal, Pierre Prévert, Denise Tual, Eugène Lourié, and Jean Oser. Some of these have since passed away.

Two groups of faculty participating in NEH summer seminars that Steve Ungar and I led contributed to my ideas and their expression. Peter Christensen, Janice Morgan, David Slavin, and Robin Bates continue our discussions, years after those seminars ended. A succession of graduate research assistants, several now professors on their own, collected and organized my materials, becoming working partners in the process: Charles O'Brien, Claire Fox, Neal Baker, Jim Lastra, Janette Bayles, Sylvie Blum-Reid, Georgia Gurrieri, Didier Bertrand, Ursula Hardt, and Shoggy Waryn. Heather McKay and Anne Alfke helped ready the manuscript for Mary Murrell's editorial scrutiny at Princeton University Press—which had been convinced to take on such a large book thanks to Joanna Hitchcock, who believed it could be something special.

Composing these acknowledgments reminds me how privileged my life and project have been. To the institutions and the people mentioned here, but even more to Stephanie and our children, to Angelo Bertocci, to Donald and Christine Costello, and to those unmentioned who have been with me in a special way throughout this period, I owe the dare of trying to live up to the fullness and the imagination of the films treated here. In the dominant chord of those films, I regret the passing of these years that have been so rich for me and for the field I work in. That regret is condensed around the three extraordinary figures who died while I was writing this book and to whose memory I dedicate it—as different as they were from one another, they shared, in addition to their nationality, a passion for films and for talk about the cinema. They shared as well a generosity of spirit that touched me personally as it did so many others. In our epoch, if I can use the refrain that concludes *La Règle du jeu,* "ça d'vient rare, ça d'vient rare."

A portion of several chapters appeared, often in quite different form, in journals and anthologies previously published. I would like to acknowledge these here and thank the publishers.

> For chapter 1: B. Palmer, ed., *The Cinematic Text* (New York: AMS, 1989); translated in J. Aumont et al., eds., *Histoire du cinéma: nouvelles approches* (Paris: Sorbonne, 1989).
>
> For chapter 4: *Yale French Studies* 60 (1981)
>
> For chapter 6: *Postscripts* (Fall 1987) and *Esprit créateur* (Spring 1990).
>
> For chapter 9: *Yale Journal of Criticism* (Autumn 1990) and *Mana* (West Germany) (Summer 1987).
>
> For chapter 10: David Klemm and W. Schweicher, *Meanings in Texts and Actions: Questioning Paul Ricoeur* (Charlottesville: University of Virginia Press, 1993).
>
> For chapter 11: G. Vincendeau and S. Hayward, eds., *French Cinema: Texts and Contexts* (London: Routledge, 1990). Translated in *CinémAction* 66 (Spring 1993).

The following abbreviations appear with the illustrations to identify their sources:

BFI	Stills, Photos, and Designs section of the British Film Institute
CB	Courtesy of M. Claude Beylie
CF	The Collection of La Cinémathèque Française
MOMA	The Motion Pictures Stills Collection of The Museum of Modern Art

MISTS OF REGRET

1

Introduction: A Compass in the Mist of Poetic Realism

Poetic Realism . . .

whether good or bad,

gave glory to French

cinema and was sold

around the world. It has

been imitated abroad but,

God knows why, nobody

makes this kind of movie

better than the French.

—PIERRE BRAUNBERGER,

Cinémamémoire

OPPOSITE PAGE:
Hôtel du Nord. MOMA

1938: THE APOTHEOSIS OF POETIC REALISM

Poetic realism hails us with a most nonchalant greeting, one that few of us take time to acknowledge. Most scholars nod in recognition and then move on in the crowded marketplace where films are hawked on all sides. But if one were to stop and answer back, as I have chosen to do, and if one hoped to gain or build whatever is possible when a rapport with anything or anyone is accepted, then a process of acquaintance, suspicion, and comprehension will be initiated that might be termed a cultural hermeneutics.

There is no reason to hold an allegiance to poetic realism. Neither the name itself nor the films huddled under the porous umbrella of that name should be taken as sacred. Nevertheless, to distrust, and even to disparage the term, while following out the directions it indicates, is to proceed in good faith. It is to proceed as students of culture always should: without the illusion that our constructs are solid, and without the greater illusion that we can do without constructs altogether.

Let us summon poetic realism, then, by letting it summon us. Let us gauge the power of this kind of film in 1938, when it was at its apex, by looking not at a sublime instance but at Marcel Carné's *Hôtel du Nord*, a standard star vehicle, neither high-nor lowbrow. *Hôtel du Nord* was meant to slipstream behind the phenomenal and rather unexpected success of his previous effort, *Le Quai des brumes* (1938). Evocative locations, characters from the lower social class, a downbeat ending, and a quartet of fabulous actors constitute the recipe for both films. *Hôtel du Nord* was not to be lionized by critics the way its predecessor had been. It was too patently a commercial venture

Hôtel du Nord: "Atmosphère. . . . Atmosphère."   *Le Quai des brumes*: More atmosphere. BFI
MOMA

full of compromises, little jokes, and lapses in taste to aim at the formal unity
achieved by *Le Quai des brumes* and *Le Jour se lève*, that third "somber tale"
Carné delivered before the war.

Some of those jokes seem aimed right at the high seriousness of the style
itself. The film's most memorable line, one of the most memorable in all
French cinema, comes out of the broad Parisian mouth of Arletty when she is
tired of the way her cultured and taciturn protector, played by Louis Jouvet,
has treated her. As he leaves to go fishing for "a change of atmosphere," she
calls out in a saucy voice: "Atmosphère. Atmosphère ... bonne pêche et
bonne atmosphère." Is she spitting not just at Jouvet's pretensions but at the
studied gloomy atmosphere suffusing *Le Quai des brumes*?

Yet the success of *Hôtel du Nord* was exactly one of acting and tone, whereby
Jouvet, Arletty, Jean-Pierre Aumont, and Annabella exuded the kind of fluency
yet familiarity that characterized James Stewart, Gary Cooper, and Claudette
Colbert in this same epoch. As in a Frank Capra film, we relish the dreams of
these down-and-outers, in this case dreams of voyages and double suicides.
Beyond the dramatic contrivances such dreams lead to, we relish the social
celebrations that provide their backdrop: a first communion, a Bastille Day
street dance.

Quietude distinguishes *Hôtel du Nord* from its American competitors at the
festivals and box offices around the globe. Those raised on Hollywood fare
might have allowed the fated lovers to mumble their despair to one another
but must have awaited a dramatic surge to carry them away to their glory or
their doom. *Hôtel du Nord* withholds any such surge. It scarcely has a denouement to point to; rather the Bastille Day dance swings each character out
toward some corner to await the final fade-out. Jouvet arranges his own end,
smirking at the smiling gangster whose gunshots are mistaken for fire-
crackers. The lovers return to their bench beneath the bridge on the canal and

ponder a bleak future. Arletty packs and leaves the hotel for good, leaves it to the peculiar proprietors and guests who inhabit this milieu and make it worth our attention.

Hôtel du Nord replaces a cinema of events with one of people, language, and milieu. It asks its viewers to enjoy the ordinary interplay of social types on the ordinary streets of Paris. Of course neither those streets (the picturesque canal Saint Martin and le quai des Jemappes that runs beside it) nor those types (Jouvet as the pimp, Arletty as the whore, Bernard Blier as the cuckold, and so forth) are ordinary at all. An idealized, poeticized reality encourages viewers to measure the reach and aspiration of their own ordinary lives, to look for the picturesque details in their own homes and neighborhoods, waiting for the chance to blurt out to a friend, a lover, or an enemy their own versions of the colorful repartees and tender sentiments Henri Jeanson had written so "naturally" for the cast.

That an unmistakably commercial venture such as *Hôtel du Nord* could triumph so readily in 1938 certifies the epigraph that opens this chapter. The French did indeed know how to make dark films and sell them worldwide. Compared to the highly plotted and gaudy American cinema, poetic realism promised far more integrity. For example, it promised authenticity in its sets, which were recognized at the time for their detail, their nuance, and for the way they seemed to participate in the dialogue and action played out upon them; whereas Hollywood sets, at least those the industry lauded with awards, stood off as added attractions that the audience might applaud, as when the curtain goes up at the overture of an opera.

No one applauds *Hôtel du Nord* that way, though the magnificent footbridge on which the film opens will carry us across to a fascinating world of people and incidents. When we return to that bridge in the finale, we are satisfied that this is our *quartier*, or could be ours, and that it is worthy of our attention and imagination. Few Hollywood films of the time draw us in quite the same way,

Hôtel du Nord: "The Discourse of Sets." BFI   *Hôtel du Nord*: "The Spectacle of Actors." BFI

or were meant to. Hollywood's classic prototype of this genre, *Grand Hotel* (1932), features standard studio elegance as the setting proper to showcase its cast of stars. Exceptions, such as *The Informer* (1935) or *Peter Ibbetson* (1935), were deemed "European" in look.

Hôtel du Nord is not a classic but just a very good film produced at a moment when it seemed easy to make good films. Its quietness and poverty of incident mask its self-assurance. In the same year and in another, much more complex film, *La Bête humaine*, Jean Gabin and Simone Simon would exchange some of the most violent and erotic language and looks the cinema was then capable of, yet they would do so in an equally subdued, whispering tone, letting audiences monitor the incredible pressure underneath the sad routine of ordinary life.

Such calculated repose in even the most violent or exotic films identifies the poetic realist sensibility. It is a sensibility that flourished in France in the 1930s, involving more than the internationally celebrated directors we have mentioned. Pierre Chenal, for example, had little reputation outside the industry in which he labored. But his relentless, nigrescent *Crime et châtiment* (1935) makes one want to apologize for Joseph Von Sternberg's ostentatious version, made the very same year. At the decade's end Chenal adapted James M. Cain's *The Postman Always Rings Twice* (*Le Dernier Tournant*) with a tone of understated but general discontent that in their versions neither Tay Garnett (1946) nor Bob Rafelson (1981) would care to imitate or, for that matter, be able to fathom.

American cinema has always invested in maximum shock effects, in bursts of song, violence, eros, or language. Poetic realism diffuses such energy in a warm mist of style that mutes the sound and brightness of every effect, even as it washes over us and seeps down to the roots of feeling.

A National Project

Every identifiable aesthetic originally develops within a national context, even if it later bleeds across political borders. Thus cinematic expressionism is first of all German, and only later does it serve as an apt way of describing, among others, Eisenstein's final films. It is in this sense that poetic realism is properly identified as French.

A history of any national cinema written from the perspective of political economy necessarily tells a debilitating story, because it views the past from the standpoint of the conquerors of that past, the Classic Hollywood Cinema and its avatars. But there is more to the history of French cinema, or any national cinema for that matter, than political economy can tell. There is a cultural and psychic economy that demands another form of history, one that accesses the French cinematic mentality. A proud nation, France has always proclaimed the difference of its institutions, or at least the difference of its style of participation in institutions. In a word, it believes in its "distinction."

Claims about the special nature of French cinema continually ooze from right-wing and left-wing magazines, from official governmental proclamations, and from the announcements put out by the film industry. They establish a virtual, if phantasmagoric, axiom: French cinema may obey the laws of international economy, but it retains an inner purity exempting it from the debasing consequences of that system. Its purity is thought to descend from the hallowed traditions of literature and painting that underlie filmmaking in France more than in any other country, lending it a subtle moral edge that it has occasionally exploited against Hollywood businessmen. In addition, the cinema spreads French culture to new audiences at home and abroad.

A typically soothing response to the fear of sound film can be found in a 1929 article called "Toward a French Style of Cinema," which warns producers not to imitate American films by turning to ersatz theater, particularly of the boulevard variety. To recover its cinematic mission France needs but two elements, organization and style, both of which aim at "unity of expression," something that is practically a national instinct. What is the French style? We are quickly told: "a certain precision of contour and rhythm, a mixture of darkness and poetry, occasionally a quality of eloquence that seems to be ours alone, and above all a sense of architectural line, a genius for simple sturdy construction."[1]

Poetic realism took up this standard in the 1930s, and on a battleground of uneven terrain already staked out by other kinds of movies representing sizable economic forces. On the one hand, this new, delicate French strain asked for special attention and consideration from audiences and critics alike. On the other, these same films had to compete with Hollywood at the box office. Hence, their appeal fell somewhere between the sophisticated and the popular, an elusive target that French cinema has aimed to hit ever since the founding of the Film d'Art company in 1908, and especially since the *ciné-club* movement of the 1920s. The leader of that movement, Louis Delluc, may have been responsible for recruiting intellectuals to turn to the cinema, but he was also adamant that the medium maintain its lifeblood through connection to the lower classes. It was he who first announced that "the cinema will be a popular cinema or it will not be at all."[2]

To negotiate this middle zone, those responsible for poetic realism adopted a literary demeanor. Its very name referenced literature or, at least, literary ideas. It would be up to poetic realism to prove that serious cinema, taken with the seriousness generally accorded to literature, could at the same time be as irrefutably alluring as Hollywood films.

To define French cinema with Hollywood in mind, then, is not merely a heuristic exercise, for French cinema has developed in relation to this explicit competition. Arguments over the very invention of the medium pit Louis

Lumière against Thomas Edison, the victor determined evidently only by the chauvinism of whatever historian you are reading. There is no argument, however, regarding the early mastery of the field. The French dominated the world hands down. Centrally located, and with far more experience in international entertainment trade, they were without rivals up to World War I. Georges Méliès opened an office in New York, and, at least up to 1911, Pathé Frères distributed more films from its New Jersey offices than any of the American companies, including Edison.

But 1914 put an end to all that as it did to so much more. Four years of hostilities left the cinema business open to the nonbelligerents. Sweden and America prospered, making films in untroubled circumstances, selling them to all countries. When the rest of the world awoke from the nightmare of World War I, it found itself caught in the midst of a gentler dream spun in a land of sorcerers: Hollywood. Forever after the world would look to Hollywood as it would to any sorcerer, with a mixture of fascination and fear.

Hollywood played on these feelings, manipulating the international market to suit itself. Just consider the unilateral reconfiguration of the medium to include sound. With this stunning business gambit, Hollywood incurred the wrath of smaller industries unable to afford the required audio technology. The French were most vociferous. The cinema was their invention, or so they believed. Now a cartel of crass studio heads from across the Atlantic were intent on starving the already anemic French production. In the process the art of cinema was being permanently disfigured.

And so the period of concern to us could not start on a bleaker note. In 1929 only sixty of the four hundred films projected in France were French, and 80 percent of all receipts found their way back to Hollywood. Bringing with it both immense capital and up-to-date technology, Paramount of Paris immediately became France's leading production company. As a consequence the French populace must have assumed that the movies were a rightful Hollywood phenomenon: they routinely watched more American than French films. In contrast, although Americans went to the movies more often than the French (some twenty-three times annually per capita in this era), they most likely would never encounter a French film.

How had such a situation developed? First of all, the structure of Hollywood gave it an unbeatable advantage. A virtual monopoly held by what would eventually amount to eight vertically integrated studios kept foreign films from all but a few designated import theaters in New York. Production, distribution, and exhibition in France, on the other hand, competed with one another, permitting foreign interests a foothold. Since 95 percent of theaters in that country were independent and unchained, power lay in distribution. Subsidiaries of Hollywood studios quickly began to control distribution, pressuring theaters into exclusive deals with them. After all, they could provide Hollywood stars and spectacle. Soon second-line genre pictures began to perpetuate themselves through this system. Audiences became used to westerns and Mickey Rooney vehicles and routinely went back to see them.

And so, while their facilities and personnel were easily capable of turning out 250 films a year, in the 1930s France produced half that number. Not only was this a financial loss and a failed opportunity for idle artists, the massive importation of American films had invisible consequences for cultural identity, that is, for "French" ideology. From 1925 on an alarm decrying this situation was sounded in French trade papers, an alarm that continues to this day. A panoply of emergency strategies has been deployed. Most of these have been economic in nature: taxes on imported films and on the dubbing of films; the required employment of French personnel in dubbing; quotas limiting imports, then limiting the number of weeks theaters might play foreign films; the blocking of funds made by American companies from leaving France.[3]

Far more interesting are those textual strategies aimed at product improvement and differentiation. This was defense by counterattack, with consequences for the history of film style. Since, with its vast technical and financial resources, Hollywood was unassailable in the realm of spectacle, certain French producers introduced guerrilla tactics, launching distinctively French offerings that emphasized regional characters, dialects, tales, and lore that Hollywood could never copy or assimilate. Because the international language of the silent film exploded in 1930 into a Babel of dialects, the possibility was raised of innumerable independent fiefdoms ruling over local terrain. French stage plays, cheap to reproduce on film, could bring to a large French audience the witty and often socially attuned dialogue that playgoers in Paris enjoyed. And this dialogue could be spoken by actors the whole country had heard about but few had ever had the opportunity to see in person. From 1930 to 1934 the national theatrical genius flowed onto film in the form of farces, satires, boulevard comedies, and melodramas. Many, such as Marcel Pagnol's, were spiced with regionalisms.

A second strategy flowed from the magic words "cinema of quality," first pronounced with missionary zeal in this context of trade around 1930. With "quality" the French would dare to strike back not at regional outposts but at the center of the American power. Quality was to match up with, and defeat, the ungainly American cinema of "quantity," and not just in France alone, for this would be designated an export line of movies. Hollywood was pictured as an assembly-line factory, whereas all films made in France were thought to develop in an individual, hence more natural and human, manner. The standardized genres and studio styles of the factory were countered by the healthy diversity of French subjects, each treated in a style tailored specifically to it. As for working conditions, the alienated writers and contract performers in Hollywood were said to lack the morale maintained on French projects by talent who considered themselves artisans, heirs of a medieval guild system. Furthermore, these artisans could take pride in their devotion to a grand project as well as in their relations to co-workers with whom they formed a team or *équipe*.

Such an argument had a material basis. The absence of an integrated studio system in France meant that each film gestated as a unique venture. In 1937 only a handful of French producers were involved in more than one film, no producer involved in more than six. Hollywood studios, by contrast, turned out as many as fifty films each. Everything in a French film of export quality was built around the writer-director team who offered a project to a producer (frequently a friend). Jacques Prévert and Marcel Carné formed the most famous of such teams, but there were many others. Often an actor was included in the package, which, once under way, grew with the addition of a trusted cameraman, designer, and composer. Such teams frequently traveled together from project to project, getting to know and respect one another. This contributed to that wholeness of atmosphere that bathes each of the famous poetic realist films of the late 1930s, this and the fact that in a system of such liberty, where projects develop along lines of friendship and acquaintanceship, often the very best artisans were eager to join in. Take music, for instance: cinema attracted prominent composers like Darius Milhaud (who in his career composed 24 scores), Georges Auric (125), Maurice Jaubert (19), Arthur Honegger (40), and Jacques Ibert (29). The composer, along with the rest of the *équipe*, met frequently with the director to contribute to and share the overall design of the film.

The difference between the systems stands out visibly in set design, as we saw with *Hôtel du Nord*. When the technical shooting script is handed to the designer and properties manager in Hollywood, they outfit the sets with the backdrops and props available in the studio warehouse. Every item may be of first-rate quality, but nearly every item has been used in earlier films and few would be constructed with the current project in view. By contrast, to take an illustrious French anecdote, when Jean Renoir asked Eugène Lourié to construct the château set of *La Règle du jeu* (1939), Lourié started from scratch.

La Règle du jeu: A prop comes center-stage. CB

Perhaps the limits of the budget show; certainly the château does not have the brightly lit expanse of a Paramount set, but Lourié's château grew up around the possibilities inherent in the script and contributed possibilities all its own: a staircase to separate (and connect) the servants from the aristocrats, redoubts and closets to permit the camera its hide-and-seek game with the action. Furthermore, Lourié's wife combed Parisian antique shops in search of the mechanical toys collected by the Marquis. Indeed the role of the Marquis was enlarged once Renoir saw what Mme Lourié had collected. Its natural childbirth, so to speak, gave this and the better French films an artistic edge over Hollywood products that were doctored by specialists working serially and in increments.

How successful was this strategy? French cinema even today likes to measure its strength by the stir it creates. Box-office statistics were not even tabulated and published during most of the 1930s; so the luminous image that French cinema projected was thrown primarily by the discourse kept up by critics, journals, and official proclamations.[4] Films made for export naturally received far more critical attention than others, shaping an impressive "front" of the industry that was often disproportionate to their commercial success in France.

What is the artistic "image" of French cinema worth? Under its lure some producers were tempted to take on striking projects proposed by writers and directors looking to raise the cultural stakes of the cinema. No matter what the economic realities of poetic realism, then, its image was not only a source of pride, most critics were certain it upgraded the importance and impact of the national cinema.

ETYMOLOGY OF AN AESTHETIC

I do not believe the words "poetic realism" ever entered into the discourse of producers, distributors, or exhibitors, in the way that labels like "western," "musical," or even "neorealist" certainly did. Symptomatically, the origin of the term came by way of literature. It was conferred by Jean Paulhan, editor of the prestigious *La Nouvelle Revue française*, on Marcel Aymé's *La Rue sans nom*, a 1929 novel about a handful of forgotten people who languish in the dark suburban streets of Paris. When Chenal adapted this work late in 1933, relying on location shooting, the reviewer for *Cinémonde* declared, "This film, in my view, inaugurates an entirely new genre in French cinema: poetic realism."[5] He then distinguishes the "artificial realism" of standard cinema from Chenal's breakthrough and he links that breakthrough to a concentration of the caldron of contemporary social life seen at its most squalid but most lively.

This was a quiet baptism, very unlike the case for a movement like Surrealism. Intellectuals who knew little about cinema were apt to pay attention to Surrealist films because its name brought with it debates in both literature and painting. Moreover, filmmakers began to think of, sometimes to promote, their new projects in relation to the ongoing sense of the Surrealist mission, as though that mission were an entity one could adhere to, carry forward, and be rewarded by. Poetic realism, in contrast, commanded no adherents, promulgated no doctrine. Its name did not arise in the workplace, so to speak. It did not accompany the films associated with it, cuing the way they should be read or indicating in advance their projected import. It was in effect a fabrication of the critical establishment, and it remains so today.

A fabrication, however, is by no means a fiction. Some label was required to help sort out the increasing number of films that displayed at least a common ambition. Without the convenient genre categories of Hollywood, without a governmental body to speak for it (the only major European cinema left to fend for itself in this way), and without a vertically integrated industry (indeed without a substantial production company after 1934), French cinema appeared on screens in piecemeal fashion, only the names of stars guiding the viewer and the critic in their efforts to harmonize what they saw week after week.

One can imagine the anxiety pervading a filmmaking community that could scarcely predict what, or how many, films it was liable to bring out each year. The fact that production remained constant (between 110 and 140 films each year from 1934 to 1938) suggests that certain economic and marketing factors were quietly regulating the flow of this laissez-faire industry, but its identity was another matter. Certainly, successful ventures were repeated with variations (military comedies, for example), and producers made sure to concoct scripts congenial to the dominant presence of certain stars, whose names unquestionably served as the one reliable lure capable of catching the attention of prospective viewers. But since no single producer planned for more than a couple of films each year, French cinema developed haphazardly.

In such apparent absence of constraint, independent initiatives could sprout and take their chances. Nothing in the system could have predicted *Le Quai des brumes*, for example. It belonged to no nameable genre. Its astounding success sent critics searching their memories of earlier films to give substance to the feelings it aroused. Adjectives like "romantic," "moody," "pessimistic," cropped up. Understandably, poetic realism became a concept to latch on to.

Should it surprise us that foreign critics more comfortably identified this trend than did the French? Politics split French critics on every film, fragmenting an already fragmented situation. With a haughtiness born of the recent ascension of the Popular Front, the communist critic Georges Sadoul saluted the triumph of Jacques Feyder and Carné over German competition and even over the alluring but vapid Hollywood films of the time.[6] While he was singularly aware of the stylistic pedigree of these directors (he mentions Emile Zola, Louis Feuillade, D. W. Griffith, F. W. Murnau, and German expressionism), he was much more anxious to applaud their realist (and "antifascist") temperament. Yet other critics, and not just right-wingers, found poetic realist themes and characters puerile and evasive. Renoir went so far as to contradict Sadoul, labeling *Le Quai des brumes* "fascist," and thereby initiating a rancorous response, as we shall see.[7]

Foreign critics ignored such differences. At the Venice Biennale, for example, appearing against the background of Italy's "white telephone" genre, Julien Duvivier, Carné, and Renoir stood out for their astounding seriousness and pessimism. Meanwhile, "French films of the late 1930s became the first substantial body of foreign-language pictures to interest American audiences. In major American cities, a few little 'art theaters' sprang up to show them."[8] One after the other, *La Kermesse héroïque* (1935), *Mayerling* (1936), *La Grande Illusion* (1937), *Regain* (1937), and *La Femme du boulanger* (1938) received the New York Critics Prize as best foreign film.[9] As different as they may be, they were taken as sharing a particular sensibility, one that distributors knew how to direct to a certain class of viewers. A survey of the *New York Times* reviews for the whole decade shows not only the large number of films that played in the city (170 are reviewed) but also how highly they were valued: a great majority are praised, often for outscoring Hollywood in artistry, taste, and maturity of content and execution.[10] Especially after 1935 the *Times* repeatedly gives the impression that something about French mores, tradition, education, or language destines its better films to be serious, candid, atmospheric, and strangely dark. The review of Jacques Feyder's *Pension Mimosas*, to take an example nearly at random, speaks of "the fondness of the traditionally gay French for films of somber tragedy." *La Bandera* is praised for "its camera consciousness . . . its ability to suggest mood and regulate tempo," that makes it "possible to get behind the externals, to develop the drama psychologically, to build up steadily to the close of the chase and then with typical Gallic fatalism and irony . . . leave the solution to destiny." Perhaps most telling is the *Times*'s reaction to Jeff Musso's *Dernière Jeunesse*, since this was a rather ordinary film of 1939. Although it received little attention in its own country, the American reviewer seemed predisposed to its poetic realist tone: "A macabre, shadowy drama of jealousy and fear, with a certain somnolent attraction which we can attribute to the performances and to its director's conjuration of mood."[11]

Outside France, then, a "cult" value began to accrue to "the school of poetic realism," as it came to be known in the 1940s.[12] Paul Rotha snidely says, "French films were thought to have something to do with 'culture,' something to do with sophistication. The word most often used to describe them was 'mature.'"[13] He found this aesthetic jejune: "[These films] all focussed on the individual against a background of poverty, crime, and violence. . . . These misty waterfronts and low dives were excellently rendered and photographed, but their 'life' was a subjective one. . . . Beautifully made, sensitively acted, they were films of defeat in which the British and American intelligentsia discovered poetry."[14] Evidently large audiences in Buenos Aires and Tokyo were also drawn to this defeatist sensibility. When World War II cut off French exports, foreign critics froze poetic realism into a single, solid, and dazzling block. Even in postwar France, the politically motivated dissension these films caused at their premieres evaporated; suddenly everyone regretted "the school of poetic realism" that had brought such glory to the nation.

Textbooks and coffee-table volumes[15] could now size up its impact in an overall history of cinema. They have made the movement official by citing a small catalog of traits and a few canonized films. *Le Quai des brumes*, because of its single-mindedness and concentration, has dominated these appraisals of poetic realism. When, in its very first scene, a bedraggled Gabin shuffles down a foggy road, he evidently ushered in a new morality, a new, anonymous hero, and a new style of filmmaking, comparable to the change wrought twenty years later by Jean-Paul Belmondo in Jean-Luc Godard's *A bout de souffle*.[16] "With its moon-lit port town enveloped in fog and inhabited by symbolic people with exotic-sounding names, *Quai des Brumes* [*sic*] creates a fantastic, stylized world in which reality and imagination merge into one, but which is still essentially real and true. The most tangible quality is the sense of anxiety and finality. . . . All the elements of style are perfectly blended and balanced."[17]

The sheer gravity of this film is sufficient to attract a plethora of others coming before and after. Jean Vigo's *L'Atalante* (1934) may seem closer to magic realism, for the objects crammed within its frame convey not fatality but a liberating sense of possibility; still Vigo's only feature film confirms the movement of the best French directors away from action or intrigue and toward milieu. The same point has been made for the bucolic lyricism of Pagnol and the tragic naturalism of Renoir: even though neither fits willingly or comfortably into the poetic realist camp, their films belong to an era dominated by its conception of story and character, and by its attention to evocative physical detail. Similarly, less well known examples, like Jean Grémillon's 1930 *La Petite Lise* can now be taken into the movement; after all, it was reviewed at the time as a film that "created an atmosphere surrounded by destiny, *fatum implacabile*."[18] Thus for the historian who can make use of it, a large galaxy of films swirls around the textbook constellation of dark stars that Carné released in the waning years of the Third Republic. Alan Williams's authoritative *Republic of Images* provides a catalog of both traits and films putatively belonging to poetic realism, although he is careful to point out that "few labels in film history are as vexing," and that "it is arguably not a school. . . . Nor is it a genre, yet it is something more than a style."[19]

As for film theorists, their reach is always centrifugal. André Bazin, we have seen, was attracted to *Le Jour se lève*, because it exemplified in a supreme way that "balance" between attention to the everyday and a heightened concern for subjective mood that he felt to be definitive of modern cinema. Jean Mitry was prepared to extend this balance outward in his expansive and sympathetic survey of poetic realism. Because of its moody romanticism, Mitry mingles this style with that of Von Sternberg, Frank Borzage, and the German *Kammerspiel*.[20] He calls it an "attenuated expressionism inserted into the norms and conditions of the immediately real where symbolism is reduced to things, to objects."[21]

Mitry came to such wide-ranging ideas in the very milieu of Popular Front Paris. A schoolmate of Pierre Chenal, frequent critic for *Pour Vous* and *Cinémonde*, and co-founder of La Cinémathèque française, he was on hand to witness and publicize what he saw as the progress of French sound cinema. And so it is hardly surprising that poetic realism should take its place literally in the center of his massive *Histoire du cinéma*,[22] where it functions as a touchstone, the most indicative and progressive use of the medium in the first decade of sound. Unlike related genres of the time such as social realism, psychological realism, and psychosocial lyricism, which he judges ponderous and tendentious, poetic realism maintains contact with social experience analogously, not directly; it models social experience by means of a cinematic experience that chemically transforms whatever facts make up its climate.

Like Carné he would gladly exchange the term "poetic realism" for Pierre Mac Orlan's more precise *fantastique social*. The stories Mac Orlan concocted between the wars, *Le Quai des brumes*[23] foremost among them, were designed, like all tales of the fantastic, to engender "disquiet and mistrust" but to do so in the manner of nocturnal street photography rather than eldritch lore. In the twentieth century, our own urban landscapes exude the eerie more readily than do the Gothic settings of traditional tales of this genre.[24]

Le Quai des brumes. BFI   "Le Fantastique social."   *Le Quai des brumes.* BFI

Poetic realism earns Mitry's respect because it respects cinema, whereas propaganda, social or psychological realism, and the fantastic all commandeer the cinema to transport spectators outside the movies to some recognizable or foreign land. Poetic realism, on the other hand, promises to drive its enfolded spectator into an ever-deepening cinematic world. For this reason its impact on film history was the greater, for it developed an interplay of registers that led to strikingly concentrated effects.

In his theoretical writings, Mitry went on to hypostatize poetic realism, a term so haphazardly introduced at the time of the Popular Front. Whether specifically French or not, this kind of cinema fulfilled the dual role of the medium signaled in the title of his treatise: *Esthétique* (the appeal of the poetic) *et psychologie* (the need for realism) *du cinéma*.

The version of film history that Mitry narrates and that textbooks have disseminated brushes dangerously against both formalism and narcissism. This history of the great tradition of poetic realism values formal developments which point the way to the cinema that, in all senses of the term, "becomes us." In this process the bulk of movies fall into oblivion, since 80 films, 100 maximum, are all one needs of the decade's 1,275 to establish this tradition.

Social historians of every stripe have come to challenge this hegemonic view of the decade by opening up the full archive for inspection. To the student of popular culture these 80 films stand as a mere genre (films of "dark pessimism")[25] within the larger system of the French film industry and the larger needs served by a range of genres. Moreover, when treated as one part of the chief "popular entertainment medium" of the day,[26] poetic realism hardly fulfills the vaunted social claims made for it by the likes of Sadoul.

Shortsighted and morally anemic, this genre, like nearly all the films of the time, evaded pressing political problems and wallowed in regret. Few French films, none of them commercially viable, lifted their heads out of the sand to confront the economic depression and the fascist threat head on.[27] None of the poetic realist writers or directors came from the working class; this is evident when one tallies up the problems they fuss over (virginity, for example), problems that apply aptly to the petit-bourgeois moral code that was officially promulgated in the country but that did not keep the proletariat awake at night.

As Rotha was quick to note, because it appealed to an international and literate audience, including later generations of film lovers like us, the poetic realist canon is suspect. Berated as too lax in its "social" ambition,[28] or as too pretentious in its "cultural" ambition, poetic realism has been consecrated by a purely formal appreciation that has obliterated whatever work cinema as a whole performed in its social context.

In exploding the canon, the modern historian may appear to exercise a professional obligation to recover the entirety of the past, yet here too self-interest asserts itself. The "us" that the past helps constitute has changed even in the few years since Mitry, Bazin, and Sadoul assessed it. If today's historians are likely to emphasize the social dimension of the films of the Popular Front era, one can thank changes in the politics of academic life since 1968 or the inspiration of François Mitterrand's socialist government that came to power in 1981. To use the title of Geneviève Sellier's provocative article, after Mitterrand we all suddenly became "remarkable inheritors of the French cinema of the 1930s."[29]

But what we have inherited is certainly not everything that the 1930s tendered; rather it is what we require: a socialist vision in politics and the aspirations for the cinema it gave rise to. For better or worse, this vision and these aspirations descend from the films that made an impression so indelible it can be retraced today; that is, the films of Renoir, Carné, Duvivier, and Grémillon remain with us, not the "cinema du samedi soir." Even in their most powerful moments, these directors were not in direct touch with the heartbeat of the masses (a case that could be made for a Fernandel) or with the key issues confronting Europe (as was the *cinéma engagé*).[30] Instead their social relevance—hence, their relevance to Mitterrand's France, Sellier argues—must be indirect, through the importance of particular narrative strategies and investments. The ideological density at the heart of Grémillon's *Gueule d'amour* (1937), for example, derives from an inspired script that conjoins in the same female figure (played by Mireille Balin) both the object of the hero's desire and the representative of the cavalier upper class that oppresses him. When the enraged hero (Gabin) strangles her, his doomed gesture can be read as deeply revolutionary. Admittedly, Grémillon's assessment of his era's social problems may be partial, and his "solutions" may be escapist. Nevertheless his film remains powerful for its ingenious, yet precarious, balance of individual aspirations, social forces, and the destiny of sentiments. Sellier believes that he learned this balance from Honoré de Balzac and Zola whose aesthetic precedent allowed him to sculpt a sophisticated model of subjectivity that indirectly gives us access to a Popular Front perspective. To study a film as clairvoyant as *Gueule d'amour* is to seek to understand indirectly the social and psychological sensibility of a particular past. This may also tell us about our sensibility as we return, with nostalgia or obsession, to a former time.

We have reached the forking paths in film historiography. In one direction lies the canon, for even with social issues in mind, to focus on a figure as substantial as Grémillon[31] inflates the specific power of a certain cinema above other films, other modes of expression, and perhaps even above its culture. The danger is that "indelible" masterpieces and their auteurs are all too easily taken as transcending their era. The other direction veers toward a sociology that claims to establish (often statistically) a rapport between cinema and the social trends of the day. The danger here is that, no matter how comprehensive such a study may be, or how attentive to the myriad genres and topics of a complete archive, the social touchstone it employs neuters whatever it is that films bring to culture, reducing them to evidence, the equivalent of votes in an election or public speeches or caricatures found in newspapers.

Anyone who takes films seriously surely conceives of them as involving more than the unpredictable intuitions of inspired artists and more than the fully predictable output of a social mechanism of popular culture. For the one concerns itself with masterworks as though they were autogenetic and the other treats the movies as engendered by social forces and laws. Those who credit the cinema with having, if not a mind of its own, at least a body of works and practices, must look beyond the hypotheses of either autogenesis (in the case of auteurism) or social engendering. The body of films within the larger body politic of culture has something to say about the way we should assess French cinema of the 1930s. This is the point of departure of a team of scholars who have arrived at what they call, in the very title of their stunning book, a *Générique des années 30.*

The term *générique* refers in the first instance to the "generic" network that interrelates films by topic and theme. The authors—Michèle Lagny, Marie-Claire Ropars, and Pierre Sorlin—deliberately unknot this network and even unravel the threads of individual films in order to retie them in various "series" that model the mechanism of an industry of the social imagination. Without qualms, they manipulate the films so as to look behind them (at their staging) and in front of them (at the investment of audiences paying to see them). The series they draw up are intentionally diverse and include depictions of collectivities (such as the army), individual stars (like Harry Baur and Gabin), thematic taboos (as in the representation of the colonies), and repeated narrative rituals (the public/private reversibility of main characters). These are not formal traits but structures of representation that "generate" the figural possibilities of the films of this era. These possibilities, it turns out, are concentrated in the credits (*générique*) of each film. It is here that production hierarchies, audience fetishes, and dramatic structures stand revealed.

In modeling the unconscious system at the root of French cinema, *Générique des années 30* treats filmgoing as a repetition compulsion driven by the names of a coterie of stars. The limited roles that could be scripted for them inevitably congeal into still more limited dramatic and imaginative possibilities. Stars, roles, plots, and themes are shown in case after case to rise into the spotlight, then split apart, motivating a quest for unity that absorbs but never fully satisfies spectators. The "lack" structured in each film requires the production of further films with modified *génériques*. Thus, once off the ground, French cinema of the 1930s was virtually self-sustaining, but it was also, and for the same reason, monotone. Under the spell of an ingratiating narration that asked little from them, under the greater spell of a *générique* that froze them in their seats, spectators of the time admired, but did not enter into, the feigned sacrifices of the actors playing before them on the screen.

The ingenious critical coup of the *générique* exacts a price paid for by history, or by the possibility of historical development. Discounted in advance is the importance of variety both in films and in audiences; in this kind of structural analysis, a single mass spectator sits mesmerized before the single block of "the film of the 1930s."[32] To recover variety and change, without resorting to the kind of "exceptionalism" implied by the masterpiece approach, and without abandoning the scorching attention to films implied by the *générique*, I need to introduce another French term, *optique*, so as to give French cinema access to something outside itself, access precisely to the culture of the 1930s.

CULTURAL SPHERES AND THE NOTION OF *OPTIQUE*

In his first major book, *Le Degré zéro de l'écriture*, Roland Barthes called on the concept of *écriture* to open a wedge in Jean-Paul Sartre's binary literary theory.[33] For Sartre, literature could be reduced to an interplay of language and style: the one general, universal, and impersonal (as in a *générique*); the other idiosyncratic, spontaneous, authentic (as in a masterpiece). Barthes found this view suffocating and ahistorical. By *écriture* he meant to designate the limited plurality of literary options available in any epoch. Barthes's term motivates both my investigation into cultural history and my understanding of aesthetics as these work together to locate what was artistically or rhetorically available. Because it is dependent on cultural history, the notion of *écriture* allows for the development of movements, for shifts in taste, for competition and variety among audiences. It helps make concrete the mysterious operations of the auteur (who chooses a particular aesthetic option before contributing personal style), while at the same time it specifies the aesthetic and cultural fields within which artworks make their mark.

By *optique* I designate *écriture*'s equivalent in the domain of cinema. *Optique* is meant to retain the original structuralist connotation Barthes first intended for *écriture*, a connotation that has been largely lost after the term's assumption into the complex theories of Jacques Derrida, Julia Kristeva, and others. More pertinently, *optique* suggests the ocular and ideological mechanisms of "perspective," both of which aptly play roles in the medium of film. Finally, its position in the dictionary allows *optique* to carry an echo of *option*, of a limited set of possibilities alive at a given moment in a specific cinematic situation. Although it can be conveniently used to differentiate groups of films, in fact the most genuine application of the term *optique* as I conceive it involves the specification of audience expectations, needs, and uses.

It is in this sense that poetic realism can best be seen as an *optique*. Among types of filmmaking in France during the 1930s, it exercised the option that has most deeply fascinated film scholars and international audiences. The restricted narrative scope of these films, their heavy atmosphere and sustained largo, hamper the vision and the understanding of audience and characters alike, forging a complicity between spectator and drama that one does not find in any other type of film in that era. For example, "entertainments," whether comic or social, catered to a spectator who paid to enjoy and judge what was displayed, while historical films and propaganda were meant to impress and instruct a spectator whose applause or assent was requested. Renditions of boulevard theater successes, to take up the most ample genre of the decade, aimed to set admirable acting, dialogue, and plots before an audience that gathered precisely to admire such performances.

These representative types of films traded in different ways on spectatorial distance and discernment, be it the discerning of quality performance, or of tough political analysis, or of the pattern in a clever intrigue. Poetic realism, on the contrary, does not flaunt its talent or authority. It is, as I shall repeatedly show, and despite appearances, nontheatrical in its methods and, more crucially, in its mode of address. When examined alongside other films of the 1930s, the poetic realist text seems to invite its spectators onto the screen, seems to invite them to merge with the sensibility it expresses. The spectator plods forward hand in hand with such a film, unconscious of any voice behind the screen, be it satiric, consoling, analytic, or knowledgeable. The spectator of *Le Jour se lève* is as helpless as is its doomed victim.

Who was this spectator, and why was this somber cinematic *optique* appealing? We know poetic realism earned prestige among sophisticated audiences prepared to take some risk at the movies. Might this not be the same audience who would shortly applaud the closely related existentialist aesthetic of Albert Camus and Sartre? Poetic realism lays claim to such an elite reception by disingenuously laying itself open as a type of direct "experience." The ordinary tragedies of daily life, so deliciously repeated in such films, are not rendered homiletically as in a sermon about the poor and downtrodden, but are figured directly. Poetic realism promises to deliver not a message about frustrated desire, or oppression, or bartered hopes, or helplessness, but the very experience of these feelings.

Such an aesthetic function was neither forged by the genius of a handful of auteurs nor inevitably ground out of a mindless moviemaking machine. It owes its existence to historical and cultural circumstances that involved strong directors and the conditions of the industry, to be sure, but that, more specifically, were characterized by the particular rapport the cinema developed with renegade literary, musical, and artistic figures during the heady days of the Popular Front. In turn, the aesthetic forms spawned by this *optique* affected the standard films of the day, the other arts, and the whole cultural atmosphere. In order to find these films consequential, one does not have to believe that poetic realism helped bring the Popular Front to power (its heyday came about only later) or helped the Third Republic fall (though this is what the right wing claimed). The press they received at home and abroad testifies to their public prominence. I plan to look at both the films and the culture for the source of that prominence, practicing a hermeneutics that strives to understand the culture from the films and reciprocally that teaches us how to watch the films from the culture.

Between the high road of political history and the folk path of personal biography lies the varied landscape of culture, a landscape whose ecology features the complex and contradictory interplay of institutions, expressions, and repressions all subject to the force fields of power. The cultural historian bears, to the limit, the burden of the contested middle, by insisting on a stance between the already hermeneutic enterprises of the critic and the historian. Refusing to stop at the boundaries of texts, as do most critics, yet unwilling to seek an era's "imagination" by direct, disinterested investigation (philosophic or historical), the cultural historian proceeds, by methods of supple interpretation, to read and weigh culture in texts and texts in culture. In this way the logic of changing values can be understood as felt.

Every history that treats the cinema must calculate the importance of films within a world larger than film. From the perspective of the film scholar, culture surrounds the film like an atmosphere comprising numerous layers or spheres, as numerous as we want. One may identify these as though they successively encompass one another moving from the center (the individual film) out toward the stratosphere of political structures and events. Intermediate layers might include the film industry, film history (the tradition of genres, the biographies of filmmakers), the status of the other arts, the institutions of culture, and the organization of social classes.

My revision of French film in the 1930s derives in part from the spheres I choose to emphasize (the nebulous zone between high art culture and popular culture), but it derives more certainly from a belief in the permeability of all spheres. The fluidity of its object forces any cultural hermeneutics to abandon the hope of full command over its "material," but by devoting itself to complex interaction, it can observe disturbances in one sphere affecting the situation in another. Moreover, the direction of this interactive flow is reversible, although it is usually tracked from the top down. For example, a change of government may bring in a new minister of education or of leisure who promotes the expansion of literary journals. These journals may, in turn, promote an aesthetic that works its views on the legitimate theater. Ultimately film acting, including the kinds of roles created for, or chosen by, key actors may literally encourage a specific cinematic style, amounting to a significant alteration in the way the culture represents itself on the screen.

Cultural interaction can be treated as a continual trickle-down process from government to popular expression only in states exercising the most rigid political control. The fact of censorship is a notorious reminder of how governments themselves can be disturbed by images bubbling up from beneath the cultural surface. Who can forget the way the French ministry flinched at violent filmic discourse or at local vigilante groups whose intermediate discursive spheres might include the Church (the case of Luis Buñuel's *L'Age d'or*, 1930) or the educational establishment (Vigo's *Zéro de conduite*, 1933). Censorship is an index of the power that films evidently deploy beyond the sphere of the strictly cinematic. No history with aspirations of thickly representing an era's cinema can ignore this traffic among spheres, in this case between texts and institutional structures.

Beyond keeping all spheres actively in mind the film historian ought to identify the most pertinent sphere within which to track the (shifting) values of cinema. Pertinence depends both on the researcher and on the topic under scrutiny. Take the period that concerns us. In establishing the special relevance of a particular cultural sphere containing subgroups such as the Surrealists and the novelists published by Gallimard, I mean to challenge a study like that of Francis Courtade, for example, whose *Les Malédictions du cinéma français* examines French films within the atmosphere of official history (political proclamations, censorship rulings) and official events in the film world (technological innovations like sound, economic developments like the fall of Gaumont). In certain revolutionary eras such as that of the Soviet Union of the 1920s, Courtade's focus seems apt; the Soviet film historian ought to follow very closely the major events of public life, since cinema explicitly participated in a national reawakening. But in the interwar period of France, cinematic values were forged and debated less in the political sphere than in the cultural sphere, or rather in the nebulous zone where transactions between high and popular culture were possible. The effect on cinema of personalities from the established arts outweighs, from my perspective, all governmental and most economic pressures. And so the involvement in cinema of novelists and publishing houses, classical composers, painters, architects, and playwrights is more than anecdotally significant and is meant to do more than validate a popular art. Such involvement testifies to changes in the function of cinema and helps specify the direction such changes took. This cultural sphere is pertinent precisely because it identifies the site of development in a cinema that, from the perspective of other spheres, can hardly be said to have changed at all.

In brief, a cultural history of cinema must reconstruct the options of the times, neither through the direct appreciation of its products nor through the direct amassing of "relevant facts," but through an indirect reconstruction of the conditions of representation that permitted such films to be made, to be understood, even to be misunderstood, controversial, or trivial.

I have determined to put into focus the address of films, because, as a spectator myself, it is the films that seem to address me. By examining the event of their broadcast, the situation in which they first spoke in the way they do, one avoids the narcissism of teleological histories that force the past to submit to the rule of the present and that neatly suggest a single world of the movies.

The films that beckon us are entrances to a different way of being a spectator, not totally different (else how could we ever intuit that something lies there for us?) but different enough to tempt us to construct the spectator to which they are addressed. Thus the historian must understand not their style so much as the *optique* that makes them possible, and that at the same time models a possible world that can still be fleshed out. As a historian, I am a spectator ready to become another spectator.

2

Impressionism and Surrealism: The Origins of an *Optique*

EVERY redescription of a phenomenon succeeds in overcoming the shortcomings of its predecessors only through the help of a key concept or word that must itself remain unquestioned and in a sense magical. My word is pronounced in the title of this chapter, *optique*. Untranslated it retains an essential imprecision, throwing its arms around films, events, persons, and other elements that, when seen globally, construct a significance for the movies that is pertinent to the past and the present.

As an *optique* poetic realism encompasses more than a style or a genre, though only certain styles and genres could conceivably belong to it. By introducing aspects of cultural function and audience address, *optique* involves a plethora of heterogeneous elements that interact in making up in this case "poetic realism," embedding it in historical and cultural life. I say "embedding," rather than "dissolving," for the term *optique* credits the presentiment that what we call poetic realism is more than a concoction of the critics, that its sensibility—a manner of representing and valuing experience in pre–World War II France—can be intuited by attentive viewers from other places and later times.

As an *optique* (a sensibility, a function, and a mode of address) rather than a genre or a style, poetic realism belongs to more than the four years of its abundant flourishing (1936–1939). To explore the historical possibility of what I have called a cinematic possibility surely involves identifying elements of style or subject matter that bear a "family resemblance" to aspects of the definitive films of Marcel Carné, Julien Duvivier, and Pierre Chenal; but it equally involves the search in the years prior to 1936 for something equivalent to the particular role poetic realism assumed in its heyday. Specifically the neighboring *optiques* known as Surrealism and impressionism can be scrutinized not just for the themes and techniques that later show up in the films of the late 1930s, but for the attitudes toward the cinema inculcated by what can only be called the "cultures" of these movements.

Why not begin with a hint provided by the critics of the time? "Poetic realism" ingratiated itself with audiences through the "calculated naïveté" with which it represented life, one oxymoron fertilizing the other. In this lies both its charm and its limitations. And in this it drew on attitudes and strategies that preceded it in Surrealism, in impressionism, and in the films both these movements in turn had valued.

FEUILLADE: A SOURCE DISOWNED AND RECLAIMED

Asked in 1962 to assess the specifically French contribution to world cinema, Alain Resnais was only too happy to count himself one of the inheritors of that combination of popular instinct and intellectual mantle which I have claimed as the most salient features of the national pedigree.[1] Resnais would amend the cliché about French cinema's double parentage in Louis Lumière (realist) and Georges Méliès (fantasist). For him, as for me, Emile Zola is the name of the father of the French cinema, Zola and such popular "spiritual descendants" as the authors of *Fantômas*, Marcel Allain and Pierre Souvestre. At the very moment Lumière and Méliès were exploiting the technology of the *cinématographe*, these popular storytellers were preparing the tastes of the nation for large-scale social melodramas that employed the familiar and quotidian details of life as a lure into a world full of exciting and often disturbing surprises. Resnais singles out Louis Feuillade as "one of my gods," because he brought this sensibility into the movies.[2] This sensibility would inform the work of many of the most revered French directors and would give shape to the nation's most characteristic cinematic proclivity, ultimately labeled "poetic realism." Carné, René Clair, Jean Vigo, Jean Grémillon, Jacques Becker, and Jean Renoir form the trunk of this great tree to the top of which Resnais adds the comic Jacques Tati and among whose roots he implicates Feuillade's two antagonists of the 1920s, Louis Delluc and Jean Epstein.

Despite his reputation as one of the most coolly intellectual of directors, Resnais likes to date his own interest in the cinema from a childhood experience in 1936 with the exciting serials of Feuillade. He could not resist "in Feuillade this prodigious poetic instinct that allowed him to fashion Surrealism as easily as he breathed."[3] Regretfully Resnais ruminates, "I could have been made a member of SAF, that imaginary Society of the Friends of Fantômas which was founded before 1914 by Guillaume Apollinaire and Max Jacob."

Resnais inherited this hybrid fascination (with the popular Feuillade and with the avant-garde Apollinaire) from those Surrealists who in the late 1920s were already reminiscing about Feuillade's anarchist villains.[4] The disdain for the moneyed classes, the conspiracies and paranoia, indeed the hatred of growing up that Feuillade evinces, were perfectly tailored to the Surrealist personality and worldview. These feelings would seep into poetic realist movies when Surrealism had largely run its course.

Feuillade's impact on the industry, particularly his blending of studio decor with location shooting, had an indelible effect on French cinema. The mythology disseminated in his films shows heroes and villains surfacing and disappearing across a dangerous topography of streets, alleys, department stores, warehouses, railyards, and townhouses. It is a seductive mythology that even the impressionists drew on in their own way. As critics, the impressionists had dismissed Feuillade's serials as lowbrow, but as filmmakers they often adopted a general atmosphere of mystery and alienation hovering above modern city life. The differences between the two can be reckoned in the split personality of melodrama, the Ur-form both descend from. On the one side lie Feuillade's convoluted plot reversals, misconceived identities, and epic scope. Impressionist melodrama, on the other, reduces plot to a skeleton that protects within it a delicate motif. It then emphasizes "melos" rather than "drama," excessively

Les Vampires: Urban anxiety. BFI

and redundantly expressing the emotional significance of that motif through multiple stylistic registers.

These two distinct avatars of melodrama served two quite different cultural functions. Like ballet and opera, the stylistically complex impressionist films appealed to an elite audience, whereas Feuillade specifically saw the cinema within a mass entertainment context. It was primarily on these grounds that the Surrealists were proud to support Feuillade and satirize the impressionists. One must not forget that the Surrealists, peculiar and extreme though they may have been, traded in popular images and motifs even while proclaiming a utopian cinematic project that could only outrage a public looking for comfortable diversion.

The Surrealists hoped to reestablish something akin to Les Amies du Fantômas, perpetuating the sensibility of cutting-edge figures like Apollinaire and Pierre Reverdy who, even before World War I, had pointed to the popular cinema as the site of activity for any culture worthy of the twentieth century. Impressionist cinema they found unworthy, a throwback to old-fashioned ideas of tortured subjectivity, delicate expressiveness, and fussy images. By contrast, in their artistic production the Surrealists aimed for what today we might call hyperreal representations, claiming Jean-Jacques Rousseau and Erik Satie as forebears. Recall *Un Chien andalou* (1929). In the non sequiturs of its intertitles ("Au printemps," "Huit ans aprés," and so on), it pokes fun at the convoluted tenses and moods invented by such serious poets of the cinema as Epstein. At the same time these intertitles playfully recall the childish narrative drive exploited by Feuillade, a drive that the impressionists perverted in their allegiance to the purportedly higher aims of *photogénie*.

The Surrealists were only too glad to come to the rescue of Feuillade, who was treated with disdain by the critical establishment of the 1920s. In 1929 André Breton and Philippe Soupault paid homage to Feuillade by writing a play, *Le Trésor des jésuites*, for Musidora, the head Vampire of Feuillade's serial. This was the second script dedicated to the haunting actress; in 1920 Colette had authored the screenplay *La Flamme cachée* for the actress she believed best represented the modern era.[5] In 1932 producer Pierre Braunberger remade *Fantômas* with Paul Fejos as director. Although Fejos's film disappointed Braunberger's hopes, attracting neither support nor critical discussion, it can mark for us the idea of an integrated audience that arrived with the decade of the 1930s and the technology of sound.

Between these two vehicles for Musidora, and between the original and the remake of *Fantômas*—during the period Richard Abel calls "the first wave" (1915–1929)[6]—a drastic differentiation of audience and art function developed. Colette gave way to a new, haughtier type of critic. Intellectuals insisted on their own film culture and produced their own films. For most of them Feuillade and his virtually interminable serials (*Tih-Minh, Judex, Barrabas, Les Deux*

Gamines, all shot between 1917 and 1921) became the emblem of a mindless and aesthetically dull commercial medium. He was the target at whom Delluc aimed his clarion call for the development of a superior national cinema, led by men and women not afraid to take chances with their images and stories.

Delluc employed a vocabulary of "risk" in attacking Feuillade, concluding one barrage: "You have at your disposal all the means necessary to undertake and carry out great things. What are you going to do?" Feuillade answered in his own way: "I consider the cinema to be a place of relaxation, of pleasure, of sweet emotion, of dream and forgetfulness. Others want to make of it a temple of the abstract, the bizarre, even of hallucination and deformity. That's their business."[7]

Now the Surrealists were certainly given over to the bizarre and to hallucinations, but not so much in the realm of film form. They thought of themselves as ethnographers (à la Georges Bataille and Michel Leiris) rather than as poets. They wanted to explore cruelty, sexuality, and obsession, Feuillade's stock-in-trade. The pure successivity of the plots of his serials fascinated them. Feuillade's storytelling must have seemed as primitive as sexuality and ritual, which they also studied and furiously celebrated.

Les Vampires (1915–1916), for example, is studded with uncanny occurrences and motifs that later would show up in films by Luis Buñuel. When one of the villains falls into a booby trap as he tries to enter a forbidden room, a large nail pierces his hand. An extreme close-up of the oozing wound prefigures the ants that crawl from the center of the hero's palm in *Un Chien andalou*. The perverse close-ups of the villains' bright lips that bracket this image add to the incipient Surrealism of Feuillade's narration. Buñuel must also have been thrilled by a gratuitous flashback later in this same film wherein a bull is mercilessly killed, its carcass cluttering up the outdoor set. Such strange and abrupt occurrences, strung together by farfetched intertitles, would fuel the Surrealist imagination. Robert Desnos wrote a fabulous poetic tract called "Complainte de Fantômas" for radio broadcast in 1933, just after Braunberger's unsuccessful remake of that subject.[8] Earlier the great Surrealist poet had written a hymn to Musidora in her role as the voluptuous villainess Irma Vep: "How beautiful you are in *Les Vampires*! Do you know that we dream of you and that, evening come, in your black outfit, you enter our room without knocking and that, on waking the next day, we seek out the traces of that troubling mouse that visited us in the night?"[9] Desnos was only taking seriously what Breton and Louis Aragon spoke about in 1929. "You will understand soon enough that there is nothing more Surrealist and at the same time poetic than the filmed serials which not long ago were the joy of those strong of spirit. It is in *Les Mystères de New-York*, it is in *Les Vampires* that we must search out the great reality of this century."[10] As they all pointed out, there was hardly a street corner in Paris that was not haunted by some mysterious adventure from *Les Vampires*, making for "a complex interpenetration of the real and the imaginary, a transmutation of the lived by a transfiguration of quotidian space."[11]

Clair, the filmmaker most tied to Parisian geography, began his career as an actor in Feuillade's troupe. His first experiment in directing, *Paris qui dort* (1924), tells a tale worthy of Feuillade in which a mad scientist holds the hypnotized metropolis hostage. In *Entr'acte* (1924) Clair's debt to Feuillade is visible in the animated cannon that fires on Paris, a motif lifted directly from the Marseilles adventure of *Les Vampires*. But the most memorable images linking these two filmmakers are surely the haunting silhouettes that both photographed of outlaws scurrying across the distinctive rooftops of Paris. Climbing down rainspouts, Feuillade's vampires create the kind of futurist designs Clair was only too happy to emulate in *Le Million* (1931). Tellingly, it was not until the end of his life that Clair deigned to credit Feuillade as a master, and to deprecate the chic avant-garde in which he himself had participated.

> The young filmmakers of the period [the 1920s] were not at all interested in the popular vehicles manufactured by the prolific author of *Judex* whom they spoke of with some disdain. But what can be predicted? Today the esthetic experiments of that era are forgotten or no longer arouse much interest, whereas film societies show *Fantômas* or *Les Vampires* to respectful houses. Louis Feuillade was not that wrong: his works still have an audience and a particularly alert audience! That would really have surprised Louis Delluc and his friends (that is it would truly have surprised *me*), if some fortune teller had predicted it to them.[12]

This is not to say that Feuillade's technique of narration was ahead of its time. On the contrary, its premodern tenor is precisely what attracted the Surrealists who wanted to recover the pure possibilities of cinematic astonishment that had been bartered away by the sophisticated cinéastes of the 1920s. His scenes, shot in ordinary locations, take no shortcuts, but inch forward predictably until they reach a culminating moment in some memorable tableau. In the final scene of the first half of *Les Vampires*, for example, the wealthy of Paris have come dressed in their finest to a ball; suddenly fumes can be seen seeping up from the floorboards. Noblemen lose all decorum in fighting their way to exits. Naturally they find these locked. The Vampires' greatest victory, gloriously photographed in longshot, calls to mind newspaper drawings of the disastrous Bazar de charité of 1897 wherein 140 well-to-do Parisians lost their lives in a cinema fire.[13] The first audiences of *Les Vampires* must have looked around uncomfortably as the lights went up.

Feuillade found in hypnosis an even better way to unnerve his spectators, by showing how readily an alien control can, through concentrated vision, utterly take over an innocent person. An engaging scoundrel named Moreno

Les Vampires: The Vampires' greatest victory. BFI

hypnotizes a cohort. Then at the Gaumont Palace our hero Philippe intently watches a newsreel of a burial at Fontainbleau after a shocking assassination. Gradually the diegetic screen grows to full frame, as the Grand Vampire he has been tracking seems to stare directly at him from the graveside. Instantly now Philippe appears on the scene at Fontainbleau, as though sucked into the screen. What an allegory for hypnosis and for storytelling too! André Bazin put it best after experiencing a marathon screening, without intertitles, of *Les Vampires*.

> This story, the meaning of which was a complete mystery to the audience, held its attention and carried it along purely and simply by the tension created in the telling. There was no question of a preexisting action broken up by intervals, but of a piece unduly interrupted, an inexhaustible spring the flow of which was blocked by a mysterious hand. Hence the unbearable tension set up by the next episode to follow and the anxious wait, not so much for the events to come as for the continuation of the telling.[14]

Bazin points to something apt. The sheer size of these narratives, requiring hours and hours (actually weeks and weeks) to unravel, confers on them a stature that supports the institution of storytelling beyond any given episode. Off and on *Les Vampires* acknowledges this contract. Marcel Levesque mugs directly to the audience on numerous occasions and in doing so he gains our affection not just for his clownish character but for the storyteller as well. At the same time, such gestures assert the theatrical origins of melodrama. In one of the tale's most charged moments—when Irma Vep at last lays her hands on the lost treasure map—she winks twice at the audience to signal her success. As was the case with many Film d'Art productions and other French silents, the set design underscores its rapport with theater. Several important scenes that pit characters in adjacent rooms are shown in cross section, dollhouse fashion, so that we see both spaces bisected by the interposing wall. One of these scenes has the villain peep through a hole in the wall at a young boy who hides himself in the adjacent room. We observe the observation.

Les Vampires: Haunting silhouettes. BFI   *Les Vampires*: Generating paranoia. MOMA

Playing, like Alfred Hitchcock, with the spectator's knowledge diminishes Feuillade's ability to render character subjectivity. His serials generate paranoia by marshaling evidence (inserts of newspapers, maps, and diagrams) and by testing explanations of an evil so pervasive that it seems beyond the powers of civilization to comprehend and control. Poetic realism will express much the same incomprehension before its dark world, but this time from the restricted point of view of a single, ignorant character.

While it developed a completely different mode of narration from Feuillade's, poetic realism inherited his ingenuous way of employing settings to suggest the stable qualities of the characters living there and the dramatic surprises that put those characters in danger. The home apartment of the journalist hero of *Les Vampires*, for example, is replete with bourgeois appurtenances, offering both him and us a place of refuge and rationality. Here he collects his evidence and makes his plans. Feuillade employs a box set here and in other places that serve a similar function, such as hotel rooms and police offices. The simplicity of the staging allows our eyes to rest after the unpredictability we are subjected to on the streets and in public places. The camera setup in these scenes never varies, with the journalist sitting at his desk directly before us in the front plane, writing up a report, talking on the phone, or poring over the facts. This tableau recurs at regular intervals to punctuate the plot and to permit us to assess the complexity of his dilemmas and to consider possible measures yet to be taken. Moreover, the stability of the composition works like a musical motif that becomes increasingly familiar. It is as comforting as the chair where the journalist sits in his dressing gown. But even these privileged spaces of rationality are never utterly safe. The enemy, disguised as a servant, or hidden behind a retractable wall, or dangling down from the roof, can always appear. The ubiquity of evil makes us scrutinize the details of even the most innocuous compositions. Someone may be peering through a painting on the wall. The floor may be booby-trapped.

Feuillade's taste for simple compositions, repeated gestures, and reused sets naturally serves the economy of a complex filmmaking project. Beyond this, such simplicity results in an aesthetic gain by challenging the viewer to read the moral contour of this universe. The obvious anagram making "Irma Vep" the leader of the "Vampires" encourages us to look twice at billboards and other signs in the city. More important still, the repeated sets and gestures are timed to satisfy a need for sameness and novelty that defines the literary mode of the *conte* that Bazin alluded to in his homage to this film. When the repeated motifs are visually evocative as well—for example, a gently curving street down which a man may flee on bicycle or a lone automobile may carry a kidnapped victim—the film's epic quality stands out and with it the poetic genius of Feuillade.

Georges Franju, whose remake of *Judex* opened in 1964, understood completely Feuillade's importance for later developments in film style:

> Precursor of fantastic realism, Louis Feuillade has remained unique. He left on me the impress of a magic that was black, white, and silent . . . an orthochromatic magic, a poetry, an aesthetic unalterable in time. . . . In his shots where nothing happens, something can occur that profits from this nothing, this inaction, this void and silence, something that profits precisely from the waiting, from inquietude. This something is called mystery.[15]

The "Milieu" of Impressionism

Would any cinéaste of the 1930s have recognized Feuillade as a "precursor of fantastic realism"? Jacques Prévert perhaps, but hardly anyone else. The form and the function of the cinema had changed too much in the intervening years. Feuillade's mass appeal was unwelcome in the refined *ciné-clubs* of the 1920s where ideas about the relation of cinema to the other arts incubated under the tutelage of the so-called impressionists. Certainly the key impressionist critic, Delluc, recognized that cinema was one art that needed to be popular, but most of those over whom he had such influence took pride in the strides they felt they were making to bring the cinema into line with the music, painting, and literature, and with the avant-garde sensibility of the times.

"Narrative avant-garde" more precisely labels the aesthetic directions taken by the largest coterie of ambitious French filmmakers of the 1920s. Experiments in editing, point of view, temporal structure, and subjective images can be found in domestic melodramas like Germaine Dulac's *La Souriante Madame Beudet* (1923) and huge historical epics like *Napoléon vu par Abel Gance* (1927).

La Souriante Madame Beudet:
Subjectivity on view. BFI

The inexact and problematic term "impressionism" is worth retaining, however, just because of its pretentious association with the homonymous movement in painting. As a self-styled "school" or "movement," the French film critics of the 1920s were among the first to produce manifestos concerning the function of cinema, manifestos that owed a good deal to what were by then well-worn arguments about the aesthetic, as opposed to realist, mission of art.

No matter that the subjects of their films were frequently urban and contemporary, the impressionists by and large did not want to fall into any standard sort of "realism." When the most prominent members of the narrative avant-garde (notably Gance and Marcel L'Herbier) failed to contribute whatsoever to poetic realism in the 1930s, no one should have been surprised, for their real concern all along was with style, visual tempo, subjective states, delicate textures, and private sensibility. These traits would interest Carné, Grémillon, and Chenal, but in the service of "popular" storytelling. For example, Carné's devices for dipping into the mind and the past of his hero in *Le Jour se lève* seem crude in comparison to the dissolves, superimpositions, splitscreen formats, and other tactics that constituted the silent syntax of Gance and Epstein. Similarly, when Renoir and Prévert set *Le Crime de Monsieur Lange* within the brackets of a flashback, it was in the manner of recounting a folktale and had nothing to do with the literary modernism of, say, André Gide that had guided Epstein in *La Glace à trois faces* (1927) or L'Herbier in *L'Inhumaine* (1924).

Melodramas treating the tribulations of the lower classes compose a genre of impressionism with clear resonances echoing down to poetic realism. Although they would never have confessed it, in the early 1920s the impressionists shared this genre with Feuillade and with another popular melodramatist, the theater director André Antoine. Antoine too was unappreciated by Delluc and his followers,[16] yet his films incorporated many of the beliefs about melodrama and natural landscape that became important to the tradition leading to poetic realism. *L'Hirondelle et la mésange* (1920), for example, is set on the barges of the canals of Belgium and northern France. The family that sails the *Hirondelle* to Antwerp and back seems as calm, earthy, and uncomplicated as the land and villages they glide past day after day. Disturbing this harmony, the barge's newly appointed pilot soon shows himself an utter miscreant, by lasciviously pushing himself on the captain's wife (even though he is affianced to their daughter) and by eventually trying to steal the diamonds being smuggled across the border to France. Yes, smuggled. The innocent little family is party to a smuggling ring from which they quietly benefit. Antoine treats this activity as part of the everyday life of ordinary people. But the fact that the contraband is hidden out of view in the water upsets the visual clarity of the photography. Just as the seascape conceals a reef of disharmony, so a scarcely submerged passion lurks behind the eyes of the criminal pilot.

L'Hirondelle et le mésange: Heaving rhythms of the barge. BFI

Antoine was clearly more interested in expressing the pace of a life lived on the canals than the pace of passion and punishment familiar to all moviegoers. He submits his melodrama to the languorous rhythm of the barge, just as he subordinated sexual drama to the slow description of rural landscape in his screen adaptation of Zola's *La Terre* in 1921. (At one point in *L'Hirondelle et le mésange*, he diverts his narrative completely in order to take advantage of a marvelous festival in Antwerp that probably caught his eye while he was filming in that location.) Nevertheless, the melodrama must raise its head out of the water so it can be resolved before being permanently resubmerged at the end. Under his direction, crime and lust are debris floating on the waters of life and permitting us to gauge the heaving movement of its deeper rhythms.[17]

Antoine affected an unsophisticated photographic approach to landscape and emotion that was very well received by the public but that many critics found insipid. Delluc was suspicious of such success, wanting him to go further in his use of nonactors and outdoor shooting.[18] D. W. Griffith's popularity, however, was never suspect. The Parisian *ciné-clubs* found in Griffith an international powerhouse director more akin to them than any French precursor. Léon Moussinac beatified Delluc's *Fièvre* (1921) simply by comparing it to *Broken Blossoms* (1919),[19] Griffith's most influential film in France, and arguably the first major film explicitly intoning the poetic realist appeal. He was smitten by the transcendently vulnerable face of the beaten virgin (Lillian Gish) and by the ritualistic suicide of the sensitive Chinaman (Richard Barthelmess) who adores her.[20] *Broken Blossoms* sublimated its crude masochism into delicate figures of lighting and acting that lift it effortlessly into the realm of art.

Ever since the success of *Broken Blossoms*, character vulnerability has provided the dramatic predisposition for an audience identification that is rewarded by touches of atmosphere and by the masochistic pleasures of dark fatalism. In this way virgins and urchins have been included in the range of topics that producers can bank on. This subject matter in turn encouraged an introspective visual approach. First of all, the quietness required of a relatively passive hero or heroine calls for an acting style of reduced gestures and subtle facial expression. *Broken Blossoms* exemplifies this unmistakably, coming as it does just after the era of theatrical histrionics that the early cinema had borrowed from the Victorian stage. In the 1930s poetic realism would distinguish itself in large part for the more natural brand of acting it brought to a national cinema that, as we have seen, prided itself on the professional stature of its performers. The silent grimace of pain (tinged by a perverse pleasure) that comes over Jean Gabin's face as he twists the knife into his stomach at the end of *Pépé le Moko* (1937) recalls the Chinaman's suicide in *Broken Blossoms*. Their exquisite deaths reveal more generally the workings of sublimation as the (spiritual) refining of lower instincts. For it is not just suicide but also its stylish preparation that satisfies, through intensely introverted displacement, the outrageous sexual urges blocked by the moral codes guiding these respective stories. In *La Bête humaine* Gabin's Lantier literally displaces his psychopathic urges through hushed whispers that express a dark world around him and a darker one within. His paroxysms of violence, including suicide once again, shatter the veneer covering the social and the textual order, and they do so irrefutably since they burst from such a gentle and self-tortured man.

If the subject matter calms the actors by turning them inward to con their own reactions in the midst of overwhelming passion, it affects the mise-en-scène to an even greater degree. Although the cinema seems virtually destined to exploit its twin expansive potentials for showing the variety of forms and objects this world has to offer and for showing off what its own magical apparatus permits, masochistic tales of the downtrodden pull the medium quite the other way, pull it, we might say, back into itself. Forgoing spectacle, indeed forgoing its broadcast out to the audience, the mise-en-scène of poetic realism lures the audience into the screen. The limited number of characters and objects circumscribes the system of signification and overcharges the elements that have been chosen. Coordinated lighting and set design then bathe these objects in an atmosphere that seems to emanate from something deep inside them. Once aroused, the spectator strives to penetrate this atmosphere to read the inscrutably unexpressive faces of the players and props. *Broken Blossoms* is the prototype of this sort of cinematic experience.

In a remarkable unpublished text (a 1926 lecture given at a *ciné-club* outside Paris) Grémillon can lay claim to bearing the spirit of poetic realism from Griffith through the French impressionists, handing it on to the directors of the great features of the 1930s. Two years before his own first major effort, Grémillon showed his thorough comprehension of the possibilities Griffith opened up in *Broken Blossoms*, possibilities that the better French directors of the 1920s occasionally exploited and that he would strive to realize over the next three decades.

Grémillon first singles out *Broken Blossoms* for its concentrated effects. "It is satisfying to find a work where such purely cinematographic means carry expression to its maximum intensity. . . . What strikes us in *Broken Blossoms* is the profoundly human expression obtained by such simple and stunningly balanced means. . . . For the first time, nothing appears that is useless, that is without photogenic value."[21] It is hardly surprising to hear Grémillon salute the film's "photogenic value" and "purely cinematographic means" since these are catchwords of the criticism generated in the clubs run by Delluc, Epstein, and Ricciotto Canudo. In line with the discourse rife in those clubs he can applaud the film while disparaging its "stupidly moralizing" plot as a kind of libretto on which Griffith composed his magnificently expressive visual music.

In Grémillon's discursive community, the analogy with music comes up naturally: the need in the face of such a film "to speak of rhythm, of 'timbres,' of 'luminous melody,' of visual counterpoint, and even of 'visual symphony.'" But he finds that "there is nothing more gratuitous than hypotheses about the correspondence of music and cinema,"[22] particularly those that promote such tropes as superimpositions or metrical editing. *Broken Blossoms*, on the contrary, distinguishes itself by its balanced use of standard techniques, proving that "the cinema is not yet so old that it is necessary to call on odd techniques so as to infuse it with new blood."[23]

Instead of music, Grémillon calls on the words "poetry" and (transfigured) "realism" to characterize the film's delicately balanced cinematic language. Here he proleptically conjures up the poetic realist sensibility that opens the pores of the screen to allow free passage from the outer to the inner:

> Griffith has put before us his three characters by a few perfectly chosen traits. He has delivered them to us. Nothing has been spared, nothing overdone. This is exactly an admirably measured approach. Despite his realist tendencies, he has not forced an art so expressively subtle as the cinema to try stupidly and vainly to rival nature. He reveals three beings, describing them from the out-side while also bringing forth the inside. . . .
>
> Every creator of moving images carries in himself the power to conceive the world from the exterior or the interior, and in a new manner the power of putting in place of the existing world a new world, which belongs to him, in which his characters evolve.[24]

This personalized world takes form under the poetic light that must be the filmmaker's chief preoccupation. "I would begin to study the new atmosphere that the light creates in Broken Blossoms," Grémillon says. And then, identifying several key sequences, he does just this. "Griffith was the first to discover this spirit of light and to understand the expression that is thrown in rays from floodlights or from the ambience of lamps on simple objects or on a face. While evoking a person, through the ensemble of the natural and social as-pects that constitute him, he diffuses around that character an atmosphere that silently circulates an indefinable expressive quantity."[25] In the idiom of the day, an idiom that largely persists into our own day, Grémillon associates such uniqueness with the personal vision of the creator, the film poet. In contrast to a "realistic" approach to a subject that always leaves open other avenues by which to examine it, the poetic realist approach, essentially interior, is irre-placeable. "The composition in space of the images of Broken Blossoms seems to us to create an effect of a wonderful dream. We feel intensely the presence of a living thought, of a human heart, but equally the presence of a poetry of values unique in the cinema."[26]

Existing more as thought than as vision, the film, we might instead say, envisions its subject. Thus the subject is unthinkable except as it emanates from the visual thought that is the film. This is why the specific character of the subject is indifferent to Grémillon, and why when we speak of beauty in the cinema, "we are not talking about the beauty of things in themselves (a sunset, for instance, clouds, the reflection in water, close-ups of branches of fruit) but we mean this special beauty that a certain attitude creates, that light multiplies, that the organization and composition of forms situate. The beauty of the transfigured subject. Thus for the cinema there is no such thing as a beautiful or an ugly subject . . . [since] cinema elevates its material inflating it in its own atmosphere."[27] The specific quality of the atmosphere of Broken Blossoms will haunt Grémillon's own films, especially *La Petite Lise*. Indeed much of the movement of poetic realism as a whole might be summed up in Grémillon's description of the mysterious visual subtlety of *Broken Blossoms*: "Griffith uses blurred images . . . to render an invisible presence that gradually manifests itself like a shadow of something that approaches but which we are yet unable to recognize, the shadow of a reality that in a moment will annihilate it."[28]

This "pathos of death" hovering over the film, threatening "to annihilate it at every moment" will govern the mood of poetic realism; first of all it will govern the mode of representation, by a suggestive, coordinated appeal that is opposed in every way to the standard theatrical aesthetic that directly reaches out to the paying customer. *Broken Blossoms* is the Ur-text of poetic realism because it can be experienced only by the spectator who agrees to float into the misty images that quietly beckon. Instead of being part of an audience entertained in the theater, the spectator watching *Broken Blossoms* brings the film to life in the intimacy of his or her own consciousness, taking on the thought of the film in the way one does when reading a poem or a short story.

With his future films in view, one can readily steer Grémillon's discourse on *Broken Blossoms* onto the path leading toward poetic realism. But had he taken another course, one might be tempted to bring his remarks to bear on such movements as German expressionism and Surrealism that were available when he spoke in 1926 and that equally, though in very different ways, promised to bring the viewer into the dream of the film.

The specific recipe of poetic realism differs from other cinematic *optiques* in its modestly documentary and ethnographic interest. *Broken Blossoms*, we must recall, opens with a carefully reconstituted Chinese urban set and then moves to a specific location, the Limehouse district along the Thames in London. The literally thick "atmosphere" of opium smoke and fog that the characters of *Broken Blossoms* breathe condenses all the pathetic sociologic and geographic conditions that we are invited to explore with sympathetic imagination. The *Stimmung* of *The Cabinet of Dr. Caligari* (1919) or *Waxworks* (1924), on the other hand, might better be thought of as constituting a dreamscape, an inner landscape whose referent is fictional, phantasmic, or even psychoanalytic. In contrast to these German counterparts, *Broken Blossoms* was considered too realist and not "lyrical" at all during its first run in France. In an otherwise laudatory review, Moussinac chides Griffith: "The overly acute sense of observation absorbs and suppresses the film's *élan*, [suppressing that] penetrating poetry . . . that one day will seize hold of the simple grandeur and radiant power which can be achieved on the screen, and impel the truth of our new times to emerge out of the marvelous world of images, in a breath of irresistible lyricism."[29] *Broken Blossoms* may exhibit a perfect sense of "atmosphere" and a peerless virtuosity in its palette of black and white (Moussinac compares Griffith to Duccio di Buoninsegna and Cimabue), but to the avant-garde sensibility of the 1920s it remains too "observational." The reigning aesthetic of the day preferred that reality be "transposed into the dazzling and magnificent dreams of [the poet's] imagination." Impressionism, expressionism, and Surrealism aim for a cinema of the imagination, and in this Griffith must be said to have stopped short; but along with those other masters of atmosphere, Stiller and Sjöström, he had set the cinema moving toward another goal, in Grémillon's mind a more proper one.

In presenting this Griffith film Grémillon was inculcating a French sensibility that he among others would soon begin to satisfy. In 1932, the critic Emile Vuillermoz would recommend to all readers of *Pour Vous* that they immediately go see *Broken Blossoms* nine times in a row.[30] He ought to have told them to see Grémillon's *La Petite Lise* as well, for this was the French equivalent of Griffith's masterpiece.

Even before Grémillon's lecture a number of impressionist films set about refining the aesthetic that *Broken Blossoms* pointed toward. Delluc's *Fièvre* bears the strongest relation to the Griffith work, featuring a Chinese heroine and a smoky barroom alongside the Marseilles docks. While a brawl rages around the girl, the camera shoots from her optical point of view. Cowering in a corner, she focuses on a single flower on the bar, the only comforting sign (of nature and poetry) in this new land. After her husband is killed (a boot crushes his throat), she obliviously crawls forward to the flower, much as Gish in *Broken Blossoms* had held to her breast the delicate little doll she had seen, and identified with, in the Chinaman's store window. The flower in *Fièvre* turns out to be artificial. Delluc, like Griffith, makes use of flashbacks and multiple points of view to build the drama to a pitch of desire and aggression. In his review Moussinac used painterly terms. He also invoked the words "poetry" and "realism":

> *Fièvre* . . . demonstrates that in order to "make cinema" by no means is it necessary to carry a camera to the most extraordinary sites and that from the emotion of faces and gestures in a decor which encompassed them all together one can derive effects of real power through the simple play of light and shadow, of black and white. . . . the realism of the character types and the action does not exclude a kind of solemn poetry, heavy with an oriental nostalgia, an ennui of drunkenness and debauchery, and a violent disgust with sensual pleasure.[31]

In *Film in the Aura of Art* I could not help but point to Lillian Gish as the "broken blossom" emblem of masochistic sublimation wherein a certain conception of art is deliciously ravaged by the crass industry of cinema only to win a final spiritual victory in the hearts of those capable of experiencing art.[32] *Photogénie* would bring such delicate art to the cinema, and right within the harshest subject matter imaginable. The art of the cinema altogether might then resemble Gish as the delicate, if artificial, (blue) flower in the land of technology. At its worst, this sort of emotional slumming, which would uplift melodrama by means of style, produces mawkish effects fawned over by effete

Fièvre: Violence. CF

Fièvre: Vulnerability. MOMA

ciné-club audiences. At its best, it paints the moral landscape of modern life for everyone to see. This was the goal of *photogénie* and it soon became the goal of poetic realism.

How self-serving is this scenario of sublimation wherein film art is at the mercy of a crass public and crasser businessmen? In 1929, a trade journal like *Pour Vous* could "meditate with tenderness on French cinema, this little plant buffeted by storms but ready to withstand all insults, the weight of snows and even the foul care of a malicious gardener."[33] Walter Benjamin would scoff at the kind of aesthetic enterprise represented by this metaphor and even more by Delluc's *photogénie*, since it so obviously calls up a religious, "auratic" function for art that is inappropriate in this century, particularly given the industrial basis of the medium.[34] Even the name used to identify them, "impressionists," suggests a function for cinema that is at least a quarter century out of date. This is exactly how the Surrealists saw them.

When Dimitri Kirsanov concluded his *Ménilmontant* (1926) with a shot of impoverished and exploited young women fashioning artificial flowers in the poorest district of Paris, he provided us the most comprehensive image, aesthetic and social, of this form of cinema. Through a panoply of stylistic experiments and through glorious close-ups of the incomparably fragile face of his wife, Nadia Sibirskaïa, Kirsanov thought he had shaped a harsh milieu into an exquisite flower. But a flower for whom? *Ménilmontant* "soon became a major film on the *ciné-club* and specialized cinema circuit"[35] but never played to the people of the working-class *quartier* that gave it its title. This was not Kirsanov's public anyway, for he came from the Russian aristocracy. In 1919, having fled the Revolution, he was reduced to playing his beloved cello in movie houses just to be able to eat. He must have been tempted to imagine himself and his music as an unappreciated flower in the crude milieu of mass art.

Ménilmontant: Destitute
madonna. BFI

Seen this way, *Ménilmontant* becomes a personal triumph of art over industry, of the icon of the madonna Sibirskaïa over the brutal world of plot and spectacle that constitutes ordinary cinema. That triumph is signaled in the miracle of the film's narration, the first French film without titles, a tale told completely through the eloquence of its images. The dark alleys of the nineteenth arrondissement, the streetlights glistening on the Seine, and the pathetic decor of shabby apartments are all redeemed by art. No silent film more clearly bewails the fate of art in our century, more obviously appeals to connoisseurs of the emotions roused by artificial flowers.

Kirsanov would retain this personal aura into the sound era, directing one of the most poetic films of the decade, *Rapt* (1934), taken from a celebrated novel by Charles-Ferdinand Ramuz, and adapted for the screen by the religious Surrealist Benjamin Fondane. When *Rapt* premiered, *ciné-clubs* were no longer à la mode and the specialized theaters were gone. Forced to compete in the standard market, *Rapt* was smothered by the 135 other French features of that year, and the nearly 300 American imports.

The lesson of *Rapt* and of Kirsanov is that impressionism may have provided the poetic realists with an image of cinematic lyricism, but not with an image of a public to be served. Delluc was right when he proclaimed that the cinema would have to be popular or not be at all.[36] When the industry shifted to sound, impressionism had already run its course. Ambitious film production would need another model and would need a public. But impressionism had given French cinema a taste for style and for a certain subject matter that would come to life all through the 1930s, from Clair's *Sous les toits de Paris* (1930) to Chenal's *Le Dernier Tournant* (1939), films celebrating the "milieu" of tough criminals and poor girls.

SURREALIST PEDIGREE FOR A POPULIST MONGREL

Where impressionism, following modernist writers like Gide and Paul-Ambroise Valéry, had bartered its social and spiritual mission for the surface effects of "art for art's sake," the Surrealists employed a familiar vocabulary of "profundity" to characterize their aspirations and entice the sincerest members of their generation. They preached that life might be penetrated to the core through art, that consciousness must give way to the depths of the unconscious. In a dash to hurdle familiar barricades of the mind/body relation, Surrealism proclaimed the primacy of symbols and images; and with the extra propulsion accrued from Freudianism, they developed concrete measures to drive the mind through the body of the universe and to find in the universe the scattered signs of a larger mind they might become.

Surprisingly, Surrealism so quickly attained cultural credit that even mainstream French cinema felt repercussions from its incipient program for the cinema. That program, we know, begins by affirming that the secret world of the mind (or soul) is proximate. We experience it in dreams, in moments of clairvoyance, and occasionally in art where it can be promoted through such well-known strategies as automatic writing, bizarre juxtaposition, and hyper-realistic description. The cinema was an art form ripe for the Surrealist project and particularly attuned to precisely this new semiotics. A childlike art, cinema indulges wild juxtapositions; it offers the hope of a utopian language of images that, as everyone noted, has much in common with the logic of dreams. "Everything that is foolish about the cinema is the fault of an old-fashioned respect for logic," wrote Jean Goudal in 1925.[37] Breton's search for the marvelous leads straight to the movies, a medium that in the 1920s appeared pristine, unspoiled by stodgy aesthetic traditions.

The Surrealists wanted to keep it that way. They regarded the impressionists as pretentious throwbacks and opposed every initiative to upgrade the cinema. They saw cinema's popularity, its mass entertainment appeal, as one of its most winning attributes. Aragon claimed that real art "ought to be read like the morning paper." The cinema, moreover, was "read" like newspapers by millions each week. This gave it capital strategic importance to any group whose designs lay in "the service of the revolution." And the Surrealists proclaimed such an allegiance. With this in mind they excoriated the life and work of Jean Cocteau with whom they loathed to be linked. Soupault was merciless: "*Le Sang d'un poète*," he said, "like his later films is counterfeit Surrealist currency. Cocteau erected an obstacle, a barrier to our efforts. We became disgusted with and alienated from the cinema because it fell into the hands of 'charlatans' like Cocteau."[38] But in actual fact, most of the Surrealists shared with Cocteau a class background that dulls the edge they put on their self-righteous rhetoric. Many of them lived on inheritances received from the wealthy families they all loudly renounced.

Tellingly, artists like Man Ray and Cocteau who banked on their "amateur" status to guarantee the sincerity of their cinematic output worked under commission for a dying aristocracy. This single link helps explain the frailty of the Surrealist cinema. For as the depression and the rise of Adolf Hitler forced the aristocracy to concern itself with other interests, the enthusiasm that these fashionable artists had displayed for the cinema waned. Surrealist cinema may have had revolutionary aspirations, but it was hardly more than a pastime of the elite.

Cinema requires a discipline; it requires recognition of the laws of image flow that come from its machines more than from personal dreams and wishes. At best, and history has shown this repeatedly, the exigencies of the medium necessitate compromises that amount to intricate detours on the dream's path to the screen. At worst, cinema's own logic, a machine logic, will swallow up whatever designs and intuitions the wide-eyed Surrealist might have hoped to imprint directly on the screen.

The Surrealists did not abandon cinema after 1930; rather they returned to their original interest in it, dynamic spectatorship. It was first and always as adept viewers that the Surrealists came to depend on movies. These were the men who wandered in and out of theaters haphazardly, seeking odd dramatic effects; the men who would half shut their eyes, or blink rhythmically to produce a hallucination in front of the screen. These were the writers who loved to describe the bizarre images available even in common serials and genre pictures. The cinema goaded their search for fascinating interconnections. They were, in short, what we have come to call, following Charles Baudelaire and Benjamin, *flâneurs* at the cinema, anonymous travelers in the crowd, turning this mass spectacle into private illumination. Alienated, they controlled their experience in their own way, manhandling the films they loved to see.

Loath as they were to surrender their childlike fascination with the screen by learning its techniques, for most of them the cinema remained a magic drug, a portal to marvelous visions. To labor over it as a means of expression would demystify it, and they valued their dreams above any films they might produce. In this Buñuel, by his own admission, was no exception. "My *amour fou*—for the dreams themselves as well as the pleasure of dreaming—is the single most important thing I shared with the surrealists."[39] Still Buñuel stands apart from his confreres as an authentic filmmaker. Having dirtied his hands as an assistant to Epstein among others, he had become fascinated by the medium and did not mind its resistance to his will, its limitations and frustrations. And he did not even think of it particularly as an art form.

Even before the Surrealists brought him to self-consciousness, he ridiculed Epstein, Cocteau, and the entire cinematic avant-garde for its fealty to "art" either as something traditional or as something "chic." Instead he initiated an anthropological cinema. His documentary *Las Hurdes* (1932) is of a piece with the dream film *Un Chien andalou*, since both locate and exemplify the violence that is at the heart of life. The ants, scorpions, bees, and beasts that infest his screen are not symbols in the customary sense (the sense we would grant them were these films authored by Cocteau); instead they lodge the life struggle as far down the biological scale as you like.

Buñuel's stark films help verify the link James Clifford has made between

Le Sang d'un poète: Counterfeit Surrealism? BFI

Las Hurdes: Surrealist ethnography? BFI

L'Age d'or: Primitive sexuality. BFI

the Surrealists and the founding of modern ethnography in Paris.[40] Like Bataille, Leiris, and Roger Caillois, Buñuel learned to explore himself through the study of bizarre rites and foreign peoples. One finds in his films, as one does in such journals as *Documents* and *Minotaure*, a reverence for the mystery of experience and for the power of primitive art to confront us with that mystery. At the same time he openly outrages those basking in the comfort of their beliefs and privileged life-styles. The shock of the very first scene of his first film, the notorious eye slashing of *Un Chien andalou*, deliberately turns the fat stomachs of the bourgeoisie and cuts the threads that make up the delicate web of their precious subjectivity. But at the same time, such violence respects the power of human and inhuman urges. The blood that bursts through Gaston Modot's eye and covers his face as he swells in sexual passion in *L'Age d'or* besmirches the romantic feelings of civil people, while it serves as an offering to the gods of primitive sexuality.

Violence, the Surrealists preached, can generate as well as destroy possibilities. If there exists any excuse for the cruelty that Buñuel so disturbingly displays in the manner in which he films the poor people of *Las Hurdes*, it must stem from this need, this instinct, to make us shudder. In speaking of the morality of Surrealism, of its strictness and logic, he recently said, "The idea of burning down a museum, for instance, always seemed more enticing to me than the opening of a cultural center or the inauguration of a new hospital."[41]

If he could, Buñuel would send a psychic shudder through his audience directly. This is the intent and effect of such scenes as the slitting of the eye or, in *L'Age d'or*, of an orchestral performance interrupted by copulation, or the outrageous presentation of Christ as the marquis de Sade's most decadent lecher. The syntax of Buñuel's films engages our desires and lifts the images toward a dream to which we unavoidably succumb.[42] Only then are we sharply wakened, as the tricks that entranced us are cruelly exposed. In *L'Age d'or* Lya Lys and Gaston Modot, although separated by the authorities, nevertheless make passionate love entirely through Buñuel's crosscutting. Their increasingly aroused faces are accompanied by merging sounds of a cowbell (her), a dog barking (him), and the rising wind (their intercourse). When, at the moment of her most visible excitation, that wind miraculously and visibly enters Lya Lys's room through the mirror to blow her hair, we are uplifted in eroticism, only to be quickly let down. For in the next shot the mirror is shown to trick us: it reflects her toilette bottles and (inexplicably) a distant sky with clouds, while she sits fixed before it somehow unreflected.

This visual trick, taken directly from René Magritte (who lived next door to Buñuel for a time),[43] teases and makes us wince. For we too are excited and we too are deceived. It is all masturbation: lonely, imaginary, finite. Unlike Cocteau, Buñuel's interest lies not in the magic of art but in the moments when the magician is exposed and we waken to a sickening realization of the banality of things. He is an ethnographer of subjectivity; his films are uncivil because they not only depict but also exemplify the cruelty of all living organisms and the crueler repression of civilization.

The climax of the relation of cinema to Surrealism came in November 1930 with the notorious premiere of *L'Age d'or*. Actually there were two premieres, each explosive. The first was a 10:00 A.M. screening for the producers of the film, the elegant vicomte and comtesse de Noailles and their invited guests, held at the Panthéon theater recently purchased by Pierre Braunberger. Buñuel recalls the count and countess shaking hands and embracing their friends as they entered the theater, but watching them all hastily depart. "The day after, Charles de Noailles was expelled from the Jockey Club. Apparently, the Church also threatened to excommunicate him; his mother had to go to Rome to negotiate with the Pope."[44]

The official run of the film was set for the Studio 28. After numerous violent confrontations with right-wing groups, during which several paintings by Yves Tanguy lining the entryway were destroyed, a manifesto defending the film was sent out, authored by Breton, Paul Eluard, René Crevel, Aragon, and André Thirion.[45] Other radicals (including Georges Sadoul, Tristan Tzara, and René Char) signed this document, which, as much as the flagrantly combative tone of the film, brought about its official ban two months later. Evidently in this film and his earlier *Un Chien andalou*, Buñuel really did make good on the Surrealist ambition to fight for a revolutionary representational strategy featuring the scandalous expression of outright desire and its more scandalous suppression. Moreover, these two films, as the manifesto so brazenly proclaims, go right to the heart of the interminable dispute between private and public life. In their stark images and in their associative, mysterious, but convincing internal logic, Buñuel attained the "ideorealité" that the Surrealists had been proposing for the cinema since 1925.

L'Age d'or marked the culmination of the first period of Surrealist filmmaking; for the impressive ciné-club network in Paris foundered in 1931 with the death of La Revue du cinéma.[46] And the group, aside from Buñuel, had neither the time nor the talent to make films or build an audience for them. From the perspective of the cinema, one may be tempted to accuse the Surrealists of the very dandyism they despised in the culture at large. Toying with the cinema to inspire their painting and their poetry, did Breton, Desnos, Eluard, and Aragon ever really take their proclamations concerning its extraordinary power to heart?

I have dwelt on the Surrealists, because, peculiar and extreme though they be, they provide the best starting point for a cultural history of the cinema of the 1930s. Outflanking the avant-garde on the left, they baldly posed troublesome questions about the relation of cinema to the traditional concerns of art and to a mass public. Even as extremists, they still represent the distinctiveness of a national cinema that we have characterized as balancing concerns for the broadly popular and the aesthetically rarefied. The artists and intellectuals responsible for poetic realism took up these same issues in a less hysterical, more subdued manner.

Soupault helps make the transition. His first "poème cinématographique" dates from 1917 and is thought to have motivated the experiment with Breton two years later, Les Champs magnétiques, from which the origin of Surrealism is conventionally dated.[47] As a film reviewer he led the Surrealist offensive for a new cinema throughout the 1920s. It is important, then, that two of his final reviews promote early examples of poetic realist cinema: Grémillon's La Petite Lise and Duvivier's David Golder.[48] But it was in Vigo that he found the heir of cinematic Surrealism. Together they worked out a scenario taken from Edgar Allan Poe's The Stolen Heart, which would have gone into production in 1934 had Vigo survived.[49]

These tenuous links between the founders of Surrealism and the cinema of the 1930s[50] are immeasurably strengthened by the presence of Prévert, an unmistakable cinematic emissary of Surrealism, bearing to poetic realism the legacy that had been absolutely central to his formation. The fabled lightness of his images and the limpid directness of his language belong to an imagination that was carefully uncultivated and absolutely Surrealist. To the dark vision of Carné and Grémillon, Prévert supplied the "poetic" contribution that made their films renowned.[51] To Renoir's increasingly complicated political

vision he offered the airy esprit of Amedée Lange. And in his outright Surrealist features, *Drôle de drame* (1937, suggestively titled *Bizarre, Bizarre* in English) and *Adieu Léonard* (1943), he persisted in his lifelong pursuit of serious
absurdity.

Although Ado Kyrou singles out Prévert's lightness in tracing the legacy of
Surrealism into feature filmmaking, the poet's undisguised rage against the
civility of contemporary bourgeois life amounts to a deeper influence over the
renowned scripts he wrote for Renoir, Carné, and other directors. Characters
such as Batala in *Le Crime de Monsieur Lange* and Zabel in *Le Quai des brumes* are
the sort to have been invited to the elegant banquet satirized in *L'Age d'or*. As
played by Jules Berry and Michel Simon, both characters glisten with a veneer
of cultivation; both can twist language to suit their designs, especially when set
off against the simple direct phrases spoken by René Lefebvre and Gabin.
Their manners and power make the bourgeoisie suspect in a way that brings
to mind the films of Feuillade as much as those by Buñuel.

Black humor, cruelty, and outright rebelliousness are constitutive traits of
Surrealism, distinct strategies of asserting individual will and spontaneity that
Benjamin claims have their source in Fyodor Dostoievsky, Friedrich Nietz-
sche, and Arthur Rimbaud.[52] Prévert indulged in these during his years with
the Groupe Octobre. After *Drôle de drame*, however, his films march to the
slow drum of implacable destiny. Here individual will is celebrated only as it
is crushed. Did the darkening political sky cloud the exuberance of Prévert's
Surrealism? Unquestionably the poetic realist aesthetic exploits the sentiments
of passivity over and against the aggressivity of Surrealism.

Here Cocteau returns in a more favorable light, for *Le Sang d'un poète* (1932)
addresses the issue of "the poetic" within its very title. Opposed to the "pro-
fane illuminations"[53] and the confrontational tactics of Surrealism, Cocteau
offers a strategy of suffering whereby the "unveiling" of inner truths occurs
like the passage and the pangs of birth.[54] While this aesthetic is apparently
congenial to poetic realism, Cocteau's grand pathos and sublime truths lie
only in the unconscious of exceptional souls (artists like himself), whereas the
poetic realists were fascinated by the destiny of "everyman." And the destiny
they felt prey to was a social, even a historical one rather than the mythical
"death and transfiguration" Cocteau arranged for himself.

In following out the fate of ordinary people on ordinary streets, and in
transmuting both into something extraordinary, poetic realism pursued a Surrealist goal; but in its delicacy of sentiment, and in its aesthetics of suffering
rather than confrontation, of poetic logic rather than poetic spontaneity, another influence is felt, Cocteau's, or, more surely, that of the impressionists.
Surrealism we might say is an ethnography of violence, whereas poetic realism
is a phenomenology of pain.

Though hardly a direct influence, Surrealism helped prepare the terrain for
poetic realism to flourish. In their book *Les Surréalistes et le cinéma*, Alain and

Odette Virmaux make the point for me: "Vigo and Prévert are readily arrayed within that French school of the 1930s that we have grown accustomed to calling 'Poetic Realism': a rubric that is scarcely distant from Surrealism in the large sense of the term, in the sense given to it for example by Apollinaire."[55] Apollinaire, we must recall, had found in *Fantômas* the prospects of a better spiritual nourishment for the twentieth century. He is credited as the first to recruit poets to participate in the redirection of this "popular art . . . to compose images for meditative and refined minds that the clumsy imagination of the movie moguls will not much longer be able to satisfy."[56]

Apollinaire's complex relation to cinema may serve as an indication of the mixed origins of the school of poetic realism. From Chenal and Carné to Resnais, the most distinctively French cinéastes have been cousins both of *Fantômas* and of Apollinaire, of naturalism, impressionism, and Surrealism, of those aspiring to create a refined cinema and those eager to maintain the popularity that makes cinema the art of the century. Poetic realism is the mongrel whelp of these opposite impulses, carrying within its various styles an array of traits that constitute the family resemblance we recognize and adulate.

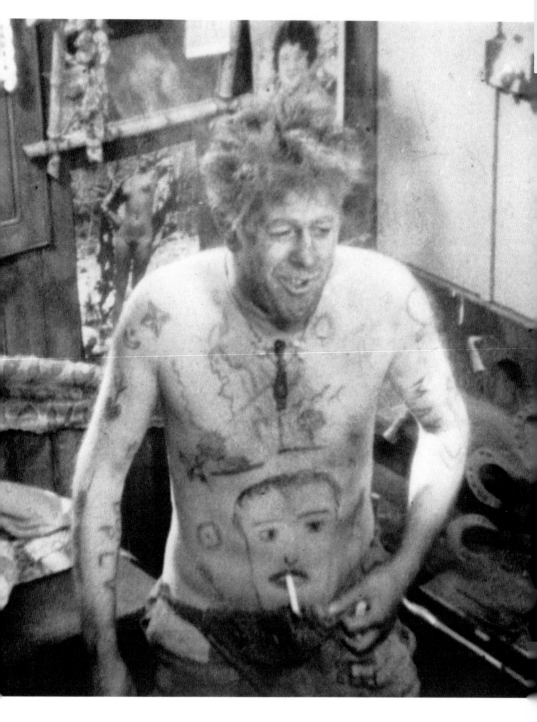

3

Adolescents in an Adolescent Industry

AT THE START of the new decade what must savants or ordinary citizens have thought the cinema might be like by its end? All bets were off now that sound had come on stage. Despite *L'Age d'or* and *Le Sang d'un poète*, who could expect the Surrealists, or any avant-garde faction for that matter, to direct the energies of this new hybrid form? Experimental cinema declined, we know, in the face of complex and expensive technology on the one hand and of an apparent entrenchment of mass entertainment on the other. *Ciné-clubs* could no longer sponsor amateur efforts; *ciné-clubs* in any case were no longer prominent, their cultured memberships having deserted them in this moment of economic and technological crisis.

In the inevitable shuffle of studio heads, theater owners, and distributors that the depression as well as sound brought about, the way was clear for the ascendancy of the crassest businessmen to direct the future of this art, and to direct it naturally toward crass spectacle. Such at least were the frequently pronounced fears of those intellectuals who monitored the cinema, who rued not just the passing of the silent film at a moment that it seemed to be reaching its maturity, but the passing of a profound cultural mission for this medium that now would go the way of the circus and the music hall.

But no one knew for certain how it would all come out, what movies would look like or what their social impact might be. And amid the malaise and cynicism of the moment, one can recognize certain far-flung hopes that the apparently total reorganization of the medium might benefit significant new forms of film. Poetic realism hovered as an unnamed presentiment in the minds of some individuals who were caught between the strictures of the business cycle being put in place and the evanescent dreams spawned in the cinephilia of the 1920s. It hovered as an image of a popular and populist form that would draw on the subtle possibilities of the medium, including now the possibilities of sound recording. Mainly it hovered as a potential serum to counteract the rampant spread of the standard theatrical movie of the day, which nearly everyone found facile and puerile. Of course there were many presentiments, as many no doubt as there were individuals dedicated to a strong view of cinema. Poetic realism is perhaps the name of a composite image of these many hopes for the cinema, hopes one could recognize in a few movies made each year by a few strong individuals who struck out on their own against the norm. All cultural concepts exist only insofar as they pass through individual cultural subjects, but in a moment of transition like that of the cinema in the early 1930s, the instincts of individuals take on an even greater prominence, since the concepts (the *optiques*, in this case) are nameless and as yet without definition.

If the 1930s are viewed as a decade of maturation, its first half would thus be the tale of a troubled adolescence, as aspiring directors found themselves having to deal with weak, dissolute, and ultimately absent biological fathers, by which I mean French producers.[1] Paramount and Tobis Klangfilm may have stepped in to play rich uncles for a time,[2] bailing out a collapsing cinema economy, but as foreigners they were regarded with suspicion, and in any case within a few years their presence dwindled to nothing, leaving the field to scores of independent producers. Amid gross industry corruption and indirection, the avant-garde of the 1920s was a touchstone and a resource for the most self-directed filmmakers, the ones we need to examine in this chapter.

From his very first Dada exercises, René Clair's films exude, however disingenuously, an aura of innocence that accuses the wayward complexity of modern, adult life. Purity is at the heart of Jean Vigo's ethos and Jacques Prévert's as well, but it is a fiery purity of contentiousness and rebellion. These three delinquents held standard, mature cinema in contempt, releasing onto the screen, almost as a challenge to the system, unforgettable images of absolute love and grotesque satire. They drew their inspiration from the avant-garde of the 1920s (Clair as filmmaker, Vigo through his *ciné-club*, and Prévert as avid spectator). They believed in the centrality of the medium to modern life. All three rejected the aesthetic pretensions of the likes of Abel Gance, Jean Epstein, and Marcel L'Herbier, convinced as they were that the cinema was born for popular subjects and a light but magical touch.

Clair was the most advantaged of the three, having gained credibility as a commercially viable director with *Un Chapeau de paille d'Italie* in 1928, and commanding a peerless arrangement at Tobis that allowed him to write, coordinate, and direct his sound films without interference and with substantial budgets. Vigo's situation was the reverse. An underling at a production house, he kept afloat a small film club in Nice. Through gifts from friends and relatives, and through outright begging, he managed to gather what he needed to make a few "homemade movies," the effect of which would ultimately equal or surpass that of Clair's highly publicized features. Prévert stands between these two. Entering the cinema slightly after Vigo, he negotiated his early *raconteur* reputation into a modest freedom that, while not rivaling Clair's, did permit him to choose his subjects. As a writer, of course, he was in the business of choosing subjects.

All three men provided French cinema with a sense of the gymnastic possibilities of the sound film, with a liberty of feeling and movement that belongs to cleverness and swift wit as well as to cinematic inventiveness. All three were concerned with the men and women of the street as subjects and as audience. At the outset of the decade their ambitions for cinema were prophetic. Yet by 1934 Clair would move to England and Vigo would be dead. Prévert alone would carry an alternative idea about the cinema into the Popular Front and beyond.

RENÉ CLAIR

Of all France's prominent directors in the 1920s, Clair and Jacques Feyder were the ones who proved most capable of steering the country into the uncharted seas of a cinema that now had to sail on waves of sound. And until he returned with a huge impact in 1933, Feyder was in Hollywood where MGM had lured him with mostly false promises. Aside from intermittent successes by Julien Duvivier and Jean Choux, Clair upheld the prestige of French cinema in the first years of the decade. He was arguably the most celebrated film artist in the world during these transitional years. Clair's status, which grew until in 1960 he became the first filmmaker inducted into the Académie française, rests on this early sound work.

No doubt due to this prestige, he has retrospectively been lodged at the forefront of the poetic realist movement. Georges Sadoul may be responsible for this, in the way he characterized the 1930 *Sous les toits de Paris*: "Clair, with the aid of some fine sets by Lazare Meerson, *realistic* and *poetic* at the same time, has succeeded in recapturing enchantingly the atmosphere of the Paris suburb—the furnished rooms, the children playing, the crotchety concierges, the window boxes, the idlers, the small shop-keepers, the respectable youths and the less so, the street-singers with their accordion in every square."[3] Few viewers would argue with the attribution of a certain "poetry" to Clair's discourse; it is the "realist" aspect that remains troubling. The earliest overview of the period available to us is that of Maurice Bardèche and Robert Brasillach, who feel compelled to salute Clair's realism only to qualify their judgment immediately. Speaking of *Sous les toits de Paris*, they allow that "every detail is based on real life, the most vulgar incidents of real life. . . . But if we compare this realism with that of the settings in German pictures we see that in them the realism was dignified by a loving care for lighting and by a prodigious use of the pictorial medium. Theirs was the realism of a painter; but Clair's realism is . . . that of the ballet. He stylizes [his characters], simplifies their outline, and leads them into that choreographed world which is peculiarly his."[4]

Clearly the topics Clair chose to film, the lower-class characters and locations, were responsible for his being labeled a realist of any sort. Sadoul depicts him serving as a relay in "the 'popular' tradition inaugurated by Ferdinand Zecca and Victorin Jasset and handed on via Louis Feuillade to the young Clair."[5] If poetic realism is defined topically, as films about the streets and roofs of Paris and about the milieus of gangsters and lonely girls, then Clair must be its most proximate parent; but if we insist, as we should, on treating style as a mode of representation and of spectatorship, then his paternity is put in doubt.

For Clair's style makes use of realist elements but has very peculiar aims. The community songs that arise spontaneously in all of his first sound films imply a folk-art conception of storytelling. For a brief moment Clair would have us think of him as orchestrating a collective story that rises out of those who gather round the screen, just as the street singer in *Sous les toits de Paris* elicits the songs whose sheet music he sells. This "populist" narrative voice protects the characters from real danger and turns the dark street corners and back alleys of Paris and its suburbs into a charming miniature set, the terrain of the good people who sing along. In what has become a common comparison, one can say, "German streets are always menacing, but not Clair's. His is a Paris that is protected and amicable."[6] And so certain likable "undesirable elements" are allowed to take their place within the guarded borders of the screen and within an overall rhythm to which every element submits. The community cares for its petty criminals the way medieval villages sheltered their hunchbacks and idiots. Sources of anecdotes and legends, their potentially destructive impulses are disarmed by the charming tales they inspire.

Sous les toits de Paris: Amiable Paris. BFI   *Backstairs*: Menacing Berlin. Courtesy P. Petro

Clair's personal world in fact is built out of preestablished cultural forms such as the vaudeville skit and the operetta; he reaches beyond his own experience to tap into transpersonal traditions in French art and entertainment.[7] And so he juggles the public and the private, the popular and the avant-garde, the traditional and the modernist. In this he is part of an age that was accustomed to exploring the effects of such mixtures, as in the collages of Georges Braque, the wallpaper music of Erik Satie, and Igor Stravinsky's puppet ballet *Petrouchka*. In cases like these, popular forms or motifs test the limits of the system of art.

Clair's *Entr'acte* was clearly made in this spirit. And, less clearly, so was *Le Million*. In both films Clair's personal sensibility comes out through his inimitable way of treating cinema as dance. It is dance that gives him the public (traditional) right to display that sensibility. And curiously it is by emulating dance aesthetics that he could champion a notion of pure cinema through the phrase "cinema of pure movement." In the 1920s dance meant "ritual." Both Sergey Diaghilev's Ballets russes and, more pertinently, Rolf de Maré's Dadaist Ballets suédois promised to depersonalize the excesses of the romantic style of modern dance sometimes by imitating vaudeville routines. At the same time stars like Diaghilev turned choral movement into highly personal expression. This tension between the social forms of media and their recondite employment to express individual, complex sensibilities characterized this period.

A film style founded on an aesthetic of dance, and on a pastiche of "numbers" associated with the musical comedy, would tend to link Clair to the

Sous les toits de Paris: Cinema as popular dance. BFI

theatrical mode of French cinema that, in my schema, stands opposed to poetic realism. But Clair's musicals homogenize the movement of all his characters into a single flow, rather than opposing types of characters (male/female,
rich/poor) through types of movement in the manner of the American musical comedy. Moreover, Clair achieves his flow through an orchestration of
camera movement, sound effects, lighting patterns, and set design. To characterize this aesthetic, Marcia Butzel rejects Clair's own term "counterpoint"
and claims that he "channels" the multiple registers of his composition into a
unified choreography whose true medium is the mind of the spectator.[8] The
personal is thus an effect of a certain use of the social, and private experience
becomes foregrounded over public display. In this way Clair's work from
Entr'acte up to and beyond *Le Million* is of a piece, and can stand as an inspiration for poetic realism.

   Clair himself promoted this view of his work, for a more virulent opponent
of filmed theater can hardly be found. His homages to Charlie Chaplin,
Douglas Fairbanks, D. W. Griffith, and Mack Sennett are based on their understanding of images and rhythm. His early film reviews explicitly praise such
poetic realist predecessors as *Broken Blossoms, Sir Arne's Treasure* (1919), and
The Outlaw and His Wife (1917). All these films gather intensity in an unbroken
accumulation of the most natural and simple cinematic elements. Concerning
a little-known American film, *The Girl I Loved* (1923), Clair wrote, "It moves
very slowly in front of the lens, yet the film is endowed with intense motion,
the expression of the incessant motion of that inner life."[9]

   Clair would never be known for quiet rhythms, yet even his exuberant
Entr'acte choreographs its optical display, gestural reflexes, and object displacements under the form of the chase so as to control the perception of the
spectator via the mechanism of cinema. Seven years later, a worldwide audience would be equally choreographed by the magistrally measured *Le Million*,
set in the imaginary Paris of Louis Aragon, who celebrated precisely the
"breakneck career of Surrealism over rooftops, lightning rods, gutters, and
weathercocks."[10]

   Clair never seriously entertained either Aragon's Surrealism or his Marxism.
Rather than a serious cultural program, he brought forward from the 1920s
an aesthetic one, having to do with vision in movement. A devotee of pure
cinema, he had nevertheless undertaken the adaptation of Eugène Labiche's
Un Chapeau de paille d'Italie because he saw in it the chance to combine a Mack
Sennett chase structure with a Chaplinesque comedy of manners. (*Woman of
Paris* was among his favorite films.)[11] Although he was on record as abhorring
the idea of adaptation, he had confessed early on that a good film could be
drawn from a play if it were completely reconceived according to the very
different principles of light and motion that constitute the cinema. The director of the madcap *Entr'acte* was drawn to the acceleration of dramatic problems and reversals that defines Labiche's formula. By funneling his roam-

ing imagination into the material of the bourgeois drawing-room comedy, Clair was able to master a style that rhythmically organized an assortment of elements from a variety of often common sources. The plot sets off a chain reaction involving long shots of galloping horses, close-ups of minuscule gestures, a ticking clock, a formal quadrille, and so forth. In this film for the first time Clair made good on his intuition that careful attention to the effect of seemingly insignificant objects, particularly in their placement within a series of other such effects, could create an undeniable momentum. And so when Clair dipped into theatrical material, it was only to discipline his visual-aural genius. The schematic plots of *Sous les toits de Paris*, *Le Million*, *A nous la liberté* (1931), and *Quatorze juillet* (1932) serve as libretti for his choreographed creations.

Despite his affinity for Labiche, if Clair is to be tied to theater it is certainly not to the boulevard tradition but to the anarchist theater championed by the Groupe Octobre. Films like *A nous la liberté* and *Le Dernier Milliardaire* (1934) share with Prévert's skits a simplicity of subject matter, a readable decor, and an acting style based on cartoons. *Le Million* is said to "link up—in the sequence of the commissariat for example—with the politely anarchist tradition of the Parisian avant-garde. This will explain soon after the kind of jokes one finds in Prévert's group."[12] In fact, if Prévert took anything from Clair, it was his cultured primitivism, not his politics, for Clair sealed his films off from the winds of pressing social issues. He shaved and polished the edges of every element so it would fit tightly into place and not budge. Thus the particulars lead immediately to the achievement of a clear and satisfying design. And as Prévert knew above all, genuine political analysis lies precisely in those particulars and the critical space that can be opened up between them.

Clair ran directly into the consequences of his purely aesthetic, apolitical attitude when he took on major social issues in *A nous la liberté*. André Breton loathed the ingratiating facility of this film,[13] and Clair meekly apologized that its operetta form was too flimsy to bear the weighty subject matter of mechanization, leisure, and social governance. He believed the film's genuine aesthetic and thematic conclusion lay in the penultimate sequence. Here the hoary dignitary's honorific testimonial, praising Louis's breakthrough in concocting the automated production of phonographs, is drowned out when an unforeseen windstorm brings with it the famous shower of currency. The controlled mayhem that ensues, everyone chasing either the blowing bills or Louis, recalls the absurd funeral race of *Entr'acte* and may recover some of the force of that film's social allegory.

But once again, Clair became more concerned with the aesthetics than with the function of allegory. By definition the frame is sovereign in pictorial allegory, as it hierarchizes the values that shuttle from low to high. The fussiness of Clair's framing and his penchant for adorning that frame with filigree keep the spectator's attention from wandering. Recall, as a marked example, the heroine as seen from Emile's prison cell. Her third-story window is framed by a flower box and by vines of morning glories to set off her lovely face and to amplify through its imagery the song we suppose her to be singing. The surface attractiveness of this scene results from the single effect produced by the ensemble, particularly when this shot is itself framed by shots of Emile in prison. The bars on his window are made to contrast with the vines that enclose as well as honor her. The little flower he holds may stand for the garland that surrounds her. His upturned face seeks her downward glance. Because of such graphic matches, no detail—not even the woman's perfectly lit visage—promises to reveal anything in itself. Instead these elements add up to an unmistakable signification: in this case, the general imprisonment of authenticity and innocence in the industrial world. Moments later, when the source of the lovely song is revealed to be a phonograph, that signification is rudely reversed. Although the girl has not shown herself to be inauthentic, she has been resituated in another design that contradicts our first impression of her.

This semiotic and aesthetic legerdemain has immediate thematic consequences, for it initiates the film's lighthearted but caustic interrogation of authenticity in a world controlled by business. The cardinal emblems of ancient values, carried by a blond woman's face and by the strains of song, are shown to be compromised by modern technology. The phonograph mechanizes music, removing it from its source, and the young girl is revealed to be a trivial possession of her obsequious father who uses her as his chief counter in the exchange system of modern capitalist life.

The abstract geometry of Meerson's sets effectively equates all spaces, just as the abstract value of money equates all labor and objects, right up to the rationalized apotheosis of the automated assembly line capable of turning out an endless stream of phonographs all blaring the same recorded music.[14] Individual identity means nothing in a world where "position" accounts for everything. This is the lesson of the file drawers that contain the identity papers of thousands of interchangeable workers; it is also the lesson Louis learns as he trades on his own false identity, inflating his position to a stature equal to the overblown painted portrait in his home, a portrait that will be betrayed by the prison photo that blackmails him. Throughout this cynical exposition, Emile stands as the ingenuous reminder of the simple joys of life outside the money economy. For this he is first incarcerated, then later expelled from the utopia of the finale.

Clair must surely have been aware that his own aesthetic conspires with the cold rational modernism he pretends to satirize. For geometry rules his films, and character identities matter only because of the patterns that give them temporary significance. Hence characters and actors are largely interchangeable, and the motion of Clair's movie machine takes precedence over every-

A nous la liberté: Chaos of currency. BFI

A nous la liberté: Geometry of business. BFI

thing else. Gilles Deleuze goes so far as to cite Clair as the epitome of French cinema's inhuman drive to pursue the consequence of pattern to its limit:

> French cinema uses the machine to attain a mechanical composition of movement-images. . . . A first type of machine is the automaton, a simple machine or clock mechanism, a geometrical configuration of parts which combine, superimpose or transform movements in homogeneous space, according to the relationships through which they pass. The automaton . . . illustrates a clear mechanical movement as law of the maximum for a set of images which brings together things and living beings, the inanimate and the animate, by making them the same. . . . It is obviously René Clair who gives this formula its greatest poetic generality, and animates geometrical abstractions in a space which is homogeneous, luminous and grey, without depth. The concrete object, the object of desire, appears as a motor or spring acting in time, *primum movens*, which triggers off a mechanical movement, toward which an increasing num-

ber of characters contribute, appearing in turn in space, like parts of an expand-ing mechanized set (*Un Chapeau de paille d'Italie*, *Le Million*). Individualism is the essential element throughout: the individual holds himself behind the object, or rather himself plays the role of spring or motor developing its effects in time; ghost, illusionist, devil or mad scientist, destined to be wiped out when the movement he determines has reached its maximum or overtaken him (*Paris qui dort*, *Entr'acte*). Then everything will return to a state of order. In short, an automatic ballet, whose motor itself circulates, through the movement.[15]

In the final scene of *A nous la liberté* Emile and Louis, now hobos, entertain some picnicking workers by shyly singing one of the theme songs of the movie. Collecting a couple of sous, they turn to the open road and, after a moment's regret, playfully cudgel and kick each other out of view under the recorded choral strains of the title song. The last word belongs to the sound-recording technology capable of drowning out the voices of the heroes. They must leave the modern world in search of the authentic primary experiences afforded by the open road. But if Clair is right, the road to the past goes nowhere, and his heroes, like the prime movers of Clair's early films that Deleuze cites, are meant to disappear. Their service performed, they are no longer relevant to Clair's world of mechanical motion. Neither are their senti-ments relevant to the modern world.

A nous la liberté: Fantasy of an open future. BFI

This concluding topos, made most famous by Chaplin, conventionally freezes the image of the characters for their possible future appearance in a sequel. But what could this pair do in a sequel? Completely defined by the filmic and economic system of *A nous la liberté*, they are in the end defined out of the machine altogether, discarded down the road to the dross pile. Liberty has been banished from the rationalized factory system and from the modern film based on the precision of moving parts. Neither Emile nor Louis is strong enough to hold our interest beyond the film in the manner of Chaplin.

A year later, Jean Renoir's vagabond, Boudu, would likewise doff his tuxedo and wander down the road in scarecrow's garb. But this character is indeed ready to reappear, and will do so irrepressibly as the magnificently anarchic Père Jules in Vigo's *L'Atalante*. Unlike Clair, Renoir is fascinated by both his actor and his character, obtuse elements that are more powerful than the society and the film set around them.[16] Boudu's inexhaustible imagination and spontaneity force a breaking of cinematic as well as social rules. Liberty thrives in his body and pushes out from it, whereas Emile and Louis are abstract ciphers of liberty, hence factored out in the final equation.

Was Clair's "decline" due to a loss of inspiration and execution, or was his genre exhausted and unresponsive to a changing culture? For one thing he had sacrificed everything to the god of rhythm and handicapped himself by ignoring the cult of the star. Important players stud his films, Albert Préjean and Annabella foremost among these, but no star is allowed to command attention in an aesthetic based on shifts of attention. The stunts, skits, and routines in his films fail to stand out since they are so carefully intercalated into the larger flow, whereas American films had learned to slow down for stars and set pieces. In contrast, Clair proposed to transform each actor's gestures into pure musical notes that he could call on in his orchestration. He was disappointed that audiences preferred to single out top-ranked actors, stunning set pieces, odd characters, and even individual gags that they could applaud or take home in their memories. He worried lest the cinema become an auditorium for this parade of the grand or the peculiar to which the director was beholden.

Clair was determined to be beholden to nothing but his notion of visual movement. He followed that notion to England, when in 1934 he could see that his operetta style had lost popularity with the French public and had not gathered many followers among filmmakers. In that year *Le Dernier Milliardaire* opened to disappointed reviews. Moreover, the only veteran director who could be counted in Clair's aesthetic camp, Augusto Genina, decided to return to Italy.[17] Clair left behind him the international prestige he had built almost single-handedly for the French film industry but he left little else. If we need to look for it, Clair's influence on poetic realism comes from his conviction that directors should perpetually strive for a single effect, but he was not a poetic realist for all that. As a narrator he stood back from the cinematic flow under his baton with humor and irony, an attitude that the poetic realists would be unable to muster.

Although no Clair school of film ever developed, he did help many of France's premier technicians to mature (Georges Périnal and Meerson the most renowned). They always credited his genius, as did Georges Lacombe, his assistant on some early films, who in 1934 made *Jeunesse*, the one film

Sous les toits de Paris: Clair's crew, Meerson's set. BFI

Jeunesse: Streets and a street song in the Clair tradition. CF

clearly indebted to Clair's sensibility. *Jeunesse* opens on a quintessentially French street scene, complete with street singer, à la *Sous les toits de Paris*. Lacombe's romantic comedy is more bitter than Clair's prototype, however; its peripeties include attempted suicide and an unwanted pregnancy. The restrained acting style, the constantly moving camera, and the picturesque but realistic settings (cheap hotel rooms, an airy café—a *guinguette*—on the Marne) give us a better preview of the poetic realist concerns than had any of Clair's films.[18]

As they would with the poetic realists, viewers of the time found Lacombe "less ironic" than Clair and far more tender in his depiction of disappointed

Jeunesse. CF

love.[19] Lacombe retains from Clair the imposition of symmetry not only on a plot that matches two men and two women, and that arranges satisfying but unbelievable repetitions and coincidences, but also in sequences organized with geometric clarity. The first two sequences of *Jeunesse* open on a contextualizing icon (a street singer in the first, the pendulum of a clock in the second) and, after the drama has made its point in each, Lacombe returns to the key icon and fades out. Such careful patterning never becomes a delight in itself, as it does in Clair, but rather frames this "milieu of Parisian quarters, Sunday boating parties, open air dances, and the fleeting poetry of life."[20] Lovingly attentive to Clair's populist themes, *Jeunesse* maps them onto a genuine French landscape and by doing so maps out the turn French cinema was taking away from Clair's more abstract allegorical style.

Jean Vigo

Vigo has been called the natural child of Surrealism and anarchy, so that the radical expression of his films became the exhalation of an unconventional life and upbringing more than the consequence of a considered program. While committed thinkers of the 1920s like Léon Moussinac, Henri Goudal, and Robert Desnos ineffectually prophesied a glorious future cinema, Vigo with his more casual relation to Surrealism and socialism had an effect that can still be felt today.[21]

Vigo's reputation as a prodigy of the cinema rests on less than two hundred minutes of film. In his first venture, the twenty-five-minute *A propos de Nice* (1930), one can see immediately the energy and aptitude of this great talent. Confined to Nice on account of his already advanced tubercular condition, he made the trip to Paris in the summer of 1929 ostensibly to consult medical specialists. Haunting the *ciné-club* showings at the Vieux-Colombier and at the Studio des Ursulines, he met Boris Kaufman, a Russian émigré and brother to Dziga Vertov. Kaufman, already an established cameraman in the kino-eye tradition, was enthusiastic about Vigo's plan to film an incisive essay on Nice and accepted the latter's invitation to move into his apartment during the project. Since Vigo worked for a small company as assistant cameraman, he had access to ends of film stock. He also possessed his own Debrie camera, purchased with $250 of a cash wedding present meant to help the Vigos in their poverty. During the autumn of 1929, the two men and their wives labored over a script, and shooting began by year's end. Before the takeover of sound, one could still cobble together such a cottage enterprise. If you ran a *ciné-club*, you were almost expected to try.[22]

Vigo's single surviving proclamation is the introduction he gave for the premiere of *A propos de Nice* at the Studio 28, entitled, "Toward a Social Cinema." In manifesto style, he lashes out against commercial cinema, of course, but is more aggressive in his attack on that portion of the avant-garde pursuing art for art's sake. Like Breton he demands an energetic cinema capable of doing damage to reigning ideas and of penetrating the skin of nature and society. At first, his plea for a "documentary approach" might remind one of John Grierson, but Vigo's notion of a "document," let alone a documentary, is worlds away from straightforward realism.[23] Against the passivity of the camera lens he opposes the hyperactivity of the filmmaker's passionate eye darting about in a worldly but calculated search for new and magical relations among objects, moods, words, and actions. Again echoing Breton, Vigo insists that such relations exist independent of the designs of the artist; they hover in a heretofore invisible space. The artist documents them, forcing viewers out of their habitual indolence, making them respond to the vibrancy of a film form that expresses the true vibrancy of social and natural life forms. Such a strong notion of documentary boldly attacked both its subject matter and its audience. Vigo proudly proclaimed his own effort as a continuation of the film he most admired, *Un Chien andalou*. He implied that French producers and spectators needed their eyes slashed. In 1930 they needed the energy of direct, even adolescent, visions.

Vigo and Kaufman originally planned their film as a variant of the city symphony complete with three distinct movements (sea, land, and sky). *A propos de Nice* was meant to be far more politically aggressive than earlier films in the genre like *Berlin, Symphony of a City* or *Rien que les heures*. One thing was certain, the audience must not be given room to soften their images into a travelogue. A rigorous thematic scheme, pitting the ennui of the upper classes at the shore and in the casinos against the struggle for life and death in the city's poorer back streets, was to keep the film and the audience on a critical keel.

Not many days into the shooting, the clarity of such a programmatic script idea was abandoned. Unable to film "live" in the casinos, Vigo and Kaufman concentrated on the strength of particular images they discovered in their rushes, rather than on the continuity of a larger design. They were certain that design would emerge in the juxtaposition of the charged images themselves. They looked at each shot for its particular charge, weighing its iconographic significance as a "social document" and its visual quality as a composed photograph with internal rhythm. In keeping with the dialectical impulse that served as the script's starting point, the figure of antithesis was used to point the chosen images in a rhetorical trajectory; for example, pictures of hotels, lounging women, wealthy tourists, and fancy roulette tables stand out against tenements, decrepit children, garbage, and local forms of back-street gambling. In the carnival sequence that ends the film, the bursting energy within the city's filthy belly spills out onto the streets of the wealthy to dramatize a conflict that geography tries to hide.

At the level of form, an opposition develops between a two-dimensional optical schema, used primarily for the wealthy facade of the town, and a tactile, quasi-three-dimensional approach that renders the city's interior. The aerial views that open the film are the epitome of the flat, optical style that characterizes the form of life of the wealthy who stroll voyeuristically along the famous Promenade des Anglais. Indolent observers of sport and fashion, they keep away from the city center where everyone including the camera participates in the carnal dance of life, a dance whose eroticism is made explicit toward the film's end.

Vigo's explicitly Buñuelian aesthetic and Kaufman's Soviet constructivism account for the shock cuts of symbolically laden images, such as towering smokestacks and baroque cemeteries. A woman can be stripped nude by a stop-action cut, or a sunbather can instantly metamorphose into a lobster. Swift tilts flip a grand hotel as though it were a picture postcard. Yet moments later a hidden camera delivers covertly recorded shots of people at their leisure. *A propos de Nice* presents several striking styles but manages to recruit them for its own purposes. Its experimental techniques and frequently clumsy camerawork exude the energy of its creators and blare a guttural cry. The city is built on fashion and gambling; ultimately it is built on death, as its ornate cemetery advertises. But beneath this surface, somehow beneath even the cemetery, flows an erotic force, the force of seething life that one can almost touch and smell. This force drives the film.

A propos de Nice advanced the cinema not because it gave Vigo his start and not because it is a beautifully crafted art film. It remains one of those few examples where the several powers of the medium (to record the unknown, to clarify relations, to proselytize and arouse) come together with an irrepressible strength and ingenuity. Its premiere brought Vigo the recognition from critics and devotees of *ciné-clubs* that he needed to launch the larger projects he had in mind. But *A propos de Nice* received only minimal distribution; the age of silent films, even experimental ones like this, was at an end. Still, every director should begin his or her career as Vigo did, with the commitment, independence, and sense of enthusiastic exploration fostered by the era of *ciné-clubs*.

Commonly one traces in Vigo's three important productions (*A propos de Nice*, *Zéro de conduite*, and *L'Atalante*) a line descending from the most politically and aesthetically radical to the more settled and assimilated. The three genres these films draw from (the city symphony, the allegorical short, and the feature love story) would tend to confirm this descent into commercial production. And the same might be said, as a corollary, for the distribution they received, or, more aptly, failed to receive. *A propos de Nice* had one big night at the Studio 28 and after that only a few art-house showings. *Zéro de conduite* was banned by the censors but in any case could have anticipated little more than a marginal commercial release, given its clumsy length and questionable production values. *L'Atalante* alone was publicized and released in standard fashion, though only after the producer had renamed it, recut it, and totally reworked its music track.

Despite this apparent aesthetic softening and this increasingly friendly outreach toward commercial distribution and broad audiences, the best critics of the day saw in *Zéro de conduite* and *L'Atalante* the same concerns that howl from the belly of *A propos de Nice*.[24] Hardly a concession, Vigo's more agreeable and seductive films responded to changes in the situation of cinema in the first years of sound. The death of so many *ciné-clubs* and journals, the end of the experimental era, and the birth of significant new genres presented Vigo with an altogether different arena in which to make himself felt. Yet the excitement of directing films, the joys of surprise and spontaneity, of strong images and stronger breaks with convention, are as visible in *L'Atalante* and *Zéro de conduite* as in *A propos de Nice*. In all three we find a powerfully sensual politics of the image, Vigo's greatest contribution to, and legacy from, anything that might be called the Surrealist revolution.

Such a politics had its consequences. In 1933 *Zéro de conduite* was one of just eleven films (out of 583) removed from all distribution by the official governmental censorship board.[25] Its irreverence, which at first blush seems harmless compared to that of *A propos de Nice*, rightly distressed the censors. Indeed its rhetoric is all the more subversive for arising directly within the image world it portrays, whereas the rhetoric of the more stridently politicized city symphony had sounded from the side of the screen, as it were, a commentary on the conditions of life it documented. *Zéro de conduite* does not comment on anything; rather, it directly expresses a revolutionary sensibility.

Unique among films of "school days," its tone is not that of an adult reflecting on the insults suffered long ago. Nor is there the slightest hint of nostalgia for those frolicking days of misspent youth. The reason is clear: *Zéro de conduite* unfolds with a genuinely childish narration. Where *A propos de Nice* was cocky and flippant, *Zéro de conduite* is winning and outrageous. In essence Vigo has become one of his adolescents, seeing with their eyes, exaggerating things with their sense of truth, impressed by whatever impresses them. In the earlier film, the city of Nice was analyzed across a range of its aspects (economic, social, ritualistic, architectural) but *Zéro de conduite* analyzes nothing. Truly a dream film, it calls on just enough facts of social life to spawn its imaginary adventures. Its triumph, though, is to present the imaginary in the most commonplace way. In the first sequence the boys transform their innocent toys into sexual props (the balloons, the feathers, the horn, the ping pong gun), before fading into a fog of cigar smoke. The choo-choo train inspires Maurice Jaubert's score, which in turn will continue to inspire the children by insisting on the rhythm to be found in the structured dullness of their surroundings. The full narration (like the music that is its principal emanation) is as alive as the children, joyfully complicit in their pranks, sensitive to their observations. At one point Vigo goes so far as to animate a teacher's cartoon drawing; next, the teacher magically stands on one hand with which he doodles. The children applaud in glee, as do we.

The moral dimension of this universe is transparent, revealing itself as a matter of course to the camera's darting eye. All adults are caricatured, not just to satisfy some childish urge to deform, but to satisfy the stringent demands of a childish morality that literally does see adults as dwarfish or greasy or sniveling and surreptitious. The polymorphous sexuality of the children stands out against the vaguely submerged pederasty of their teachers, who continually cringe and look askance, all the time fearing that with these children "anything can happen!"

It is tempting to recall only those moments when anything does happen, particularly the glorious feather pillow procession that celebrates in slow motion the children's accession to power, and then the release of that power outdoors that sends the old "stuffed shirts" reeling. But Vigo also shows us

Zéro de conduite: "Anything can happen." BFI   *Zéro de conduite*: Anarchy does happen. BFI

their dead-time so as to make us wonder if some day they, as alumni, might not become stuffed shirts themselves. Dawdling in the kitchen while the cook prepares the unvarying and tasteless meal, or sitting bolt upright on a Sunday visit in the parlor of a girl, these children remind us of the insufferable boredom childhood involves.

Is such boredom and are these insupportable authority figures prerequisites for the life of the imagination that rises up in response? Refusing to fly off to some post of wisdom or even of understanding, Vigo cannot tell us if the prison of the schoolyard is the happiest plot of ground for human souls, but he stands in wonder beneath his triumphant children, looking on as one kid among others, imaging their imagination, giving body to their beautiful bodies.

From the moment of its screening at the censor's board, no one has doubted the radical intentions of *Zéro de conduite*. Vigo's producer, Jacques-Louis Nounez, still believing in the talent of the young man, decided to protect both of them by dictating the tame subject of their next venture, *L'Atalante*. This seemed the responsible thing to do and, because of that fact, *L'Atalante* for a time suffered a comparative critical neglect, for Vigo's notoriety has been based precisely on the moral thrust of his irreverence, which the earlier films so salaciously exhibit.

L'Atalante's structure and theme are undeniably conventional: the conflict of love and liberty and the maturation of sexual desire into domestic harmony. A decade earlier such a film might find critical acceptance on condition that its theme be subverted or its structure formalized—in short, that it be sculpted into an impressionist "art film." But we know from his speech at the Vieux-Colombier how Vigo loathed the aestheticism of the impressionists, and we can tell from a sympathetic viewing of the film how he honored the sentiments of the subject put before him, trite though they be. In *L'Atalante* Vigo took up the stage of life just beyond the marvels of childhood, the stage, treated seldom by the Surrealists but often by the poetic realists, in which human beings must define themselves by the commitments they make. The plot of *L'Atalante* schedules this problem as the eruption of sexuality into civilization's most basic social structure. Can marriage sustain itself without repressing the innermost longings of each partner? Moreover, can it make use of the energy such longings generate? Vigo refigures these as problems in his work as a filmmaker by submitting the demands of narrative and logic to the power of imagistic play and spontaneous flights.

Whereas he goaded on the young characters of *Zéro de conduite* with visual antics equal to their own play, in *L'Atalante* Vigo follows the lead of the three actors confined on the barge. As skipper of the barge Jean represents the need to organize and discipline. He encloses Juliette in his cabin and would frame her irrepressible joy, keeping it safe and for himself. He represents the well-schooled and responsible storyteller Vigo could never become.

Juliette, on the other hand, embodies in her lithe way Vigo's fascination with the sheer beauty of the image. Her thrill in being aboard, her anticipation of their arrival in the metropolis, and most important, her amazement in front of Père Jules and his cabin of exotic memories bespeak the grand adventure of the movies. Juliette gives herself to the untamed possibilities of the imagination and threatens the tidy life story Jean had scripted for her as his wife, as she responds literally to the disturbing sexuality exuding from Père Jules and the helter-skelter sex offered by the peddler.

L'Atalante pursues these character instincts and filmmaking aesthetics until their inherent conflict nearly overturns both the marriage and the film.[26] The pressure peaks when a hallucinating Jean dives desperately into the Seine to seek Juliette, while Juliette, lost in the loneliness of Paris, finds only her own reflection in the store windows. Subsequently crosscutting between their separate beds, Vigo arranges the couple's union through simultaneous autoeroticism, bridged by Jaubert's soaring love theme. Imagination here transforms desire into the very image of love.

This third and finally triumphant way of life, overcoming Jean's paternalistic control and Juliette's narcissistic childishness, descends from the director only after it emerges out of the hold with Père Jules. Superstitious and spontaneous, Père Jules is the real power source aboard the barge. His wisdom is not that of age but of the ages. Music flows from his fingers; Juliette's song finds its way to his ear from miles away. In tune with his instincts he lives with the naturalness of a cat. Vigo is no romantic. The natural man, if Père Jules is that, is graceless and clumsy. But he belongs with cats because he knows how to tread. The paraphernalia he surrounds himself with and the impulses to which he responds possess a hidden logic. One cannot impose that logic (as Jean would wish) nor can one arrange for it on the spot (as Juliette seems to hope). Père Jules alone knows that it must be elicited from the imagination and the truths it reveals of life. This is the core of Surrealism in *L'Atalante*.[27]

Vigo designed just enough narrative and just such imagery as to net the unexpected in his film. The final result represents an advance over impressionism, for *L'Atalante* listens to the possibilities it evokes rather than arranging all its effects in advance. What Luis Buñuel termed "the inviolate moral exigency" of Surrealism surfaces in Vigo's wise innocence.[28] Refusing to discard the ordinary pleasures of narrative or the equally ordinary beauty of images, he refuses even more to refine these into fetishes. Instead he hovers about his story and his images with that excess of attention François Truffaut termed "a fever," waiting for the marvelous to emerge.[29] "Fever" does indeed emerge in Juliette's night walk on deck, in the bursting smile with which she greets the sunrise the next day, in the extraordinary beauty of the locks of the canal Saint Martin in Paris, and continually, in the character of Père Jules.

The price of this approach is clumsiness. By classic standards, *L'Atalante* is an ill-shaped film. The music it strives to make is made with an audible effort. We hear the scratches of the phonograph, the static of the radio, the breathing of the accordion, just as we can see Vigo strain to bring the chaos of reality into a provisional order. At times we sense him growing excited at the order he has discovered, as when blotchy spots suddenly appear on the flesh of the separated couple in their bipartite love scene. Vigo is an "obscene director" in that his films are aimed specifically at some need in our own bodies. He has a faith in bodies, in a hidden reason of the flesh. He has the instincts of Père Jules.

Exactly where these instincts come from Gilles Deleuze tries to pinpoint: "If there is any reconciliation between land and sea, this takes place in Père Jules, but only because he knows how to impose spontaneously on the land the same law as the sea."[30] Vigo has refigured a simple narrative into a complex problem of vision and movement, using the barge as an intermediate space between two sexes, two moralities, and two centers of gravity. "On the land there is not the same regime of movement, not the same 'grace' as on the sea, in the sea: terrestrial movement is in perpetual disequilibrium because the motive force is always outside the center of gravity . . . while aquatic movement is like the displacement of the center of gravity. . . . This accounts for the apparent clumsiness of this movement when it takes place on land or even on the barge—a crab-like walk, snaking or twirling—but this is an other-worldly grace." Deleuze goes on to salute the film's achievement of "grace under a coarse appearance."[31] To clinch his view and mine, he might have described the apotheosis of grace as displaced gravity when Jean seeks Juliette in the waters of the Seine, crossing the screen from bottom to top, top to bottom, and side to side, while her image in a wedding dress turns slowly before him in superimposition.

L'Atalante presents a mature Vigo, where maturity comes to confirm the earliest intuitions of the man. The wisdom of old Père Jules expresses Vigo's faith that a lasting life upon this barge of a world is possible once we have renounced our need to dominate. Thus runs the final message of his perpetual but nuanced anarchism. Out of a brief, difficult life, he managed to concoct three uncompromising and marvelous films, the last of which may serve as a direct transit from Surrealism to poetic realism. Officially listed along with films by Buñuel and Man Ray in the special issue of *L'Age du cinéma* consecrated to Surrealism,[32] *L'Atalante* was further singled out as a summit of Surrealism by Alain Virmaux.[33] In Ado Kyrou's still more official account, *L'Atalante* was praised as "one of the most penetrating dreams of love the cinema has produced."[34] French critics proudly cite not just Breton but Arthur Rimbaud and Gérard de Nerval in recounting its poetry of objects (the pickled hands), its unsettling fogs, its unpredictable cats, and its more unpredictable characters.

We may claim populism for Vigo, if not poetic realism, by looking at his producer. While Man Ray, Jean Cocteau, and Buñuel depended on the largesse of the artistic and aristocratic communities, Vigo negotiated with the industry, working his way in from the periphery of his *ciné-club*. Furthermore, he took himself as one of the people about whom and for whom he made movies. The vignettes of *Zéro de conduite* draw on popular memory of school days. The vision he crystallized of those tender yet horrid years, with their childish yet utterly serious call to revolt, was a shared vision of millions, one whose articulation the censors needed to suppress.

In *L'Atalante* Vigo offers Père Jules as a gift to the working class. Larger than life, a popular genie, he has no aspirations to raise his station above the ordinary because he transforms everything into the extraordinary. *L'Atalante* trades in popular mythology, but it also digs its hands in the life of those whose toil leaves little room for imagination. It represents the labor of those millions who keep alive a Paris they have neither the time, the money, nor the culture to enjoy, a city that calls to them from the scratchy sounds of a radio. Where the river rises Jean is subject to the suffocating traditions of Juliette's village. Where it empties into the Atlantic he is at the mercy of the laws of commerce. Between mother-in-law and boss, Jean, like countless Frenchmen then and now, is proud of his independence. Just forty feet in width, his barge sustains this independence the length of the Seine. Jean carefully lifts it through the locks in Paris and steers it through fogs. Between the narrow banks of the river and the narrow time of its strict schedule, this barge holds passions of love and jealousy as large as any tale of princes. It holds, as a reward, the magnificent Père Jules.

Many have recognized that *L'Atalante*'s Surrealism, its discovery of the magical character of ordinary people, expands into the poetic realist sensibility that would dominate the rest of the decade.[35] It might be more accurate to recognize in poetic realism a retreat from the opening Vigo made in the fabric of French cinema, a visible retreat that lets us see the point of light through that hole growing smaller every year. For as much as Vigo's imagery inspired later filmmakers (think of the bridge over the canal in *Hôtel du Nord*), and as much as his focus on the beleaguered lives of poor but strong-willed characters would reappear in the roles Jean Gabin made famous, Vigo's tone—and hence the social force of his films—is distinct.

In an article on Vigo,[36] Bruno Voglino raises the central issue of individualism in French cinema. The optimism of individual creativity that characterizes the avant-garde of the 1920s did not survive the depression. As Aragon made so clear, two options presented themselves to the French: either to renounce the avant-garde as he did and submit utterly to the Communist Party, or to fall back on a pessimistic evocation or analysis of individualism. The poetic realists, including Renoir, chose the latter way. And one can feel it in the pathetic tone of their narration. Vigo's tone in contrast rings out confidently. Voglino believes it rings in harmony with the people. The poetic realists for the most part were disappointed children of the bourgeoisie; their weak pessimism shows itself in the terminal fatigue that overcomes the hero of *Le Jour se lève*, a fatigue that shows up in the very title of Duvivier's *La Fin du jour* (1938). Vigo's people are never tired. Juliette, the purest of these, explores Paris with a reckless curiosity. "Juliette is exactly the antithesis of the individualist heroes of Duvivier and Carné who pull away from contact with the socially ambient milieu."[37]

Vigo's tactile sensibility comes through his characters who subordinate order to adventure. The poetic realists scarcely relished adventure at all. Men of the people like Père Jules and Vigo had far too much going on in their imaginations for the notions of despair and suicide ever to settle into focus. Vigo's Surrealism does not evade social issues in poetic flight; it attacks them with its energy. As he was completing *L'Atalante* and just a few months before he died, Vigo signed Breton's "call to arms" against fascism, addressed to the organizations that would make up the Popular Front.[38] For Vigo Surrealism and politics were both at the service of a poetic realism that constituted an ethics as much as an aesthetic.

Jacques Prévert

A wonderful 1925 photo shows Breton standing beside a youthful Prévert. One could hardly demand a more pertinent affidavit for the origins of poetic realism. It is a tribute to the French film industry that a talent as wildly undisciplined, disdainful, and seriously Surrealist as Prévert's could be harnessed to drive the most successful films made in the years around World War II. Whereas Vigo was constitutionally unassimilable, and whereas Clair became perhaps too assimilated to constitute that radical difference he had sought to make in the 1920s, Prévert—to paraphrase his own self-description—stands with one foot inside French film, one foot outside French film, "and a third foot in the butts of the imbeciles."[39]

Unlike Vigo and Clair, but very like Breton, he had no patience for the discipline of the medium. Even after he had achieved great fame, Prévert was never known to make suggestions during the shooting of his scripts. Nor did he particularly socialize with the film community. He thought of himself as a more or less permanently invited guest of the industry. Yet whatever he offered the cinema seemed precisely what it needed. Guy Jacob reminds us that although he is always paired with Marcel Carné for their seven poetic realist masterpieces, Prévert must also be credited for the very best films done by more pedestrian directors like Marc Allégret, Christian-Jaque, André Cayatte, Jean Delannoy, and even Tino Rossi.[40] He worked on nearly thirty completed features in his life, virtually every one of which is memorable. One can only regret the numerous scuttled projects.

Despite his success and notoriety, Prévert also stood aloof from the official literary scene. A playwright, he was always taken for a gagman or a farceur, who dabbled cleverly with the craft of the stage but was not schooled enough to merit attention. A poet, indeed France's most widely read poet of the century, he was for years unrecognized by the critical establishment. And this suited him well, for he refused to recognize that establishment in return. He loathed sophisticated criticism, had no use for academics, and claimed never to have understood the value of artistic discipline. His writing came easy, and he flaunted the term "facile" to describe it. But in Prévert facility is raised to an aesthetic principle, one that permitted him to slide with ease from verse to song to the stage and then to the screen.

His facility was due not just to an incalculable talent, but to a milieu marked by speed and disposability, a milieu in which the cinema was the native art. In this context Prévert can be described as a cinematic poet; his verse travels from evocative object to object (a key poem is entitled "L'Inventaire"), building an interior decor within which one discovers a sentimental anecdote. Such a formula is nothing other than the "poetic" seed of poetic realism, out of which would blossom its limpid dialogue, Manichaean dramatic equations, and atmospheric effects. Other poems have been described as miniature scenarios complete with implied sets and fade-outs.[41] Such a mixture of poetry provides continuity of theme and style to his work in all media, governing his ethereal songs, his satires and caricatures for theater, his sketches for ballet, his commentaries accompanying the published drawings and photographs of his friends.

His diversity flowed from the exuberance of a mind so verbal some felt it talked only and continually to itself. Talking to oneself in fact is exactly the habit of poetry, at least when one is intent to say things just right; and so it is no wonder that Prévert's first and last publications should be in verse, and that his scripts should inform a movement known precisely as "poetic realism." Moreover, the distinctively lyrical quality of those scripts separates them from the theatricality that was standard throughout a decade of French cinema dominated by professional playwrights like Jacques Natanson, Marcel Achard, Yves Mirande, and Henry Bernstein. Next to these Prévert seems a naïf. His method of recounting stories by sketch, of evoking values by simple words and creating atmosphere by charged objects ignores the central criterion of drama: carefully developed characters expressing sophisticated dialogue. Sitting at his accustomed café, cigarette in his lips, his wineglass before him, Prévert was at once too ingenuous and too bored to follow such conventions. Nevertheless his subjects are ever and always the traditional ones: innocent love, societal repression, hypocrisy, fate, and the triumph of the imagination.

In a different register, Prévert's urban romances sing the same song of the common people one hears in Clair's ethereally abstract ballets or Vigo's obscenely tactile tales. All three rely on eloquently self-sufficient images (a bride in full wedding dress tripping across the length of a barge in moonlight, the silhouettes of silent criminals picking their way across the roofs of Paris).

Prévert's imagistic clarity stands out in a style of writing that owes more to the visual arts than to literature or the theater. He lived a life with painters of strong images, with Yves Tanguy, André Masson, Pablo Picasso, Joan Miró, and Marc Chagall.[42] He had the lightness, optimism, and swift imagination of Chagall, conjuring in bright words and brighter anecdotes the flights of lovers above a city, or the cynical reach of wily animals in cassocks and decorated uniforms. It is in this painterly, musical, and curiously nonliterary sense that he was a poet; it was in just this sense that his vision grafted itself onto the French cinema.

Prévert is the unmistakable child of the 1920s, spontaneous, iconoclastic, disdainful of success and of everything that comes from the establishment. He partook of the Surrealist emphasis on experience over artifact, on activity over system, and on perpetual revolution in search of the marvelous. Unmoved by the sublimity of natural landscapes or artistic monuments, Prévert tracked the marvelous in the realm of words and representations. He was prepared to go to the end of drunkenness and foolishness to come up with a single image or pun to delight and inspire his remarkable companions. His days and nights were parades of brilliant wit and satire.

Prévert's magnetism sets itself against the cult Breton fostered through his notorious credos, commandments, and encyclicals. Breton's tantrums and vendettas, theatrical though they were, disciplined his followers and kept the seriousness of their rebellion in view. Not so much younger, Prévert neverthe-less seems a full generation beyond Breton. Where Breton had been assigned as medical aide to deal with psychotic soldiers at the war's end, Prévert's disillusion with that disaster was more distant and ironic, for he was assigned to a military post in Constantinople from 1919 to 1922 where he pondered in leisure the absurdity of the struggle that had brought France victory but had ended her way of life and scuttled her traditional values.

In the army he met Tanguy and Marcel Duhamel, the friends with whom he would explore Europe's new (non)culture. Together with Jacques's younger brother, Pierre, they set themselves up in a communal house on rue du Château near Montparnasse. It was *La Bohème* 1923 for these future lumi-naries (Tanguy would soon be a key Surrealist painter; Duhamel, a novelist and founder of Gallimard's "série noire"). By all accounts[43] their nightly ribald "soirées" grew in notoriety from 1923 to 1928. Makeshift meals, followed by liters of cheap wine, led to dramatic rituals that served as models for the skits the Groupe Octobre would mount a few years later. Jacques inevitably mapped out the characters and the premise of these plays, and Pierre played the most complicated roles. But everyone took on at least one role, including the women who shared the flat with them, the visitors who heard about these nightly events, and their friends who lived with and around them.

Rue du Château soon grew in reputation to rival Breton's notorious Surreal-ist salon at his rue de la Fontaine apartment. Blaise Cendrars ambled cross-town when he tired of the haughty high-seriousness of the Surrealists. Breton himself took to showing up so as to monitor the situation; he declared that never had he felt an atmosphere more naturally Surrealist, with its easy spontaneity and its total liberty of expression. He marveled at Prévert who "masterfully aimed his verbal gems that were so charged as to show us perceptibly in a flash the right direction to take, and that radiated straight out of childhood, sustaining indefinitely the reservoir of revolt."[44]

For their part, and despite their interest in Breton, the rue du Château group scoffed at his intimidating manifestos; soon they attracted many of Breton's disaffected followers. In a notorious proclamation called "Un Cadavre," Prévert, along with Desnos, Michel Leiris, and Georges Bataille, sealed their excommunication from the main line of the Surrealists by publicly ridiculing Breton. Somehow Breton retained an affection for Prévert, perhaps because he was, like Raymond Queneau, a modern-day troubadour so delightful to listen to, and so in touch with the rhythms of contemporary speech, that his doctrinal errors could be forgiven.

In 1928 Sadoul and André Thirion bought the flat at rue du Château and the Prévert group moved on to rue Dauphine. By this time, though, theirs had become a café culture. Sitting in a corner of Les Deux Magots or Le Flore with a view of the old church of Saint-Germain-des-Prés, Prévert would be surrounded with members of the intellectual subculture of Paris. Fanning out from his table were successive ranks of those enthralled to hear him comment on people, invent anecdotes, and pun mercilessly. He was an oral poet, whose reputation grew by word of mouth, for by 1930 he had yet to publish a single line of verse or prose.

Picasso recalls first seeing Prévert at Le Flore discussing a recent ballet, *Rendez-vous*, with the painter, Mayo, and with Alexandre Trauner, soon to become the most famous poetic realist set designer. Also there was Georges Ribemont-Dessaignes, the editor of the avant-garde journal *Bifur*. He whispered to Picasso, "[Prévert] brings a new sound to French poetry . . . even when he writes, you have to say he is really talking . . . he comes out of the street and not out of literature. . . . A case apart, he adores life and despises 'good folk.' With his simplicity, his taste for joy, his corrosive humor, he can't be classified at all."[45]

Those pressing around him increasingly spoke of the cinema. Even on rue du Château, films had been a staple as nourishing as food and drink. The American cinema and the standard French serials drew them, generally to the cheap midnight screenings. Like the Surrealists Prévert had been marked in his youth by *Fantômas* and *Les Mystères de New-York* and continued to fawn over popular movies rather than the recherché experiments of the European avant-garde. He and his "bande," as they grew to be called, found in Buster Keaton and Harry Langdon styles of acting they would emulate in their own skits. They felt at home with the liveliness and vulgarity of the standard cinema.

The images of urban landscapes and the faces of stars haunted them. They lived the Surrealist dream of walking through movies and through life as spectators to a mysterious scene that only their attentiveness and imagination could begin to put together.

Prévert's favorite Surrealist companion at the cinema was also one of the cinema's stars, Pierre Batcheff. Despite his growing fame Batcheff dreamed only of making his own films, and making them against the grain. As the lead in *Un Chien andalou* his face has impressed itself on all our imaginations. It also impressed Prévert who immediately embarked with him on a scenario worthy of the actor's talents and ambitions. The two of them would go off to a corner table or even an unknown café to work out the scenes of *Emile-Emile*, as the script was called. This would have been Prévert's first foray into the public world, and Batcheff seemed exuberant at the prospect of scandalizing Paris with his friend's bitterly satiric wit and with an openly physical comedy associated with Laurel and Hardy and with Charley Chase.[46] But financing depended on Emile Natan, the most influential producer in Paris and Batcheff's boss. Natan was not amused by the script, was shocked that its title took aim at him, and scuttled the project.[47]

Batcheff saw this rejection as an ultimate roadblock in the way of the authentic life and work he craved. His behavior became erratic. Decrying the stupidity of the films he was forced to act in, trying to rouse the masses to respond to the liberating representations of countercinema, he would carry a projector on weekends to the prisons and ghettos of Paris. His wife Denise Batcheff (later married to Roland Tual) claims that he was a victim of Breton's fanaticism. In the end he hardly slept, alternating nights of wild dancing with interminable sessions of "automatic writing." His death came in an overdose of drugs. Perhaps he had long been subject to their effects. In any case, Surrealism was to him, as it was to many others, an addiction he would not forsake for all the fame and money that was repeatedly offered him.

Prévert was crushed by this loss and put *Emile-Emile* away forever. But the public would be hearing from him soon, indeed immediately. On the day of Batcheff's death, Raymond Bussières led a group of young actors to rue Dauphine to ask Prévert to write a script for a worker's theater spectacle. Although he was not up to greeting them that afternoon, within two weeks the first Groupe Octobre production, *Vive la presse*, lightened the heavily didactic soirées that passed in that era for "théâtre engagé." This intersection of Prévert's improvisatory talent with the worker's theater movement in 1932 was decisive for both. It gave Prévert an audience and, quickly, an unprecedented fame. It gave to a growing theatrical tradition precisely the spirit required to lead it toward the glory years of the Popular Front.

The early 1930s saw theater worldwide inflate itself with political ambition. This was the great era of socialist dramaturgy, following on the experiments of Erwin Piscator and Bertolt Brecht in Germany, and Vsevolod Meyerhold and F.E.K.S. (the Factory of the Eccentric Actor, inaugurated in 1921) in the

U.S.S.R. The most promising French site for revolutionary theater was surely the Théâtre Alfred Jarry, but its avant-garde productions staged by Roger Vitrac and Antonin Artaud carried scant political overtones, striving instead to liberate actors and spectators from the strictures of the text so as to promote something they termed a "communal action." Their notion of action had more to do with spiritual flights than with concerted, rational, political behavior; still, they inspired the more politically conscious theater groups around them.

One such group, Prémices, underwritten by Gaston Baty, mixed professional actors and amateurs in productions ranging from comedies by Prosper Mérimée and satires by Mirbeau to ensemble recitations of contemporary *engagé* poets. Their first production in 1929 allied them directly with the national labor unions, for whom they regularly prepared holiday spectacles. Henri Vaillant-Couturière, soon to be the head of cultural affairs for the Popular Front, suggested that a disgruntled portion of Prémices ask Prévert for material, after they had come into conflict with the troupe's more formalist wing loyal to Baty.

Thus Prévert came on board a splinter troupe, Groupe de choc Prémices, sustained by Vaillant-Couturière's money under Moussinac's supervision. Moussinac gave Prévert and his brilliant friend the director Loup Tchimoukov a free hand, which for the next few years they waved wildly about the union halls, factories, bistros, and *grands magasins* of Paris. No one has ever written and produced plays faster than the Groupe Octobre, the name they adopted late in 1932. When Adolf Hitler burned the Reichstag, Prévert composed a mock "reportage" the very next day. When the workers on strike at Citroën were beginning to falter and a friend asked Prévert to give them something, he whipped up a complete drama in the morning, rehearsed it all afternoon, and had it presented that very evening, with a set cleverly designed to permit the actors to read portions of the imperfectly memorized text unnoticed.[48]

His most famous piece was *La Bataille de Fontenoy*, a spoof on the origins of World War I (businessmen, clergy, and overstuffed generals, of course). But Prévert wrote in other genres as well, scripting mime plays for the dancer Georges Pomiès, composing songs for the music hall sensation Gilles Margaritis (who played the peddler in *L'Atalante*, a film for which the Préverts were hastily recruited as extras). He wrote larger roles for Jean-Louis Barrault whom the group paid to participate in their more impressive spectacles.

Prévert's contagious personality and his manifest (but manifestly nondoctrinaire) sympathy for the causes of the Left disarmed insinuations about the shallowness of his political awareness. As had been the case with his lax Surrealism, this easygoing attitude brought to him a number of actors and friends disenchanted with the more intellectually sophisticated and "responsible" leftist theater groups that abounded in the Paris of 1933. The Groupe Octobre never affiliated itself with the Parti Communiste, nor even with the trade unions whose members constituted the bulk of their audience. Their plays, then, were not dictated from above but grew in symbiosis with a popular audience they respected and increasingly knew how to please. Still, they were invited to the Moscow Olympiad of workers' theaters in 1933 where their antics won them top prize.

After the fascist riots of February 1934, they bartered some of their independence for solidarity with the Popular Front. At the behest of Vaillant-Couturière, they joined in the famous Bastille Day spectacle of 1935, which attracted an audience of over 100,000 citizens. But by 1935 the Groupe Octobre had lost much of its cohesion. Financial troubles grew with the size of their productions. Duhamel, who had in the early years personally underwritten their losses, looked for work in the film industry, as did Yves Allégret, Jean-Paul Le Chanois, and a good many others. Unemployment was so severe that anyone who could find a job simply had to give up the luxury of working in the bistros with Prévert and company.

Pierre had actually been the first of the Prévert brothers to break into filmmaking. He had produced a short in 1929 with Duhamel, had assisted on Buñuel's *L'Age d'or* together with Jacques-Bernard Brunius and Claude Heymann, and then had moved over to work on Jean Renoir's first talkies, *On purge bébé* (1931) and *La Chienne* (1931), a film Denise Batcheff (Tual) helped edit.[49] Even before this Duhamel had secured a temporary job as a production manager at Pathé-Natan thanks to Batcheff and to Prévert who had come to know the studio head, Charles David. It was this same David who in 1932 would permit the Préverts to shoot their thirty-five-minute *L'Affaire est dans le sac* on a set already in use for a standard production.

This slide into professional filmmaking was inevitable, as scores of independent French producers, most looking for cheap personnel, rushed to fill the void left by rumors of the retreat of Paramount that surfaced in 1933. Nearly every member of Prévert's "bande" had a working knowledge of filmmaking gained from marginal productions; moreover, they all had logged years of informal café talk about movies, often with industry figures like David or with intermediary figures like Claude Autant-Lara who shuttled between the bewildered industry and the bewildering avant-gardists in these first wild-west years of sound production.

It was in fact through Autant-Lara that Prévert and his "bande" rose in the profession. Born into the scintillating world of theater to which his illustrious parents gave him access, Autant-Lara had come to know Marcel Duchamp, Satie, and other legendary figures of Dada. His own first efforts in design were for the unknown Clair (an amateur unproduced piece of 1919) and then as assistant to Robert Mallet-Stevens and Fernand Léger.[50] Soon on his own he concocted costumes for some of the better films of the 1920s, including Renoir's *Nana* (1926). Called to Hollywood in the first years of sound, he returned to France in 1932 a very attractive talent to producers. He was, no matter how radical his ideas about art, both well connected and technically up to date. Almost immediately he was drafted by the well-known music critic Emile Vuillermoz to direct a lightweight operetta, *Ciboulette*. As a first-time director, he found himself subject to the imposition of a cast he scorned but could not alter. However, as a caustic avant-gardist he had his own response. Calling on Prévert to deform the play into a farce, he recruited a full contingent of the Groupe Octobre to play secondary roles. *Pour Vous* reported that no professional production had ever taken place in such an atmosphere of freedom, exuberance, and near anarchy.[51] The young Trauner built the sets with the help of Meerson. Yves Allégret took care of the costumes based on Autant-Lara's own designs. Jean Lods, Duhamel, Moussinac, Pomiès, Bussières, and Tchimoukov contributed their commedia dell'arte antics to spice the saccharine tale, so much so that Vuillermoz completely recut the film in anger and disgust.

It would be ten years before Autant-Lara found his way back to directing. *Ciboulette*, however, seemed only to hasten the entry of the Groupe Octobre into the mainstream of the industry. It moved en masse to Marc Allégret's *L'Hôtel du Libre Echange* (1934), introduced both by Marc's brother Yves and by Denise Tual who had edited the director's recent success, *Lac aux dames*. The sixth Georges Feydeau farce to have been adapted in the sound era, *L'Hôtel du Libre Echange* was easily the most spontaneous and vaudevillian. Jacob credits the cast and crew with lifting this film to the summit of its director's long and otherwise fussy career.[52]

L'Hôtel du Libre Echange:
Groupe Octobre vaudeville.
CF

A number of opportunities came to Prévert after *L'Hôtel du Libre Echange*, the most significant of which linked him in a single but legendary collaboration with Renoir. In 1935 each man sat at the center of devoted "bandes," and both were committed to communal action and art. Among the few individuals with allegiance to both groups was Jean Castanier, Renoir's set designer and a member of Prévert's café circle where he was once described as too social to put up with the loneliness of painting, and perhaps too lazy. Castanier and his friend Jacques Becker drew up the treatment for the film that would become *Le Crime de Monsieur Lange* while Becker was working with the Groupe Octobre on the short spoof *Le Commissaire est bon enfant* (1935). When Renoir was handed Castanier and Becker's treatment, he turned to Prévert, whom he had seen at the Billancourt studios when *L'Hôtel du Libre Echange* was in production and about whom he had been hearing so much. Becker was removed from his own project (and alienated for some time from his mentor), while Prévert converted the skeleton of a story into a script that was the basis for a film which enthused a good segment of the public, the critics, and the leftist politicians. This was a watershed movie for nearly everyone involved. Joseph Kosma contributed Florelle's song to the film, initiating a lifelong collaboration with Renoir. The actors who form the cooperative in the film came from the core of the Groupe Octobre (added to those who had worked on the Allégret film and on *Ciboulette* were Max Morise, Sylvain Itkine, Sylvia Bataille, and Jean Dasté).[53]

One of the clear triumphs of French cinema by every standard, *Le Crime de Monsieur Lange* reaches a plateau on which we can momentarily rest and survey the decade. For in the collective enthusiasm that it so ebulliently represented just before the elections of 1936, it stands as a peak of artistic and political optimism. A few months later the Popular Front government came into power behind an unprecedented union of intellectuals and workers. Even the politically diffident Prévert was ecstatic.

Le Crime de Monsieur Lange marks the decade's caesura, after which a newly professionalized Prévert would play a major role. How are Prévert's two dispositions reconciled: the adolescent poet of the cafés, author of amateurish satires like *L'Affaire est dans le sac*, and the polished scenarist whose name stands behind the most canonical—and some would say conservative—of French films.

Roger Leenhardt posed this question in an essay that came out in 1945 following the premiere of *Les Enfants du paradis*.[54] Must success automatically connote capitulation to mass taste and conservative politics? he asked, citing the cases of Victor Hugo and Emile Zola. There is, he ventured, a pure Prévert and then there is another Prévert whom the most interesting directors of the time used to their benefit. The pure Prévert is to be found in his early work with the Groupe Octobre, where burlesque and acid wit are played out as social allegories by actors who emulate marionettes. This acting style can be seen as the theatrical counterpart of the "pregnant commonplace" that characterizes Prévert's poetry (and hence his dialogue). Lines like "Un vrai béret français" that the peripatetic Brunius recites as a narratively detached refrain throughout *L'Affaire est dans le sac* strike us at first as pungent satire. After all, the "commonness" about such a commonplace is the vapid bourgeois sensibility that its emptiness indexes. Heard repeatedly, however, such a line acquires a truly poetic ring and so is assumed to take its place in a world of simple but tenderly plump expressions and sentiments. Leenhardt compares this to Francis Ponge's interest in the proverb as a form in which values and language are peculiarly concentrated.

The closed space of the set in *L'Affaire est dans le sac*, the distant camera angle observing "marionettes" (the word is Leenhardt's) who seem happily caught within that set, and the flat lighting that dedramatizes the plot in the manner of the Marx Brothers—all these are visual correlatives of a language of commonplaces and all are capable of working beyond satire toward the poetic assumption of the image. This should be evident in the film's final scene taking place "a few years later." The satirical screw is turned to the limit as the hero is shown trapped in a silly marriage. But the two babies who peek from their prams suggest an innocent and raw power alive in the little square. And the dense snow that covers the square converts the screen into a glass ball we can gaze at affectionately.

This is Prévert's personal world, a lovable world of typical human stupidity. It would reappear, greatly inflated, in *Drôle de drame* and *Adieu Léonard*, which his brother Pierre directed.[55] *Drôle de drame* did try to raise Groupe Octobre burlesque several notches. This time, among the marionettes one could count such popular stars as Michel Simon, Jean-Louis Barrault, Françoise Rosay, Jean-Pierre Aumont, and Louis Jouvet. This time there was a good deal of money to design the sets. The German master Eugen Schüfftan led a photographic unit that also included Louis Page and Henri Alekan. Jaubert composed the score. One could hardly ask for more propitious circumstances, and indeed *Drôle de drame* was a pampered project, set in motion by Roland and Denise Tual and financed by the dashing Édouard Corniglion-Molinier, close friend of André Malraux and Antoine de Saint-Exupéry. Yet *Drôle de drame* was the only failure, commercial or critical, that its director Marcel Carné experienced among his first seven features.

It may be blasphemous to advance the comparison, but in some respects the fate of *Drôle de drame* predicts that of Renoir's *La Règle du jeu* two years later. Both were large-scale works from which much was expected; both played out their satiric visions through an essentially theatrical aesthetic. Both found favor with critics and audiences after World War II but were hissed at their premiere screenings at the Colisée theater. The standard explanation for these reactions mentions that both films were "ahead of their time," leaving the audiences of the day baffled.[56] But Edward Turk disputes this in the case of *Drôle de drame*, a film he finds so darkly pessimistic in its humor that it could please only the small band of leftists who managed to preserve their cynicism in 1937, even after the Popular Front election.[57] Brutally ironic, the plot and the sets combine to suffocate the film's only imaginative characters: the

Drôle de drame: Michel Simon,
Louis Jouvet. BFI

Drôle de drame: Françoise
Rosay, Jean-Louis Barrault.
BFI

amorous milkman who spouts the exciting popular stories that trigger the
drama in the first place, and Molyneux, who prefers to be left alone in the
greenhouse with his beloved flowers. The milkman, because of his social class,
and Molyneux, because of his sincerity, are hemmed in by a hypocritical
bishop, a straitlaced tyrant of a wife, and a coterie of incompetent but tenacious detectives and journalists.

Amid the antics and the satire, Carné's sober camera rather deadens the
effect of Prévert's language run wild. Consider the first scene in the church
where we learn that Molyneux has written on "le mimesis des mimosas," and
that the ethereal William Kramps sitting behind him is none other than "the
terror of the stockyards; the man who butchers butchers." Carné records such
dialogue humorlessly alongside the inquisitorial bishop, who imperiously surveys the crowd before him. The genuinely imaginative characters are contained within the logic of the frame and the more perverse logic of a "respect-

able" morality embodied by the rigid Jouvet. Had the film been made by Vigo
one can imagine the difference; its narrational center would certainly have
been the energetic and spontaneous milkman. As it is, Jouvet can only respond
to a world that resists his domineering categories by exclaiming several times,
"Bizarre, bizarre."

Turk insists that *Drôle de drame* bears the stamp of the later Carné/Prévert
films, especially *Les Enfants du paradis*,[58] and so he emphasizes the dark seriousness of its point of view. Leenhardt suggests, as we have seen, that *Drôle de
drame* belongs rather more to Prévert's Groupe Octobre sensibility and so fits
clumsily into Carné's world. If *Les Enfants du paradis* somewhat resembles
Drôle de drame in the way it exhibits its commedia dell'arte characters, indeed
in the way it theatrically exposes its sentiments to the throngs on the boulevard du Crime, we should look first to Prévert's extroverted aesthetic.

Prévert, Leenhardt insists, is not a man of letters, but a man of the "word,"
of the word publicly expressed. Hence his poems find their true fulfillment in
the songs Kosma composed around them, and his prose comes to fruition in
his screenplays.[59] One of the dramatic consequences of Prévert's peculiar
"poetic" voice, a string of pearls plucked from the murky sea of commonplace
language, is the suppression of psychological development in his characters.
From *L'Affaire est dans le sac* through *Les Enfants du paradis* a crystalline symbolic pattern rules the behavior of all characters and annuls temporality altogether. *Le Jour se lève* can be taken as the paradigm case, since its absolute
moral geometry is elaborated through flashbacks that are anchored in the few
minutes that intervene between the opening gunshots and the final suicide.
From this perspective, the moon, streets, flowers, mime shows, mirrors, and
duels of *Les Enfants du paradis* concentrate, via poetic not dramatic logic, all the
characters and actions that range across the years of its plot. The clarity of
dramatic presentation (symbolized by the theaters on the boulevard du Crime)
cuts through the novelistic complexities that the film's sheer size produces as
a mirage.

Brecht as social poet and playwright might seem to stand behind Prévert's
early street theater aesthetic, yet Leenhardt suggests that his later poetic dramaturgy reminds one far more of Jean Giraudoux, who, in plays like *La Folle
de Chaillot* and *La Guerre de Troie n'aura pas lieu*, staged a world transparent
with essences and moral options. His translator could be writing about
Prévert's poetic realism when he describes Giraudoux as constructing "a
drama of delightful surprises, somewhere between the art of the candid camera and the art of the fairy tale."[60] Prévert's moral world relates readily to
Giraudoux's, if we accept Kyrou's memorable characterization: "The Prévert
mark is always synonymous with lightness, fantasy, love, and total revolt."
Thus Jouvet and Simon could pass easily from the set where *Drôle de drame*
was filmed by day to the stage where they performed *La Guerre de Troie n'aura
pas lieu* each night.[61]

Yet Prévert was always prepared to upset this delicate world with a congenital explosive anarchism that would have made the urbane Giraudoux squirm uncomfortably. For Kyrou goes on: "He brings to life extraordinary personages who have pockets full of fireworks, lips ready to kiss, and hands loaded with itching powder meant for cops, clergymen, and decorated officials. The serious types in Prévert are no less poetic and no less revolutionary ... he remains the film-poet of revolt."[62]

Can one remain "the film-poet of revolt" when the era of revolt has passed? For many, nothing was more disheartening and debilitating than to be for so long "révolutionaires sans révolution."[63] But, if Leenhardt is right, Prévert's revolt was general enough to persist beyond the particular political configurations that came and went in his lifetime. For his was a revolt of commonplace language against the commonplace. He thereby could live a veritable anarchism that neither electoral nor military victory could quell.

Prévert projected a poetic future to French cinema that was hard to envisage in 1934 when he and Clair and Vigo had all felt blocked by the direction of the industry and its aesthetic norms. By 1938 one could witness the astounding success of *Le Quai des brumes* and feel justified in having expected (albeit erroneously) the acceptance of a vision like that of *Drôle de drame*. How do we account for such changes in production and reception? Three directions of inquiry should help answer this question. The first examines the film industry itself, its structures, needs, and fears. The second ranges into the aesthetic traditions that dominated French cinema, specifically the theatrical entertainment tradition. The third searches in the other arts (especially the novel) and in the few darker realist films that stand out brilliantly from the early sound years, for the power capable of mobilizing the inspiring rage and tenderness I have chronicled in these three adolescents of French film.

4

French Cinema and the Sonic Boom

THE IMAGE OF SUPERIORITY

In 1937, flush with the success of *La Kermesse hé-roïque*, Jacques Feyder proudly claimed, "Sound film has allowed France to become once again the center of world cinema as it was its birthplace. Everyone can see that we have hit our stride."[1] In the second half of the 1930s, French films routinely won international competitions;[2] their export sales (if one excepts Hollywood) led the market in the rest of Europe, in Japan, and in Latin America. They dominated the "Best Foreign Film" lists of American critics and garnered four straight Academy Awards in that category.[3]

But did the international critical establishment project a mirage? Economic historians point out that the conditions that kept French film in arrears in the first part of the decade persisted right up to the war, conditions such as exorbitant taxation, diminished capital investment, the lack of any industrial or governmental body to coordinate and regulate activities, and so on. From this point of view, France increasingly gussied up an essentially bedraggled cinema until World War II. One survey discovered that only 7 percent of the French attended films regularly in 1937, compared to nearly half of all Americans.[4] While some French films may have been beautifully polished, most were haggard, trying to manage with budgets averaging only a quarter those of German or British films and a sixth of Hollywood pictures.[5]

Still, French production doubled between 1929 and 1937, so that native offerings finally surpassed imports in box-office receipts at home.[6] This statistic grows in importance when coupled with figures showing how the sound cinema pulled spectators out of the music halls and the boulevard theaters at a tremendous rate from 1930 to 1936. Establishments that once were café-concerts, music halls, and theaters were refurbished for talkies; in five years cinema receipts more than doubled while live entertainment saw theirs halved.[7]

When we get away from statistics, we find even more "evidence" for the resurgence of the national industry. Semiofficial lists show France fifth (and falling) in world cinema in 1929,[8] whereas in 1937 it was considered second only to the United States, outdistancing in reputation the declining industries of the U.S.S.R., England, and even Germany.[9] I emphasize the word "considered," for no matter what the economic conditions of international entertainment competition, the prestige of French cinema soared in the period of poetic realism. The real question, then, concerns the value of prestige. What is an "image" worth in bankable terms, and what leverage does it provide directors, producers, and distributors in their negotiations with one another as they struggle to expand the scope of their ambition?

Without adjudicating this dispute over the financial health of the industry or adding to the many economic histories devoted to this period,[10] I want to insist on the importance of the appearance of French film by first enhancing the image of a national cinema that came into focus mid-decade. Examining sources as different as autobiographies of producers, economic histories, and aesthetic overviews, one finds that the undeniably chaotic first years of sound project a weak and diffuse picture of French film. Repeated in all sources are accounts of a disoriented industry struggling with bankruptcy (including the giants Paramount and Gaumont), with scandal (Pathé), and with the widening effects of economic depression. In 1936, however, critics start to render a harmonious image of a national cinema on the verge of breaking forth in glory. Was this sheerly a public-relations effort? Writing retrospectively, Henri Fescourt, one of France's key directors in the transition to sound, argued that the fame bestowed on French cinema after 1936 was based on the "appearance" of artistic evolution, an appearance trumped up by advertisers who had finally begun to promote a cinema that had been exceptional right from 1930. "I don't share the opinion according to which our cinema began to rebound only in 1936. It rebounded little because in fact it never really fell. The truth is that in this famous year exporters began to deploy real effort to sell our films to foreign countries."[11]

One instance of this harmonious picture concerns a film few people today would recognize, Marc Allégret's *Gribouille* (1937). General expectations about the strength of French cinema had advanced so far that the critic for *Beaux Arts* could write: "Here is a great French film, a very great film which proves that we possess all the qualities and all the resources that are necessary to succeed in national production. . . . In brief, a film without willful aestheticism, nor concessions to the large public, but which should satisfy both the most refined spectators and the masses because it is a total work that marks a date in the history of French cinema."[12] After having floundered for half a decade, French cinema had at last managed to negotiate a middle course between extremes of style and of audience. Or so this critic thought: *Gribouille*, like French cinema as a whole, stood out as both distinguished and popular.

And so, despite the disturbing findings of the governmental commission charged at that very moment with helping the cinema survive what economic authorities believed was a deathbed crisis,[13] by decade's end many people shared a genuine pride in the achievement of French cinema. The most clairvoyant critic of the time, Roger Leenhardt, breathed a sigh of relief in the February 1938 issue of *Esprit*, noting "the general upgrading of the average French film and the renewal of this national cinema via a return to the 'film d'essai'" crowned by the flower of "several works that had reached a status which belongs to films of that mysterious international class."[14] He dates the beginning of this resurgence at 1935, attributing it in part to complicated market conditions that flow around the globe in waves. At this juncture, the tides favor France and its native genius for genres that are related to the essay and to tragedy. His idealist explanation is balanced by a slightly more grounded one, as he asserts that "superiority in cinema moves, like the Davis Cup, from continent to continent, depending on cinematographic ambience, including technical equipment, the education of the public, the overturning of one generation by another."[15]

"Cinematographic ambience" is a term that should be resurrected, for it calls up all those contextual aspects, thought to be incidental to art, that have of late taken center stage in the materialist rewriting of film history. While Leenhardt was not insensitive to the institutional and business conditions of filmmaking, he would never hold that an understanding of the film industry, including the popularity of genres, is a sufficient, or even a first, step in explaining the strength of a nation's cinema. For him that strength rises and falls on the depth and power of the films produced. In his estimation there is no question that French cinema in 1937 is far better off than it was in 1933 because the average quality of every film has advanced and the opportunity for passable directors, like Allégret, to arrive at something truly interesting, like *Gribouille*, has vastly increased. So, despite the fact that according to various industrial indicators (such as amount of capital invested, number of films produced, average profit per film, and so forth) the French cinema had declined since 1934, Leenhardt writes of a nearly glorious ascendancy, because the French system in 1937 routinely gave life to more complicated and accomplished films than it had earlier.

From Leenhardt's standpoint the effects of industrial conditions are most visible in the work of prolific, second-line directors, like Allégret, Pierre Chenal, and such émigrés as Robert Siodmak and Anatole Litvak. Leenhardt reasons that, no matter what the conditions, one must always expect an un-abashedly commercial baseline cinema on the bottom rung, what the French refer to as "les films d'alimentation." These feed a popular taste for entertainment that, in the 1930s at least, appeared timeless.

The highest rung brings us to another timeless zone, that of serious art. In all eras a few brilliant films may be made, thanks to the genius and tenacity of their directors' aesthetic vision and despite adverse conditions. This characterizes the films of Jean Vigo and René Clair in the otherwise pitiful national cinema scene of 1930–1934. But no national cinema can ride the shoulders of such figures. As the *Beaux Arts* critic implied, one should look between top and bottom to note the health of the industry. Leenhardt's optimism about French cinema in 1937 derives not from the fact that Jean Renoir or Marcel Carné made a few peerless films, but from the premise that it was difficult to make mediocre films in this era. His point is corroborated by a man known for producing low- and mid-level movies, Henri Diamant-Berger:

> In 1938 French production reached an apogee. Its technical capability allowed directors a freer utilization of the image, comparable to the great epoch of the silent film; the scripts were competently written by good authors; moreover, we possessed a generation of remarkable actors and actresses. . . . I had the impression that year that the French output had become tops in the world. Russian, Italian, and German films were hampered by an unfavorable political climate. As for America, it produced nearly 800 films a year, exporting at most 180. Out of this number there were perhaps ten really good films. In France, out of a total of 160 films you could put thirty in a strong class all of which were quite good and at least worthy of real attention.[16]

Now Diamant-Berger felt himself pulled forward by this trend. His success early in the decade had been with admittedly superficial, low-budget comedies that, as he said, played much better in the provinces than in Paris. After a visit to the United States during the stressful year 1934, he determined to regain his power as a producer. But the "ambience" Leenhardt spoke of had changed in two years, so that the arrangements Diamant-Berger had made with his usual financial backers (who were by and large regional distributors) needed to change as well. "My 'regionnals' had gotten through the crisis period without grave damage; as 1935 began, they proposed that I work once more with them. Naturally they preferred small-budget films again, but now competition forced us to aim at quality, that is, at larger investments."[17] From 1936 to 1938 the average cost of a French film rose nearly 75 percent. While this indubitably led to the demise of dozens of small producers,[18] it also may have helped push a large number of French films to a stature that was recognizably superior to what it had been a few years earlier. Valéry Jahier, one of the most respected critics of the decade, felt able to salute France for its "progress" in his summary of the 1937–1938 season.

Never before has one seen in the ensemble of [France's] output so much good work, including perfect casting, great care in details, in the work of minor roles, in the quality of dialogue. And the result seems even more admirable because it has come about according to means that are proper to the genius of our country and without the flat imitation of the American cinema.[19]

How had the French film industry, scattered though it was, settled into a configuration that was in accord with its "genius," and that permitted or even encouraged the kind of ambitious film that poetic realism best exemplified? Even images have their start in the workshops of artisans laboring in vividly stark conditions. What were those conditions?

SOUND WARS: FOREIGN POWERS IN PARIS

The stark condition facing everyone in 1929 was Hollywood. Hardly a new adversary, Hollywood in this year had begun deploying its newest and most deadly weapon, sound, threatening to dismantle what was left of its competition around the world. As it surveyed the globe, Hollywood looked increasingly to France, a territory it coveted above all others. France generally consumed over 50 percent of the "foreign picture news" in *Variety* each week. American audiences were so fond of stories set in Paris that Paramount maintained an elaborate Parisian *quartier* in its back lot. More than ever before, Hollywood executives fancied business trips to Paris, since the remnants of France's once dominant cinema industry were so badly guarded. Studios, laboratories, theaters, and subsidiary businesses were still available a decade after the postwar decline of Pathé.

The German company Tobis Klangfilm represented its only serious rival in quest of the fortune that could be made in equipping the six thousand French theaters and fifty-five production stages. With neither an organized strategy nor significant resources, the demoralized French could only watch themselves be "taken" while the entire nature of the cinema changed around them.

I follow the standard military vocabulary employed to characterize the era in which cinema became sonorized. The smaller French companies consolidated their forces, forming alliances such as Pathé-Natan-Ciné-Romans and Gaumont-Franco-Film-Aubert, but even so they could hardly keep at bay the far more powerful American and German companies, since these came armed with the dreaded technology. For cultural and economic reasons the great patent wars between Tobis Klangfilm and three Hollywood studios were waged largely on French soil.

Trying to work in a battle zone is risky. The few independent French producers who had survived the mergers of 1929 were at the mercy of powers much larger than had been known only months previously. Pierre Braunberger showed more courage than the French majors (the Gaumont and Pathé consortiums) by quickly moving to purchase the Billancourt studios and prepare them for sound recording.[20] He and his partner Roger Richebé planned in their first phase of operation to enter the market with cheap, popular films based on successful plays. But whose equipment should they use? They preferred Western Electric's but learned that all films made on such equipment might be locked out of Germany and all other Tobis-dominated countries; this they could not risk. In buying German Tri-Ergon process equipment through Tobis, they ran into initial problems with the compatibility of their products in American theaters or in any theater equipped by Americans. But compatibility was only the technical side of a much more sinister situation. Since only a small percentage of theaters had been equipped for sound in 1930, the independent producer was in competition with large distributors, many of which were linked to or owned by the giant studios. Thus Paramount refused to play pictures produced by Braunberger (or Jacques Haik or Osso) in its large block of theaters, thinking to squelch them at the starting line.

The conservative French exhibition system (made up of small family concerns for the most part) was likewise at the mercy of the distributors, traditionally the strongest sector of the film industry in France. To amortize the investment in sound projectors and speakers, a theater needed to quadruple its box-office receipts. Early in 1930 only two hundred French theaters had taken the plunge, though by the end of the next year well over a thousand were sonorized. As in all countries, sound spelled the end for hundreds of independent exhibitors. Distributors played on this fear, as one can imagine.

The most blatant expression of the threat Braunberger and other French businessmen felt at the time can be found in a crudely direct *Film Mercury* article that announced Hollywood's master plan for world conquest:

> Slowly but surely, thanks to a clever and uninterrupted plan, we have learned to build bases in Europe which permit us to direct according to our desires the commerce of cinema in that continent. At a certain moment we had to fear that the sound film, sliced into many fiefs according to different external markets, was going to uproot our world mastery. Happily for us the countless financiers who are interested in cinema are always ready to listen with a complacent ear to American offers. There are certainly independent producers in England, in Germany, and in France, some of whom fight with all their strength against foreign invasion; they are without weight compared to those who, without even thinking about it, sell their own industry to Uncle Sam. We will arrive at our goal no matter what the cost; the foreign market is from now on just as important as our internal market. It will bring in receipts doubled compared to those at home, and it is for this reason that day and night our businessmen work with tenacity to get the reins of control in hand everywhere. Economists will certainly protest; the avarice of Europeans for American gold is such that

their cries of alarm will continue without echo. We know already what language is being used in England, in Germany, and in France against the American intrusion. And we know as well that those who clamor the loudest have been, and still are, our best clients. We are following, after a few cautious steps, a campaign strategy which is very simple; we are buying theaters in the capitals and in the important big cities first; from there we will spread out everywhere. Let's leave them little respite so that our financiers can quickly force the extermination of what little remains of what used to be called the European film! We won't permit ourselves, you say, to grab their theater circuits! Aren't we doing just that right now in London, in Berlin, and in Paris? The heads of the European film industry moreover hold out their hands to the all powerful American dollar with such greediness that they don't even see opening before them the grave into which they will soon stumble. Another part of our plan consists in luring to Hollywood all European artists of any renown. When silent films were king this tactic worked marvelously and it should be perfectly suited to the talking film as well. In the theaters of England, Germany, and France will resound national sound tracks made in the U.S.A. What European producer will vie with us when we have captured their greatest actors with our money?[21]

In this climate those concerned with the "art" of the French cinema could only hold their breath. They watched most writers and directors quickly re-tooling to emulate the new Hollywood model, while others, more haughty, turned their backs on the cinema altogether. They saw a defensive alliance develop between a sector of the French and German industries. But despite the fear, the rhetoric, and the lawsuits, for the first two years of the decade nearly everyone reaped profits. The French thronged to see sound films, no matter where or how they were made. From the standpoint of the French industry even though Hollywood seemed to be cornering far too great a portion of the market, the exponential increase in the value of movies insured that smaller, local investors like Braunberger could share in the bonanza. Naturally there was concern about the kinds of films being made, particularly among critics and directors. In general they stood stridently opposed to the very existence of the sound film, if for no other reason than that it meant further dominance of themes and styles by a Hollywood industry that had several years' jump on them.

Hollywood's strategy to control the European market included three phases. At first foreign versions of certain designated scripts were filmed in southern California. Personnel from every country were imported for the hasty rewriting, acting, and direction needed to turn a $300,000 English-language film into four $100,000 European versions. Feyder and Françoise Rosay were the best-known French names to be lured into working on what amounted to used sets.

Even personalities with avant-garde backgrounds were conscripted by Hollywood. Claude Autant-Lara spent several acrimonious years there;[22] somehow Luis Buñuel did also.[23] More typical, though, was the case of Yves Mirande, an established playwright in the boulevard tradition. He sat in an empty Hollywood room for three months, picking up a weekly check of $500: recompense for refraining from turning out original French scripts in Paris.[24] He also was used as bait to lure larger talents to California and to lure French audiences to MGM pictures. Eventually Mirande became a rewrite man for French versions of MGM pictures and contributed at least two original screenplays to the studio, driving his salary up to $1,500 weekly. But no studio, not even MGM, could long keep a stable of personnel from every key nation. In 1932 Mirande, like so many others, was sent home where he immediately found work, writing fluff for Paramount's plant in Joinville.

Jesse Lasky and Walter Wanger, chiefs of this wealthiest and most cosmopolitan of studios, were responsible for Hollywood's second European strategy.[25] They equipped the Joinville studios with the same Western Electric sound that the company used at home, and before 1930 the plant was refurbished until it rivaled the best in Hollywood production facilities. Bob Kane, who had been actively organizing French production for nearly a year and had long been in Paris as a Paramount distribution executive, was installed officially as head in the first months of the new decade.

The next twelve months at Paramount in Paris are fabled, as that studio turned out an incredible one hundred features and fifty shorts in as many as fourteen languages. Locals called it "the Tower of Babel." Paramount's expenditures in Paris at this time were staggering. In April 1931, for instance, it allocated $8 million for French productions, a sum equal to around 20 percent of Paramount's total production budget. This infusion of money into Parisian production was an obvious boon to French technical and artistic personnel. *Variety* gloated that Paramount was keeping European film afloat and that for the first time Continental workers and artists were getting a taste of real production methods. "They like the money," *Variety* wrote, "but they are upset at the strictness of the operations, unaccustomed as they are to coming to work on time."[26]

Variety might have added that although the French were happy to have jobs, they were also ashamed of the shoddy work and insipid subjects that came off this production line. The American obsession with efficiency reached a peak in the single-take, multiple-version method that stationed four teams of actors in glass booths surrounding the sound stage to deliver, in their particular tongues, simultaneous versions of the action taking place. Diamant-Berger warned Kane that multiple versions of "prototypical plots" would soon tire audiences eager to see regional, or at least national, concerns and subjects.[27] What he objected to is exemplified by one of Mirande's fluffy scripts, called *La Chance*, which featured Rosay as an elegant society woman with a gambling problem. Her virtue is threatened by several Continental suitors in luxurious settings from Paris to Nice, although every scene was shot at Joinville. Paramount turned out multiple versions of such international, high-life comedies at the rate of more than one a month.

This curious phenomenon, replete as it is with innumerable paradoxes involving image, voice, colonialism, originality, and nationalism, has become a subject of research all its own.[28] But, despite the fanfare with which it began, the multilingual film was only a proto-dubbing process that was bound to give way to actual dubbing technology in 1932, Hollywood's final colonization strategy. By that date, however, Paramount was starting to reel from the first effects of the depression and nearly ceased production of original French films at Joinville,[29] which became instead its dubbing center, still supporting many technicians but no longer dominating European filmmaking.

If Paramount is remembered as the most potent force in French cinema at this time, it is due not to the films produced in Joinville, but to the massive and efficient system that produced them. Several young directors received their training in this hectic system: Allégret, Autant-Lara, and Serge de Poligny. Older renegade filmmakers from the silent days found a second chance at Paramount, especially if they were polyglot. In Alberto Cavalcanti's case, this only led to disappointment, for the bureaucratic impersonality and American haste that he encountered every day turned every interesting idea he had insipid.

Alexander Korda, however, was more fortunate. He had come to Europe after being informally blacklisted in Hollywood.[30] His old friendship with Kane paid off in an offer of work: the direction of *Marius* (1931), the one Paramount title that has survived in everyone's memory. Paramount decided to produce *Marius* when they saw the truth of Diamant-Berger's prediction about the falling interest of American and "international" subjects played out by second-rank French look-alikes. *Variety* conceded that "films with a strictly local background are preferred to those adapted. We are receiving increasing competition from native producers and will have to change."[31]

Korda knew nothing of Marcel Pagnol or *Marius* when that property was given over to him. After watching a command performance of the play, he was so moved that he talked Paramount into hiring the entire original cast, including Raimu and Pierre Fresnay. In addition he convinced his brother to design the memorable sets that contribute so much to the physical atmosphere of this wonderfully southern drama, an atmosphere so earthy and different from the neutrality of the white sets used in many Paramount films made at home or abroad at this time. *Marius* capitalized on the flavor of its Marseilles setting by emphasizing the accents of its characters. The use of natural sounds, especially those of ships at sea, forms a rich track that both renders the place in an audible way and works toward a level of sound symbolism that was genuinely innovative in these first years of the talkies.

Marius. BFI.

The flavor of
Marseilles's port

Marius. BFI

Korda understood that a single shot of the sun-drenched harbor was all the vista he needed to provide the horizon of this particular locale and of a set of characters at one with that locale. *Marius* still strikes us as "true" to its subject and region largely because of its restricted point of view. We are made to see and hear with the characters, not above or beyond them. *Marius*'s script was so strong that it needed only a small measure of special treatment to come alive, even under the Joinville assembly-line conditions. It was truly a harbinger of a kind of realism that would become crucial to French cinema soon enough, a realism spiked with Pagnol's inimitable poetic dialogue.

The success of *Marius* bolstered Paramount in its ongoing battle with Tobis. Very early on, the German firm had bought a studio in Epinay that was equipped with its Tri-Ergon sound system, and had begun leasing it to all comers. Although Tobis was producing sound films in Berlin (many with simultaneous French versions) at a reasonable rate, it entered the Parisian market cautiously. Tobis's strategy involved making dual-language films in Paris using the top personnel and scripts available. Through their association with French film during the 1920s, its managers knew French film artists well and picked Clair to launch its first French efforts. Within the space of little more than a year, Clair directed *Sous les toits de Paris*, *Le Million*, and *A nous la liberté*. All were filmed at Epinay in French and German versions. All were aimed at a rather sophisticated reception. As opposed to *Marius* whose regional flavor won it immediate success in France, *Sous les toits de Paris* was underappreciated at home until the Germans hailed it. Before long it became the most discussed of all early sound films, arousing the jealousy of *Variety*, which asked how the Germans could afford to spend such time and money on an individual film destined for an educated audience. The Hollywood mouthpiece scoffed at the momentary prestige *Sous les toits de Paris* had brought Tobis, intimating that Paramount's ability to turn out film after film would in the long run win it the public whose head Tobis and Clair had undeniably turned.[32]

Variety had indeed understood Tobis's tactics: its list of French films is not long, but it is stunning. Feyder directed *Pension Mimosas* (1934) in both French and German at Epinay, where he next built the magnificent sets for *La Kermesse héroïque*, another production that he personally directed in the two languages. G. W. Pabst and Julien Duvivier also benefited from the largesse and artistic freedom associated with this firm. Although Tobis was clearly not going to rule the Continent through its Paris studio, it was at least committed to high-quality products and happy to lease its facilities to other parties when its own schedule lagged. By 1936 Tobis was no longer a factor in Paris, although its German competitor UFA-ACE had moved in to become the most consistent force in the French industry.

FRENCH DEFENSES TO SOUND ON THEIR SOIL

Chauvinistic historians like to point out that, despite being reluctantly drawn into what was an international trade war, the French (in the persons of two future Academicians, Clair and Pagnol) provided an intelligence and intuition about sound that contributed far more to the history of film practice than did the standard products of either of the dominant foreign companies in Paris, Paramount and Tobis. Putting aside the issue of art, the chief long-term effect of those foreign companies was the opportunity and training they provided for hundreds of French artisans to learn a craft they could carry with them to the scores of feeble but native production companies that inevitably sprouted on the newly bulldozed terrain. Without strong government or banking support, and amid the debris of ruined careers and crass business deals that character-ized these early years, the shoots of this French "industry" would outlast the American and German colonizers and grow toward a future that included, among other things, poetic realism.

In this environment, then, the trade papers speak of three different sorts of competition: between Hollywood and Germany, between France and its would-be colonizers, and among the various French investors. Even before the Pathé and Gaumont consortiums could reorganize their clumsy bureaucracies and set up their soundstages, several silent films were partially sonorized through the addition of songs or intermittent postsynchronized dialogue sequences, so as to allow exhibitors in the few wired theaters to charge higher prices.[33]

Although shot in Germany, Pathé's *Les Trois Masques* (1929) has gone down as the first 100-percent-French talkie. Essentially a filmed play with no visual adventure, *Les Trois Masques* nevertheless made enough money to encourage Pathé's ambitious new president, Bernard Natan, to back more films of this genre. After the huge success Maurice Chevalier enjoyed with *Le Petit Café* (a 1930 film actually made in Hollywood under a German director), Pathé poured all its efforts into the transposition of vaudeville and boulevard comedies like Pierre Colombier's *Chiqué*, the first such subject filmed entirely in France. Even Marcel L'Herbier, who a year before had been among the loudest in decrying such hybrids, found himself adapting Henri Bataille's diverting play, *L'Enfant de l'amour* in 1930.

Pathé's plan was to give popular entertainers and topical themes an extended life on the screen. These were the films that *Variety* claimed were driving MGM to abandon its strategy of cosmopolitan subjects duplicated in multilingual versions. The French public demanded familiar songs, singers, and stage routines. These could be cheaply transposed to celluloid since they required little rehearsal time and even less script writing and set design. Finally, their previous stage-life gave such films an immediate advertising advantage. By and large lost and forgotten,[34] as a genre such films launched local production and gave innumerable producers, many of them harboring aesthetic ambition, both experience and hope.

In all, eight sound films were made in 1929, though only five of these were fully synchronized and none was made in France. The year 1930 was hardly stronger, with but nine sound films financed by French companies. All nine, however, were produced in the modified Parisian studios that were finally ready for a massive changeover. The year of that changeover was 1931, when Pathé alone accounted for nineteen sound features and when a total of 159 films came out of France, compared with 62 in 1929.[35]

In this period of incubation, Pathé was not inclined to give its directors free rein to experiment with new forms. Natan made sure that newcomers like Jacques Tourneur as well as experienced directors such as L'Herbier and Raymond Bernard obeyed Hollywood's "sound man" who accompanied the Western Electric installation. Every setup had to be "okayed" by this foreign technician while the director sat helpless in the huge camera booth.

Pathé's ground-level response to the new technology was challenged by many people in search of the appropriate cultural function of sound cinema.

Discounting certain unrealistic visionaries,[36] it fell to a few people like Pierre Braunberger to challenge Pathé. Braunberger, who would ever describe himself as an "idealistic businessman," was instrumental in helping Renoir launch his career with *Nana*. In 1927 he had founded what was probably the first avant-garde distribution house in the world, Studio Film, to promote the wildest efforts of the "pure cinema" movement, including works by Man Ray, Cavalcanti, Germaine Dulac, and Eugène Deslaw.[37] His close contact with the avant-garde was to influence the shape of his feature film projects when he turned commercial in 1929. It was Braunberger, for instance, who distributed Gide's *Voyage au Congo* (1927), directed by Marc Allégret. The notoriety garnered by the film at *ciné-clubs* fed Gide's ambitions for the cinema; moreover, on the basis of this little film, Braunberger entrusted to Allégret a series of half-hour comedy shorts that soon developed into larger-scale commercial projects such as Pagnol's *Fanny* (1932).[38]

Whether drawn by its artistic or its financial potential, Braunberger eagerly entered the scavenger hunt brought about by sound technology. Not knowing how to proceed, he telegraphed Robert Florey, inviting him to return from Hollywood to become the first to make a French film. Florey, a French expatriate, had worked in Hollywood for nearly a decade as an assistant director on many projects and, more importantly, as a special-effects expert. His technical acumen increased his personal stock at a time when producers were in awe of the problems posed by sound films. In 1929 he co-directed the first Marx Brothers comedy, *The Cocoanuts*, and shortly thereafter received his summons from Braunberger, whom he had met years earlier when the latter had come to Hollywood as a wealthy teenager to acquire a feel for the business. *La Route est belle*, shot in London, missed by a few weeks being the first French sound film, but it outdistanced *Les Trois Masques* both critically and financially.[39]

Florey's contract called for two films beyond *La Route est belle*, if possible to be shot in Paris. At this time only Gaumont and Pathé possessed soundstages there, and Pathé's were monopolized by their own frantic production schedule. Gaumont would rent its studio only under the condition that it could distribute the final product. This was unacceptable to Braunberger, who jealously guarded his independence. Florey began shooting *L'Amour chante* in Berlin while Braunberger linked himself to Roger Richebé so that their third production could be shot in the Billancourt studios that the new partners risked buying and modernizing.

Richebé brought more than money to his partnership with Braunberger. He had started like so many producers in live entertainment, converting his resources (and his theaters) into a profitable chain of movie houses centered in Marseilles. In 1928 he went to London to investigate this new invention. It was there, during the filming of *La Route est belle*, that he and Braunberger discussed a merger. Richebé agreed to show *La Route est belle* at his immense theater in Marseilles where it broke all records. Soon he had sonorized a dozen theaters in the region; now the problem was to fill these with sound films, particularly French ones so that his audience could enjoy their own language and so that he would not need to pay the exorbitant distribution fees charged by American and German companies.

The Braunberger-Richebé partnership was a natural. The former was a dynamic, experienced producer who had friends both in the business world and in the arts world and who had studied Hollywood firsthand. Richebé could provide an important circuit of theaters and the business sense needed for distribution and exhibition. Financing actually came from a shoe magnate, a cousin of Braunberger, who underwrote the reconstruction of the Billancourt studios in Paris. Within fifteen months les Etablissements Braunberger-Richebé had risen to third among native companies, behind Pathé and Gaumont. These two young men, way over their heads in debt, negotiating with banks, exhibitors, artists, and technicians, found themselves determining what French films would look and sound like for the next ten years.

They also found themselves disagreeing precisely over aesthetic matters. Richebé knew popular theater and operetta through and through, having arranged for actors and troupes during the 1920s. Now making decisions about subjects and talent for sound movies, he naturally aimed to please the same non-Parisian popular audience. His pet project for his new company was drawn from an operetta he had put on the stage with great success at his Capitol theater, *Mam'zelle Nitouche*. He gloated to his partner that not only had he shown an instinct for material (the film was a hit), but he had recruited for the male lead one of the foremost actors of the era, Jules Raimu. A noted comedian in boulevard theater whose popularity in the south had brought him to look for fame in Paris, Raimu had never been approached about the cinema until Richebé, who had engaged him in Marseilles in the past, signed him for three films. Before *Mam'zelle Nitouche* was ready to go into production, Richebé tested Raimu in a light comedy, *Le Blanc et le noir* (1931) by Sacha Guitry, to be directed by Florey. Since Raimu had played the lead in the stage version in 1922, the producer was certain he could pull it off on the screen and carefully monitored the shooting.

Indeed he monitored it perhaps too closely, removing Florey from the project and replacing him with Marc Allégret. Richebé contends that Florey was high-handed in dealing with him, and in fact wanted to test the authority he had recently acquired as co-head of a Parisian studio. He adamantly refused to film on a location set that Richebé, in one of his first "creative acts," had gone out of his way to make available. The proud Florey expected to be implored to return; the prouder Richebé locked him out of the studio.[40]

Florey has always held that the conflict was essentially financial, that he had not been paid the 5 percent that was his due from the immense profits of his first two films, the money going instead into completing the Billancourt studios.[41] He refused to complete *Le Blanc et le noir* until he got a check. For his part, Braunberger alleges money had nothing to do with the affair. Florey was simply unable to handle the temperamental Raimu, whereas Allégret had shown himself incredibly politic in dealing with powerful personalities.[42]

No matter which version is accurate, this argument displaces a more fundamental competition over values and power. The repudiation of Florey is a repudiation of Hollywood by French producers. He simply was no longer needed, since a native French director (Allégret) and native French talent (Raimu) were now sufficiently initiated into the mysteries of sound to be responsible for their own future. In fact the film was quite successful, gaining for Allégret a reputation he was able to parlay into a string of important productions. It also prepared Raimu for the dazzling career he no doubt would have had anyway. And it sent Florey back to Hollywood denigrating the Continental system.

Richebé's pet project, *Mam'zelle Nitouche*, turned out to be the last of the three films for which Raimu was contracted. Sentimental and overplayed, like so many operettas of the period, the film scored powerfully at the box office, proving to Richebé that his "provincial" notion of popular cinema had won the day. Braunberger, in constant dialogue with the Parisian literary culture, believed that the system was just learning its way, and was eager to experiment. Marc Allégret would be his means, as would Pierre Prévert and Renoir. He wanted Richebé to mind the finances while he took charge of the artistic end of the business.

Naturally Richebé could not comply. At just this time, Raimu was negotiating a deal that Richebé intuited would set the course of much of French cinema. He meant to stay involved. That deal was initiated by Pagnol, who approached Richebé in 1931 to ask him to release Raimu from his contract so that he could play César in the Paramount production of *Marius*. It was mainly Pagnol's meridional accent and background that won over the tough Richebé, together of course with exclusive rights to distribute the film in the south. Through this venture Raimu, Pagnol, and Richebé became a serious force in French cinema, for Richebé was slated to produce (with Marc Allégret directing) the second film of the series, *Fanny*. Richebé was certain of success after the stunning career of *Marius*. He lavished funds on promoting the film, accompanying his writer and star to Brussels for its export premiere, and opening at the same time the largest theater in Belgium. These were expansive times for Braunberger-Richebé, the fly-by-night company that in 1931 found itself leading French cinema toward its future.

But they were not times that would last. As with so many other firms, smaller and larger, bankruptcy, or at least its threat, cramped muscles they had been flexing with such apparent power. The shoe magnate was unable to renew his guarantee on their huge credit, so that the banks now became co-partners of the enterprise. Since distribution and exhibition were by far more secure financial concerns, wary bankers vetoed numerous production ideas. *Fanny* actually was produced by a ruse, using the Billancourt studios under the banner of "Films Marcel Pagnol," an organization quickly devised to launder the project. Ironically, within two years Richebé would be directing operations at the flourishing "Films Marcel Pagnol," while les Etablissements Braunberger-Richebé had foundered.

In the unruly, unregulated, and utterly speculative conditions of the infancy of sound, a tough businessman like Richebé was able to play not just an effective but a formative role in the aesthetics as well as the economics of French cinema. While he soon was at odds with Braunberger on every count, for a while he trusted the latter's intuition about directors and writers. Braunberger had hired Florey, Paul Fejos, and Allégret, who had all contributed inventively. Allégret's connections widened the talent pool to include among others the Préverts and their friends. In the absence of well-defined traditions and working methods, experimental ideas and people came to play a major role at a small studio like this.

Of all the films produced at Billancourt from 1930 to 1932, none was more important than *La Chienne* (1931), for it ushered in a type of cinematographic naturalism that would lead to *Toni*, *La Bête humaine*, and Italian neorealism. It was conceived as a key film by both studio heads, Jean Renoir's first significant sound movie. *La Chienne* was a long time in the making and consequently cost a good deal of money. Much of this time and money went into experiments with location sound, the first such experiments in France, according to Renoir, who refused to shoot street scenes in a studio and refused to shoot them with simulated sound effects. His fanaticism for "real sound" drew the attention of Western Electric's consultant, who believed that Renoir might extend, in *La Chienne* and later films, the capabilities of the medium. If he were to do so, it would be not in search of technique for its own sake but in his lifelong pursuit of traditional values: "I welcomed sound with delight, seeing at once all the use that could be made of it. After all, the purpose of all artistic creation is the knowledge of man, and is not the human voice the best means of conveying the personality of a human being?"[43] As André Bazin was to point out,[44] sound became the natural complement to the realist style Renoir was intermittently searching for in the 1920s. It allowed him to become "the most French of directors,"[45] and attuned him to the solidity of a world that resonated with sounds carrying distinctive accents and timbres. To producers sound meant theatrical sound; whereas *La Chienne*'s tawdry melodrama took place within a sea of noises that risked swallowing it up. The heralded naturalism of this film, like that of *Toni* a few years later, comes less from the plot than from the way we must struggle to follow that plot while it competes with countless other voices, dramas, and inconsequential vibrations making up the chaotic chorus of social life. Renoir would work with that chorus like no other filmmaker of the 1930s, pitting class against class in highly mixed genres to express the complexity and thickness of the modern world in an audiovisual medium that

La Chienne: A chorus of social life. BFI

was itself complex and thick. Because of this he would always look affection-ately at *La Chienne*: "[It] was to be a turning point in my career. I believe that in it I came to the style that I call poetic realism."[46]

La Chienne stirred up critical controversy and, after its delayed and hesitant release, stirred up the public at large. Richebé was certain he knew this public; they were not ready for the "cacophony"[47] of such a sound track, nor for the dark treatment of the film's sordid characters. Even the sympathetic Jean-Georges Auriol in his article in *La Revue du cinéma* reprimanded Renoir for not taking enough care to lead the audience along.[48] In his view the producer was right to complain. But Renoir was equally certain he had succeeded in locating a new vein for French cinema to mine in the future. He summed up this vein in the word "realism," which, with respect to *La Chienne*, would include the fullness of the sound track, the Montmartre exteriors, and the carefully re-searched studio decor. The film's so-called lack of rhythm (according to com-plaints by Richebé and Auriol) was in fact a new rhythm altogether, the sense of time's ineluctable and eroding flow, that was out of step with the flow of the standard melodramas and musical comedies that ruled the era and kept audi-ences comfortable. *Variety* declared *La Chienne* to be so detailed in its exploration of degradation that it was probably undistributable in America.[49] Yet even though uncomfortable, Auriol had to admit that *La Chienne* was without question the most significant sound film the French had produced to that moment.

PATHÉ'S PROPHETIC *LA PETITE LISE*

La Chienne's production and reception was generous when compared with that of another dark, prophetic work, Grémillon's *La Petite Lise* (1930). This film displeased its producer and consternated its audience to such a degree that only recently has it risen again to view. In fact Pathé recruited Charles Spaak and Grémillon for a historical epic. When this project dissolved, the pair left a series of scripts in the Pathé offices hoping that a shift in policy might open up this studio to the kind of intimate films they were intent upon. Nothing that could be called a shift came about; nevertheless, in the constant administrative turnover of that first year, a breach did momentarily open up for *La Petite Lise*, when a sympathetic producer who liked the script found himself in power for what Spaak recalls as a period of three days.[50] This was all it took to launch such an inexpensive movie. After its completion, however, *La Petite Lise* found itself friendless in the studio offices and subject to Bernard Natan's ire. He never gave it the courtesy of a premiere, treating it as an aberration, an illegitimate daughter.

Natan's incomprehension before the film was not purely idiosyncratic. Auriol would review it in terms similar to those he later used for *La Chienne*, praising its intricacy and sensitivity to the medium, but questioning its apparent disdain of the popular audience:

> No doubt loving the cinema in itself more than what it serves as instrument or means, Jean Grémillon develops copiously and complacently the atmosphere of his story even to the detriment of the story itself . . . so that the drama loses its way in his mise-en-scène. . . . *La Petite Lise* may move individual spectators but it leaves indifferent or even irritates the masses for whom it like all films is destined.[51]

Auriol particularly objected to the lengthy prelude in the Cayenne prison with its aimless tracking camera, its "nerve-wracking music," and its isolated sound effects. He understood that this film's interest was utterly unconventional. As Geneviève Sellier aptly characterizes it, the dominant mode of discourse in *La Petite Lise* is description rather than narration.[52] Hence the ambiguity and atmosphere, not to mention that "complacence" of development that so put off Auriol, are calculated effects of the first sequence and carefully maintained throughout. This helps account for its tempo. A composer himself who scored some of his later films, Grémillon avoided nondiegetic music altogether, turning the various registers of the medium into a piece of audiovisual chamber music. Sellier claims that the film's misreception stems from its completely cinematic construction, whereas nearly all other early sound films, including *La Chienne*, were able to rely on the audience's familiarity with well-known forms of theater, fiction, vaudeville, and so on. A truly experimental piece of cinematic lyricism, *La Petite Lise* orchestrates its melodrama like the libretto of an opera, minimally structuring an experience that owes its power to multiple elements of design.

This makes of the opening and closing sequences (the prisoners' song with its hypnotic percussion and the frenzied jazz at the black nightclub) a kind of primitive psychic ocean out of which slowly lumbers the equally primitive Oedipal drama. One can even read that drama as an incestuous dream of Berthier the prisoner, provoked by this music to imagine himself back in Paris for one day of longing and tragedy.[53] No matter how we accept that drama, its darkness and muffled sounds express an incredible undercurrent of repressed sexual power literally depicted in the prologue. This is just the kind of energy that would fuel *La Bête humaine* and indeed drive the Jean Gabin character in all his poetic realist incarnations. Like Gabin, all the actors in *La Petite Lise* mumble their sparse lines, frequently facing away from the camera. It is a film overheard, one that is viewed obliquely, even from behind, the opposite of the direct frontal presentation that dominated the theatrical adaptations of the day.

Natan, exasperated by such arty direction, accused Grémillon of deliberately holding back the tale in so limiting the sounds and camera angles. Yet this was just the strategy required to compress and bottle up the emotions set in play by the melodrama. Evidently most spectators, like Natan, felt themselves ignored or toyed with, and they hissed the film.[54] Some were amazed. Henri Langlois speaks of the film reverently and regrets that neither it nor Grémillon ever exercised the influence over French cinema they ought to have. In an essay entitled "Les Chefs-d'oeuvres perdus," Langlois wrote:

> It was 1930. In the local cinema that had just been given a fresh shine. In only a few weeks all had changed: the public and the films, and every Saturday one regretted still more the [silent] cinema that had been lost. It was at this time and place that there appeared on the screen a film which had no exclusive run and because of that, one about which no one had spoken. Armed with sound and speech the cinema once again commanded attention, and created emotion. . . . It was in seeing *La Petite Lise* of Jean Grémillon that I forgot *Sous les toits de Paris* and stopped regretting the passing of silents. In the history of French cinema, *La Petite Lise* marks an essential date. It is the first work of a school that after 1936 would definitively come to the fore and make French cinema the best in the world.[55]

Its screenwriter Spaak is the most direct and obvious link between *La Petite Lise* and the poetic realist school, connected as he was to Feyder, Renoir, and

La Petite Lise: Mute fate. CF   *La Petite Lise*: Mute incomprehension. BFI

those halcyon years Langlois mentions. The film announces the poetic realist school in its rhythm, tone, and dramaturgy, which together create a tension between the drive toward realism and an impulse to essentialize reality. The theme of fate, worked out coldly in the lives of uncomprehending characters, is set in an atmosphere of regret in which the audience, if not the characters, is compelled to meditate on the inevitable. The specific tension between realism and transcendence, fate and regret, mechanism and atmosphere, became particularly viable after the introduction of sound.

Grémillon was precocious in sensing so immediately the power of an understated style of sound film. Resisting the temptation so many fell into of letting the sound track etherealize the image, Grémillon used sound to slow down, and in one sense weigh down, his film, establishing a rhythm and counterpoint that make the notion of "tone" absolutely literal. Refusing to impose a tone on his film from above, in the manner of Clair, he also rejected the clutter of *La Chienne*'s realism, wherein the sound track absolutely anchors each scene to a particular place and moment. Instead he sought a tone by which a simple melodrama would have a clarifying rhythm capable of universalizing the situation and our response to it. This would be the formula of the poetic realist school.

The structural simplicity of *La Petite Lise* is especially notable when compared to the denser naturalism of *La Chienne*. The credits list but four characters, who will be locked in intense interplay. As would be typical of poetic realist scripts, they are socially marginal: a convict, his prostitute daughter, her petty criminal fiancé, and the Jewish pawnbroker robbed, and then accidentally murdered, by the young couple.

But it is the pace and indirection of *La Petite Lise* that mark it as an indisputable precursor of the later movement. The rising din of voices and noise in the tropical Cayenne prison precipitates a plot that will culminate tragically in the equally stultifying atmosphere of a Montmartre nightclub. In the first sequence the plot's motivations (the father's imprisonment, his hopes for release and return to his daughter) are given in dialogue that must compete with the songs, squabbling, and noise of the other prisoners. In the finale, the confrontation between the guilty couple and the father is overwhelmed by the ambient sounds of the jazz club. Without speaking, the father leaves his daughter with the pulse of that club and takes himself to the prefecture to confess to her crime. An insert shows his hand slowly, fatally, closing the door behind him while the frantic pace of the music accelerates. The closing shot tracks back from the prefecture office to frame his hunched figure in silhouette. Then the prison bell of Cayenne tolls.

Even before the first sequence, Grémillon signals the fatal key to his tale by sounding the ticking of a clock for nearly a minute, during which we see nothing but black leader. Always a signifier of fatality, the ticktock in this instance is doubly so, since it prefigures the treasured watch that will bind the destiny of the four characters: as a gift of love from father to daughter, as the central prop in the murder of the pawnbroker, and as the key to the father's discovery of that murder.

But beyond these narrative overtones, the opening ticktock sets the steady mechanical rhythm the plot will follow, a rhythm measured in the extraordinary and complete silences between speeches and sounds. No music or contrived ambient noise coats the track; yet there is an impression of continuity, even inevitability, in the pulsing intermittence of sounds against this silence. Whispered speeches, lone train whistles, the closing of a door, all create a clear rhythmic chain leading away from the confusion of the first scene and toward that of the finale. This concatenation of sounds finds more complicated expression in its interplay with the film's images and suggests an altogether single-minded fatality behind the world of the senses. The opening three-minute pan shot of the prison, for instance, is accompanied by a single bell toll fading into the offscreen voice of a guard. In the first Parisian sequence, the rumble of an approaching train interrupts an intricate editing pattern in which three isolated characters are interrelated in the dark. The sound of the train focuses their glances, linking them to a common fate. Moments later, with the camera tracking their heels, Lise and her fiancé walk into the gloomy night while we overhear an expository conversation motivating their plan to rob the pawnbroker and start a new life. In this single long take of the characters' backs, Grémillon clearly found a way to avoid a difficult sync-sound problem; but, more interesting to us, he was able to express the weight of doom through the very length of this shot and through the quality of the pathetic voices over it.

Sound has here created atmosphere by conveying information to the side of the image, so to speak, setting the tone for our response to the image but not interrupting that response with titles or with intercutting between the characters. Similarly, the reunion of father and daughter profits from the possibilities of sound. As Lise dejectedly climbs the dark staircase, the camera remains on the landing. We then see her shadow thrown into relief by the light streaming from the opening door. She enters, leaving the screen, yet the camera refuses to budge. The little spot of light, the hope that it expresses, is the only visible source of the father's tear-choked greeting and Lise's offscreen cries of surprise and glowing pleasure. The slow fade-out punctuates this scene's overall darkness, lending it according to one reading the ambiguity of a forbidden sexual encounter.[56] In any case a brief glow is all that is allowed these characters, a momentary sigh of joy and fullness fading in the fuller silence of the night.

Grémillon intuited the dramatic as well as the atmospheric potentials of sound. In the murder sequence, suspense is built less through cutting than through the reactions of characters to their milieu, largely a sound milieu. When the pawnbroker goes into his back room to get his money, we stay with the desperate but uncertain couple. Their doubt and determination visibly redouble at the sound of the opening safe. During the ensuing struggle we are always kept to the side of violence, Grémillon once again preferring an oblique presentation that insists on his narrative prescience and, consequently, on the fated aspect of the deed being performed. During the fight itself we chiefly watch Lise's face and hear the drama she witnesses. When she takes action and prepares to bludgeon the pawnbroker from behind, the camera moves discreetly to the window. Only after the thudding blow is heard do we view its consequence: in silence, blood trickles in a pool on the floor. As the horrified couple looks on, the doorbell rings. Without having to cut away as in the silent days, Grémillon gives neither his actors nor the characters they depict the space of a moment's relief. The concentration achieved by alternating the drama between what is seen and what is heard limits cutting and visual scope. We do not need to see the safe that opens, the doorbell that rings, the train whose whistle continues to haunt Lise. Meanwhile, the fewer images we do see affect us with greater pressure. As the father goes to retrieve the watch, we hear its ticktock as in the opening of the film, its fatality now fully directing the action. It is only a short step from this to the father's silent sacrifice in the noisy club and to the final tolling of the bell to close the film.

The sound track of *La Petite Lise* alternately breathes atmosphere into the tale and maintains narrative tension in even the most atmospheric shots. Such elasticity of image and sound, of the dramatic and the poetic, was achieved through a more subtle appreciation of the potentials of the expanded medium than that displayed by either Clair or Pagnol. More important, it also foretold a type of sound film that would appeal at once to a mass audience and to a more cultivated elite which had threatened to defect at the coming of sound. This was evident to one of its first viewers,[57] and it would in seven years be evident to a host of producers seeking both gain and prestige in backing the poetic realist school.

In 1930, however, *La Petite Lise* was too delicate a movie to stand up to the hard realities of distribution. In this it bears comparison with the first great poetic realist film, Griffith's *Broken Blossoms*, which Grémillon, as we have seen, studied and venerated. Both films sought to wed a delicate lyricism to blatant melodrama. The passive suffering of *Broken Blossoms*, what I have termed its sublimation through masochism, characterizes the acting style of Nadia Sibirskaïa and the style of *La Petite Lise* as well, yet Grémillon failed to protect his art in France while Griffith, having just formed United Artists, succeeded in Hollywood.[58] Griffith, in short, was himself a powerful businessman whereas Grémillon was truly the masochist. He must have presented his little film to its inevitable fate at Natan's office knowing what would happen. One can imagine him hunched over in the doorway of that office, like Alcover, playing the old escaped convict turning himself in at the police station. There would be no last-minute rescue; *La Petite Lise* was crushed by the crass entrepreneur who was certain that the cinema had permanently abandoned its dalliance with art, now that sound had made it the mass entertainment medium par excellence.

In fixing the image of the French film industry that I have been developing, one can hardly keep from dwelling on the uncannily apt case of Natan. At the moment when poetic realism was beginning to recover for France some of its international cinematic stature, Natan would fall victim to a lurid set of circumstances that might have come out of one of his early pornographic films.[59] A buyer and seller of desires, he could readily have traded in drugs rather than films, or so it has always been alleged. I have made him face the gentle Grémillon, most beloved of French filmmakers, so as to emphasize the contest between art and industry.

And yet Natan too can claim our sympathy, victim as he was of political and economic forces far greater than even he could manage. In 1934 he was dismissed from the industry in a financial scandal that would ultimately send him back to prison. There the Nazis found him in 1940. A Romanian Jew, Natan was exterminated during the Occupation. Many of those who noted his death did so in a tone of foul self-righteousness.

The lesson from this biographical allegory should be clear. The art of the cinema may well have been at the mercy of the business conditions and businessmen of the time, but the film business, for its part, was the plaything of much larger forces: uncooperative banks, testy union heads, uncaring government officials, inconsistent censors, international business giants, whimsical foreign policy makers, and so on. It would be hard to say that such conditions improved during the decade. What did improve was the perception of the strength of French films in the international market, a strength that was based on artisanal and artistic "quality." And this improvement owes itself to a host of people, many of them studio executives. The aesthetic heroism it is so easy to applaud in Renoir and Grémillon had little economic impact, and one might want to applaud just as loudly the cumulative business venture that managed under horrendous conditions to turn out a thousand *films ordinaires* during the decade. While poetic realism can be said to amount to but one type of film amid a dozen other types, its moral and aesthetic claim to realism and poetry allowed it to play a highly visible cultural role. One historian feels compelled to conclude a nine-hundred-page thesis on the business aspects of French cinema in the early years of sound by raising what he calls "the temptation toward realism" in an industry characterized by "irrealist entertainment dominated by stars."[60] To put it another way, from the standpoint of its producers and consumers, La Petite Lise was an average project and a minor casualty in a year when over a hundred other films vied for attention. But Jean Dréville spoke for a culturally influential elite in 1930 when he wrote that La Petite Lise was "a precocious child in the dollhouse of French cinema,"[61] for he sensed that Grémillon had intuited a significant optique that would need a few years yet to carve out a space for itself in studios and at theaters. He called it "a film that opens vast horizons based on a new formula for tomorrow." Quite unlike the avant-garde quest of the 1920s, that search for tomorrow would take place not on the margins, but within the very industry that seemed so hostile to it and against the backdrop of the entertainment films with which it indubitably shared a great deal.

5

Theatrical Models for French Films

The Rise of the Performer

One cannot overestimate the consequences of the technological revolution that sound brought to the film industry worldwide. As I hope to have demonstrated, in France bare statistics mask the extent of the change. For although from 1928 to 1938 nearly the same number of theaters (4,500) continued to show nearly the same number of films (500), the entire technological and administrative mechanism by which those films reached the screen had been completely revamped. And the aesthetic consequences of these changes were permanent.

Given the need for capital outlay and the increased cost of film production that sound required, many small companies inevitably consolidated into conglomerates. Immediately the opportunities for independent production, for its diversity and artistic freedom, diminished. The expense of shooting with sound, not to mention the limited number of soundstages, restricted production to projects carefully scrutinized for their potential financial return. Sound itself was deemed a sufficient artistic novelty to preempt the search for fascinating styles or material.

I have already chronicled the difficulty encountered in 1930 by strong directors like Grémillon and Renoir in circumventing those in charge of studios and the technicians they employed. But the successes that such struggles eventually produced, the "realist" films of the decade, reached an immense audience in comparison to the art films of the 1920s to which both men had proudly contributed. Looked at sympathetically, poetic realism can be counted as a rare instance wherein those most devoted to the social and aesthetic advance of the cinema were constrained by the prevailing circumstances to reach a popular audience. The even rarer coincidence of this popular descent of art with the rise of the populace into a political "Front" made few important filmmakers wish for a return to the freer days when their struggle was mainly with the limits of the medium and when their avant-garde efforts were seen primarily at *ciné-clubs*.

Whatever the blessings and the banes, real-world economics sucked those filmmakers who could be considered artists into the center of an entertainment industry that many, including Grémillon and Renoir, had previously temporized with from the margins. Now the industry was clearly in control, playing as it might choose with the artists. As Clair said in 1934, "The liberty which is accorded in these matters to private initiative is a caricature of liberty; it has as its net result the reign of an absolute dictatorship of several financial groups in a domain which is not merely that of finance."[1] Clair's fears were specific: the sound film was on the point of liquidating the advances of the silent art by returning to a theatrical model. He was certain that the word would dominate the image and that the producer, as impresario or head of the company, would prevail over the director. These linked fears may have been understated, for another force, the actor, rose to a mighty position between director and producer, skewing an already unbalanced set of relations. In the talking cinema, those who could talk (and sing) would have the last word. And those who had mastered that word on the stage would spew it forth on the soundstage.

Theater has always served as a model for the business of cinema. Contracts with actors and exhibition houses are based on nineteenth-century stage traditions. The year 1930 witnessed a migration of businessmen from the theater to the multiple offices of cinema management as they scented a lucrative but cognate enterprise. And film producers, whether they possessed a stage background or not, quickly turned to theater directors and actors, certain that these would be able to adapt best to the new format. This worldwide phenomenon was particularly prevalent in Paris, a city abundant with international theater talent, a city that was in fact arguably the European capital of both media. A play seen one night by a studio executive might the next day be bought for the screen, its actors transported en masse to a nearby soundstage. Shooting previously staged material was comparatively easy, requiring minimal set design and casting. On the technical side, only as many camera setups might be employed as were needed for facial emphasis, dramatic cutaways, and the like. Given the clumsiness of the blimped camera and the delicate requirements of microphone placement, static group shots became the norm, at least until 1933.

And so subject matter (raw material) that the sound cinema needed to process in a hurry came from a ready source: the full repertoire of stage plays, from boulevard farces and light musicals to serious drama. Adaptations of this material served as the staple in the industry for several years. Every alternative, including documentary and poetic realist efforts, needed to take this norm into account. No one could afford to neglect the "star system" that bloomed in the 1930s, fertilized by these theatrical adaptations that sound had made possible. Although a surprising number of the key actors and actresses composing this system had performed in silent movies, their relative importance to the industry's self-conception escalated exponentially when amplified by the microphone.

If you let yourself be inundated with French films of the 1930s, you will remember primarily the actors that come back film after film. And you will remember them largely because everything about the lighting, the mise-en-scène and, above all, the plot and dialogue has been arranged to accentuate their presence. Particularly when compared to the more visually complex direction of the silent era, the 1930s thrived on the hegemony of the actor, the scenarist, and, even more crucial, the dialogist.

Scrutinizing a randomly chosen film, or calculating the global effect of hundreds of them, you can be charmed or annoyed by the egregious manner with which they play up to the audience. In this they hardly differ from the Italian cinema under Mussolini or from standard American television fare today. Had the French thought of laugh tracks, these would surely have been added to help guide the spectator as do the obvious camera angles, explanatory cut-ins, clearly miked dialogue, and unmistakably articulate grimaces and gestures.

In fact the bulk of these films do rely on an early progenitor of the laugh track, the diegetic audience. Within most of the hundreds of films built around or including formalized songs, dances, recitations, and the like, simple reverse shots display an original audience whose admiration or disapproval of the performance serves as a model for our own reaction. Even most straightforward dramas that avoid such scenes of entertainment include reaction shots (often to bit players standing by) to channel or punctuate the signification of events. It could be said with only slight exaggeration that the French cinema of the 1930s, as opposed to Hollywood, is a cinema of reaction. Even violence is more often signaled by its effects on those who see or hear it than by direct representation. For example, Danielle Darrieux swoons in *Le Duel* (1939) when messengers at her front door announce her husband's airplane crash. Although this crash was prophesied in her nightmare, the tension of the event is released retrospectively upon her, not in the moment of its actual occurrence. One can imagine the Hollywood rendition, with the spectacular display of the fiery crash.

Motion Picture Almanac recognized this difference between French and American films when it reported on the enlarged French industry of 1933: "The best features . . . are many times direct and exact copies of stage plays with much dialogue and little or even no action at all."[2] French cinema, it goes on to imply, exists on the faces of its familiar actors, for its plots are projected on their expressions, which announce emotion or react to it. Naturally we are speaking of a limited spectrum of emotions: love, anxiety, national pride, jealousy, and only a few others. This tidy range of articulated feeling, based on endlessly repeated themes, substituted for the system of genres that governed Hollywood. And these themes developed in relation to character roles that in turn were laid out to fit the bodies of the twenty key actors of the period.[3] It is the actors who serve as the ultimate guarantee of value in the federal reserve bank of cinematic pleasure. One's twenty-franc ticket is theoretically redeemable for a star's handshake or autograph, the way the twenty-franc note itself ought to bring one a certain morsel of silver or gold locked away in some vault.

The producers of French cinema, small and large, were all too sensitive to this economic structure at the base of the psychology of entertainment. Those films that bucked this system, such as the precursors of poetic realism, were difficult to distribute. *La Petite Lise* features no real stars, no diegetic audience, nor any performance values whatsoever, and consequently ran aground. Other maverick films accommodated themselves to the star system at a superficial level (as did *La Chienne*, which put Michel Simon in a role that masqueraded as comic and theatrical). Later on, poetic realism would reach its apex only by adding key actors to its particular imagistic and rhythmic predisposition. Thus the primacy of the actor was never seriously challenged in the decade. Poetic realism may have learned to discipline this force to serve a specific aesthetic goal, but for the most part the actor remained the goal itself.

Inertia kept French cinema sliding down this inclined plane. Sound had renewed enthusiasm in the audience for cinema mainly through its ability to present notable acts and actors to a populace that either was in the habit of diverting itself at vaudeville and music hall houses or wished to be able to do so. *The Jazz Singer* and *Broadway Melody* had been successful worldwide; and producers like Braunberger, as we have already seen, quickly copied them. *La Route est belle* featured a popular singer playing himself as a singer, followed by *L'Amour chante*, trading on the same formula. Even the most exceptional (i.e., artistic) films of the period, like Mamoulian's *Applause*, Vidor's *Hallelujah*, and Von Sternberg's *The Blue Angel*, made performance an integral part of their plots.[4]

In this rather sudden overvaluation of "performance values" in the cinema, the director was bound to suffer at the hands of the producer. The aggressive control we saw Richebé exercise over *Le Blanc et le noir*[5] became common as producers continuously monitored the desires of the stars they engaged and the "sound men" they hired. With Paris serving as the world center for multiple versions, the very job description "director" was de facto demoted in France. All too often it referred to a routine of "following directions" laid out in advance by writers and technical personnel. Set designers—who had contributed so much to French cinema in the 1920s—were now likewise hampered by the sound man. They complained at being reduced to providing suitable backdrops for speeches and songs.

The dominance of the theatrical model in French cinema has been attributed to the particularly powerful entente between actor and audience that claims precedence there over all other considerations, outweighing obligations to the film as a well-made object or work of art.[6] A Jules Berry, a Raimu, or a Pierre Larquey might be pleased to act in films only so long as each could on occasion act out to the spectator. Plot, dialogue, and decor were designed to prepare for those moments when the actor could play himself and remind the audience of the special relation they enjoyed. The music hall training of Julien Carette shows up even in Renoir's most sophisticated and serious films: *La Grande Illusion*, *La Bête humaine*, and *La Règle du jeu*.

Chotard et Cie. CB   The Little Theater of Jean Renoir.   *La Grande Illusion.* CB

This pact between actor and audience Ginette Vincendeau sees as the chief component of an unbroken popular theatrical tradition that, after 1930, fed what amounted to a new and lucrative venue, the motion picture theater. She puts into relief the continuity of a kind of popular presentation whose function changed little as it fluctuated between stage and screen, and whose economic weight was sufficient to bend the delicate light of French cinema toward the more luminous careers of performers.[7] Henri Jeanson was not exaggerating when he declared with customary bitterness that "the French cinema moves forward on the backside of Georges Milton."[8]

Jeanson, a journalist turned dialogue man, was in a particularly good position to reckon the strength of performers like Milton, Bach, and Maurice Chevalier. Their momentum as stage personalities in the 1920s pushed them to the forefront of the new sound industry, right past the key directors and scenarists. These actors were unquestionably the most reliable weapon producers could deploy in their war with foreign competition, since French audiences staunchly preferred French material seemingly without considering its quality.[9] The overwhelming response to Florey's primitive *La Route est belle* in 1929 and a year later to Colombier's *Le Roi des resquilleurs* was enough to convince them and their investors that this was the main road to follow.

Such a retreat from a conception of cinema based on photography, set design, and mise-en-scène was immediately noted by disheartened connoisseurs of the art. Valéry Jahier, one of the most intelligent and prophetic voices of the era, excoriated lazy producers for their reliance on theatrical material. He challenged his fellow critics to educate the public to appreciate the possibilities of an art that must mature beyond the mere filming of plays, or worse, of "original" scripts that might as well come from plays.[10] Jahier pleaded for a cinema not of the star but of the common citizen, a cinema that would "poeticize" (his word) the details of everyday experience. The star, he maintained, "mechanizes sensibilities," especially in films that bear the mark of an "international style." He clamored for a national, provincial, and ultimately personal cinema that would have to be founded on a very different social and economic base. Like so many other critics in his day and in our own, he invoked "realism" as the alternative to the conventional "theatricality" that ruled the image factories.

As for opportunities for flashes of realism, Jahier found more appetizing the menus available in the Hollywood system and in Germany than in Paris. He was not the only critic to blame the commerce of adaptation and of stars for usurping financial and creative resources and precipitating the decline of the 1920s countercinema that had established itself as a relatively separate economic as well as aesthetic system. Adaptations are treated by such critics as we might treat "fast food." Stage adaptations, fried in fat, salty, and appealing to coarse tastes, quickly became the habitual diet for the unrefined spectators whose money motivates the decisions of producers. Virtually addicted to comedies and song-and-dance vehicles, the populace ignored films aimed at different taste buds and providing another kind of nourishment.

Léon Moussinac immediately perceived the negative political valence of star vehicles and the reasons these were to dominate production even in an era of social agitation such as the 1930s.[11] Unlike the standard image of the masses hypnotized by Hollywood's realism, the image given off by French films is one in which spectators really are addressed in their seats by a familiar face on the screen. The "cinéma du samedi-soir" was a *popular* but not a *populist* cinema, and working people learned from it very little that would help them bring into existence a culture of their own. Its actors exhibited the high life of the bourgeoisie in their real-life personae and the values of that same class in the roles they played.

For Vincendeau the joy French viewers took in applauding their stars is the most visible symptom of the regressive function played by the movies in this decade, a decade she aptly sums up with the phrase "a cinema of nostalgia." She refers here naturally to the way the past is evoked as a lost haven in serious films such as *Pépé le Moko, Gueule d'amour, Le Jour se lève, Un Carnet de bal,* and *Paradis perdu* (1939). Less obvious is the pervasive presence of nostalgia not as a theme but as a form of entertainment experience one can locate in comedies, musicals, military farces, and, it seems, most films made in the decade. Through the direct address of stars, the cinema evoked the memory of simpler forms of pleasure, of a lost community surrounding street singers, of revelers at spontaneous outdoor stage shows, of good times in the army, and so forth. As France's economic and international situation grew more disturbing, as its increasingly urban populace became more alienated, the cinema conveyed the security of a former identity, the persistence of an endless Belle Epoque. It may seem ironic that one finds in the most politically retrograde movies of the decade the same search for community that the leftists were trying to represent as the search for tomorrow. Evidently nostalgia was far easier to market even during the Popular Front than were hope and struggle.

One final twist multiplies the significance of nostalgia. Popular theater went into unmistakable decline in 1930, owing in part no doubt to competition from sound film, but owing also perhaps to fears of a depression around the corner.[12] When music hall entertainers (such as Florelle or Chevalier) and boulevard actors (Alerme, Arletty, Harry Baur) began to appear regularly on the screen, they found themselves catering to a very different clientele, an impersonal mass of viewers hidden in dark cinemas around the country. Yet their cinematic presence immediately conjured up memories of those better days when they played live on stage to groups of socially bonded neighbors.[13]

Among historians the state of cinema in 1930 is relatively uncontroversial: sound did widen the audience for a medium that began taking on many of the functions formerly served by popular forms of theater. And sound did demote the director and art director in favor of the actor. Controversy begins soon enough, however, for this situation has traditionally been characterized as the temporary "regression" of French cinema requiring a laborious march toward a purer aesthetic during the decade. Tired of this argument, finding it elitist and unresponsive to popular tastes, a newer brand of historian dismisses the artistic pretentions of this "purer cinema" at the decade's end. For them the culture's values remain securely and constantly lodged within the popular cinema. They rightly erase the line strictly separating a serious "pure" cinema and the popular one that kept the industry alive, but they risk submerging the aesthetically advanced wing of the industry (the populist films of Duvivier, Carné, Grémillon, Chenal, Feyder, Clair, and especially Renoir) within the more numerous films of diversion. While there is no denying that filmmakers with different backgrounds and ambitions drew on common resources during this decade (sharing actors, writers, situations), a serious cinema did diverge from the "cinema d'alimentation" in its appeal to new values and to a new function for viewers. Since it extended this appeal within an entertainment world dominated by theater and theatrical adaptation, however, any history of poetic realism needs to account for the types of theater alive in France between the wars, from the lowliest farces to the most pretentious productions of the Comédie-Française.[14]

POPULAR THEATER AND THE CINEMA

Without apology Bernard Natan cultivated Pathé Studios' reputation for crude farces. While Pathé was large enough to diversify its output with occasional prestige productions like Raymond Bernard's *Les Croix de bois* (1931), it relied on cheap entertainments adapted from the music hall and vaudeville. In its contest with foreign competitors who turned out "international" dramas, the specifically French nature of the Pathé entertainments gave them an immediate edge with the French public.[15] Moreover, Pathé considered itself the studio traditionally in touch with the national mass audience. During the 1920s Charles Pathé had built a rural distribution network across which he sent low-quality but very French films. One must recall that of France's 4,500 theaters only 500 could be considered large. All the major companies fought to buy these higher-priced, urban venues. But Pathé, while launching its products in the major cities, put its efforts into sustaining their momentum in the rural areas, even though prices were much lower there and many theaters exhibited only thrice weekly. Pathé even established a special exhibition wing of mobile projectionists (9.5-mm) to reach communities without any theaters nearby. Even after Charles Pathé relinquished the reins of his enterprises to Natan in 1929, the company continued to profit by providing this less sophisticated rural mass what it wanted, and at low prices. What it wanted above all was farce.

It is all too easy to assign an ideological valence to French farce. Except for the Groupe Octobre (whose work, inspired by Brecht, is often compared to that of the Marx Brothers) and later Jacques Tati (likened to Keaton), French comedy is seldom very physical or anarchic. Contrived domestic (parlor) situations, abrupt changes in class, and witty dialogue link it to dramatic traditions that flourished in the eighteenth century, traditions that have always tended toward political and aesthetic conservatism. Unlike Laurel and Hardy, France's crude comic bumblers must be said most often to capitulate to the status quo and to work ultimately for its expansion. Fernandel, the most sensational actor of this sort, played a mentally slow bumpkin in film after film. Yet in film after film, instead of disrupting the system, or showing up its willfulness and blindness, he finds himself rewarded by mistake. In *Un de la Légion* (1936), he not only survives a tour of military duty, despite his ineptitude and the idiocy of his missions, but he goes on to reenlist. Such a film may spoof the earnest military films that flourished in the mid-1930s, but it does so affectionately and in an infantile (that is, submissive) rather than adolescent (rebellious) way. By contrast, remember that a truly rebellious film like *Zéro de conduite* was banned by the censors. It would not have had a good commercial run anyway.

Could producers, much less audiences, distinguish Vigo's or Prévert's polit-ically astute anarchism from the sheer juvenile humor of a comic like Georges Milton, who was likely to fart or burp at any moment to solicit a laugh? For whatever reason, Milton was the very type of performer on which French cinema depended throughout the decade for consistent box-office returns. A "versatile butterfly, never worried about tomorrow," he was confident that his Parisian genius for "getting along" could overcome such annoying circum-stances as a depression and escalating international tensions.[16] The indomita-ble French spirit, exemplified by Georges Milton, was a product of neither discipline nor sacrifice, but of expediency and cleverness.

Although he appeared in film only once during the 1920s, Milton's career on stage was firmly set at the coming of sound. He required only the dependable direction of the seasoned Pierre Colombier to rise high at the film box office. For his part, Colombier used Milton in *Le Roi des resquilleurs* (1930) and *Le Roi du cirage* (1931) to solidify his position at Pathé-Natan. He was known as an actor's director, turning out two films a year, the most famous of which fea-tured Raimu. When *Le Roi* vied with Pagnol's *César* as the most lucrative film of 1936, credit should go to Raimu (who starred in both) rather than to Colom-bier's visual inventiveness. Most often his direction amounted to the duplica-tion of a theatrical setting. *Le Roi* contains not a single shot / reverse shot to lure the spectator onto the stage. Instead all its conversations are played out in medium two-shots or group compositions, with suitable time allowed be-tween speeches for the viewer to weigh and judge the wit of each. In *Le Roi du cirage* Milton, an errant shoeshine boy, finds himself in a loge at the Palla-dium where he interacts for over thirty minutes with the music hall revue he has come to watch. Later, he ascends to the very summit of the social ladder and attends an aristocratic masked ball. Once again the theatrical aesthetic takes over as characters perform for the entourage (and for us). As the film's single star, and in his iconoclastic role, Milton rather than Colombier controls this aesthetic, shifting its tempo by means of the ostentatious excess of his often lewd and always sophomoric behavior. Following his actor, Colombier startles the audience by going beyond the bounds of taste in occasional silly gestures of mise-en-scène. Consequently *Le Roi du cirage* displays moments of real spontaneity. Its first twenty minutes contain live-action street scenes, in the most memorable of which Milton madly pursues a taxi while driving a bus full of outraged and terrified riders. Reminiscent of Keaton and even of the Keystone Cops, this sequence combines some daring outdoor footage with an escalating series of gags.

Colombier, we might say, represents the lowest common denominator of French cinema at the coming of sound. He was ready to slap together a film with whatever resources he could muster; his methods and style, like his mate-rial and performers, came from the music hall and vaudeville theater. In fact

Le Roi du cirage: Milton winks at his fans. BFI

his style might better be termed "technique," a set of production practices that served the actors and the tastes of his time. And in this he can stand for the numerous forgotten *metteurs-en-scène* upon whom Pathé-Natan, Osso, Gaumont, and Haik relied.

In 1937 Colombier reached the summit of his craft when he cast Fernandel in the incomparably successful military vaudeville, *Ignace*. Vincendeau highlights this genre as perfectly suited to director and actor alike, since it consists of regular interruptions of plot by showcased spectacles (songs, "improvised" sketches, routines, dancing girls).[17] The often outlandish contrivances that hook such set pieces to the thread of the drama provide an additional comic element to French audiences who had been raised on revues masking as dramas in popular theaters and music halls. Provocatively Vincendeau points out that this "low art" formula adulterates sophisticated films like *La Bête humaine* where, in the climax, a crooner sings of Ninon's tender heart while in parallel montage we witness the literally bleeding heart of Severine.[18] If, as I believe, the poetic realist impulse achieves a unified and concentrated aesthetic effect, it must have learned to discipline such heterogeneity at play in its scripts. Renoir's strict editing in *La Bête humaine*, to take our example, forces the innocuous *caf'conc* ditty into a powerfully pathetic relationship with the murder.

Indeed, many of the most highly regarded films of the poetic realist era accumulate their energy on the different acting styles authorized by the variety that is literally contained in and by their scripts. *Un Carnet de bal* (1937), known precisely as an episode film, plays Louis Jouvet off against Andrex and Fernandel against Harry Baur. In this way poetic realism did not avoid the popular theater tradition so much as learn to harness its well-known effects in the service of a greater effect and a more sustained mood. Poetic realism also fell in line with 1930s theater in emphasizing male roles and stars. One can hardly ignore the fact that men alone are represented by the names I have listed for the popular theater and—even more—the ones that I will discuss for the serious theater. Each level of theater and each tier of cinema certainly developed female stars and roles, but few became dominant enough to have vehicles written specifically for them,[19] and no woman in the French cinema of the 1930s stood in a position capable of taking the industry in one or another direction, the way Jean Gabin or Raimu did. It goes without saying that women were excluded from the camp of writers, directors, and producers in theater as well as cinema, Colette being a notable exception.

The "variety" associated with vaudeville, its quickly changing and diverting acts, earned it a consistent popular—but little critical—following. (No film trading on its formula aspired to the export market.) A step higher in prestige and more in league with the "better" films of the decade, stage melodramas and well-made bourgeois comedies included plenty of performance pieces but subordinated these to the movement of plot. These genres thrived at the boulevard theaters, where a more discriminating audience than that of the music hall paid a somewhat higher price for a brand of entertainment that seemingly owed as much to its writer as to its performers.

Marcel Achard, the most prolific boulevard playwright to lend his talents to the cinema in this period, shared with music hall and vaudeville not only a taste for surprise effects but also a sense of the priority of discrete scenes. The critic André-Paul Antoine claims that Achard developed his scenes in detail without considering their interrelation until he had accumulated a sufficient number to constitute a play of the proper length. At this point began the arduous search for a substantial connecting conduit to give these scenes not just continuity but accelerating development. Antoine and Achard agreed that only those of his plays with an unbroken chord carried the electricity that could illuminate each scene so as to tingle, then shock, the audience.[20]

Achard, whose peer group was literate—not high—society, wanted to be taken seriously, even while appealing to a broad public. At twenty he had landed a menial job at the most forward-looking theater in France, the Vieux-Colombier. Within a few years he found recognition for plays at once light and psychologically penetrating. *Jean de la lune*, memorably produced by Louis Jouvet in 1929, stands out among these in part because, given its date of composition, it was among the first popular plays that film companies vied over to bring to the screen. And it came to the screen first-class, with sets by Lazare Meerson and an incomparable cast: Madeleine Renaud, Réné Lefebvre, Michel Simon, and Jean-Pierre Aumont. Extraordinary in an enviable role, Michel Simon would always take credit for the film's overall conception. Apparently he did more to shape the result than did the competent but weak director, Jean Choux. Nevertheless, most critics understood that this theatrical adaptation stood out on the strength of Achard's lucid, deliciously disturbing script.

Already an important stage dramatist, Achard instantly secured a reputation among producers as a reliable craftsman in the new medium of sound film. He was brilliant, yet very much in touch with the sensibility of his age, or at least of the bourgeois class he represented in both senses of the word. As his apprenticeship at the Vieux-Colombier and his association with Jouvet would indicate, he was anxious to live among the makers of literary culture. The publisher Gaston Gallimard, a devotee of the theater, became his lifelong friend, and he penned an influential column for the distinguished Gallimard journal *Marianne* in the mid-1930s. Achard had doubled as a journalist in the 1920s, at *Le Figaro* and *Le Peuple* among other places. For *Marianne* he carried on a discriminating dialogue with the popular cinema of the day—primarily Hollywood—predicting its directions, criticizing its various turns, praising the professionalism of the writing and acting. He surely saw himself in the company of René Clair, despite their very different origins. Both men aimed at a large audience; both were students of the arts, full of opinions about acting, rhythm, the avant-garde. Both would be inducted into the Académie française. Yet a key difference between them remains: whereas Clair spent a lifetime in search of the unique principles of the art of the cinema, Achard felt there to be no aesthetic barrier between stage and screen. Like most of his fellow playwrights in the boulevard theater, he worked prolifically in both media without hesitation. After all, his métier consisted of fashioning words and actions no matter where these might appear; the differences that concerned him were primarily sociological. Without sacrificing one's reputation among critics, yet without adopting a supercilious tone, just how subtle ought one be when writing for the less-schooled film audience? Achard, together with fellow playwrights like Henri Jeanson, Steve Passeur, and Jacques Natanson, sought (and generally found) solutions to this problem throughout the decade.

Yves Mirande represents a quite different, friskier specimen of theatrical animal. Mirande was from first to last a bon vivant for whom the theater was an extension of life: a place to dress up, flirt with society, seduce with words, and score financial and amorous triumphs.[21] As with the playwrights of the Restoration period in London, Mirande's talents were his entrée to the society he depicted, and he was careful not to overvalue them. Facility was the virtue he most cultivated, together with a certain diffidence. So determined was he to charm that even his satires are ingratiating. After all, it is only entertainment, he would say.

The entire output of Yves Mirande is a display of upper-class life that, even when treating its foibles, reinforces the desirability of the class structure. Modestly educated, he knew the literary and artistic set more through cocktail parties than through an examination of their works. After the success of a few light comedies on the stage, he sold his time to film producers as a dialogist.[22] By 1936 Mirande was rewriting some of the most famous comic authors of the French stage (Courteline's *Messieurs les ronds de cuir*, most memorably), concocting his own films, and occasionally directing them. As a director, he emphasized broad acting styles, like Jules Berry's in *Café de Paris* (1938). By his own admission, Mirande gave no thought to social issues or to any culture other than the sophisticated society his films invariably concern. So hermetic is Mirande's world, its elegance can give way occasionally to a kind of paranoia. This is the case in *Café de Paris*, where the Jules Berry character and his fancy date on New Year's Eve find themselves accused of the murder of her husband. The entire movie takes place within the swank club as the police interrogate the guests in turn. One after another, each reveals a hidden life full of assignations, obsessions, hypocrisy, and unexpected motivations. Nevertheless, it turns out that none of them is guilty; the murderer in fact is the club's pianist—a servant, so to speak—around whose melodies their high life gaily spins. As soon as he is taken off, the revelers return to their diversions, in full consciousness of their shared deceptions. Mirande evidently longed to live in a world of divans, fancy restaurants, witty talk, and bejeweled mistresses. Hypocrisy was an art to be cultivated, a theater of life, which in his best-received film, *Café de Paris*, only the pianist was too crass to understand.

No one traded more openly on hypocrisy and appearances than the "Prince of Paris," Sacha Guitry, by far the most illustrious personality of the boulevard stage. Far outdoing Mirande as playwright, actor, and bon vivant, Guitry flaunted theatricality, certain that audiences came not for realism, but for sparkling dialogue and elaborate and ironic twists of plot. For an exceedingly verbal playwright like himself to please the large audiences that were his target and the critics who alone could confer on him his place in the world he cared about, he required absorbing scenes linked by a clever dramatic structure. The formula for which he became renowned in such films as *Ils étaient neuf célibataires* and *Remontons les Champs-Elysées* allowed him to share highly personal confidences (played directly to the audience) that comment on the bizarre characters and incidents the plot contrives to surround him with.

The credits of some of his films read like an actors guild register, yet his were essentially one-man features—monologues—or at best, concertos in which his voice not only predominates but gives each film its reason for existence. In 1937, *Les Perles de la couronne* was cited by the American correspondent for the *Film Daily Yearbook* as the year's most significant French product. What made it significant to this critic was the presence of Arletty, Marguerite Moreno, Renée Saint-Cyr, Raimu, Jean-Louis Barrault, Marcel Dalio, and sixty other actors and actresses playing nearly a hundred roles in a ribald historical pageant. More important than this collection of stars, though, is the playfully sardonic voice of Sacha Guitry that conducts us from 1560 to 1936 and from the court of England to the very Parisian soundstage from which the film emanates. As narrator, Guitry projects toward the audience a presence so central that his cast (whom we always take to be his guests, as it were) seem mere shadows of his prolix, fanciful historical imagination.

The title of *Faisons un rêve* (Let's create a dream, 1937) takes advantage of the conspiracy Guitry builds with his audience, and the credits predict his unique deployment of actors. A tantalizing list of names (including Michel Simon, Marcel Levesque, Renée St. Cyr, Marguerite Moreno, and Claude Dauphin) promises to spice a drama of but three characters, two men and a woman. In fact, all the spices are used in the first sequence, an elaborate party to which Guitry invited his many friends in the film community, or so it seems. The famous actors of the credits are glimpsed by an exceptionally mobile camera that prepares us for a film of size and spectacle. But the second scene permanently reduces the social drama to husband, wife, and suitor played loquaciously by Raimu, Jacqueline Delubac, and of course Guitry himself. Against a minimal interior set, static setups (some running a full ten-minute reel) test the inspiration, memory, and sheer verbal dexterity of these actors who perform in soliloquy, in dialogue, or on the phone for the film's remaining eighty minutes. Guitry brings theater and "society" face to face, animating the latter with witty drama and genial, if dangerous, plays of words and sexuality over which he exercises a rather naughty authority.

Guitry's utter neglect of the larger world of society, let alone of nature or the outdoors, has given his films an almost renegade look and reputation that curiously has found favor with recent film historians. The hypnotic drone of his low voice is meant to evoke, rather than to follow from, the sets that have been amateurishly thrown up around him and his characters. Particularly when meant to represent spectacular moments in European history, the cheap quality of these sets adds to the charm of Guitry's character and makes more acceptable his ridiculously chauvinistic view of history. The cinema, he tells us openly, is just one more facile instrument for narcissism. To the large audiences of his own day, and to cinephiles today, Guitry's forthrightness, at once ironic and naive, excuses him. But these same personal qualities can, and have, condemned him, most seriously after 1945 when he went to jail for having flirted with the Nazis. He would flirt with anything just to stay in the limelight. This was his persona if not his actual character, and the theatrical basis of French cinema permitted and flattered him until he really could do with it what he would.

Guitry's chef d'oeuvre, *Le Roman d'un tricheur* (1936), imitates a confessional novel, spoken in our ear by the author, whose voice overarches the picaresque scenes that fade in and fade out one after the other. The audience has no

Le Roman d'un tricheur: Guitry
writes his novel. BFI

Le Roman d'un tricheur: Guitry
lives his novel. BFI

choice but to accept unquestioningly the value of Guitry's perceptions, tied as
they are to those of the character he pretends to play. Many filmmakers, like
L'Herbier and Gance, wanted to break out of the theater mold that had been
constricting cinema since 1930; Guitry loved this prison for amplifying his
irrepressible energy. Because he so flagrantly pushed theatricality as far as
could be imagined in that era, Guitry crystallizes the politics of comedy and of
the presentational discourse of cinema. This discourse, demurely hidden in
other directors, trades on audience submission through its bewitched fascination with stars (adroit, older males and desirable females) as these play out
comedies or melodramas of sexual and class transgression.

Social comedy of this sort is central to the cinema of evasion, dubbed "the
ostrich cinema" because it buries its head in the sand to avoid treating the
serious issues of the day. Guitry never apologized for such a response to his
confusing times, claiming personal prerogative (he felt himself too expansive

to be ground down by the depression) or social utility (the cinema being in his view the one place beleaguered citizens may divert themselves and dream). The professionalism of his theatrical calling and the long French tradition of sophisticated comedy put Guitry beyond the zone of social conscience. Or so he was convinced.

Less self-possessed purveyors of social comedy could point to the satire inherent in the genre, but Guitry's satire always encompassed his own persona; this is a chief reason for its disarming tone. On the other hand, the charm of Bernard-Deschamps's *Monsieur Coccinelle* (1938), to take a memorable example related to Guitry, stands as an embellishment to the side of its satire.[23] While this film establishes a winking rapport between actor (Pierre Larquey) and audience, while it uses narration, choreographed sound effects, and two-dimensional sets on which its actors ham it up in the Guitry manner, one cannot help but feel that those responsible for the film are patronizing their easy target, the defenseless petit-bourgeois class. In an opening sequence commemorating the fall of the Bastille, the title character refers to himself, and dresses up, as "a revolutionary of the happy middle." In the course of the film he will valiantly protect his aging—indeed dying—aunt, not to mention his class, from the unacceptable suitor, Illusio by name, for whom she has pined throughout her boring life.

The defense of domesticity against threats from the outside appears in many other comedies concerning beleaguered father figures.[24] Such films are always played frontally to an audience happy to see the social order confirmed whether through the punishment of the eccentric or through the victory of the man in the center. *Circonstances atténuantes* (1938, dialogue by Mirande) portrays the clash of two social orders represented by a conservative barrister and a band of *apaches* (ruffians). This confrontation results eventually in mutual understanding that satisfies the logic of the plot but that neither questions the law nor searches for the causes of delinquency. Food, wine, seduction, and song are homogenizing French qualities that bring tolerance. And from tolerance springs the enjoyment of difference in behavior, accent, and mores that has actually been structured into the production as a function of casting (Arletty plays an *apache*, while Michel Simon is the stuffy barrister).

Against such ingratiating, well-made social comedies as these, Guitry seems more radical and more authentic, there being no hypocrisy in his treatment of hypocrisy. His totally theatrical self-presentation stands opposite the poetic realist *optique*, but both offer significant alternatives to the soft, patronizing "boulevard" sensibility that dominated French film in the 1930s.

One possible cause of the inauthentic tone conveyed by the bulk of these films may stem from the fact that many of the filmmakers who contributed to the boulevard theater model of French cinema did so reluctantly. Their ambitions for the medium soared beyond that of light entertainment. One of the direc-

Circonstances atténuantes: Dramatic clash of classes. CF

tors most constrained by and contemptuous of this theatrical stranglehold was Marcel L'Herbier, whose tendency toward ornate embellishments had made him the darling of the 1920s narrative avant-garde. But his assumption of directorial privilege was quickly squelched by the sound man and the scenarist who came to power with the new technology. No producer would give L'Herbier the carte blanche he customarily demanded. Even after the success of his 1930 *Le Mystère de la chambre jaune*, a lightly comedic *policier*, he found himself 'humiliated" by powerful new producers whenever he proposed his more "cinematographic" projects. Paris was full of new producers, he notes, many unable to understand the delicacy of his French sensibility, coming as they did from central Europe![25]

In 1933, after two years of unemployment, he had a play thrust upon him, a stage success written by Francis de Croisset. As he himself points out, the more perceptive critics were ready to condemn from the outset this adaptation of *L'Epervier*. It just was not the sort of play that lent itself to the screen.[26] L'Herbier agreed, but he managed to wrest more than the usual authority away from his producer, and, working with Jean-Georges Auriol on the adaptation, he infused the rigid script with a variety of tones that made even Henri

Langlois count it among the most important of early French sound films.
Auriol, we must recall, was the *Revue du cinéma* critic who had cautioned both
Renoir and Grémillon against their aesthetic purism, suggesting that a balance
was needed between popular appeal and cinematic innovation.[27] *L'Epervier*
evidently found that balance, for even de Croisset was fulsome in his praise.
L'Herbier claims, and contemporary critics agreed, that he had broken free of
the theatricality of the original and had taken flight with certain redolent images, particularly in the "transcendent," silent love scenes played out through
glances between Charles Boyer and Natalie Paley.

   L'Epervier opens inauspiciously in the massive Hungarian palace of an eccentric prince, a bizarre but absolutely conventional locale for French films of the
time. Candelabra cast wild shadows on the enormous walls, while a diegetic
orchestra plays somber music for an annoyed audience of one, the aging dem-
agogic prince. Charles Boyer, the prince's decadent son, toys with his weapons
in a firing range, while his bored wife tries on jewelry in her ornate dressing
room. To regain the fire of their love (and to renew their funds, we later
learn), they embark upon a trip to Rome. Thus begins an anthology of luxurious scenes that move from Italy to Paris and down to the Côte d'Azur.
L'Herbier is right at home in the overdone decor such scenes call for, as was
the French public, addicted as we know they were to fairy-tale exoticism. We
are even treated to an evening with an avant-garde dance troupe, which
further establishes the alluring decadence of the chic class these characters
represent.

   But the play's premise, that the source of such princely wealth is card
sharpery, eventually shifts our attention from decor to the inscrutable figures
who inhabit it. When Boyer and his reluctant wife clean out a French diplomat
(with whom she is having an affair), the film becomes a poker game of faces
that reveal, and more often conceal or fabricate, sentiments of love and honor.
L'Herbier's direction becomes exceptional when he abandons his clumsy
rhythmic editing and his art deco compositions (the actors posturing languidly
in longshot on banisters) for the intense close-up drama of this complex
ménage à trois. He instinctively focuses down on the translucent and pained
visages of his high-stakes players, entering their emotions and motivations.
L'Herbier goes so far as to interrupt what has become a luxury cruise, in
deluxe automobiles and train cars, with an explanatory flashback showing
how Boyer had earlier botched an assassination of the French diplomat and
was injured in the process. The film turns darker after the flashback, darker
and more interior, L'Herbier now suppressing the musical accompaniment
and high-key lighting that was always the norm for such upper-class dramas.
No doubt this is the reason de Croisset approved this "fidelity to the spirit" of
his piece, especially in comparison to the irreverent way his other play, *Ciboulette*, had been adapted that same year by Autant-Lara and the Groupe Octobre. Recall that Autant-Lara had been contemptuous of de Croisset even
before the latter had him removed from the project.[28] L'Herbier, however,

L'Epervier. CF

Chic life-style of
inscrutable gamblers.

L'Epervier. BFI

respected the playwright, even if he began by undervaluing the transposition of any play.

L'Epervier's success was enough to change L'Herbier's mind on the question of adaptation. He immediately took on Henri Bataille's *Le Scandale* and then the incomparably melodramatic *Le Bonheur* from the stage hit by Henry Bernstein.[29] With actors who knew the cinema as thoroughly as did Charles Boyer and Michel Simon, L'Herbier now believed that a resourceful director could create something that floated on the eloquent wings of a well-made play's plot and dialogue. He notes in justification that one of his country's most celebrated novelists, François Mauriac, claimed exactly this in the acceptance speech he delivered on being inducted into the Académie française in 1934.

L'Herbier continued to proclaim the primacy of the "cinematographic" over the "theatrical" even as he learned to compromise with adaptations of plays. Abel Gance, that other giant of the narrative avant-garde, showed less patience. True, in 1934 he devoted himself to the adaptation of two plays, Henri Bataille's classic *Poliche* and Alexandre Dumas's *La Dame aux camélias*, but he would spend the rest of the decade striving clumsily to burst the boundaries of this form. Even *Poliche* concludes with pyrotechnics worthy of the "silent era" Gance, including superimpositions, time distensions, quick cutting on body parts, expressionist lighting, and significant camera angles. His pet project, *Un Grand Amour de Beethoven* (1936), and the remakes of his silent triumphs (*Mater Dolorosa*, 1932; *Napoléon Bonaparte*, 1935; *J'accuse*, 1938) look ludicrously overblown today, even if they fetched official respect in the 1930s.[30] These

Un Grand Amour de Beethoven:
The artist as romantic hero.
MOMA

films derive from a heroic conception of art that was on the wane in the film world and in the culture generally. That Gance had to be reckoned with throughout the decade is a testimony to the power of a magnificent early career that tied him to a vast network touching all levels of the culture industry. Curiously, many historians and critics find Gance's most powerful expression of the 1930s to lie in his impersonal films, especially *Poliche* and *Paradis perdu*, which he tossed off while waiting to put together his epics.[31] Evidently even a style as muscular and idiosyncratic as his could be buckled within the reigning theatrical *optique*.

To characterize the "boulevard influence" on French cinema by focusing on directors like Gance and L'Herbier neglects the more central role that scriptwriters came to play in the 1930s. As already noted, Mirande and Guitry were playwrights, as were Achard, Natanson, Jeanson, Passeur, and Louis Verneuil. All of them viewed the cinema as an extension of their public careers writing for the stage and for journals. They were the Noel Cowards and Robert Ryskins of Paris. Their prestige in the world of theater often earned them priority over the directors chosen to film their scripts. Achard, for example, considered himself (and was interviewed as) the creative force behind *Gribouille*. He claimed, patronizing the director, "I was able to do nearly what I wanted . . . it is a film I conceived and executed freely and I'm probably one of the only writers who can take responsibility for their work in film. Marc Allégret shot the film admirably, just as I conceived it. I watched the shooting to make certain everything in the dialogue was expressed to perfection."[32] *Gribouille*, like the next Achard-Allégret production, *Orage* (1937), exhibits more than a hint of the poetic realist tone, the credit for which must go either to Allégret or to the fact that by 1937 Achard had absorbed tendencies coming from sources other than the boulevard theater with which he was primarily associated. Perhaps by watching earlier efforts by Allégret, such as *Lac aux dames* and *Sous les yeux d'Occident*, or in discussions with fellow writers—his close friend Jeanson, his acquaintances Pagnol and Spaak—he was led to venture more complex solutions to the melodramatic intrigues that bubbled annually into his fertile imagination.

Whether or not it directly affected the poetic realist aesthetic, we can credit the boulevard theater model with nurturing the system of production by *équipe*, so important to the better films the French produced in this and later decades. The most professional playwrights of the time would customarily collaborate with a single stage director and often with a small band of actors. Set designers and even composers frequently attached themselves to a particular theater or troupe, lending a definite style to a run of plays across a number of years. As I have already noted,[33] Renoir, Carné, and many other strong filmmakers of the 1930s adopted this model as their chief way to control the fluctuations of an industry that had no strong studio legs to stand on. While the music hall cinema can be said to have been dominated by the actor (and to have been affiliated in its early years with the major studios, especially Pathé, holding actors by contract), the more expensive films of the decade by contrast are to be found in certain independent productions where the producer pulled together an *équipe* based on the nucleus of a writer-director team.

This "system" of filmmaking accounts for the perception, one I have already described, that French cinema was produced in tiers, at the bottom of which were the vaudeville quickies, and above which stood a writer's cinema with pretensions to quality.

The most famous and successful exponent of this writer's cinema was unquestionably Marcel Pagnol. Despite his reputation as a regionalist, Pagnol from the beginning wanted nothing more than to conquer the stages of Paris. It was for this that he moved from Provence to the capital and joined Les moins de trente ans (those under thirty), a noisy group of ambitious playwrights who had coalesced around Paul Nivoix, the drama critic for the journal *Comoedia*. A good share of France's future scenarists (including Achard, Passeur, Natanson, and Jeanson) participated in Nivoix's meetings, manifestos, and programs. They aimed to develop an alternative to the predictable theater of the boulevards and to the pretentious, often impenetrable, experiments of the cubist and Surrealist avant-garde. The group pursued a dramatic ideal based on the well-made, naturalist plays of Scribe and Dumas *fils*. While each playwright in the group professed a singular style, they shared a concern for crisp dialogue, tight but inventive structure, and devastating irony.

Pagnol and his cohorts stood in line to inherit, by altering, a postwar theater that had lost its way. Jacques Copeau's Vieux-Colombier went out of business in 1924. Antoine's experimental Théâtre libre could not sustain itself past his old age, as productive as that had been. The boulevard houses were taken over by businessmen (many, it is often pointed out, immigrants to France and insensitive to national stage traditions). And so the business climate of French theater in the 1920s had much in common with that of the film industry of the 1930s; once he had made his way in the former, Pagnol was determined to have an enormous effect in the latter.

Sound cinema arrived at a summit in Pagnol's career, for his great plays *Topaze* and *Marius* both opened in the 1928–1929 season to the unanimous acclaim of the critics and the public. Spreading his feathers, he announced his conversion: "The art of the theater is reborn under another form and will realize unprecedented prosperity. A new field is open to the dramatist enabling him to produce works that neither Sophocles, Racine, nor Molière had the means to attempt."[34] Pagnol's plot of land in this field came to him through an offer from Robert Kane, the executive producer of the European branch of Paramount Pictures. Kane secured the rights for the screen versions of the two plays, retaining Pagnol as writer for *Marius*, to be directed by Alexander Korda,[35] but then excluding him from participation in the *Topaze* project. This neglect spurred the volatile ex-schoolmaster to look to take control of his own productions. At first he required financial and technical nurturing, which, as we have seen, Pierre Braunberger and Roger Richebé were eager to give him in their struggle against Paramount. Pagnol served as line producer in the adaptation of *Fanny*, the second title in the *Marius* trilogy and a film that made money, but not enough to float the foundering Braunberger-Richebé company. Retaining Richebé as an executive producer on his next project, Pagnol, in 1933, leaped over his bosses to form Les Auteurs associés,[36] modeled on United Artists. Centered in Marseilles, this firm would control both the production and distribution of all his future projects, thumbing its nose at the Parisian film establishment. Employing a steady troupe of Provençal performers, he triumphed with his ingenuous canticles of rural life. It was at this moment that Pagnol also founded *Les Cahiers du film*, a journal dedicated to the propagation of "cinématurgie," Pagnol's name for his theory of filmed theater. He was bubbling with confidence.

Jofroi (1933) and *Angèle* (1934), the first two projects of the fledgling company, established the tone for much of his ensuing career. Adapted from stories by Jean Giono and set in the countryside northeast of Marseilles where Pagnol was born and raised, these films subject the manners and diction of the simple farmers and shopkeepers of the south to the precise principles of dramatic structure Pagnol had developed in his years with Les moins de trente ans. At the same time, they subject a kind of dialogue that Pagnol had cultivated to please Parisian audiences to the raw but evocative terrain of southern France. Pagnol banked on a faith that contact with this soil would authenticate his dramas. The cast and crew of *Angèle*, it is always recalled, helped build the farmhouse that became the setting for that film.

This then is the formula to which Pagnol would return with increasing popular and international success in *Regain* (1937) and *La Femme du boulanger* (1938): a tale by Giono, inevitably pivoting on the redemptive power of a woman, honed into a taut drama carrying the folkish tone of "le coeur meridional." Shot on location in Provence, and cast with the repertory company Pagnol had assembled from the Marseillaise music halls (including Raimu, Fernandel, Charpin, and Orane Demazis), these films develop at a relaxed pace with a disingenuously limpid visual style. It is reasonable to claim that Pagnol's early success on stage and in the first sound films was primarily dramaturgical.

Angèle. MOMA   Redemptive canticles of rural life.   *Regain*. BFI

True, he had introduced an entourage of characters not normally seen or heard on Parisian stages, but he treated them without a program in mind. Pagnol thought of himself at this time as simply a good craftsman working as every craftsman should, on material he knew intimately. In the melodramatic *Marius* trilogy, his inspiration was to take shopkeepers and fishmongers seriously, and to let them display their aspirations, conservatism, and manners in rich detail. That this riveted audiences around the globe astounded the reigning Parisian critics.

In time, of course, critics were tempted to speak of Pagnol's worldview, but only after his adoption of Giono's deeply social vision that went beyond sympathy for his characters, bordering on a full cosmology. At the moment of the Popular Front, of disturbances in Paris and organized factions fighting for supremacy in a depressed economy, Giono preached a return to the soil and a pacifism that was so thoroughgoing it would ultimately land him in jail. Pagnol was a natural ally, and in the films they put together from 1934 until the war, one can speak not only of a Pagnol style but of a myth and a social project flowing from that myth.

These larger concerns parade openly in *Regain* whose lumbering plot line is chained to the movement of the seasons. In an abandoned hillside village the eruption of springtime from winter coincides with—indeed seems to bring into existence as an epiphenomenon—an elemental love story between the last remaining villager and a lonely itinerant woman who happens on the place. Their affection is expressed sacramentally through the cultivation of the fields and the production of bread. The crude, almost brutish villager, under the spell and affection of the woman, turns from hunting to farming and so resurrects the wasted fields around them. In gratitude, the land gives back in abundance a grain so rich that its quality stands out at the local market. The farm thrives; the seasons turn; the couple sow more grain; naturally they conceive a child. *Regain* is a film without suspense but with an elemental power that rolls forward the minute the couple listen to nature within them and heed the religious obligations brought on by their vague desire for fertility. Pagnol films all this ritualistically, reducing the props to a limited number of charged icons (bread, a plow, a bubbling spring, a church steeple).

Amid the calls and programs for social change that were increasingly heard from Left and Right alike, the solid moral understanding evident both in Pagnol's characters and in the sure craft of his technique seemed a haven that attracted both the simple and the sophisticated. Where Sacha Guitry justified theater through its artifice, Pagnol justified it as the human expression of a cosmic drama. One dealt with Parisian life in urbane dialogue; the other with rural life in elemental speech.

Flanking the standard films of the decade from quite different sides, Pagnol and Guitry likewise upset those progressive critics who wanted to overthrow standard theatrical cinema with specifically "cinematic" strategies. They might be said to represent the limits of the theatrical tradition in French cinema. They derive from an essentially comic tradition and a confidently conservative one. You can locate the source of Pagnol's confidence in his luscious pantheism and Guitry's in his deification of (French) culture; in both cases their theatricality makes use of the cinema for the direct presentation of human potentiality and need. Nature in Pagnol and culture in Guitry justify and amplify the sentiments that their engaging characters pronounce with neither hesitation nor qualification. Human beings may be flawed, as every satire aims to demonstrate, but in Pagnol and Guitry those flaws are so clearly audible and visible that they shed all hint of menace, becoming the occasion for celebration by the delighted auteurs and the huge public those auteurs so proudly and directly address.

Serious Theater, Cinema's Conscience

One might forget that for every proponent of a pure cinema freed from noxious theatrical influences, there was a proponent of pure theater, horrified to watch a crass film industry undermine an art form dating back to Aeschylus. One of the theater's most notable critics, André Lang, declared that the cinema, popular medium par excellence, had thankfully returned the theater to its rightful (that is, to its serious) mission and to its predestined (highly literate) audience.[37] Lang, at the very moment adapting *Les Misérables* for Pathé, convinced himself that the boulevard theater was a viper's nest just as treacherous as that of commercial film production. The boulevard theater deserved to be victimized by the cinema and by those writers (himself included) whom it had spurned in the 1920s, many of whom now worked at major studios. Lang believed that playwrights with substantial talent should be nurtured in conservatories and in state-supported theaters. The compromises so many of them had made with the boulevard theater during the 1920s blurred the difference between the cultural functions of these media, demeaning the theater and not setting sound cinema on a sensible path either.

To many disgruntled critics of the early French talkie, theater was certainly the culprit, but it could also serve as the solution. It was a matter of trading in the model of the popular music hall and boulevard stages for that of serious drama. In France between the wars this in fact consisted of three separate enterprises, each of them mercilessly serious: the experimental laboratory theater of the likes of Artaud, the patrimony of the Comédie-Française, and the several endowed artistic theaters.

Before 1930 the sharpened blade of the avant-garde had carved out for itself in theater as elsewhere a realm of independent critique, experiment, and pleasure. But fatigue set in with the turn of the decade and strident visionaries lost their edge, some of them even being absorbed by the enemy. One of those temporarily absorbed, Benjamin Fondane, is particularly exemplary because in the silent era he had denounced even experimental cinema as compromised. To retain his purity he had composed instead a series of unfilmable *ciné-poèmes*, or "fetuses" as he referred to them, a genre he proudly announced that culture could never tolerate. Yet by 1930 he could be found working at Paramount Studios evidently hoping for a chance at independent expression if he stayed on long enough.[38]

Did Fondane have scruples working for an industry producing and selling images he loathed? And why would Paramount have taken a chance on such a spirit as Fondane's? Probably because he was affordable and they were desperate for literate writers, particularly those with language skills. Fondane could adapt completed films into Romanian, could comment on new ideas by the stable of writers Paramount kept on the payroll, and, if things worked out, could develop scenarios himself. In fact things did not work out. After three years at Paramount, having worked on over a hundred projects, he had no screen credit to boast of. In 1934, however, a major film bears his name, Kirsanov's *Rapt*, a remarkable film independently produced, which was a distinct progenitor of poetic realism. Fondane was proud of his script and of the film as a whole, because for once it did not slavishly cater to some vague mass taste.[39]

Fondane's search to transcend cinema with his essays on the art and with his *ciné-poèmes* (not to mention an uncompleted experimental effort launched in Argentina) scarcely intersects the story I have been telling of French cinema. How remarkable, then, that during the years 1930–1933 he could have been drawn into the commercial sector. Producers and studio bosses certainly were not out to convert Surrealists and anarchists to popular art; but they must have felt that the sound film could use imaginative and literate writers and that the temptation of an audience would bring these nonconformists into the fold. For their part, most free thinkers lost interest in the cinema immediately.

It is always difficult to chronicle disinterest. The fate of Antonin Artaud, passionate about everything, is an index of the lethargy that sound brought to some former aficionados of cinema. In 1928 Artaud played major roles in the two swan songs of the silent era, Dreyer's *La Passion de Jeanne d'Arc* and L'Herbier's *L'Argent*. He had the means and the ambition to use the cinema as he thought it should be used. But just as he published in the prestigious *Nouvelle Revue française* his scenario for *La Coquille et le clergyman* together with an essay "Cinéma et réalité," sound came to disrupt everyone's beliefs and hopes about the art form. As a well-known actor, as a *metteur-en-scène* with innumerable connections (his uncle was the important film producer Louis Nalpas), and as a scandalous personality, Artaud might readily have played a serious role in the transition to sound. For a time he tried: he adapted Robert Louis Stevenson's *Master of Ballantrae* and came up with a French version of Lewis's *The Monk* that was published in 1931. But no producer bit on either project.

Artaud was not locked out of the industry. He landed parts in the French version of double-language films shot in Berlin, including Pabst's *L'Opéra de quat'sous* (1931).[40] Pierre Braunberger, Charles David, and Paul Fejos nearly engaged him for their 1932 *Fantômas*, a role that would have fully guaranteed the pedigree I have traced descending from Feuillade through the Surrealists into the 1930s.[41] But too few interesting prospects like this turned up, and in any case Artaud had become increasingly intransigent. Discouraged with cinema, he returned to his experimental theater, to the spontaneity and ritual it provided. The sound cinema, especially in the way it was developing, quite simply would not be for him a locus of important cultural or aesthetic research and expression. Instead he ventured, and lost, everything on his staging of *Jet of Blood* in 1935. Artaud was not alone in his feelings, as many intellectuals and artists demoted the cinema to the status of insignificant pastime. They might despise it or indulge in it patronizingly, but no longer would they employ it in their efforts to redirect culture.

Where Artaud and Cocteau were the most famous theater personalities interested in the aesthetic possibility of experimental cinema, and while both saw their hopes dashed in the 1930s, another radical direction lay open to counterculture figures like the Prévert brothers. They sought to develop a socially committed theater and cinema practice, inspired by the communist drift of Breton and Aragon. They wanted to bypass (or destroy) the vapid world of middle-class entertainment, and devised a program to do so without a permanent venue or even a regular schedule of performances. In effect the Groupe Octobre and other such troupes fought a guerrilla war against the theater establishment and the class it represented. While the critics ignored street antics and union-hall performances, we have seen how imagination and spontaneity gave guerrilla troupes a certain notoriety in Paris. The fact that their audience was working class, rather than "the chic" to whom the likes of Cocteau and Artaud appealed, paved the way for their eventual entry into more mainstream moviemaking. Unquestionably the Groupe Octobre's disdain of effete aestheticism and its attraction to burlesque brought its members into the terrain of the popular entertainment sphere, a terrain they would soon hope to conquer through the formation of a popular front.

Surfacing from the culture's id, revolutionary theater aimed to topple the middle class and its smug diversions. The world of theater contained a severe superego too in the righteous Comédie-Française, the lofty conscience of the entertainment sphere. So white-gloved was that institution during most of the interwar years that it paid cinema little attention and received little in return. As a three-hundred-year-old establishment, and France's only fully funded national company, the Comédie-Française dedicated itself to a revered past, not to fashionable trends. A literary museum, the Comédie-Française would at best, and only occasionally, showcase "modern classics." Obviously the aura

of tradition that it kept alive within the sanctuary of its holy building threatened to disperse into the general smog of modernity were its plays routinely
available at the movies. In 1929 its board voted to forbid its actors to appear
on the screen, in effect claiming rights to their bodies and their famous voices
in the name of art.

It was not until 1934, after five years of discussion, that the company's board
finally permitted the filming of one of its lighter plays, *Les Précieuses ridicules* by
Molière. A prologue to the filmed play was required—a disclaimer, really—in
which M. Emile Fabré, the bearded director of the company, sitting in front of
a similarly bearded bust, reminded the spectators that as a medium of images
the cinema could never stand in for the true art of theater, in which inspired
actors embody in the present the immortal dialogues of the past. The cinema
could at best remind them that intellectual substance was available elsewhere.
So as to seal this point, the film proper begins with a tracking shot down the
rue de Rivoli where well-dressed people have queued up for a performance at
the Comédie-Française. We follow a couple inside the famous building, into
the vestibule and the *promenoire*. They take their seats. The play begins, shot
from the wings so we can see the audience. Numerous reverse shots document their reaction to the play and cue our own, until, almost twenty minutes
into the film, we have become the sole spectators of the action. One can hardly
imagine a more patronizing enunciation, as though the Comédie-Française
had to remind not just its audience, but its own actors and administrative
personnel, of its special cultural mission. Perhaps such a reminder was necessary as its actors lobbied for a share of the easy profits in the cinema. For also
in 1934 permission was granted for actors to take on roles in films, under
carefully spelled out conditions.[42] Even after the Comédie-Française was reorganized in 1936 so that Jouvet and other strong directors had access to its
stage, it rather kept to itself, avoiding the competition of themes and styles that
beset (and enliven!) public theater and cinema. In short, this most famous of
Parisian theaters had small effect on the daily life of cinema in the 1930s.

Not everyone concurred that the soul of the theater was housed within the
Comédie-Française. The interwar years saw the rise of four artistic theatrical
producers whose vitality kept them in the forefront of serious criticism and in
a position to influence the cinema. The "cartel," as they came to be known
after their 1927 manifesto, included Charles Dullin, Gaston Baty, Georges
Pitoëff, and Louis Jouvet.[43] Dedicated to the vibrancy of drama, with its ability
to represent and inflect contemporary life in a powerful, critical, and modern
way, they opposed the anachronistic Comédie-Française just as staunchly as
they did the money-grubbing boulevard fare. Each had roots in the 1920s,
connected either to André Antoine or Jacques Copeau; each was able to muster enough backing to launch a troupe, and all but Pitoëff maintained tenure
for a time at a renowned stage in the 1930s; each sought to reform theater by
refusing on the one side to fall back on the classics as classics and by refusing

on the other side to pander to popular taste. The theater would not be a diversion; it would comfort neither the haute bourgeoisie nor the rising middle class. It would be a theater dedicated to the possibilities of the art.

As sound came to cinema, all four were poised to influence the cinema, for while most film producers undoubtedly paid attention to trends in the popular theater and music hall, any film director, writer, or actor who thought about shaping the sound cinema looked up to the studio theater. After all, because they occasionally received a measure of state aid and private support, these studio companies were able to follow through on artistic projects that could only be dreamt about over wine in the cafeterias of the film industry.

Although their work has often been referred to as avant-garde, the cartel had no wish to suppress language and plot, the way Artaud did as an exponent of visceral experimental theater.[44] In this sense, all four men were traditionalists—at least in their efforts to make possible the interaction of great dramatists with a significant public. They were thought of as avant-garde in that each had achieved distinction by threatening the status quo of French theater with a superior, modernist aesthetic, not by throwing over the standard rapport of drama to audience. And so inevitably their talent and success brought them into phase with the official culture. In the revolutionary year 1936, all four men were designated *metteurs-en-scène* at the troubled Comédie-Française. This marked a summit of prestige for the art: at the very moment of the Popular Front, the cartel could be thought of as representing the "state of French theater." The cinema, it would seem, could only gain by the association it had maintained with these men.

That association, however, had scarcely been exploited. Gaston Baty, to begin with, was a purist, refusing to enter into the least transaction with the cinema, a medium he was sure would contaminate his efforts. The sanctity of the stage—the communion it promised between actor, decors, and public— precluded its re-presentation on the screen, particularly in the crass conditions of the capitalist entertainment industry. Less closed to the cinema, the Pitoëffs, Georges and Ludmilla, also had less to offer it. Prominent Russian émigrés, their major effect on the stage was to have renewed French acting styles with the Russian forms they brought with them. They appeared in a handful of truly notable films: Jacques Feyder's *Le Grand Jeu* (1933), Jeff Musso's *Le Puritain* (1937), which starred Jean-Louis Barrault, Jean-Paul Le Chanois's communist feature *Le Temps des cerises* (1937), and the last film by their émigré compatriot Dimitri Kirsanov, *Quartier sans soleil* (1939). Rented from their genuine vocation on the stage, the Pitoëffs were asked to validate, by virtue of their prestige, one or another rather exceptional film. Evidently these cases were very few, and the Pitoëffs' influence on film acting and mise-en-scène consequently amounted to little.

The two men who trafficked most with the cinema were Charles Dullin and Louis Jouvet, both products of Copeau's Vieux-Colombier experiment that began before World War I. Dullin was the older. His fame rested almost entirely on a legendary performance style. And it was large, this fame, large enough to permit him to use his name in the silent cinema, eventually to star in most of the sensational historical epics of the day: *Le Miracle des loups* (1924), *Le Joueur d'échecs* (1926), and *Les Trois Mousquetaires* (1921). In 1927 he went so far as to incorporate himself, creating Le Société des Films Ch. Dullin whose sole production introduced one of France's greatest directors, Jean Grémillon. Dullin's career had peaked before the introduction of sound; nevertheless, he shows up in a remake of *Le Miracle des loups* and in a portmanteau vehicle called *L'Affaire du courrier de Lyon* that featured his aged mentor Jacques Copeau as well.

It was left to Jouvet, then, to effect any substantial links between the serious artistic theater and the cinema. As a director he rivaled Baty in his sense of "total theater." Gaining notoriety for his lighting effects and his set designs even before his acting, he might be expected to have had a special affinity for the possibilities of the cinema. His acting style, in contrast to Dullin's and the Pitoëffs', was subdued, or at least potentially so. He aimed for subtlety and intensity, qualities the French cinema would later try to adopt. And so a rendezvous with the popular and commercial world of cinema was inevitable.

Jouvet waited until 1933 for that rendezvous, when he starred in the second Pagnol film to be adapted, *Topaze*, and re-created his famous role in *Knock, ou le triomphe de la médecine*, a play by his friend Jules Romain. Jouvet claimed that his appearance on the screen meant to him nothing more than the check that bankrolled productions at his new Théâtre Athenée. But from 1934 to 1940 he appeared in nothing but important films, usually by directors of great talent like Feyder (*La Kermesse héroïque*), Renoir (*Les Bas-Fonds, La Marseillaise*), Carné (*Drôle de drame, Hôtel du Nord*), Duvivier (*Un Carnet de bal, La Fin du jour, La Charrette fantôme*), Pabst (*Mademoiselle Docteur, Le Drame de Shanghai*), Marc Allégret (*Entrée des artistes*), and Chenal (*L'Alibi*). His presence on the set could only have brought self-consciousness to the production and perhaps an edge to the acting.

Jouvet never directed in the cinema, but the care and clarity of his theatrical productions must have affected those directors and producers so eager to put him in their films. In the 1920s, for example, he worked diligently with a corps of composers who a few years later would be writing the most innovative film scores in the world: Georges Auric, Francis Poulenc, Maurice Jaubert, and Darius Milhaud. He gave Christian Bérard license to create stage decors that even today seem adventuresome. Bérard of course would startle the cinema much later in his memorable sets for Cocteau's *La Belle et la bête* (1945) and *Orphée* (1949). Jouvet also served as mentor to Jean-Pierre Aumont and other young actors. His discipline and standards as well as his notorious oscillation between coldness and warmth can be glimpsed in *Entrée des artistes*, where he plays himself, a teacher of aspiring actors at the Conservatoire.

In sum, Jouvet contributed directly to the "quality" of the French cinema. More important he helped bring to it a cultured audience that otherwise might

Entrée des artistes: Jouvet plays Jouvet. BFI

have been alienated. The fact that he produced several plays by Achard and by Jean Savoir, both of whom wrote for the boulevard theater as well as for the cinema, helped lessen the class distinction among media and audiences. In his pursuit of an ideal of theater, he played to, and enlarged, an audience interested in "distinction" and sensitive to the quality of the composers, painters, writers, and actors he enlisted. Many of these artists followed Jouvet into the cinema, no doubt drawing with them a segment of their cultured audience.

As an art form that lives in the interaction among people, not to say personalities, theater has always forged alliances and projects that go beyond the stage. Jouvet's magnetism proved this over and over, and occasionally to the benefit of cinema. For example, Gallimard's underwriting of Renoir's *Madame Bovary* (1933) came about largely because of his relation to Jouvet's favorite actress, Valentine Tessier. Jouvet's productions of Martin du Gard's plays led that author and his close friend Gide to dwell on the possibilities of a social cinema. From this came their involvement with Colette (another Gallimard author) in *Lac aux dames* (1934) and in the interrupted adaptation of *La Bête humaine*.

Jouvet's case, on the other hand, also confirms the limitations of the theatrical model for the French cinema of the 1930s. If he was indeed the one serious *metteur-en-scène* to devote some energy to film, then by and large we must side with those who claim that the theater's influence on the cinema was conservative. For none of Jouvet's fabled dramaturgical risks was ever systematically tried out in film. He merely acted, and by acting, acted upon the cinema through association. In the movies Jouvet was, no matter how accomplished, simply another performer. In the theater, by contrast, he was aiming for a "dramatic rite or ceremony" in which the mystery of the theater would strike at all those who dared to assemble as a group before its power.[45] This religious analogy may not have suited every intellectual hoping for a renewal of culture, but the seriousness it implied could only be a relief for those who felt overwhelmed by an anodyne mass culture. Since Jouvet could be found working in the cinema, there was hope for the cinema, reason to review films and read reviews, reason to promote its most distinctive endeavors. His presence allows us to imagine a type of spectator—not the popular spectator, to be sure, but a discriminating one—eager for an intense and probing experience at the cinema. Poetic realism would work to satisfy this spectator while at the same time addressing the larger audience.

The Literary and Artistic Sources of Poetic Realism

IN THIS PERIOD of dire financial stress, it would take more than visionary directors to open up the cinema to possibilities beyond the theatrical paradigm. After all, most actors, artisans, and writers had stage experience and banked on the theater for their conception of art and entertainment. Particularly after the diffusion of sound technology directors and producers, terrified of expensive risks, defaulted to a theatrical conception of cinema in making most of their routine decisions. Poetic realism depended on a reversal of this conception. More than is usually understood, it depended on such reversal at every level of film production. Developing a new sense of what the cinema was capable of turned out to be the responsibility of many people working in the industry, not just of a few geniuses on top. As Alexandre Arnoux pointed out midway through the decade, "In 1933 it was enough to photograph plays. Now they must contain an integral atmosphere."[1] The story of this reversal, of the general realization of other options for cinema—and the poetic realist option in particular—will take us into the domains of writing and of visual design. And it necessarily involves artisans and moneymen (producers) just as much as it does directors.

THE POETICS OF FICTION

Judgments about the worth of poetic realism may differ, but no one can doubt the critical success these French movies enjoyed between 1936 and 1939. Even though the financial outlook for the industry was at least as bleak as it had been early in the decade, critics were certain they had witnessed the transformation of an underachieving art to one that could honestly be said to lead the world. While many of the best of these films were written directly for the screen (*La Règle du jeu*, *La Grande Illusion*, *La Belle Equipe*, *Un Carnet de bal*), many others came from novels (*Le Quai des brumes*, *Hôtel du Nord*, *La Bête humaine*, *Le Puritain*, *Gueule d'amour*). More important, not a single film in the poetic realist canon was drawn from the stage. Thus cinema's rapport with prose fiction, and particularly with the *récit*, gained ascendancy, infecting even "original scripts" with an aesthetic that avoids verbosity and that mixes description, narration, and dialogue. After several years of relatively routinized production, based on the primacy of actor, dialogue, and clear sound, French cinema began to feel the influence of a novelistic aesthetic that demanded the subtle participation of visual artists, composers, and directors in orchestrating and balancing all registers.

This trend is unmistakable in the major export films, and a statistical survey substantiates its pervasiveness across the industry. In the early years of sound the theater dominated cinematic subjects in staggering proportions. In 1933 I have identified 63 films out of a total French production of 155 as deriving from popular plays and operettas while 27 came from novels. The plays are seldom classics but include in the main farces (old ones by Feydeau, new ones by Yves Mirande) or melodramas (Henry Bernstein and Henri Bataille reappear throughout the decade). On the other hand, adapted novelists in 1933 include such canonized names as Victor Hugo, Anatole France, Emile Zola, Gustave Flaubert, Charles Dickens, Guy de Maupassant. The very prestige of these names beckoned to that audacious, weightier use of the cinema that some critics were demanding. Still, this remained only a distant hope so long as producers looked first to popular theater for their material.

Four years later, however, the novel had supplanted the play in its importance to the film industry. *La Cinématographie française* categorized the sources of the 181 films made in 1936 and the first half of 1937, finding that 48 derived from the stage, 69 from published fiction, and 64 from original screenplays. They projected that in the second half of 1937 (usually singled out as poetic realism's annus mirabilis) this trend would accelerate since of 46 films in production only 4 were from plays, while 26 came from novels.[2]

The exhaustion of the theatrical mother lode must have been responsible to some degree for this trend. But let us not discount a shift in aesthetic preference among filmmakers and filmgoers, a shift really in the cultural function and definition of the cinema altogether. Early in the decade movies were linked to the music hall and the boulevard theater through more than their material. Actors ricocheted between media, playing up to a Parisian public that purportedly did the same. As the decade wore on, cinema grabbed an enormous share of the declining entertainment trade, growing large and confident enough to look beyond theater for its destiny. Audiences began to sort themselves out more discretely, as did many actors. While the Parisian first-run houses still were most crucial to the success of any film, producers realized that provincial and export audiences ultimately brought in more money, and few of these had access to the Parisian stage. Starlets like Simone Simon and Michèle Morgan became international heartthrobs without the dubious advantage of stage careers. Their delicate voices matched their fragile frames, offering directors a new register to tap, one suiting the quiet, fluid, imaginary discourse of poetic realism. Some actors, most famously Jean Gabin, renounced the stage, especially after it was clear that the cinema had far outdistanced its competitors. Gabin not only stopped appearing in music halls after 1933, but his film roles came primarily from novels,[3] or from scripts like *Le Jour se lève* that emulated a novelistic aesthetic.

To speak as I have of a "novelistic aesthetic" is premature, for there are obviously multiple notions of what a novel is and still more notions of how to conceive of the cinema novelistically. Inspired by visions of vast financial rewards as well as of reaching a huge audience, novelists have been drawn to the screen throughout the century. Unlike playwrights, however, few have had experience dealing with producers, directors, and actors. In the period that concerns us some writers understood this problem and banded together to form a power base from which to negotiate. As early as 1929 the literary giant André Gide helped form a company called La Société d'études et de réalisation pour le film parlant. Roger Martin du Gard, André Maurois, Jules Romain, Jean Schlumberger, and Paul Morand were involved.[4] Gide in fact had taken the cinema into his orbit during his 1925–1926 Congo journey filmed by his protégé Marc Allégret. He attended its frequent *ciné-club* screenings and grew to know the art-film community.

Voyage au Congo gained Allégret entrance to the industry's inside, while Gide hovered around its edges. He helped Léon Poirier[5] prepare an adaptation of his famous *récit* "La Symphonie Pastorale," which was to have been the first French sound film shot on location.[6] Although the project was quickly scuttled when Gaumont's vaunted sound system proved inadequate especially for location work, the fact that this title stands among the very first French responses to sound is indicative of the impact that "high literary culture" would later try to exert on the new medium. On a smaller scale Gide encouraged Martin du Gard to experiment with a short film, *Nu*, shot in Gide's apartment. Meanwhile he periodically passed scripts and ideas around to the group that constituted the FPF (Film Parlant Français, as the production company was also known). For two years these influential writers charted in their vast aggregate imagination the bright future of a genuinely literary cinema. This time little was to come of imagination, however. Their influence was with publishers, not producers. Although Martin du Gard completed two scripts prior to 1931 and Jules Romain one, and although Gide discussed with Jean Giono the possibility of adapting one of the latter's novels, the FPF turned out to be one of innumerable short-lived enterprises in those chaotic economic years.

When the doors leading directly to film production failed to open, novelists then as now relied on agents and publishers to sell their wares. For nearly all the authors constituting the FPF group, Gaston Gallimard was both publisher and confidant, and partly because of their fascination with the cinema, for a time he involved himself in production. Not only did he propose the adaptation of *Madame Bovary* to Martin du Gard before settling on Renoir, but with Paul Morand as an adviser he claimed to be on the lookout for other projects.[7] Martin du Gard meanwhile slid from Flaubert directly to Zola, completing a script for *La Bête humaine* in the summer of 1933. For this he was paid by Philippe de Rothschild, the dashing millionaire who owned a theater and had decided to produce a few pet film projects now that sound had arrived. Counting on the success of another literary adaptation, *Lac aux dames*, to finance the Zola project, he asked its director Marc Allégret to make plans for a big-budget movie.[8] Things progressed far enough for Allégret to alienate Gide by choosing their mutual friend Martin du Gard as scenarist over him. Gide would soon be glad to be on the outside, for *Lac aux dames* tied up so much capital that Rothschild sold *La Bête humaine* to Marcel L'Herbier, who also found it impossible to mount a production. Eventually it would come to Renoir through the intervention of the agency Synops.[9]

Synops was the child of Denise and Roland Tual, who realized that if a novel like *La Bête humaine* should have such trouble reaching the screen, even when supported by Philippe de Rothschild and involving one of France's most famous writers, much greater difficulties were being faced by worthy novels and authors of lesser stature. Synops was set up as a tiny office within Gallimard's empire at a moment when the publishing magnate was still full of the cinema. This well-placed couple assured Gallimard that they could funnel the work of his authors to the many actors, directors, and producers with whom they were acquainted. As Denise Tual recounts, Gallimard was swayed to accept the proposal after Gide happened into the office and greeted her familiarly (they had recently seen each other during the shooting of *Lac aux dames*).[10] Synops immediately began fielding scripts by Giono, Antoine de Saint-Exupéry, Pierre Mac Orlan, André Beucler, and Paul Morand. Its formation follows the general drift toward narrative fiction that took hold in the industry in the second half of the decade. In the five years of its existence, Synops was responsible for the adaptation of thirty novels into films, a large number of which figure among the classics of the decade.

This drift toward a mature, literary cinema likewise pushed along the careers of a number of ambitious young directors whose voices at the beginning of the decade were scarcely audible beneath the far louder debates over the relation of cinema to the theater. Writing for obscure journals and putting together experimental shorts, Edmond Gréville, Pierre Chenal, and Marcel Carné struggled to revive the flagging *ciné-club* culture. Gréville and Chenal were truly close friends. Together with Jean Mitry, whom Chenal had known since high school, they conspired to enter and take over the cinema. They shared a passion for fiction and a general disgruntlement with the stage. Chenal went to plays, he claimed, only to look for promising actors for his projected films.[11]

Gréville, unquestionably the most promising of these figures, had in fact published two critically acclaimed novels during the 1920s. He then helped found *La Revue du cinéma* published by Gallimard, while directing a prominent *ciné-club*. Gréville made his transit into the mainstream industry as an actor, for René Clair cast him in one of the starring roles in *Sous les toits de Paris* (1930).

Gréville's willful search for a visibly idiosyncratic style can be seen in his first feature, *Le Train des suicidés* (1931), termed "a philosophical detective tale."[12] His next French film, *Remous* (1934), immediately earned him a critical reputation as a young genius, but one who was haughty and intransigent. Evidently he had antagonized the establishment with his "vituperative" attacks on figures like Marcel Pagnol. The right-wing magazines *Gringoire* and *Action française* dubbed him "knight of the *ciné-clubs*." François Vinneuil excoriated the preciosity of the symbolism in *Remous*. Georges Champreux went further, accusing Gréville of going out of his way "so as to give the *ciné-club* audiences something to discuss."[13]

Remous certainly is peppered with attention-getting cinematic flourishes like ingenious matched dissolves, so many in fact that Gréville seems a nouvelle vague director *avant la lettre*. One remarkable sequence opens with the hero walking into an elegant room where his bored wife is reading *Pour Vous*. When he takes a seat screen right, the camera continues its movement toward her before sliding into a pan that settles on a clock which reflects her disconsolate face. Transfocusing, Gréville marks an ellipsis of a couple hours by alternately bringing her face and the advancing hands of the clock into view, before panning again to that face and then retreating to establish the full view of the room from its entryway. The scene concludes with a reverse angle longshot of the entryway, presumably taken from some impossible hole in the wall beside the clock, as the couple sadly retire to separate rooms. Such genuinely clever but often labored decoupage made Gréville a John the Baptist of "auteurism," and the establishment wanted his head: "The trouble with this director," one critic cried, "is that you don't know if you're at the cinema or at the Exposition des Arts Decoratifs."[14]

Gréville may have felt at liberty to invent as he chose because of the volatile subject matter of his "ridiculous script." A 1934 review compared it to *Lady Chatterley's Lover*, an audacious tale of deep erotic attachment and, after a haphazard auto accident, the effects of the hero's impotence on his marriage. Gréville went to great lengths to outwit the censors via his figurative displacements of the theme's open sexuality; he also worked to find a way to express

the man's seething jealousy and the woman's unsatisfied longing without dialogue, for neither character could possibly bring such topics into the open. In
the long nights they suffer together, Gréville shows the effect of wind on the
curtains and of shadows on the pillows. Close-ups of the wife's open eyes, and
later the husband's, utterly isolate them in the dark. Sounds of cats, and the
vague moaning of people making love in the next room, charge such nights—
and the screen—with unbearable frustration.

Gréville took pride in expressing cinematically what are literally unspeak-
able emotions. *Remous*'s genuinely mature erotic subject helps justify its lay-
ered sound track and dense visual figures, including the overused refrain of
swirling water from which it takes its title. A drama of inertia and pent-up
feeling—a sensibility that I have already mentioned as characterizing French
cinema—*Remous* displaces the frustration of its characters in the energy of its
editing and camerawork. The heroine is frequently caught leaning her chin on

Remous: Stylish eroticism. BFI

her hand, looking out a window in the kind of pose that obsessed Matisse in
the 1920s and 1930s. Gréville would then work to get inside this comely yet
vague stare so as to expose the whirling eddy of conflicted feelings within.

An arrogant and scandalous film, *Remous* is in the mode of the great European art films of the fifties and sixties (Louis Malle's *Les Amants*, 1958; Truffaut's *Jules et Jim*, 1961). Dramatic love conflicts force an experimentation with
new ways of representing subjectivity. *Remous* stands far from poetic realism
in its milieu and in its ornate style,[15] but critics accorded it special respect as
a new kind of film, one that should raise the expectations of all sound movies.
The same respect would soon fall on Carné in his canonical poetic realist
oeuvre.

Carné's absolutely central importance to the prewar apotheosis of French
film actually begins with the essays he wrote for his journal *Cinémagazine* up
to 1934. In the most noted of these, "Quand le cinéma descendra-t-il dans la

rue?"[16] he linked any renewal in French cinema to a literary calling. He advised the industry to look to the work of novelists like Mac Orlan so as to take advantage of the visibility of human drama right under its nose. Why not follow this novelist and "study certain Parisian *quartiers* and seize the hidden spirit under the familiar facade of those streets"? Carné goes on to mention, among other young writers, Eugène Dabit and his great novel *Hôtel du Nord* where, quoting Dabit,

> "in a decor of factories, garages, slender footbridges, and unloading carts [throbs] the whole picturesque, restless world of approaches to the Saint-Martin canal."
>
> Populism, you say. And after that? Neither the word nor the thing itself frightens us. To describe the simple life of humble people, to depict the atmosphere of hard-working humanity which is theirs, isn't that better than reconstructing the murky and inflated ambience of night clubs, dancing couples, and a nonexistent nobility, which the cinema has kept on doing as long as they've been so abundantly profitable?

A few years later, Carné would adapt Dabit's legendary novel with a generous budget, following his phenomenally successful version of Mac Orlan's *Le Quai des brumes*. Suddenly atmosphere and populism were as "abundantly profitable" as the best of the standard escapist cinema. Evidently French cinema, at least a significant part of it, had adopted Carné's advice, had gone down into the streets (generally by rebuilding those streets in studios), and had turned to atmospheric literature for its material.

Such literature had been beckoning for years. Between the wars a publishing boom at Gallimard, Grasset, Plon, Flammarion, and smaller houses sanctioned serious popular fiction coming from the pens of a new brand of professional writer. Of interest to us are Mac Orlan and Dabit, of course, but also Charles-Ferdinand Ramuz, Francis Carco, and Marcel Aymé. None of these could be called well-educated, nor did any of them aspire to be intellectual. One might say that they flaunted an anti-intellectualism in their lives and work, writing of workers, peasants, sailors, and criminals on the run.

Much of this was an affectation, for in fact their audience was highly literate. *Hôtel du Nord* was not a novel that the hotel's real clientele would naturally read. Although the book is largely autobiographical in documenting the decrepit conditions of Dabit's youth, his circle of readers came from another class altogether, a class that, despite his poverty, he had infiltrated. By the time he was thirty, and before he had found modest fame with this and later novels, he was adopted by Martin du Gard and Gide. His letters to both certainly reveal class anger and socialist sympathies, but they reveal more often an intense, informed passion for literary aesthetics and the fine arts. Curiously, his illustrious friends were far readier to accept the cinema as an ally than was Dabit with

Le Jour se lève: A street in la Zone, rebuilt in studio. BFI

his lower-class background. Martin du Gard and Gide's interest in the populist novelist stemmed partly from the broadened topics, stylistic options, and audiences he sought, which they found quite close to possibilities associated with the cinema. Nevertheless, the fate of the FPF and difficulties with *La Bête humaine* soured Martin du Gard sufficiently that he warned Dabit of the pitfalls of adaptation. The labor, he wrote, is frustrating, often demeaning, and not even so well paid as people imagine.[17] The cinema might someday become a medium through which authors might narrate stories of real social and aesthetic worth, but in 1933 this seemed a distant hope, and not one worth much time or imagination. Both writers agreed these must be saved for literary art.

Dabit is often called a "populist" author; Pierre Mac Orlan, a "popular" one. But this hardly brought the latter much closer to the huge public that film producers must take into consideration. Look at his *Le Bal du Pont du Nord* (1936), which would certainly disappoint anyone looking for a racy thriller. Despite a premise involving beautiful female spies on the Dutch coast during World War I, its 150 pages expend themselves in evoking the desolate coast-line and isolated lives of its inhabitants. Across scenes set in rooming houses, cafés, antique shops, and on excursions to the gray seafront, a secret past is gradually ferreted out by a visiting Frenchman. No matter that its characters are picturesque commoners, *Le Bal du Pont du Nord* is a story written for connoisseurs of storytelling. Mac Orlan's nonconformism and even his private isolation on a farm far from Paris signal a tie to a segment of the educated middle class, not to the people about whom he so often wrote.

Mac Orlan, described at the time as "a savage bourgeois,"[18] kept to himself and never sought to enter an industry that by rights should have welcomed him. Earlier in his career in 1924 it is true that he had scripted the fabulously inventive *L'Inhumaine* for L'Herbier. But this was his only direct contact with the silent film. By the 1930s, although exceedingly well known, he wrote dialogue for just one movie (*Choc en retour*, 1937). Still, the immense success of the adaptations of *Le Quai des brumes* and *La Bandera*, together with the visual qualities of his fictional style, place him dead center in the poetic realist movement. The most characteristic of his stories take place in the sinister dock areas of foreign cities, several in the Limehouse district of London, the very setting for Griffith's *Broken Blossoms*, arguably the first film classic in this style.

One exemplary tale, *Rosario Molina*, written at the height of Mac Orlan's fame in 1936, might just as well have served as a scenario for a Chenal or Carné film. Within view of Gibraltar lives Rosario Molina, sixteen-year-old daughter of a crotchety bar-owner who spends his time with local loners and itinerant lowlife. Afraid he might be murdered, the mysterious and possessive father shows her a map he has drawn to his cache of treasure accumulated by gun running over the years. One day, seduced by a traveler with a vague military past, Rosario filches the map in hopes of sailing to America a wealthy woman. But her father has removed the treasure and she now must flee. Eventually reduced to dancing as a gypsy in Seville with her boyfriend's gang, Rosario afterwards learns that Dolores, an adventuress who has married her father and spent the fortune, has come to the seedy nightspot where she performs. Pretending to be a fortune-teller, Rosario gives Dolores only days to live, then cajoles her into a rendezvous in a desolate *quartier*. There in a dark, abandoned house Rosario dramatically reveals by candlelight the photograph she has kept of her father. Pronouncing her full name, Rosario empties her father's old automatic pistol into Dolores. She then runs unthinking into the night, until the sound of a bell tolling at dawn leads her to stand before a convent gate. The story closes with Rosario pounding on the heavy wooden gate with her fists.

Not only do the scenes and characters of *Rosario Molina* belong to the storehouse of poetic realism, Mac Orlan's cool, mysterious tone evokes such films in visual topoi like the lofty bell tower, silhouettes of gypsy dancers, photographs revealed by candlelight, and deserted alleys illuminated in the mist by isolated streetlamps. These images and episodes, for which Mac Orlan coined the term "fantastique social," recur in story after story. In an inspired pair of collaborations he authored the preface to Eugène Atget's 1930 *Photographie de Paris* and then prepared the commentary for Brassaï's unsettling collection, *The Secret Paris of the Thirties*. Although the latter project had to be deferred, Brassaï correctly intuited that he, like Mac Orlan,[19] had documented the libido of the cultural capital of the world: the *bals* with their riffraff, the fairs with their circus performers, the shabby streets and dark alleys with their prostitutes and criminals. Toned down, this would become the repertoire of poetic realist icons and images.

Carné has led us to Mac Orlan and Mac Orlan to Brassaï, the friend of Jacques Prévert, of Henry Miller, and of the dissident Surrealist writers and artists who roamed "Paris by Night."[20] The same route might take us to Francis Carco through this author's fascination with exotic locations and lowlife characters. Carco aimed to update an urban mythology one can trace back to Eugène Sue, Victor Hugo, and other romantic novelists. Master of the Montmartre crime novel, he was inevitably called by the cinema. In the early 1930s Carco scripted *Paris-Béguin* (1931) and *Paris la nuit* (1930), both involving wealthy women seduced by swarthy criminals or lured to the climate of the criminal *quartiers*. So well-known was Carco for such themes that in 1938 he actually played himself, Francis Carco the novelist, tracking down the suppressed stories of fallen women in Roger Richebé's *Prisons de femmes*.

Considered far more significant at the time than any of these authors was Charles-Ferdinand Ramuz, the Swiss writer whose novels often resemble meditative prose poems. In his mountain retreat, Ramuz had even less direct contact with the cinema than did Mac Orlan or Carco. He was responsible for the dialogue of an uninspired adaptation of his *L'Or dans le montagne* (1938), and he stood by to give moral support and approval while Dimitri Kirsanov shot *Rapt*, taken from his *La Séparation des races*. Despite Ramuz's aloofness from the cinema, Denis de Rougement claims that some of his stories are "written like a motion picture scenario. The characters slowly appear in the light, a head, an arm—the closeup of a hand . . ."[21] Ramuz carefully cultivated this influential style that de Rougement claims "mixes realism and poetry indistinguishably."

Highly metaphysical, Ramuz finds in his mountain peasants the elemental human being that Mac Orlan looked for in urban marginals. Were it not for a dark sense of catastrophe hovering above his fiction, Ramuz might be likened to Giono and Pagnol, not only because of the presence of such characters, but because they are observed in loving visual detail. Thomas Hardy has been mentioned as a more likely relative[22] since among the details of everyday life appear signs that "announce the unbelievable, yet real, presence of an invisible menace."[23] De Rougement sums up his opinion in a way that could refer equally to the darker, fatalistic side of poetic realism: "I know of no other novelist who has been able to ask the great metaphysical questions in terms of objects, elementary sensations, little everyday phrases."[24]

Because of Ramuz's reputation, *Rapt* was taken up as a prestige project, the first sound film by Kirsanov and the only sound film that dialogist Benjamin Fondane deemed worth his talent.[25] The press was struck by the location shooting and by the pedigree of the film's credits. Fondane received a lot of attention; he was described by one journalist as "a serious philosopher who stands against the cinema of commerce and strives to render the experience of the individual."[26] The noted critic Roger Regent called the film a turning point. "*Rapt* cleans the stale air of our vaudeville cinema, our silly comedies where soldiers meet up with cute girls in contrivances that amuse those who somehow still laugh at stories about cuckolds. If our movie theaters weren't crammed with adolescent humor and silly song and dance vehicles, [*Rapt* would prove] that the cinema could really be a great art form."[27]

One reviewer compared *Rapt* to *Broken Blossoms* because of its rhythm and atmosphere.[28] Kirsanov's own *Ménilmontant* (1926) is another obvious intermediate source, since no French film more resembles *Broken Blossoms* and since it starred the winsome Nadia Sibirskaïa, who reappears in *Rapt*. Maurice Stiller's *Sir Arne's Treasure* is also mentioned by two critics, not only because of its landscapes but because *Rapt* introduces a "highly poetic" handicapped character whose misshapen body "gives the film a disquieting atmosphere, like an announcement of disaster."[29] The word "poetry" also occurs to Roger Regent, perhaps because Ramuz's novels were often characterized that way. *Rapt* infuses the screen with "poetry," Regent says, "and no one since the arrival of sound has been so able to express the melancholy of the mountains."[30] Regent hastens to add that Kirsanov avoided the "salable poetry of bells in the mountains, of the Angelus echoing across the valley or of the little shepherd who plays his flute. No vulgarity contaminates the images. Yet we are led to share with the characters the agony of the summits, the absolutely pure air they breathe, and occasionally the feelings that pass over when the wind of a great fear blows from the heart of the mountains." Arthur Honegger composed the moody score.

Rapt scarcely masks its poetic address to the spectator, nor does it hide the allegory directing its plot. In this it can be seen as a singular attempt to recover for the sound film the aesthetic of cinematic impressionism. Numerous critics in fact found this to be the film's chief fault.[31] Apparently, despite critics like

Rapt: "The melancholy of the mountains." BFI

Regent, the sensibility of the 1930s was more attuned to realism than to alle-gory. "More immediacy," demanded one critic. Kirsanov was not a director to supply more immediacy.

But such directors did exist. Pierre Chenal's adaptation of Aymé's *La Rue sans nom* came out almost simultaneously with *Rapt* and was the first film baptized "poetic realist." While both films received far more critical attention than their budgets or eventual box-office earnings would ordinarily call for, *Rapt* was discussed as an inventive and precious curiosity, reminiscent of silent classics, whereas *La Rue sans nom* was instantly taken up as a significant new hope for the stagnant French cinema.

Atmosphere prevails in *La Rue sans nom* too, but not the metaphysical winds

La Rue sans nom:
Daily life and misery. BFI

of the Alps. Instead the anonymous alleyway that one never leaves for ninety minutes exudes a smell of crime and filth, of heat and close quarters, of desperation. Chenal was able to make this film only after convincing Aymé that he had discovered near the porte de Clichy a dead-end street just like the one featured in his novel, right down to the absence of any street sign. Moreover, breaking with accepted industry practice, he was determined to shoot the film principally on location.[32]

Chenal's casting and his restlessly roving camera so struck Michel Gorel, who reviewed the film at its premiere, that he effectively christened poetic realism as a form of documentary fiction, claiming that Chenal photographs "faces that are incontestably real. He has discovered contemporary passions that move us directly without the slightest taint of the literary."[33] But of course the film is fully indebted to Aymé's novel, to its cool and precise descriptions, and to the mixture of plots that keep eddying our interest out into the street, no matter how fascinating each character or incident may seem on its own. Without the aid of music or articulate dialogue, these rude characters express in their gestures and intonations the frustration of lives hemmed in, lives that in every sense play themselves out on a dead-end road. Fights, illness, and haphazard deaths make up the miserable routine of everyday existence and of the desperate plots to escape it. Chenal photographs everything discretely. Single streetlights keep the milieu in shadow. Broken railings suggest the angularity of expressionist compositions, framing desires and emotions in the characters and the spectator. Among the film's first spectators, Gorel felt himself in the presence of something that was astoundingly unified yet clearly a hybrid:

> I claim realism [for this film], but I likewise claim poetry. Because even in treating such a difficult, such a brutal subject, Pierre Chenal never renounces the poetic. And the most beautiful scenes of the film are perhaps those where

these characters, although worn down little by little like the broken stones of the hovels that imprison them, strive to break out, some by love, others by wine or adventure or revolt, or by a long ecstatic dream.

La Rue sans nom infects its fiction with an ethnographic attitude. Inquisitive traveling shots search through dingy tenements for dramatic elements. Drama itself is subordinated to description, as occasional long takes study the cragged faces that interest us even in their silence or in the way they mutter their argot. Here lies the film's claim to realism. Its poetry comes by means of Chenal's precise eyeline cutting, and through extended close-up stares at his pitiable characters, played, it must be remembered, by seasoned actors. Poetry also comes through the strategic use of melodramatic music expressing a response to the drama that is witnessed and felt simultaneously, it seems, by the characters involved, by Chenal, and by us the audience.

Aymé's novel and Chenal's adaptation of it epitomize the poetic realist amalgam that characterizes the writings of the other novelists I have mentioned and that would individuate French cinema for the rest of the decade. The peculiar conjunction of ethnographic curiosity and intimate subjectivity goes back at least to Zola, an author cited by a 1934 critic as indispensable to the renewal of French cinema,[34] and the source of what would be arguably the best poetic realist film, Renoir's *La Bête humaine* (1938). Curiously, Zola's impact in this era stems not from his status as novelist (storyteller in prose) but from the presence in his novels of two extremes: "photographic naturalism" on the one side, and the visionary, highly metaphoric imagery that, on the other side, he uses to paint his melodramas. Much the same might be said of a novelist like Dostoievsky, whose *Crime and Punishment* became Chenal's next project, one for which Marcel Aymé agreed to write the dialogue.[35]

One can readily sense in poetic realism an embryonic existentialism. Chenal's *Crime et châtiment* (1935) would support this connection. A certain vogue for Dostoievsky had infiltrated Paris with the well-educated Russian and German émigrés. Fédor Ozep and Victor Trivas, who would move with their moody pessimism to Paris around 1933, adapted *The Brothers Karamazov* in Berlin in 1931. Chenal was proud to claim allegiance both to the Russian nineteenth century and to the visual heritage of German expressionism. In his youth he devoured every Russian novel in French translation and in his teens he belonged to *ciné-clubs* specializing in German film. Intuitively he opted for a German expressionist decor in *Crime et châtiment* against the initial designs Aimé Bazin had submitted. Bazin's work, typically proper and erudite, came off as "too realist, too faithful to documents of the period. I told him what I expected from him: a St. Petersburg more stylized, rather suffused in the unreal, in the very image of the walking nightmare that Raskolnikov lived out."[36] With his cameraman Chenal was more nuanced. "He understood the kind of lighting I was after: effects of contrast without going quite to the extremes of

Crime et châtiment: "Pure
delirium" in decor. BFI

Crime et châtiment: "Pure
delirium" in acting. BFI

exaggeration we find in the German expressionists." Such a tightrope strung
between absolute abstraction and a more measured psychological realism had
to be walked by the actors as well. Today, Pierre Blanchar's extreme gestures
seem adolescent beside the more assured style of Harry Baur. But this contrast
is implicit in their respective roles (Raskolnikov and Porphyry). Moreover,
Chenal believes that had Blanchar toned down his interpretation of a character
who lives in a state of "pure delirium . . . he would paradoxically have appeared more theatrical, because more calculating."[37] Blanchar carried off the
award for best actor at the Venice film festival.

Crime et châtiment was a success at home and abroad, easily outdueling Joseph Von Sternberg's adaptation made the same year. Thus Chenal found
himself lifted up among the most promising of all French directors.[38] Pour Vous
praised the "Dostoievskian aura pervading the decor and atmosphere," an aura
Chenal claimed he instilled in all his collaborators by conveying something

like the "spirit of the film."[39] Consistency of mood came through the use of much longer takes than had been the case in *La Rue sans nom*. For the scene in which Raskolnikov slowly climbs the stairs to the old pawnbroker's room, Chenal had a makeshift crane constructed that could be operated from below so that the entire ascent could be filmed in a single, extended take. Real time promoted suspense, especially when accompanied by Honegger's music and Blanchar's virtually hypnotic identification with his role;[40] but it also brought the audience into the mind and fears of a madman. "We have to see exactly what he sees at every moment as we approach," says Chenal; otherwise the murder and not its moral significance will overwhelm us. Throughout the shot, extras come and go on the stairs and landings, but none of them distracts Blanchar's focus on the door he needs to enter and the deed he needs to perform. The railings, switchback stairs, and vaulted ceilings of the tenement building come to resemble the inside of Raskolnikov's mind. Chenal may not sustain such intense identification of camera and decor with character interiority throughout the film, but he made every effort to do so. "For twelve months I lived with this script in mind. Every day I suffered over more details of my scenes. It was an intense construction, cerebral, meditative, walled in, and ready to shoot."[41] He conceived his drama symphonically, in three separate movements whose different moods were nonetheless subject to a single atmospheric pressure, or dominant key.[42] No wonder Orson Welles studied this film—especially the murder sequence—as he came to the deep-focus method for *Citizen Kane*.[43] One can also feel it resonate in Welles's *The Trial* (1962), where the decor takes on the volume and contents of Joseph K's troubled psyche.

Chenal views cinema as a derivative of the novel, the medium best suited to representing a personal, limited view of the universe. The cinema can reach similar concentration by isolating the spectator within a cloud of autonomous images rather than encouraging a sense of the companionship with other spectators before the screen and under the tutelage of a director. Perhaps the film that best demonstrates this attachment to the aesthetics of the novel is one taken not from fiction but from a notorious court case, *L'Affaire Lafarge* (1937). Chenal proudly claims *L'Affaire Lafarge* as the first sound film told completely in flashback in the manner of a novel.[44] Since courtroom arguments are distributed as a relay among the represented incidents of the murder case, the viewer must intently examine not just the facts but the way they are presented. Chenal wanted the ambiguity and doubt associated with courtroom testimony to contaminate his mise-en-scène, literalizing a multiplicity of points of view.

Chenal is one of the first directors to calculate the benefits of relinquishing narrative authority and vision. His contribution to the genre of the *policier*, the extremely well-received *L'Alibi* (1937), results from the renunciation of directorial privilege.[45] Instead of leading the viewer through the facts to an inevitable outcome, the director invites the spectator to explore the possibilities evoked in the abundance of the images and the greater possibilities lying in the empty spaces between those images. Hence his penchant (paradigmatic in poetic realism) for the roving camera, for dark ambience, for isolated powerful moments rather than streamlined decoupage,[46] and for complex, but not necessarily consistent, point-of-view arrangements. One critic noted that in *L'Affaire Lafarge* Chenal altered the lighting style of each flashback while nevertheless "infusing the entire production with a singular novelistic density bathed in a Mauriac atmosphere separated by Simenon interludes."[47]

To generate such critical response Chenal needed to maintain unusual control over all elements that contribute to "infusing the entire production with . . . density." Like his friend Gréville, Chenal felt his credentials permitted him to supervise his project at every stage, for he had apprenticed in the design departments of film companies and had edited shorts. A pianist who adored jazz, he took special care with the scores he commissioned for his films. Beyond this quest to control the feel of his film from first to last, Chenal was encouraged by his acquaintances in what today one would call an "auteurist" belief in the mission of cinema to express the personal vision of the director. He kept company with Artaud, Auriol, the Préverts, and Brunius at cafés and screenings in the age of Surrealism. Like Cocteau, Buñuel, and Man Ray, he too had filmed a short for the vicomte and comtesse de Noailles. In the first years of the 1930s, and even after becoming a successful director, he remained a faithful adherent to Mitry's *ciné-club*, which programmed films of strong directors. And yet in his own case Chenal scarcely credits the notion of "personal vision," for he senses himself the purveyor of the visions of the novelists who have attracted him. It was his eagerness to replicate certain features of "the novelistic" that drove him to work toward a modicum of stylization and an unusual attention to the atmosphere of dramatic situations,[48] features he recognizes as characteristic of his vision but that he believes he merely picked up in his walks through the terrain of literature.

Tellingly, the novel he most wanted to take on was Thomas Hardy's *Jude the Obscure*. More telling still, in 1939 he wrested James M. Cain's *The Postman Always Rings Twice* from the hands of Renoir, for *Le Dernier Tournant*. Just after the war André Bazin, drawing on the ideas of Claude-Edmonde Magny, took account of the impact of the hard-edged American novel of the 1920s and 1930s on European cinema.[49] Dos Passos, Hemingway, and Fitzgerald, but also detective writers like Cain, can be seen as transplanted naturalists, because they rely on the accumulation of perceptual facts, on marginal characters, and on nonliterary dialogue. To this they add limited point-of-view structures and a generally dark context in which both the reader and the characters are set in an incomprehensible and uncomprehending universe. *Le Dernier Tournant* may fail to bring out these possibilities vividly; still the project itself would have been unthinkable in French cinema five years earlier. Its very existence speaks to a shift in the mission and capacity of the medium. Cinema was now ready to be affected by, and to affect, movements coming from French popular fiction, from the contemporary American novel, and from the gathering existentialism that one can track in authors as different as Georges Bernanos (*Le Journal d'un curé de campagne*, 1936) and Jean-Paul Sartre (*La Nausée*, 1938). Chenal had already expressed—via Dostoievsky—the same insistent, often bleak, and always tactile concern for individual experience. The novel had indeed helped French cinema extend the consequence of its intermittent obsession with atmosphere and with intimate soul-searching.

The most excessively atmospheric film of the era must surely be Fédor Ozep's 1933 *Amok*. Once again modern fiction provided a subject that helped the cinema mature. This time the script, deriving from a remarkable Stefan Zweig short story, ran temporarily into direct censorship problems. Set in the Malaysian jungle, it concerns a society woman wanting an abortion before her husband returns from France. She seeks out a debauched, cynical doctor who lives in a shack. When he refuses to help her, she resorts to an amateur and dies in the operation. The doctor, meanwhile, has had a change of heart and frantically combs the area's seamier sections looking for her. In a final, paradoxical act of regeneration, he manages to cut her casket loose as it is being loaded on a ship for Paris where her husband insists an autopsy must be performed. He drowns, literally tied to her corpse, in the happy knowledge that he has kept her honor intact.

Apart from what must have been the incredibly delicate matters of adultery and abortion, *Amok* tempts its alcoholic hero with drugs and topless seductresses. If this were not scandalous enough, its thematic core, coming straight from its title, foregrounds a wild and inexplicable madness. The tropical setting served as a perfect incubator for such decadent subjects. It probably also mollified the censors, who were willing to accept outrageous behavior "over there" in the realm of the uncivilized. To engage his audience in such decadence, Ozep encouraged Lazare Meerson to fashion his most bizarre sets ever so as to concoct a milieu that would be physically and morally stifling. Newspaper articles reporting on the production describe the dripping jungle, the fantastically enlarged butterflies, and the shabby dives that Meerson constructed in Pathé's Joinville studios. A typical review forgave the film many of its shortcomings in acting and exposition because of its "atmosphere, heavy with the unknown, rich in exotic splendor the likes of which the screen has not shown us before; a film both luminous and somber."[50]

Ozep's "émigré" photographic style, moody in the extreme, doubles the claustrophobia of the sets. An opening pan, minutes in duration, lingers over successive exotic details of the jungle, including insects and insect-eating plants. Eventually we edge up to a shack to discover the doctor in a stupor that

(Top and bottom) *Amok*: Meerson's "exotic splendor." CF

could stem more from this overgrown vegetation, sapping his will, than from the gin bottles strewn around him. *Amok* gives an exaggerated preview of *Pépé le Moko*, with its European hero caught in an exotic and sexually charged, irrational zone. The fatalism one always breathes in such atmospheric films announces itself immediately in the title, *Amok*, and in a title sequence that shows a native going out of control during a ceremony, unconsciously slaying several of his fellow tribesmen. With drums ringing all the while in our ears, he is shot, as much to put him out of his misery as to protect the tribe. We know with certainty that in this land the doctor will finally run amok himself. Like the title character of *Pépé le Moko*, he loses all bearings after meeting an enchanting Frenchwoman. Both men die for the dreams these women inspire. Both die in sight of ships bound for the France from which they have been exiled. Both men from the outset desire death.

By 1934 the "atmosphere film" was an established genre within the industry, and it was referred to as such.[51] Beyond the émigrés and the holdovers from the era of *ciné-clubs*, mainstream directors like Feyder and Marc Allégret were said to work within its province, though none of their films exhibit that maniacal search for mood that characterizes *Remous*, *Rapt*, and *Amok*. Still, the fact that producers were eager to finance their excursions into mood pieces suggests a change in the industry.

A good example is Allégret's 1936 adaptation of Joseph Conrad's *Under Western Eyes*. Unique among his films, this one is dominated by male figures, contributing perhaps to its greater than normal stylistic consistency. While Allégret has always been able to introduce striking atmosphere into his films, seldom does he endeavor to present the world of a single character and consciousness. For one thing, Allégret is fascinated by beautiful women whom he has never wanted to film in somber light. The Conrad novel, deeply psychological (even "Russianized"), concentrates on the shadowy Pierre Fresnay character, Razumov. Allégret worked hard to duplicate this darkness.

The opening sequence of *Sous les yeux d'Occident* in Razumov's dingy room might very well have used the tenement sets from Chenal's recent *Crime et châtiment*, with their exposed stairs and broad landings. Into this room comes the anarchist (Jean-Louis Barrault), Razumov's "double," who implicates him, an exemplary and utterly apolitical student, in an assassination plot. "I came home," says Razumov. "A voice in the dark whispered, 'Is the door shut?' And from that instant on, fate has tracked me." Allégret exploits such poetic realist material through a tracking camera and a network of point-of-view shots that open up disturbingly limited avenues of vision and knowledge. A door opens a crack; an eye looks out. Razumov peeks out the window blinds on the dark street below. The paranoia of this style doubles that of a plot that features police spies, dual identity, false passports, and emergency journeys. Unlike *Crime et châtiment*, where Raskolnikov is effectively a prisoner of his own psyche, Razumov is hemmed in by huge political schemes outside his control, a

Crime et châtiment. CF

Decor as mindscape.

Sous les yeux d'Occident. CF

hunted man forced into unforeseen locales (the government ministry, a train, a hotel in Geneva, a Swiss mountain retreat). Instead of consistent atmosphere that essentially represents an interior mood, *Sous les yeux d'Occident* delivers a sustained pursuit of fatality, ending with Razumov's death under a lamppost in the rain. Once again a point-of-view shot has pinned him down; only this time the visual sight line matches that of a pistol. Marcel Carné will end *Le Quai des brumes* in exactly the same way.

Pour Vous said that *Sous les yeux d'Occident* lifted Allégret into a group of five directors whom Hollywood considered the core of French cinema. He joined René Clair (now in England), Jacques Feyder (just leaving for England), Julien Duvivier, and Maurice Tourneur.[52] This implied that his handling of such a demanding project as a political-psychological novel, with difficult actors like Fresnay, Barrault, Michel Simon, Jacques Copeau, Gabriel Gabro, and Pierre Renoir, made him at once serious and commercially viable. In contrast, the more aesthetically ambitious directors like Chenal, Kirsanov, Gréville, Ozep, and even Renoir were viewed as too poetic ever to rival Hollywood films for international audiences.

At issue here is a confusion over literary terms and sources. Evidently, the common sense of the industry held that stage plays made the most convenient films, but that novels made the most interesting ones. Still, if the novel were too "poetic," or if the director became excessively enamored of its poetic dimension, the results were likely to be recherché, hence unprofitable. Nevertheless, there developed a peculiar notion of the "poetic," a notion involving visual and aural texture, that was used to distinguish those novels, like Conrad's, and the films that copied them, like Allégret's, that must be placed at the antipodes of theater. This confusing terminology culminates in my characterization of *poetic* realism as the product of those who were anxious to treat cinema as an art form of independent value.

We have to return to Jean Vigo as the director who most absolutely embodies this paradox for, although a "pure cinéaste" without any special literary credentials or interests, he has come down to us as the supreme "poetic" filmmaker of his generation and was credited as such almost at the moment of his death. Vigo mastered the evasive quality of "atmosphere" that stands as an intermediate term between literature and cinema. Although atmosphere at one time may have belonged more properly to the poetic and the painterly arts rather than to the novel, which was considered the medium of social analysis and intrigue, in the 1930s atmosphere had descended like a cloud on the narrative arts of novel and film. This terminological migration, suggesting a shift in the social function of the media, is everywhere apparent. When the noted art critic Elie Faure sought to characterize the feeling of L'Atalante, he immediately invoked Corot's landscapes.[53] In fact he makes the point that in the nineteenth century romanticism and realism were obverse and reverse sides of a single sensibility, one that Vigo, alone among French filmmakers, had fully inherited. Claude Vermorel felt equally comfortable in holding up Rabelais as the spiritual wellspring behind the surprising juxtapositions, the shimmering symbolism, and the "feverish" tone running through L'Atalante.[54] Both critics were responding to the texture of the film, to its delicate yet invigorating atmosphere. The atmosphere Vigo wafts across his film, not its tale (considered trivial by both critics), promotes the kind of experience provided by the painting and the verse of an earlier age.

Vigo's unassailable stature as the most poetic filmmaker of the era rests on more than his aesthetic. He was a man caught up in his age, sensitive to social problems and to contemporary ways of representing them. His attitude lines up with that of Buñuel who had completed the weird Surrealist ethnographic short Las Hurdes in 1932. Despite the quaintness of its love story, L'Atalante is a "document" in Georges Bataille's sense of the term. Recognizing Vigo as someone congenitally disposed to "shattering the habitual conventions of the cinema," one critic went so far as to agree that Vigo "stands more on the side of poetry than of the novel as traditionally conceived." And he then goes on to compare *L'Atalante* to a very special novel, a notorious one in the year 1934: Louis-Ferdinand Céline's *Voyage au bout de la nuit*.[55]

Thus, in a roundabout way, Vigo can be said to have imported for the cinema certain aspects of modern fiction—specifically, the effects of atmosphere and subjectivity that in our century the novel has learned to achieve. One might go further and agree with many observers that in the 1930s the novel was able to adopt these functions that formerly were served by poetry and painting, art forms that had become too refined to engage the social and political dimensions of life at the end of the Third Republic. The quality of *L'Atalante*'s images, but equally its focus on the bizarre marginalia of French life, links it to the anonymous streets of "the Zone" as evoked by the poet-novelist Céline.[56]

It should not surprise us that even as Vigo was finishing his film, Céline left for the United States with hopes of overseeing an adaptation of his *Voyage*.[57] It should surprise us even less to learn that on his deathbed in 1934, Vigo was preparing to adapt Zola's grimmest, most socially strident novel, *Germinal*.[58] Zola, Céline, and a certain strain of cinema interact in the 1930s. They belong together under the rubric of voyeurism, under the rubric of dark fatalism, and most of all under the fudged rubrics of poetry and realism.

ÉMIGRÉS AND THE LOOK OF FRENCH FILM

The thematic consistency of films drawing on the French literary sensibility of the times has led at least one chauvinistic historian to propose "a clearly defined French style" for the 1930s. Henri Fescourt claims that while no national style developed during the 1920s, after sound arrived "it took only five years to be able to see at a glance a commonality among the best films, so much so that *Mistrigi*, by Harry Lachmann, and *Coeur de lilas* and *Mayerling* by Anatole Litvak, all made in our country by foreigners, fell under our influence.... You can recognize in them a related '*écriture*,' a clear and direct manner of dealing with human solitude and anxiety."[59]

Fescourt's judgment of the films accords perfectly with my own, but I must reverse his explanation. It was not that foreigners came under French influence; rather the peculiar *écriture* (*optique* in my vocabulary) of poetic realism came into its own only after Lachmann, Litvak, and countless other émigrés brought to Paris a visual sensibility different from the theatrical one that was then dominant. Fescourt misses an opportunity to understand this when, in characterizing poetic realism, he goes on to say that "the method of collaboration by *équipe* has been efficacious. Nothing of the set design or the lighting is discordant."[60] Had he listed the designers who produced such a harmonious milieu for these films of fatality, he would have been struck by their decidedly foreign origins.

Fescourt forces the question on us: did a sensibility (one evidently drawn from French novels, from classics of world literature, and from hard-edged American fiction) precede and inform the movement that culminates in poetic realism? Or did that sensibility arise from new styles of acting, music, set design, and camerawork that slowly infiltrated the industry in the early 1930s? Certainly the growing reliance on the novel is not sufficient to distinguish poetic realism, since only a percentage of the hundreds of novels adapted in the 1930s bear the poetic realist look and its intimate address to the spectator. And what about the many films bearing that look and address which were written directly for the screen? We must in short credit the miraculous birth of a visual and audio treatment that the French, so dependent on their theatrical traditions, were in a poor position to provide. That miracle has a name: immigration. French cinema learned to fashion its particular style under the tutelage of foreigners. The developed skills, techniques, and visual imaginations of hundreds of artists and artisans gravitating toward Paris after World War I and later crossing over from Germany during the ascendancy of Nazism were immediately put to use.

When Chenal cited the influence of German expressionism on his *Crime et châtiment*, he meant to recognize not only the memory of films seen at special screenings but his interaction with German immigrant artists who had contributed to the many German films aiming at that "symphonic totality" he sought for his own work. Mac Orlan likewise recalls the impact made by Fritz Lang's *M*, specifically the replacement of dialogue by music, in developing an "obsessive" experience for the viewer.[61] Such strained and concentrated psychological effects, carried down from expressionism through the *Kammerspiel* films of the 1920s, are at the base of a stylistic option that meshed with the turn toward "interiorization" via the novel. As the sound era began, this option stood absolutely opposed to the "outgoing performance" aesthetic reigning in France.

And the French were poised to adopt German expertise. Given the increased belligerence that sound brought to relations among countries and among sectors of the industry, French producers were forced to take a slightly partisan position, aligning themselves with the Germans in a "European" effort to stave off Hollywood domination. *Variety* is full of notices from 1928 to 1931 accusing the French of making exchange deals with Berlin that violated the quotas they had set up to protect their industry against Hollywood. This was a natural turn of affairs, for liaisons between Paris and Berlin had been indispensable to French film during the latter part of the 1920s. One can scarcely find a director or producer of any worth who had not worked in Germany or with German capital.[62] Most of the important stars had some experience in Germany. Thus when sound upset the delicate international network of production and distribution, an already standing system of contacts naturally led the French to turn to their colleagues across the Rhine and to welcome those who needed to find a new home.

The tacit complicity of these nations was sealed by the numerous films shot in two versions between 1930 and 1932. Whether using studios in Berlin or in Paris, such ventures necessarily brought personnel from both countries into very close contact. One of the most influential of these, *Tumultes*, shares much with *La Petite Lise*. Here Charles Boyer (Emil Jannings in the German version) is released from prison only to find that his woman (played by Florelle) has taken up with a new man whom he accidentally kills in a fight. Sought by the police, he hides with a pal who also becomes the lover of his woman. Ultimately she betrays Boyer to the police. Advertised as "a film of atmosphere and action," *Tumultes* was a huge success in France.[63] Joseph Kessel, a Gallimard novelist who worked his way into the cinema, reported on the film in a newspaper series he was writing about life in Germany.[64] He testified to the film's authenticity, describing the life of the urban underworld in Germany. The French, he implied, were miles behind their neighbors both in villainy and in its representation. *Tumultes*'s oppressive darkness and relentless plot characterized a kind of street life that the French, at home with René Clair's Paris, might feel protected from. Its drama relentlessly entrapped its hero, a "thief caught between violence, an implacable law, his carnal enslavement, and his surprise at being tricked . . . [to create] a large human symphony."[65]

Thomas Elsaesser has analyzed the work of Siodmak and other émigrés after their arrival in France, finding it disappointing in comparison to their earlier output.[66] Siodmak had arrived in the glow of his brilliant directorial debut, *People on Sunday* (1929), yet his eight French films take limited aesthetic risks, often falling back on standard French ploys: *mots d'auteur*, staged theatrical effects, and a heterogeneous structure aiming to please a wide variety of spectators. Siodmak brashly arrived in Paris proclaiming his disdain for this aesthetic, saying, "I hate operettas and vaudeville because they represent empty genres, sheer gaudy tinsel."[67] Still, until the 1937 *Mollenard*, where he at last seized the chance to make a personally satisfying film, even his most popular efforts were punctuated with bits of vaudeville acting that reduced the suspense and mood of the whole.[68]

Siodmak had not totally relinquished his German heritage in France, but he had diluted it. His talent for *Stimmung*, which would make his reputation in Hollywood a decade later, does occasionally link up to the poetic realist sensibility even in the most compromised of his films. One critic claims, for example, that *Le Chemin de Rio* (1936) recalls the adventure tales of Francis Carco or Pierre Mac Orlan in the way it lays out objects and scenes for their abundant connotations. Certain characteristic images of docks in the fog, of old hotels and vague streetlamps shrouded in darkness, stand out with an authenticity not exhibited by the pawns immersed in the drama. "He concentrates on painting the milieu of crime, isolating some of its most evocative features."[69] But this film, like virtually all of those by German directors, mixes several styles and introduces motifs from different genres, dispersing the atmosphere that tries to coalesce around the plot.[70]

Siodmak was, of the émigré directors, the most integrated and consistently successful, taking his place alongside Carné, Duvivier, and Renoir. "His name had become a synonym for quality and guaranteed value."[71] Of the thirteen other émigré directors identified by Ginette Vincendeau,[72] only Pabst, Ophuls, and Kurt Bernhardt can be said to have had sustained influence in France, producing at least a half dozen films each. Regardless of the quality of their work, however, the German directors as a group bore a haughty, self-confident mien that French producers respected. They successfully asked for larger budgets, for extended production schedules, and for more professional working conditions than was customary in the French industry because producers thought of them as proven thoroughbreds. Moreover, foreign directors, unfamiliar with French conventions, were able to demand unusual concessions. Thus Litvak spent a fortune on the sets of *Mayerling*, claiming that this was the only way he knew to make a historical melodrama. And Pabst, who also went overboard on costumes and sets for a number of films, required as well an extra two months in the editing room, since this was a crucial stage in his conception of cinema.

When their films were organized by German producers like Eric Pommer or Constantin Geftman, a vague large-scale "movie look" results. Pabst's *Mademoiselle Docteur* is such a case, draped in sets and costumes (designed respectively by Annenkov and Pimenov) clearly tagged "international style." But the film also exhibits an exceptional precision of editing. Its plot complications and chase structure would have been beyond the capability of all French directors, except perhaps Duvivier. Scenes are juggled for their interrelated rhythms and each scene in itself is broken down in a fine decoupage, showing us fleeting glances, hidden objects, and quick facial reactions. Pabst actively involves the exotic city of Salonika and employs a host of props common to spy films but uncommon in the French cinema. In fact, this facility, together with Eugen Schüfftan's carefully mottled lighting and the self-defining behavior of so many star actors (Dita Parlo, flanked by Jouvet, Fresnay, Blanchar, Barrault, Vivian Romance, and Charles Dullin), makes this an impressive but impersonal showpiece. That it quickly reappeared in an American and then a British version (directed by Gréville) suggests the transportability of its theme and look.

Elsaesser knows better than anyone the differences among émigrés such as Pabst, Lang, and Ophuls. He knows the wildly different circumstances under which these "guests" were permitted to work. Yet he has tried to factor out from their varied output a few common concerns, or at least a common tone. "The German cinema which moved to France, and later on to Hollywood, is still characterized by an emphasis on the processes of narration over those of dramatization—or, rather, by a persistent discrepancy between narrated time and action time. And this double focus becomes the source of a particular kind of pathos—pessimistic and melancholy, but also ironic and cynical."[73] Could this not also apply to *Le Jour se lève*, photographed by the German Curt Courant? No other film so methodically isolates significant objects in the German manner to create a world in which the human actors and their milieu become abstracted under the force of an ostentatious narrational pattern. Carné takes this German fascination with narration, with the difference "between narrated time and action time," to the limit by representing his tale in a series of flashbacks.

Carné was poised to respond to the German cinema. Fascinated as he was by Murnau above all directors,[74] his work has always been thought to be tinged with expressionism. He must have had in mind German "street films" when he published "Quand le cinéma descendra-t-il dans la rue?" and he must have been aware of the powerful new film just out in 1933 by German émigré Victor Trivas, entitled homonymously *Dans les rues*. In the second scene of that film, a woman is elegantly settled on a divan as though in a Paramount picture. Suddenly the divan flips over and the woman tumbles into some unseen water below. We are at a street carnival where men in rough clothes pay for the privilege of throwing balls at a target to capsize pretty girls. No better figure could summarize Carné's plea that French cinema must break out of the closed well-lit salons of high society and tumble into the tough world of the people.

Dans les rues anticipates *Le Crime de Monsieur Lange* in its use of bricks as a symbol for the interlocked fates of the community and in its strident anticapitalist sentiments. Generally a reflective, quiet film, some of its dark images would reappear in Vigo's *L'Atalante* (particularly a dance-hall scene and a shot of Jean-Pierre Aumont standing by a bridge as a barge floats by in the canal). Three times Hans Eisler's modernist score takes the lead in organizing extended descriptive syntagms, where Trivas concentrates his depiction of the impoverished *quartier*. Such fancy editing is at odds with the bare photographic evidence on which Trivas more frequently relies. The heroine is introduced to us, for instance, in a straight-on medium shot lasting half a minute, and the *quartier* persists as a subject of independent interest well after dramatic moments are played out on its streets. The *Cinéopse* review is remarkable: "[*Dans les rues*] exhibits a fabulous technical mastery. First of all in atmosphere. It is difficult to create on the screen the atmosphere of a Parisian *quartier*—a popular *quartier* . . . but he did it with images of the funfair, the stunning chaos of the warehouse, where Père Schamp fences stolen goods, and above all with

Dans les rues: The drama on the streets. CF

Dans les rues: The drama of the streets. MOMA

the interiors of the houses where staircases serve as the living souls of these humble places. The staircases of *Dans les rues* are unforgettable. They bear a deep signification."[75] In one of the most clairvoyant moments of criticism in the entire epoch, the review notes that the film's "fabulous conclusion proceeds by evocation rather than by theatrical situation."

Dans les rues was by no means neorealist in style or method. Its editing and expressive visual figures show it to be solicitously constructed. Moreover, it not only starred a major young talent of the day, Jean-Pierre Aumont, its scenario derives from a novel by Prix Goncourt author J. H. Rosny, adapted for the screen by Alexandre Arnoux, founding editor of *Pour Vous*. Pierre Blanchar even helped direct the adolescent actors to give the film a tone that would be at once authentic and expressive.[76] This was a new type of French film that, after *La Rue sans nom*, would increasingly attract the attention of critics. This was the type of film Renoir had sought to make with *La Nuit du carrefour*, and that Carné would master in a few years. But despite its French adoption it was a type of film for which the Germans will always be celebrated. Their influence in the Parisian studios at this moment was substantial.

Siodmak, Trivas, Pabst, and Ophuls are the visible prow of a rather capacious ship of emigration bearing with it cameramen like Schüfftan and editors like Jean Oser. The large centralized German production system had spawned superior technicians used to working on grand projects for UFA or Tobis. And so the look of French films would be altered far more from below, by the techniques of artisans, than from on high by directors. Among these one must include those artisans from the Slavic countries many of whom worked in Berlin before moving to Paris. From wherever they came, as a group the émigrés entering the French industry raised standards and expectations. They also opened up stylistic options that would be crucial for poetic realism.

DESIGNED IN DEPTH: THE RUSSIAN INFLUENCE

By 1935 no studio was large enough to boast a style the way historians some-times speak of the Warner Brothers or Paramount style. In such situations continuity develops most often through artisanal channels. In the growth of an atmospheric look, as opposed to a stagy one, cameramen and set designers obviously played an instrumental role. Certainly they responded to new direc-tives provided by the exigencies of scripts and by the demands of directors, but just as surely scriptwriters and directors conjured up their projects in the knowledge of what they could expect from each technical department. With no powerful executives to discipline these influences into a consistent mold, the prior experience of foreign technicians played a central role.

One might be inclined to single out certain German cameramen who ex-panded the visual possibilities for daring directors. Curt Courant and Eugen Schüfftan are the most famous of these.[77] But French cameramen enjoyed excellent reputations too. Some had been trained in the experimental days of the silents (Georges Périnal), while others started in the wide-open first years of sound (Henri Alekan). Cameramen, in sum, came to French cinema from varied backgrounds and, except for the apprenticeships younger ones served under their masters, did not perpetuate any distinct schools of cinematogra-phy. Set design was another matter, however, as a powerful group of Russian émigrés came to rival the French designers. Their upbringing and sensibility, not to mention their friendships and apprenticeships, make reasonable the notion of a school of design.

One French decorator, Jacques Colombier, was later to complain that this overrepresentation of Russian talent in the industry had vitiated national ten-dencies, replacing them with a bland international look.[78] He wanted a tasteful native look to come through in French films; but it was just this conventional taste, this native type of realism, that Chenal had sought to surpass in *Crime et châtiment*. The Russian and eastern European artists, unfettered by a concern with "Frenchness," allowed their imaginations more play in concocting the milieu of a script. When the script was novelistic in its conception, these artists can be said to have designed an experience rather than decorated a set.

Numerically the Russian presence in the French film industry went far be-yond the German.[79] Shortly after the Bolshevik revolution, Joseph Ermolieff transplanted his entire company to Paris, ceding it after 1922 to Alexandre Kamenka under whom it was known as Albatros Films. Dozens of White Russian actors and artists were employed in more than forty silent features.[80] Ivan Lochakoff arrived with Ermolieff and was responsible for the decor in the first thirty of these, while the young Lazare Meerson's name starts to appear regularly in this capacity after 1926. The output at Albatros dropped in the

1930s to some fourteen films, including Renoir's *Les Bas-Fonds* (1936). But more important than the quantity or even the quality of Albatros's sound films was the stability of the studio, for by 1935 it was the longest-lived company left in a cinema sector devastated by the bankruptcy at Gaumont, the Paramount pullout, and the scandal at Pathé. For years Albatros served as a way station for Russian designers before they scattered throughout a suddenly wide-open industry. Most of these, like Eugène Lourié (later to be Renoir's chosen designer), were trained as painters in their native country and arrived in Paris needing work. Among their number were Andrejew, Pimenov, Wakhevitch, and Bilinsky.

The solidity of Albatros is an index to the size and strength of the Russian colony in Paris between the wars. They numbered over 100,000, and the privileged status many of them brought from Russia included inordinate wealth, talent, and culture. They established a dense support network to welcome new arrivals to Paris, and they maintained excellent contacts with other Russian refugees throughout Europe. All this provided a sizable core audience for Albatros's movies, but hardly one large enough to insure financial success. Still, over thirty-five films in the 1930s alone deal with Russia as a subject, often directed by such names as Ozep, Granowsky, Trivas, Tourjansky, Strijewsky, Kirsanov, Moguy, and Volkoff. Another favored subject was the historical picture involving the lives of nobility. Many historical films were set in Russia or eastern Europe and produced by Kamenka or by one of the other émigrés.[81] Here incontestably reigns the international style Colombier so deplored. One would imagine that Russian producers might have favored films with foreign or indeterminate settings, such as Pabst's *Don Quichotte* (1932), or Chenal's *L'Homme de nulle part* (1936). But Kamenka's varied Albatros list cannot be so easily typed, and by the decade's end one finds other Russian producers like Gregor Rabinovitch (*Le Quai des brumes*) and J. Lucachevitch (*Hôtel du Nord*) working dead center in the French industry. While Russian designers must have felt at home working on Albatros pictures or with Russian directors, they too fanned out across the industry, possessing ideas and techniques that may have had a common source, but applying them to problems encountered by sound films of all sorts.

Those problems belong to the general history of production design, which, according to Léon Barsacq,[82] should be told as the drama of the liberation of settings from stage backdrops in quest of mobile relations to story, character, and especially camera. This struggle occurred twice over: first, in the silent era with the success of the Italians in three-dimensional design, that of the Swedes in rectifying exterior and interior textures, and finally that of the impressionists and expressionists in transforming materials to focus visual space on action or mood. Hollywood consolidated these European gains, before utterly changing the game in 1927 with *The Jazz Singer*.

Most histories have it that production design immediately capitulated to this new exigency, regressing to its primitive theatrical stage model.[83] A 1931 *Revue du cinéma* article deplores the state of the art.[84] After the triumphs of *Napoléon*, *L'Argent*, *La Passion de Jeanne d'Arc*, and *La Chute de la Maison Usher*, who could be proud of the little boxes that served as backdrops for the sound pictures of 1929 and 1930? The designers were in despair, for they were at the mercy of the sound engineers who in those first years banned all recesses, vaults, curved ceilings, and anything that might interfere with "radio standard" voice recording. Gone as well was the use of carefully chosen exteriors, something that characterized French silent cinema above that of any other country save Sweden. Moreover, because the sound cinema ushered in a dramatic increase in the sheer number of films made, designers found their work load doubled, sometimes trebled. Men who had meticulously planned and dressed the great historical reconstructions of the 1920s now slaved in double shifts just to keep up with the daily production demands of the most ordinary projects. Their enthusiasm flagged; their artistry declined. A single star was paid more than the full design cost of a film.

This lament is doubly poignant since French set design had attained so great a reputation in the 1920s.[85] It would have to be with the help of designers that France might now struggle to free itself both from Hollywood and from the stranglehold of the sound technicians. In this struggle Lazare Meerson played a heroic role. Seldom can one so confidently point to an individual responsible for an aesthetic trend in any art. Having come to design through scene painting in 1925, Meerson's genius was instantly recognized. As early as 1928 he concocted the look of three masterpieces: L'Herbier's *L'Argent*, Feyder's *Les Nouveaux Messieurs*, and Clair's *Un Chapeau de paille d'Italie*. Working on these very different films he became legendary for his fastidiousness and for his ingenious solutions to the most truculent problems.

Budgets for films with Clair and Feyder we know were comparatively high. Nevertheless, Meerson stashed away materials requisitioned for run-of-the-mill productions so that he might later bolster the size and scope of his sets for these two directors. The results, visible in his first sound film, Clair's *Sous les toits de Paris*, gave designers and producers in France an idea about standing up to Hollywood's material riches by fashioning a distinctively French look.

That idea and that look can be named by a single word: intimacy. Critics around the world applauded the way Meerson had truly made the audience feel under the roofs of Paris. The visual tone and themes felt in the sets are engaging in the manner of the street singer's tune. Meerson has downsized the picturesque vistas of the city of light by constructing its more picturesque back alleys. He has humanized his gangsters and given us a *quartier* we might like to visit. I have already contrasted this with the German tendency, particularly in the Weimar period, to represent their cities as nightmare alleys, as in *The Street*, *The Tragedy of the Street*, or *Joyless Street*.[86] Even when the French would depict the crime-infested *quartiers* of Paris, as in Trivas's *Dans les rues*, the threats to the merchants and to the perpetual *promeneurs* seem momentary, for the city never belongs to the gangsters but to the people, and ultimately to the spectator. Following Clair's film, French gangsters will often be represented as colorful, rough stones in the urban mosaic, hence unthreatening. We are ready to enjoy a drink at a local café after seeing *Sous les toits de Paris* and even *Dans les rues*, whereas we slink back to our solitary homes after *M* even though Peter Lorre has been caught and sentenced. The German city is everyone's private nightmare.[87]

In this regard *Le Crime de Monsieur Lange* is particularly exemplary, suggesting the continuity of sensibility in French cinema. For despite enormous differences in taste and approach, Clair and Renoir share an affection for the openness of public life in public spaces. No matter that connivers like Batala rule the streets from their back-room desks, or that careering automobiles can strike down even the most carefree bicyclist, the streets are spokes radiating from the courtyard. They form a locus of commerce and companionship, built to the measure of the dreams of those who live there. This is the Paris of Renoir and Clair. It is the image of Paris the French cinema altogether projects, a great village that Meerson above all designers knew how to fit snugly around the actors.

Meerson never wanted his decor to stand apart from the characters and events it houses. He stood opposed to his great predecessor in French design, Robert Mallet-Stevens, whose sets for L'Herbier's *L'Inhumaine* (done in collaboration with Fernand Léger) are considered the cinematic apogee of the modernism of art deco. "It is much more difficult to compose a decor with ambience that, imperceptible to the eyes of the public, strengthens the scene and confers on it an authentic value than to execute a super-architecture before which everyone's mouth gapes in admiration but which totally denatures the sense and the direction of the decoupage."[88]

Meerson has been called the "realist" side of the poetic Clair, no doubt because he provided the memorable and authentic Parisian *quartiers* of *Sous les toits de Paris*, *Le Million*, and *Quatorze juillet*. His preparatory research for every project was painstaking, particularly for the finicky Jacques Feyder on *Pension Mimosas* (a small hotel in Nice) and *La Kermesse héroïque* (Renaissance Flanders). But authenticity is a far cry from realism, and Meerson saw himself breaking from the darker realistic aspects of the 1920s. He emphasized lightness, delicacy, and buoyancy, employing great quantities of illuminating gas so that the world might be seen through a veil. So great was his reputation that Lubitsch sent his designer, Hans Dreier, to learn "lightness" from Meerson, and MGM, rumor has it, even lightened the tone of the lion in its logo. Paramount's crucial decision to go with an expansive "white look" took into account the new style of Clair and Meerson.[89]

When Meerson challenged the prevailing architectural paradigm of Mallet-Stevens, he did so from a position of knowledge. Trained as an architect him-

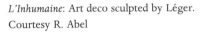

L'Inhumaine: Art deco sculpted by Léger.
Courtesy R. Abel

Le Dernière milliardaire: Lightness sketched for Clair. CF

self, he had apprenticed under L'Herbier, helping build the sets for *Feu Mathias Pascal* (1925).[90] Once assured of his own abilities, Meerson changed to the softer, more accommodating approach. Meerson would be called upon to produce modernist sets, but they became opportunities for a different form of fantasy, frequently of a satiric sort as in *A nous la liberté*. Feyder's caustic *Les Nouveaux Messieurs* tempted him to parody art deco itself, and specifically Mallet-Stevens's overblown conceptions. Art deco motifs encouraged a static "backdrop" function for sets, whereas Meerson insisted on mobile, painterly designs. Tellingly, he and his followers seldom resorted to maquettes in his preparation. Their material rigidity inhibited subtlety, imagination, and improvisation. Léon Barsacq sums up his method:

> Meerson had the vision of a painter, an impressionist painter, one might say; his small sketches were painted very freely, in a range of soft subtle colors, indicating merely volumes, principal lines, and atmosphere. From there he developed his sets little by little, with the aid of his assistants. Even during set construction he did not hesitate to modify certain proportions or details, making sketches on scraps of paper or cigarette packs while the work progressed . . . hence, no doubt, the sense of quivering life, the aerial quality of his designs, which seem never to be fixed but to pulse with the same rhythm as their films.[91]

Few designers had so dared to emphasize the overall mood of sets at the expense of their narrative function. Meerson felt that light, not volume, was the true medium of the art, light that suggested flux, spirit, and shimmering effects. In 1931, the same year that *La Revue du cinéma* held up Meerson as the only laudable designer working in France, the influential art historian Germain Bazin argued in *L'Amour de l'art* for the centrality of Degas for set design—Degas with his interest in fleeting moments, in photographic framings and haphazard compositions, in the rush of light in a visual scene.[92]

It would be hasty to try to locate the precise painting aesthetic Meerson followed. Degas seems likely; but Meerson spent his evenings in Montparnasse with De Chirico, Kokochka, and Tchewletchev. Perhaps we should be satisfied with Germain Bazin that the cinema can be seen—and in Meerson's case must be seen—as inheriting the problems and traditions that developed in painting since the Renaissance. These include movement in two dimensions, the centrality of light, and the dramatic location of the spectator. Meerson took to heart all of these problems and sought to give them cinematic expression, so as to lure the audience into a habitable space from which they might better enter the phantasmagoric space of characters' hopes and plights.

The middle zone Meerson sought between realism and stylization aims to gently seduce audiences with its rightness and its grace. Virtually every designer responsible for poetic realism would adopt this middle zone and adopt Meerson as a master, though he himself left for England in 1936 where he died the next year. In the successful constructions of poetic realist designers, characters seem to "wear" the cinematic space surrounding them.[93] In Meerson's pioneering sets for René Clair the characters literally waltz through it.

Meerson's tour de force came in 1935 with Feyder's most ambitious undertaking, *La Kermesse héroïque*. To many critics, the sets alone spell the triumph of this much-beloved movie. After months of research in museums across northern Europe and of course in Flanders where the drama takes place, he designed a town that might have once been inhabited by Peter Brueghel (a major character in the film); however, he reduced the scale of everything to three-quarters size. The result is an ironic mix of grandeur and diminution. The grandeur is owed to a few extraordinary expenditures Meerson and Feyder convinced their German backers to accept. An enormous canal was dug in the midst of the central Epinay studio,[94] around which Meerson ranged the fronts of the town, using the spires of churches in the real suburb of Epinay to extend the lines of depth. The space created is not at all like that of the standard historical epic. It is a human space, posing ludicrously as grand, imitating in architecture the view of his own times painted by Breughel—clearly a stand-in for the filmmakers—who flatters but undercuts the pompous town council and the mayor with his portraits. One sequence, identified as the mayor's nightmare of Spanish soldiers ruthlessly pillaging the town and carrying off its women, permits Meerson to concoct a fantasized decor in an unrestrained (mock) heroic style. The contrast between the look of this dream and the quaint, comic tone of the rest of the film stamps Feyder's ironic intentions unmistakably. Yet in making the characters seem to "step out of Flemish paintings," these sets turn the townspeople into lovable puppets even as they are satirized. In sum, Meerson made use of extraordinary resources to construct a spectacle that lampoons the spectacular. Far from overwhelming the drama, his magnificent town serves as a comfortable dollhouse that maintains an intimacy with the characters who inhabit it. Nothing is blown out of proportion save their egos and nightmares.

La Kermesse héroïque. BFI

At right, top and middle:
Sketching with Brueghel

Below: Satirizing spectacle

La Kermesse héroïque marks a plateau in set design. Here Meerson put to the test all his experiments using iron, glass, and oil paint on a large scale, and he found ingenious ways to adapt parts of the studio factory to give his fantasies ballast. Here he achieved that balance between authenticity and the imaginary that was his goal and trademark and that would set the tone for the work of his many disciples. "Exacting, even finicky, his pervasive influence helped establish the new direction taken by set design in French cinema."[95]

Naturally, other designers and trends grew to rival Meerson's. By 1933 audio dubbing, rerecording, and mixing had let directors regain much control over their soundstages. They increasingly convinced producers that design was not simply an annoying cost, but rather an essential ingredient in the quest to individuate any picture. Three viable alternatives challenged Meerson's balanced approach in France: the theatrical, the realist, and the symbolist. By sheer prolixity, Jacques Colombier, together with Edward Gys and Guy de Gastyne, set the standards for the theatrical approach. Chief designers at Pathé-Natan, they backed the studio's theatrical transpositions with tasteful sets and costumes that took advantage of the camera's potential ubiquity. Not so daring as Mallet-Stevens but working with his ideas,[96] they legibly designated the period of the historical films they were responsible for in their obvious choice of architectural motifs and props. When it came to modern subjects, clean geometric spaces helped separate characters into appropriate dramatic camps, while satisfying the reigning obsession with art deco fashions.

It was against such cleverness and complacent good taste that Renoir would rail, "Good taste is shit; in France we're dying of good taste."[97] He preferred malleable, messy sets, even for large-scale historical films. Barsacq recalls that during the shooting of *La Marseillaise* Renoir would never approve a set until he had physically moved the camera within it, looking for inspiration. Moreover, in that film and others he found ways to bring studio decor and natural settings into contact within the same scene, thus letting the drama breathe fresh air.[98] In contrast, when Gastyne teamed up with L'Herbier, for example, they aimed for what Barsacq calls an "official looking richness. Royal reception rooms with gleaming floors and gilded ceilings, crystal chandeliers and pompous furniture"—just the kind of thing that would later adorn the cinema of quality.[99] Some magnificent sets were built, but when seen against those that Lourié and Wakhevitch built for Renoir, or against the "Meerson balance," as I want to call it, these designs always seem to preexist and outlive the stories played out on them. They are stiff, and proud of their solidity, but they scarcely bend to the flow of the characters walking through them.

At the opposite pole from ornate, stagy decor stand the realists among whom Renoir is a chief example but a single example nonetheless. A year before Renoir took his microphone out of the studios in search of the ambience for *La Chienne*,[100] Jean Epstein had prophesied, "The simplified acoustics of the studio are no longer of any use for pursuing experiments. It's across the sound fields of the vast world that we must spread our microphones. . . . The important thing is to place oneself in conditions which do not exclude the unexpected."[101] Renoir went out in search of the unexpected most audaciously in *Toni*, which was shot on location in the Martigue; but he did so only after monitoring Pagnol's success with *Angèle*, whose "sets" were built and lived in by cast and crew. Pagnol claimed that by the time shooting took place, everyone felt perfectly comfortable in the clothes and spaces they had inhabited for weeks. It would be quite off the mark to claim Pagnol for "realism," especially after we have already explored his background and continuing interest in theater and in the classically structured play; moreover, most of his films in fact were shot in the studios he built in Marseilles. Still, like Renoir, like Epstein, and like a few other directors, he felt that cinema could only gain by avoiding the Parisian or Hollywood studio look and method. In different ratios these men aimed for a balance not unlike Meerson's, but while Meerson wanted the authentic and the imaginary to coexist in his decor, the realists were more likely to allow the sets to carry the authenticity that the plot and dialogue would then lift to varying heights of imagination.

When the balance between crude realism and the symbolic imagination arises, Jean Vigo inevitably returns as the most brilliant illustration. While both his fiction films were primarily shot in the studio, in his calculated naïveté Vigo refused many of the conveniences sets afford, always shooting as though he were on location. For example, he had the interior of the barge, *L'Atalante*, reconstructed intact in the studio, making no allowances for the possibilities of interior lighting. He and his cameraman Boris Kaufman had to punch holes in the side of the barge set so that they could photograph the inside. This accounts for the chaotic and cluttered interiors that stifle Juliette in her own room but later startle and hypnotize her in the magic box of Père Jules's room. Vigo employs flimsy sets that his characters transform. The sublime is released from the ordinary, as when Juliette emerges from the hold of the barge into the stunning sunlight and into the promise of a set as vast as the city of Paris.

If designers had competed for prizes between the wars, or if directors had been cited for their sets, no one would have paid Vigo the slightest attention, nor Pagnol, nor Renoir. Compared to the work of André Andrejew and the symbolist school he headed, their films seem undesigned. Andrejew had apprenticed in theater with Stanislavsky and Max Reinhardt before turning to the cinema. He crossed decades and borders in a stunning career in which he seemed to work only on films that would feature his genius.[102] That genius knew how to isolate and exaggerate a single element to serve as the focus and filter through which even the most immense settings had to be viewed. His impact in France stems from the triumphant *L'Opéra de quat'sous* in 1931 and rises to its greatest fame with Litvak's *Mayerling* (1936). In the latter he memorably represented the court at Vienna through a magnificent staircase, subordinating all other elements to it. Uninhibited by the "good taste" of his French counterparts, or by Meerson's belief in an underlying authenticity, Andrejew moved toward the colossal and the ingenious. In Fédor Ozep's 1938 *Tarakanova* Barsacq feels he went too far. Once again, a staircase dominates the scene, but this time it utterly crushed the actors playing on it. Ozep, another Russian, doubtless had encouraged him, just as he had encouraged Meerson to go to his greatest extreme in *Amok*. Meerson, we have seen, was motivated by a tale of delirium and drunkenness set in exotic Malaysia. But *Tarakanova* provided no excuses. Andrejew simply went overboard for sheer effect.

If we situate Meerson's style in the center of the fluctuating ratio of realism to stylization, then Andrejew and Pagnol would stand at the extremes. Yet once we except the art deco tendency, the continuity of the French approach to sets in the 1930s is more remarkable than these differences. Taken together the best French tendencies sought to carry the tone of a single character's sense of the world, while simultaneously suggesting the social web that might produce or affect that world. This tendency is consonant with "poetic realism," a term that should connote a particular look as well as a way of telling a story.

One of the few native Frenchmen to help determine the poetic realist look was Jacques Krauss. Duvivier depended on him for *La Bandera*, *La Belle Equipe*, and *Pépé le Moko*, where he created the illusion of authenticity while paying minimal attention to documentation. The Casbah of *Pépé le Moko* is a miracle of studio design, with the streets and alleyways forming a thematically pertinent and visually exotic labyrinth. Duvivier seemed inspired by the symbolic dimensions of the decor, not hesitating to employ a magnificently flowing, but highly artificial, rear projection when Pépé leaves the Casbah to descend to the sea and to his doom.

At the heart of poetic realism lies the series of films made by the *équipe* Carné assembled around him from 1936 to 1939. *Drôle de drame*, *Le Quai des brumes*, *Hôtel du Nord*, and *Le Jour se lève* owe the assurance of their tone to a system that encouraged the collaboration of a writer like Jacques Prévert, a composer like Maurice Jaubert, and of course a designer of Alexander Trauner's training and talent. Just as Carné had been Feyder's disciple, so Trauner was Meerson's. The tradition passed smoothly on to these men even if the films grew darker and less ironic.

Trauner like Krauss had first been a painter. In 1927 he moved from Hungary to Paris and to a hotel where by happenstance lived some equally indigent Russian artists. When a message arrived via his roommates that Meerson could use some assistance on a film he was designing, Trauner unenthusiastically tagged along. But Meerson's personality captivated him, as did the Montparnasse artists he associated with. He met his countryman the photographer André Kertesz alongside De Chirico and Meerson's other friends. This was the Paris milieu he had dreamt about; if cinema belonged in such a world, he was glad to make a life in it.

Pépé le Moko: Labyrinth of a Casbah built in Paris. BFI

Trauner's method has been much discussed.[103] He would characteristically seek a maximum reduction of objects on the screen, though making certain that everything that does remain is absolutely authentic to the period, class, and location the film is trying to represent. In *Le Jour se lève*, he designed the tenement building on the model of one that can be seen in the Zone, just outside Paris. Filling it with props to match his research notes taken on numerous visits to this and other such buildings in the area, he then systematically removed every object that seemed excessive to the moral and psychological drama Prévert had scripted. What was left we all remember: the great Norman armoire, the mirror, the bed in the corner, a table, and the objects that incorporate Gabin's hopes and despair: the teddy bear, the photographs, the cigarettes. It was Trauner's idea to put Gabin on the top floor, thus separating him from the crowd of his fellow workers and suspending him in an isolated vertigo. Years later Anatole Litvak remade this film shot for shot as *The Long Night* (1947), but Henry Fonda was condemned only to the second floor. The overall tone was dissipated as were opportunities for specific effects. For example, when Carné permits himself the shot down the seven floors of stairs, the vertical tunnel we see embodies the mind we have penetrated and the fall of that mind to oblivion.[104]

A general atmosphere suffuses each Trauner film, one so pervasive that it beclouds the spectator. No clear longshot lets us emerge from the fog in the Le Havre of *Le Quai des brumes*, with its isolated bar, sinister pawnshop, dirty amusement park, and old hotel by the port. We are absorbed in it, and in the aimless plight of the anonymous deserter played by Gabin. The setting of this film breathes with the poetry of its script in a single respiration. Underneath it we can feel the deep notes of Maurice Jaubert's fatalistic score. *Hôtel du Nord* is less obsessive in its search for a single hypnotic effect, but it too exemplifies the dreamy realism of the movement as a whole, with its sad bridge arching over the canal.

Novelist Italo Calvino gives one of the best accounts of the effects of these films, particularly as distinct from their American counterparts: "Having seen the Casbah of *Pépé le Moko*, I began to look at the staircases of our own old city with a different eye. . . . The French cinema was heavy with odors whereas the American cinema smelled of Palmolive." It was, he goes on to say, a serious cinema, one connected through its feeling and symbols to the life of literature and the life of the day, whereas Hollywood was a world unto itself.[105]

The French system of working by *équipe* is nowhere more important than in the integral function of poetic realist sets. Trauner would work on his designs in the same house where Prévert was finishing the dialogue. The two men were known to scout locations together. Trauner would also stick with the project until it was fully shot, thus permitting adjustments and occasional improvisations.[106] In this way the strongest French films could achieve a total, devastating effect, one that Calvino said seemed to be of a piece with the literature and even the social climate of the day.

By the time the war interrupted the increasing momentum of their international success, the poetic realist films of Carné, Duvivier, Grémillon, and Chenal seemed no longer to be played by characters on a set or actors on a stage. The theatrical model had been superseded and a novelistic, romantic aesthetic had taken its place. The visual world inhabited by the figures on the screen had become a breathing milieu, bearing down on them, often indistinguishable from them.[107] Designed to be ingested in a single hypnotic experience, this "figural space" is the visual correlate of the novels and *récits* inspiring poetic realism.

PRODUCERS AND THE PRODUCTION OF VALUES

The impressive growth of script material and visual design could also be detailed for other cinematic registers like musical composition. Obviously none of these resources for an expanded notion of cinema could have taken root without the efforts of producers. Producers ultimately purchased the properties to be filmed; they hired the visionary designers, composers, cameramen, musicians, and directors to make something new of such properties. When a poetic realist film is hailed for its extraordinary unity of conception, then one should presuppose a prior unity of effort fostered by the creative *équipe* that was gathered, sustained, and in the best cases encouraged by its producer. Not that all successful films of this sort proceeded smoothly. Carné's autobiography speaks of intermittent feuds between him and his producers or between his producers and his *équipe*. But the majority of successful projects, individually tailored as they had to be, show a sympathetic producer at their core. This was particularly true early in the decade before self-sustaining *équipes* like Carné's or Renoir's had had time to mature.

Although the resources required for sound film would seem to have reduced the number of those capable of underwriting full-blown projects, by 1933 the retreat of the studios and the increased demand for French sound products permitted a host of amateur enthusiasts and a larger host of financial charlatans to enter the arena of production. It was thanks to wealthy friends that Renoir was able to put together *La Nuit du carrefour*, *Madame Bovary*, and *Toni*, for example. And it was due to the personal faith of Jacques Nounez that Vigo's *L'Atalante* was shepherded to conclusion. Although Nounez chose what he hoped would be a safe subject for the young genius to direct, he never tampered with Vigo's conception. On the contrary, he went out of his way to provide whatever was asked. Unfortunately, his resources expired before he could prepare the premiere and distribution of this extraordinary but troublesome film. The distributor who purchased it had no concern whatever for Vigo or the cinema; a brutal but common story in the first years of sound.

Given the topic of this chapter—the development of the artistic resources poetic realism would require—I want to conclude on a film typical in its unusualness, Marc Allégret's 1934 *Lac aux dames*. Like the vast majority of the 150 films made that year, *Lac aux dames* was the single venture of its producer; indeed it was his first venture in the cinema and would be his last. But due to the strength of his reputation and involvement, the film might be said to belong far more to Philippe de Rothschild than to Allégret, the quality of whose output depended primarily on the situation organized for him by his successive producers. He could hardly have dreamt of a better producer than Rothschild.

Although it was in vineyards and wineries that he principally invested his time and family capital, Rothschild had made the theater more than an avocation. In the late 1920s he went so far as to build the Théâtre Athenée and to oversee its first productions. These involved many of the most luminous theatrical figures in Paris: Louis Jouvet, Gaston Baty, Sacha Guitry, Jean Giraudoux. Inevitably he recognized the wide-open possibilities of sound cinema; just as inevitably he discussed film production in the theatrical circles that had become his home. Extended conversations with Marc Allégret at cocktail parties and dinners made him determined to produce films, if possible to direct.

Among Rothschild's motives was a desire to influence the aesthetic direction of the cinema, especially in freeing it from its servitude to the stage. For Rothschild, good cinema required a drama set in a natural environment that would allow the photography to influence human words and actions. That is one reason he agreed to back the Vicki Baum novel, since its love story was set in the fresh Austrian air,[108] far from the moral and technical clichés of the Parisian studios. Advance publicity about the special nature of the production and its producer attracted well-known artists. Georges Auric was engaged for the score, Lazare Meerson for the sets.

Rothschild even coaxed the notoriously recalcitrant Colette into writing the dialogue. The two were already well acquainted within the theater circle and Colette shared Rothschild's antipathy for studios. She claimed she was eager to listen to her dialogue as it might sound in the Tyrol. Jean-Georges Auriol, editor of La Revue du cinéma, took charge of the initial adaptation, which Colette then continually revised. She upgraded the role of Puck, in part because Allégret was certain that Simone Simon would be unforgettable in it, and in part because that role was familiar to the author of Cheri.[109] She took advice from André Gide because he was Gide. The extent of his influence is conjectural, but we know he helped choose Aumont for the male lead[110] and later traveled to Austria to hover around the shooting. Furthermore, his nephew Dominique Drouin supervised the details of the production, struggling to keep its many powerful personalities content.

The numerous journalists drawn to such a chic spot soon began to flutter around Simone Simon. Allégret was determined to do everything possible to inject into French cinema her pure and uncultured sensuality. Thus Lac aux dames mixes atmospheric sequences involving Puck's romantic, mist-shrouded island with more traditionally dramatic plot material on the mainland. Today everything about the island seems prophetic: Simone Simon's fetching demeanor, Meerson's bizarre and evocative set, and the sheer quiet of the island's isolation put us into an interior space, a metaphor for the kind of private sensibility that is thought to be at the heart both of romantic love and of the experience of prose fiction. In this case, the cinema reaches for something new. One can hardly believe it when Allégret and his hero (the Aumont character) abandon Puck and all she represents for the more conventional goals of the mainland, where love is contaminated by social rules and where language, gesture, and costume seem so staged.

Like most of Allégret's films, Lac aux dames tries hard to shock and to please at the same time. He was a director more interested in the stir his films could cause than in the artistic advance they might make, prouder of his film's "quality" production methods and values than of its aesthetic intervention. Allégret bragged to the editors of Pour Vous that the kind of film he makes takes up to nine months to complete and requires enormous and continual attention.[111] Lac aux dames certainly exudes a delicate air that comes from being a pam-

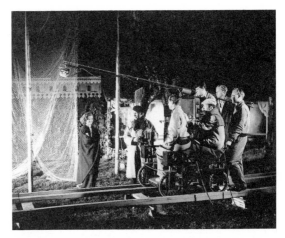

Lac aux dames. BFI

Simon Simone—making the
mystique. BFI

Lac aux dames. CF

pered and talent-laden production. But credit for this should go to Rothschild's constancy and solicitude. The expensive and difficult location work the film entailed deeply impressed Denise Tual, the film's editor, who combed through far more footage than she thought possible for a ninety-minute film.[112] Even in postproduction Rothschild's largesse seemed boundless. Days were consumed in trying first one cut of a scene and then another.

Rothschild stayed with the project all through its domestic exhibition run, guiding it into the export market. Not having secured prior distribution agreements, Rothschild was initially unable to interest anyone in the film. But unlike Nounez for *L'Atalante* or Gaston Gallimard for *Madame Bovary* (with whose production it otherwise shares a great deal), he was prepared to go another step so as to protect the integrity of the film. Personally renting the Colisée theater on the Champs-Elysées, he oversaw the film's premiere and first run. An immense billboard attracted viewers for months and secured the film's international success.

This success may paradoxically put into question the film's distinctiveness, for how could a rigorously different aesthetic achieve such wide contemporaneous acceptance? Whether in fact it did advance the artistic possibilities of French cinema, set against the standard theatrical adaptations of the day, *Lac aux dames* was an immensely ambitious undertaking. Films like it invigorated the cinema by luring important writers, composers, actors, and designers. The cultural elite could not fail to take note of such films, which billed themselves not as mere movies but as experiences worth talking and thinking about. Louis Jouvet, who, as we saw last chapter, generally dismissed the movies, confessed that *Lac aux dames* had lifted the cinema experience onto a serious aesthetic plateau, because the exceptional consistency and depth of its acting serves as just one element in a significant overall conception. Jouvet repeats his belief that artistic conception alone brings about that transcendent joy the arts should strive for and that the cinema so seldom attains. The acting in *Lac aux dames*, astounding though it may be, merely

> contributes to this nearly physical joy; it does not cause that joy. Rather one must look to the rhythm of the film, to its constantly appropriate sensitivity, to the magnificence of its natural setting which produces in a marvelously precise way a truly unusual purity.
>
> Everything in this work seems harmonious, supple, and attractive, all tied together in the most moving fashion by the delicious music of Auric. This is one of the first times that the cinema has given me an emotion at once tranquil and personal that I usually obtain only by reading a novel or seeing a play enacted. It marks a happy, a poetic moment.[113]

The very next year, Jouvet consented to play a role in Feyder's *La Kermesse héroïque*, the first time he had been lured to work strictly as a film actor. Last chapter my discussion of theater closed on the serious figure of Louis Jouvet whose presence could raise the stakes of any film he appeared in. Let Jouvet stand this time for the serious viewer demanding films that would strive for more than a secondary and convenient simulacrum of theater, that would reach for the "poetic." Thanks to the resources of a new brand of fiction, of immigrant designers, and of ambitious and independent producers, such a poetic cinema had come within reach.

Demands of
Realism

"POETIC REALISM": let us divide the name in two, the better to comprehend its joining in the second half of the decade. Unquestionably the "poetic" side yields more readily to investigation, as critics and directors had plenty to say about the goal and craft of cinematic "poesis," the shaping of a world on film. "Realism," on the other hand, despite its long association with the cinema, is a term at once more protean and more freighted with moral urgency. At the time and place that concern us, realism in all the arts could not avoid conscription into the political regiments constituting the Popular Front. The name coined for the militant cinema, "cinema engagé," sought to replace an earlier notion of cinema for which the name "reflective" serves double duty: ever since Stendhal realism has been touted as a mode of representation by which a mirror is held up to nature. The term "reflective" at the same time connotes "meditative" or "settled," as opposed to the demanding, unsettling, "engaged" cinema exacted by the Parti Communiste. As we will see, and as we might by now have guessed, a third *optique* situates itself between these extremes of traditional and militant realism, the amorphous *optique* of poetic realism that addressed a serious audience in a populist manner. To locate this particular kind of realism, I will first plot the much more obvious positions of its alternatives.

The French Realist Tradition and the Depression

OPPOSITE PAGE:
Poil de Carotte. BFI

Realism in cinema, it is easy to imagine, derives from both technological and cultural facets. The French claim to have been at the source of that technology. Bazin, for example, proudly celebrated a savant like Jules Marey, in his quest for a chronophotographic record of the flight of a bird.[1] One is surprised, then, that compared to Anglo-Americans, the French have not excelled in the pure documentary, in the scientific or social-scientific use of "their" invention. Of course famous French documentarists can be counted from Jean Painlevé through Jean Rouch, but these two names, symptomatically, are linked to Surrealism, tainting any standard scientific conception of "realism."[2] French documentaries look peculiar, strive for something peculiar; they look in fact to have been inflected by cultural concerns, by a tradition of literary and pictorial realism, and by contemporaneous aesthetic debates.

A good index of this has been provided by the French cultural ministry when it recently organized a film series entitled "Lumière's Century." The series was designed to celebrate and display to the world France's preeminence in cinematic realism; the titles and filmmakers chosen indicate a national predilection for poetic and intimate subjects. Lumière may have been an inventor, a businessman, an engineer, and an industrialist, but his progeny principally include key "poetic" filmmakers of the 1920s and 1930s together with their more recent heirs: René Clair, Jean Grémillon, Pierre Chenal, Jean Tarride, Alain Resnais, Chris Marker, Agnès Varda, Jean Eustache. If "Lumière's Century" is meant to celebrate a century of French documentarism, its aureole surrounds poetic realism in the process.

As in so many other matters, the French proclaim themselves world leaders in literary and pictorial realism. Villon, Rabelais, Montaigne, and Corneille were retrospectively inducted into the history of French realism, a movement that finally baptized itself in the nineteenth century. A range of aesthetic and social concerns and attitudes was then handed down from novelists like Balzac and Stendhal, from painters like Courbet and Manet, and from critics like Champfleury and Zola to the cinema. When the baton of realism was passed to cinema, those in the forefront of the major arts felt that that contest had been won and that their energies should engage more modern issues, fighting for or against new paradigms like *symbolisme*.

The realism that French cinema adopted would always be limited in relation to this grand tradition. From Louis Lumière's warm and funny 1895 family portraits to Maurice Pialat's grimmer family exposés of the 1980s, French cinema has made a name for itself by burrowing into intimate spaces where dramas of private feelings are exposed. Set this tendency off against the historical vision of Soviet silent cinema or against the breadth of classes and issues that arise in Italian neorealism, and you can understand why it is tempting to take poetic realism as the apotheosis of a tradition of the intimate that spans the continuum of French film history, and that has exerted pressure on even the most individual of artists—on Jean Renoir, for example.

National traditions of representation develop not according to some mystical zeitgeist, but materially, in the day-to-day decisions about what films to

make and how to make them. Nevertheless, those decisions result in an iden-
tifiably distinctive tradition. Critics have routinely tried to characterize the
national genius at play in the various cinemas of the world, claiming, for
example, that Hollywood has been obsessed with entertainment, that Germany has mastered the psychological mode, and that Moscow has given us the
greatest strain of social epics. France, we would surely conclude, has been the
source of a cinema that is simultaneously lyrical and realist. During the crisis
provoked by the introduction of sound, French critics projected exactly this
sense of national predispositions. A review of *La Chienne*, one of the films that
can open a discussion of poetic realism, explained its value in just this way:

> Perhaps it is too facile to speak of classicists, romanticists, naturalists, and sym-
> bolists. The study of human feelings has always been beyond classifications, the
> only value of which is pedagogical. You hear today, "German cinema: realism
> and sensuality; Russian cinema: social mysticism, the science of details; Ameri-
> can cinema: superficial life, pretty girls, beautiful photography; French cinema:
> lightness, incompleteness, melodrama or vaudeville." These formulas are
> handy, certainly, but inexact as much as incomplete. Still, one can underline the
> recent renaissance of French realism or naturalism with films such as *David
> Golder, Faubourg-Montmartre, La Chienne*! The old "slice of life" bursts forth
> anew on the screen. Among the genial or dull comedies, operettas, and dramas
> that sustain the current production, suddenly here we have a study of moral
> life, the strict and bitter observation of life, of a certain life composed of sorrow,
> repressed desires, injustice, and sadness.[3]

Precisely this concern for a certain national tradition led Jean Grémillon to
see French film realism as the most modern evocation of a French brand of
realism visible in all eras, from medieval architecture to modern painting,
music, and literature.[4] Recognizing the calculated imprecision of his assertion,
Grémillon immediately went on to specify that this strain of French art has
shown special attentiveness to the apparently minor and peripheral aspects of
physical and social life. Such nearly random observations are, however, raised
in French art to a level where they take on a descriptive and symbolic density
all the stronger for the humility of their origins. Grémillon's key phrase, taken
directly, I believe, from one of André Bazin's formulations about Jean Renoir,[5]
insists that French cinema is surpassingly realist and most French when it
brings out formerly hidden relations between "objects and beings," between
the outer world and the inner.

This essay, farfetched though it may be, places Grémillon within orthodox
French realist film theory. Not long after World War I Louis Delluc claimed
for cinematic art exactly this concentration on the marginal and fleeting traces
of the physical world, which, through the transformative power of camerawork, might express unspoken, unknown aspects of psychological life. In reaction to cries for pure cinema and abstract expression, Delluc settled on the

term *photogénie* to characterize the quality of the films he heralded.[6] We have seen that Grémillon learned his art under the sway of this term[7] and, in "documentaries," one of which was entitled *La Photogénie mécanique* (1925), provided French impressionism with several of its most sublime examples of the "photogenic." The final years of the 1920s saw a flowering of short documentaries successfully distributed by Pierre Braunberger to film clubs and cultural organizations. The introduction of sound completely turned Braunberger's attention to commercial entertainment, and it stopped up this stream of lyrical and satiric shorts shot on location.

In the early sound period, while there was a distinctly "idealist" strain to much of the film criticism,[8] so that critics like Emile Vieullermoz set themselves apart from realists like Carné, the vocabulary of idealist conceptions of cinema (especially in its proclamation of the "revelatory" property of the medium linking the human mind and soul) seems perfectly commensurable with Epstein's "lyrosophical epistemology" and Delluc's *photogénie*. In short, despite the placards raised for realism on one side and idealism on the other, French film criticism at the birth of poetic realism effectively developed a relatively common front.

Bazin and Jean Mitry, who dominated French film theory after the 1930s, both grew up on these versions of lyrical realism. They flagged the cinematic origins of this disposition in the pre–World War I films of Victorin Jasset and Louis Feuillade, which transformed the streets of Paris into a web of intrigue and mystery. And they both believed that, despite the impressionists' theories and the experiments they carried out, it was in the first decade of the sound era that France fully answered its vocation to realism.

Always a tendentious term, realism is subject to fragmentation into a host of related subspecies. Recall Mitry's useful, if somewhat arbitrary, distinctions among psychological realism, naturalism, tragic realism, psychosocial realism, social realism, and, of course, poetic realism.[9] These variants have in common the manner in which they signify not just the authenticity of their images, but the excess of reality beyond what can be actually seen on the screen. Particularly with Renoir we are made to feel the inexhaustible extension or surface of material life as well as the nearly infinite webs of interrelation suggested by any slice of it. In his films every shot seems to vibrate with unexplored possibilities and with the sense that something more waits at the edges of the frame. Although the key poetic realist directors—Carné, Chenal, and Duvivier—limit the material surface they choose to film, their realism derives from the depths they plumb in the everyday details that compose their works. These two dimensions, extension and depth, gave to the French cinema a look of seriousness and authenticity that made it stand out in the 1930s.

In the first years of sound, the term "realism" attached itself like a chevron to difficult and unconventional films. A decade earlier, films occupying the same critical terrain would more likely have earned the chevron "art." This shift has been generally understood as a reaction to the aestheticism of the 1920s in view of a grim economic depression. Concomitantly, cinema's new sound technology spurred many journalists and cultural critics to demand representations of the texture of everyday life and to decry not only the frivolous visual experiments of the avant-garde but more directly the vapid stage plays that were quickly becoming the norm within the reorganized studios.

Nevertheless, producers in this transitional period were more wary than ever of controversial films. So it must have been particularly exasperating for French intellectuals to watch Hollywood, the dream factory, develop an enviable strain of realist movies. An exemplary case is that of King Vidor's *Our Daily Bread*, whose reputation proved perhaps stronger in France than in America, dominating the pages of *Pour Vous* during the late summer and autumn of 1934. In the 15 November issue, one of the journal's most reflective writers, Claude Vermorel, took on the subject of realism directly by invoking the social amplitude of *Our Daily Bread*.[10] Compared to it, French movies look anemic or frivolous. The only works to merit his approbation are Trivas's *Dans les rues* and Chenal's *La Rue sans nom*, both of whose titles answer Carné's famous question posed a year earlier: "When Will the Cinema Go Down into the Street?" But even these films lack the strength of *Our Daily Bread*, Vermorel claims, because neither attains a social panorama of sufficient breadth to contextualize the problems they starkly raise. Vermorel's solution may at first seem antithetic to Carné's. He advises France to return to its literary past and particularly to the novels of Zola, which are at once "commercial, dramatic, and socially engaged," and which rely on a prodigious comprehension of the full social mechanism as a reliable undergirding for the surface effects of their realism. Excited at the prospect of Marc Allégret's directing *La Bête humaine* from a script by Martin du Gard, Vermorel proposes a new version of *L'Argent* that would directly refer to the Stavisky scandal just then rocking France, and he closes by regretting the recent death of Jean Vigo, whose next project was to have been a version of *Germinal*.

Vermorel's advocacy of literary adaptation as French cinema's best chance to contribute to realist cinema crystallizes a productive contradiction that runs through French film theory right up to its apotheosis in the writings of André Bazin.[11] Vermorel recognized that economic considerations made adaptation of realist novels a far more certain option than the documentary direction advocated by Jean Epstein among a few others. For one thing, realism in literature has always been synonymous with broad readership; cinema clearly inherits this audience and should not miss the opportunity to expose the conditions of human beings ruined by poverty and injustice even if the mode of exposition is fictional and sentimental.

Vermorel's view may be taken as the standard reflex of the day: the French were far more prepared to put their faith in the realism of novels than in that of documentary films. After all, Henri Fescourt's 1926 *Les Misérables* weighed in as the most profitable film of a decade whose documentaries screened mainly at art houses and museums. While both forms may have seen as their enemy the inane entertainment that dominated the screens of the 1930s, only adaptations employing major stars could seriously rival such movies at the box office. *La Rue sans nom* received attention, for instance, because it advertised six important actors on its posters, while Epstein's shorts about poor regions in Brittany were scarcely discussed in the press and found only minor exhibition outlets. Vermorel could have sealed his argument for literary adaptation by noting that the American film which had caught the eye of the French critics, *Our Daily Bread*, was undone at the box office by the absence of stars and by its obscure source, a newspaper essay. French realism, most mainstream critics were certain, needed to follow the proven methods of major industry productions. It should absorb the moral seriousness of King Vidor's film, not his challenge to standard industry practice. Realist subject matter, not an iconoclastic mode of filmmaking, seemed best able to redirect the industry onto paths aesthetically, morally, and economically superior to those it had been following since the sound revolution.

The richest vein of realist subject matter was thought to concern maltreated children, a topos whose roots go back beyond D. W. Griffith's Biograph films to a Victorian literary sensibility whose greatest voice was that of Charles Dickens. The French cinema had already exploited this topos in the silent era through the "orphan film" genre.[12] Cynically, it could be said that the film industry exploited a social problem in quite the way Bill Sykes took advantage of Oliver Twist, making money from his pathetic yet winsome beggarly appearance. How else can one account for the numerous remakes of such films. Remakes shamelessly exploit a topic and often build a second-level object atop an original. By strict realist precepts, they should be anathema. Take *Poil de Carotte*, a perennially popular tale. Julien Duvivier's beloved film of 1932 is a direct remake of Duvivier's own silent version of the same name, taken in its turn from Jules Renard's stage adaptation of his celebrated novel. Given this pedigree, Duvivier could only play into the hands of the established aesthetic mode, not propose in the name of realism an alternative to that mode. In a decision that frankly acknowledged this issue, Duvivier cast his scruffy but engagingly expressive child next to the most solid of French actors, Harry Baur. Baur stabilized all the performances of the film, guaranteeing the professionalism of the endeavor, while getting an opportunity to work in an unaccustomed role. Nearly fifty years later, the French would still be mining the international appeal of this formula when the aging Michel Simon played an anti-Semitic, but ultimately good-hearted "grandfather" to the little Jewish hero of Claude Berri's *Le Vieil Homme et l'enfant* (1967).

The genre of the oppressed child, then, promises a realism that, as a genre, it can scarcely deliver, if by realism one thinks of representations as striving to reach outside the conventional. The title of Marie Epstein and Benoit-

Lévy's masterful *Peau de Pêche* (1929) suggests something of the genre's problematic status in relation to realism, for "Peachskin" refers to the main character's winsome habit of blushing at the slightest provocation. Orphan films as a whole learned to blush cutely for a sympathetic audience. And so, insofar as forlorn children had become conventional in French film, their potential to release a fresh style, keyed to the freshness of subject matter, had been undermined. Only Jean Vigo seemed able to push the boundaries of subject and style, when he pulled from the young boys of *Zéro de conduite* a surplus of anarchism no conventions could completely control. The topic gave him license.

The goal Vermorel had set for a "popular realism," a term at once ambiguous and oxymoronic, was seemingly attained by Epstein and Benoit-Lévy in their 1934 *La Maternelle*. Here was a film that flaunted both serious subject matter and a documentary approach; nevertheless, *The Motion Picture Almanac* called it the most engaging French title of the year, a sure index of its export value,[13] and it topped an informal poll of "favorite films" that *Pour Vous* conducted among selected industry potentates.[14] Its advertising campaign emphasized the extensive use of location shooting and the authenticity of its subject. Added to this, however, and no doubt crucial to its success, was *La Maternelle*'s promotion of its one star, Madeleine Renaud of the Comédie-Française.[15] Little was made of its literary source, a Prix Goncourt novel, and no one mentioned that there had been a silent version. These facts point to the calculated nature of a project that was determined to promote its immediacy instead of its sophistication.

Epstein and Benoit-Lévy coarsened the literary veneer of both their source and their star. They utterly reworked the novel, turning it from the uplifting story of a woman dedicated to helping children to the much more problematic tale of a young child's psychological traumas in a Parisian slum. Then they taught Renaud how "to forget about her profession," so that she could genuinely interact with the urchins they picked up to play the children's roles.[16] The strategy worked. The *New York Times* reviewer found an incomparable power behind its ingenuous surface. Bardèche and Brasillach as well as Henri Fescourt would single it out for extended treatment in their respective histories of film.[17] Evidently it proposed a workable compromise between a kind of stark realism that had been largely effaced from cinema ever since the coming of sound and a moving melodrama that could have come straight from Freud's notebooks.

The realism consists first of all in long takes that make us discover the grimy surroundings in which the children of this poor *quartier* grow up: the dance hall and shabby hotels, the institutional schoolyard, all filmed in an exploratory, rather than didactic or even narrative manner.[18] Unwashed children scamper across the screen like small animals the camera is startled to glimpse. Then suddenly one of them stops and stares directly into the camera, un-

Poil de Carotte. BFI

Stately actors with genuine
children.

La Maternelle. BFI

abashed, perhaps uncomprehending. The effect arrests us. We are being addressed, perhaps accused.

A realism of another sort controls the script, that of a bad mother, her
lowlife boyfriend, the abandonment of a child, an attempted suicide, and so
on. As Erich Auerbach so elegantly demonstrated in *Mimesis*,[19] the most famous study of the subject, realism exhibits its stylistic endeavor only when
motivated by the urge to represent that which has been hidden or repressed.
Thus, no catalog of traits can ever adequately define realism, since it adapts its
strategies from case to case, depending on the codes of the period and the
situation in need of representation. By contrast, street urchins, ordinary laborers, classless men and women, when allowed an appearance in French films,
had generally been trained to conform to the culture's image of them. This is
first evident in their costumes, taken from literary and painterly conventions
more than from documentation and research.

La Maternelle fought strenuously against such conventionalism. Sandy Flitterman-Lewis insists that as a female director, Marie Epstein provided a double
resistance that saved the project from banality. Along with the better French
films of the time, *La Maternelle* strove to differentiate itself from the dominant
Hollywood model; more distinctly, it differentiated itself from standard
French films not just by its "documentary" conditions of production, but by its
orientation around the sensibility of a young female.[20] She argues that *Peau de
Pêche*, *Poil de Carotte*, and even *Zéro de conduite* (as the best of the urchin genre)
tended to replicate on a different plane the standard structures of viewing and
desiring that underlie the cinematic experience as it has developed in Western
countries. *La Maternelle*, on the other hand, gains unaccustomed access to the
sensibility of its heroine. Where Vigo's schoolboys may actively do violence
to the environment that constrains them, the little girl of *La Maternelle* can do
violence only to herself in response to similar conditions. If Flitterman-Lewis
is right, *La Maternelle*, evidently alone among films of the 1930s, represents not
just the hidden side of child abuse in French culture, but an equally hidden
mode of experience, the vast inscape of female perception and desire. This
would indeed make *La Maternelle* a quintessentially realist achievement by
every standard.

However, the very evidence that *La Maternelle* strikes out on its own can
also be used by those arguing that the film remains caught in an earlier and
rather predictable aesthetic, that of the 1920s narrative avant-garde. Three
times in the course of the film Epstein and Benoit-Lévy visibly manipulate the
camerawork so that it imitates a young girl's traumatized vision: when she
sees her mother and the new boyfriend carrying on, when she senses that Rose
(Madeleine Renaud) is threatening to leave her for the school principal, and at
the moment of her suicide attempt. The locations chosen for these sequences
are realist by one standard, yet subjectivized by another. Flitterman-Lewis
points out, for example, that the sequence with the mother and her boyfriend

La Maternelle: The child as
traumatized spectator . BFI

moves from a cabaret to a dingy street and then to the girl's tenement room,
locations that "resonate with symbolic intensity, and contribute to the highly-
charged emotional atmosphere of this portion of the film. These factors all
combine to create the sequence's profound systematicity and homogeneity,
and when this unity is coupled with the striking and poetic use of close-ups,
the sequence achieves the evocative power of a silent film, all the more so
because it is embedded within the larger cinematic context of a uniquely experimental sound film."[21]

Homogeneity in each of the key sequences is obtained by an ingenious
linking of the external world to the internal through such images as reflections
in a storefront window or in the water of a river. Optical identification accrues
from glance/reverse glance editing, foregrounded frames (the bedstead
through which an adult embrace is viewed), superimposition, shock cutting to
memories, canted angles, and so on. The shift to this heightened perception
already codes these as privileged dramatic moments that are nonetheless
folded into a single poetic experience. And the shift toward subjective vision
and the unconscious is mediated by the panoply of audiovisual effects that give
this film the "evocative power of a silent." In its pursuit of atmospheric effects
and subjectivity *La Maternelle* recalls the ideas, if not the images, of Marie
Epstein's brother, the *ciné-poète* Jean Epstein, or those of Cavalcanti, or even
Abel Gance.

From the standpoint of the history of style, then, *La Maternelle* stands out for
the intense way it mixes and still manages to homogenize its documentary
point of view with moments of intense subjectivity. But such an alternation
was already visible in *Poil de Carotte*, which opens with a lengthy exploratory
traveling shot of the dingy rural house that will suffocate the irrepressible
young boy. Only later does this same camera cut into extreme close-ups of the
boy's face, particularly in his suicide scene. This kind of interplay between

contextual conditions and the feelings of central characters forms one of the prime conquests of the 1920s, a conquest Marie Epstein and Benoit-Lévy had already put to use beautifully in *Peau de Pêche*, with its extensive superimpositions, close-ups, and other signifiers of poetic reverie.

That *La Maternelle* employs handy rhetorical devices to produce its intense effects should not be held against it. Compared to Pabst's 1939 *Jeunes Filles en détresse*, for example, its integrity and seriousness stand out triumphant. Pabst's film never takes seriously its analogous subject matter, the abandonment of young girls. His orphans, most of them the products of divorce, also displace their affection onto a virtuous teacher at the institution that serves as the film's home base. But Pabst's editing is lax and the histrionic excesses of its many famous actors ring false. Showing off bright, curiously ornate settings fashioned by Andrejew, Pabst reproduces the standard look and morality of the 1930s, albeit in an unexpected location; bourgeois attitudes, we may rest assured, prevail in French institutions even in the absence of virtuous bourgeois parents. Flitterman-Lewis is right: *La Maternelle* shows us another side of French life altogether.

Still the film remains a problematic case, since Epstein and Benoit-Lévy had it in mind both to attract and to shock the French industry and audience with a strong dose of serious social and psychological life. Its *optique* straddles that of institutional realism (that is, realism as a venerable way of making and selling art) and corrosive realism whereby attention to the look and sound of the overlooked aspects of social life must challenge every convention, including that of traditional realism itself. In 1934 *La Maternelle* assumed this ambiguous position between two films worth examining since they represented purer alternatives staked out at the very same time: Raymond Bernard's highly traditional *Les Misérables* and Jean Renoir's most unconventional *Toni*.

Whereas vulnerable children already had a proven track record as cinematic subjects, the immigrant workers Renoir determined to deal with in *Toni* had scarcely before been tested for audience interest. And where codes of sympathetic narration, including subjective interludes, had been refined during the 1920s until audience identification could be systematically regulated, Renoir's "antigraphic," anthropological style challenged these codes, introducing a quite different audience address. *Toni* precipitated a minor scandal in bringing immigrants, those hidden laborers, center stage; but its more lasting scandal came from the way Renoir adjusted the sacred norms of French cinema to the measure of lives that, he confessed, were so foreign he could scarcely comprehend them.

The first adjustments to be made occur in the script, which should be seen less against other filmed melodramas of the period than against newspaper reportage of lurid events. In fact the project was launched by just such an account, thrust in Renoir's hand by an old friend, Jacques Mortier, who pointed out, with embellishments no doubt, its cinematic possibilities. Mortier was particularly convincing because he had been chief of police in the Martigue area at the time. With the solicitude of another friend, producer Pierre Gaut, Renoir dared to let his script take its shape from the symptomatic yet bizarre real-life drama of desperate love and murder within an exploited community.

As a challenge to the hothouse environment of the studios, where, we must recall, even La Maternelle needed to be shot, Renoir determined to reenact this sordid drama just where and as it had occurred ten years before.[22] So as not to pictorialize the "primitive animality" of an incident of nearly naked instinct, Renoir did what he could to reduce his role from director to that of interested outsider or chronicler.[23] Letting the terrain and the drama retain their distinctive and craggy shapes, he was intent to approach both as far as possible in the manner of the ethnographer, or at the very least that of the itinerant photographer: "Our ambition was that the public ought to imagine that an invisible camera had filmed certain parts of a conflict without the human beings unconsciously drawn into this action being aware of it themselves."[24]

Toni: Craggy landscape, craggy drama. CF

Léon Moussinac was relieved that Renoir had avoided "schematizing" the drama in the conventional cinematic way.[25] He was particularly impressed that Renoir had refrained from vulgarizing the accents of his characters to play up to his audience the way Pagnol, in the tradition of Zola, Hardy, and Dickens, was prone to do. Rather than exoticize provincial peoples and foreigners, making them curious or cute, Renoir would ask his actors—who were in fact provincial—to express themselves in their accustomed way, according them "their simple human dignity," without recourse to sophisticated (and always conventional) psychology. Bazin was certain that the objective, nonpsychological treatment of actors accounts both for the film's roughness—its defects—and for its claim to be the primary forerunner of Italian neorealism.[26]

In an offhand remark about the production of the film, Renoir mentioned his growing friendship with the photographer Henri Cartier-Bresson,[27] and with *Toni* one can note a more considered photographic sensibility than in Renoir's earlier sound films. Renoir was still committed to the preeminence of acted drama certainly, abandoning his early "searching concerns [that were] above all plastic." But by the time of *Toni*, indeed even before shooting *Madame Bovary*, he endorsed a method of treating actors—professional and non-professional alike—that depended on a new photographic style. He suggests that the filmmaker consider it his job to "make a documentary" about actors "as he would make one about an animal in nature." Renoir recognized immediately that this attitude would promote the view that humankind is caught in a mechanism of social and natural destiny, and would be "contrary to the fundamental ideas of the dominant film industry."[28] But the quasi-anthropological experiments Cartier-Bresson had tried out during his important trip to North Africa no doubt inspired him and probably drew him to consider the contemporaneous work of Elie Lotar, André Kertesz, and Brassaï. This was the period of the journal *Minotaure* with its strong ethnographic stance. It was also the moment of Luis Buñuel's *Las Hurdes*. Renoir's Spanish set designer, Jean Castanier, would have kept him abreast of Buñuel's extraordinary project, a project like Renoir's that scorned the Paris studios in addressing subjects found on real locations.[29] Of course Buñuel's notion of "addressing a subject" might be termed "sadistic," his camera a sharp probe that prods the poor people and animals of the region in their most sensitive spots, whereas Renoir's cultivates his subject solicitously.

It may be too extreme to attribute a genuinely ethnographic impulse to *Toni*, but the term brings up Renoir's singular interest in the heterogeneity of the medium. Where standard entertainment films feature individual elements in a series of attractions strung together, and where the developing poetic realist aesthetic aimed to coordinate all elements into a single, orchestrated feeling, Renoir sought to force the possibilities of mismatched elements. The best example illustrating this approach in *Toni* was censored from the release print. After she has shot Albert, Josepha, aided by Toni, plans to wheel the corpse into the quarry as though it were her laundry. Along the way some poor Corsicans happen by and keep them company singing a jaunty tune. What the censors perceived as "callous" and "brutal"[30] was precisely the irony of passion in the gentle countryside, an irony heightened both by the carefully composed shot of a traditional topos, "the laundress," and by the singing of the workers. Renoir wanted our eyes and ears to be struck by the freshness of the lives of the working class. However, our knowledge that Albert lies dead underneath the fluffy pile, and that he is about to be disgorged onto the rocks,[31] would unsettle the scene with an irony played out less densely elsewhere in the film, an irony based on an active social analysis achieved through the "socialization of space."[32] Given the invisibility of the camera to the action (a tactic Renoir learned from photographers like Cartier-Bresson) and given the deep focus of the film's images of life in the quarry, Toni becomes merely one laborer among many, and his tragic tale a simple statistic bound to be repeated by other migrants coming north to the Martigues.

To say that *Toni* refuses to moralize is one way of introducing the heritage of naturalism that Renoir explicitly cites as the major aesthetic influence in his life. His sympathy for the exploited immigrants of southern France never encourages Renoir to motivate their habits and passions. Indeed in the drama of patriarchal control over virginity, and in the economy of sex this founds, one can sense that Renoir feels he has latched onto a structure that covertly rules more refined cultures. This is not far from Zola's project; but where Zola inflated his prose to the size of the passions that so fascinated him, Renoir's measured, ethnographic attitude keeps this film both smaller and "truer" to its situation than grand naturalist novels that put the spectacular resources of their medium behind their investigation into the human animal.

This attitude is also what separates Marcel Pagnol and Jean Renoir in 1934. Both worked in the south of France with regional stories and regional performers. Both were happy to acknowledge the impact of naturalist novelists like Emile Zola or Alphonse Daudet. But where Pagnol sang a modern saga of the south attracting worldwide audiences with local cadences and charming folk characters, Renoir fought his literary instincts and, if we can use the term, brought a documentary realism to a world he was quite happy to treat as foreign.

Toni is a touchstone of realism in the gestating poetic realist formula; until Malraux's *Espoir* (shot in 1939) French cinema would not come close to such a concerted attempt at the sheer description of a subject set solidly out in the material world. Compared to the much warmer *La Maternelle*, *Toni* kept a clear and unusual distance from its sad tale, and for this it had minimal immediate impact. Like *L'Atalante*, which was shot the same year, it caused a stir only among critics ready to listen to the small, distinct voices of prophets of films to come.

In ignoring *Toni* the French were not giving up on realism altogether, only on Renoir's stringent version of it. The industry still proclaimed its preeminence in this domain, despite Feyder's sojourn in Hollywood. In the first years of sound Raymond Bernard replaced Feyder as the country's main hope for a viable and traditional realist cinema. Son of the prolific playwright Tristan Bernard, he has come down to us as "un directeur à l'américaine"[33] for his ability to work in multiple genres and with projects involving large budgets and casts of stars. His first sound venture, *Faubourg-Montmartre*, explores the seedy milieu of novelists Pierre Mac Orlan and Francis Carco and of the photographer Brassaï. Its melodramatic treatment of two sisters, one good and the other bad, relies more on atmosphere than on dialogue or plot twists. In this

Faubourg-Montmartre: The seedy milieu of Francis Carco. CF

it lines up with *La Petite Lise* and with Carco's own *Paris la nuit*, all three shot in 1930, all three experimenting with carefully selected ambient sound, all three showing the somber influence of German visual design.

Faubourg-Montmartre convinced Emile Natan, Pathé's co-head, that Bernard could be trusted with that studio's grandest project to date, an adaptation of Roland Dorgelès's World War I pacifist novel *Les Croix de bois*. This was an industry event of the first order. Importantly it was also thought to represent the height of French realist cinema. Pathé, which had refused to try to sustain Grémillon's *La Petite Lise* because of its unorthodox use of the medium and its implacable fatalism, built an enormous campaign for the downbeat *Les Croix de bois* because World War I topics remained popular, and because this film featured broad storytelling techniques, spectacle, and a warm humanist message. The ads focused on the authenticity of the wartime re-creation. Reporters were invited to visit the battleground where much of the action would take place, naturally a historic battle site near Reims. The French army supplied extras, materiel, and expertise.[34] In this way the cinema could lay claim to leaving behind the protected kingdom of its studios and the tiny world of boulevard theater for a novel based on the greatest of tragedies history had known, photographed on the very grounds where it had occurred.

Natan meticulously planned the film's world premiere for the League of Nations in Geneva; he staged its first Parisian exhibition at the Moulin Rouge in front of Paul Doumer, the chief of state, and other invited dignitaries. *Les Croix de bois* claimed to speak to the Western world about the immorality of war. Beyond its topic, the technical staging of battle scenes set new standards of verisimilitude, even after the remarkable gains the year before by two celebrated war films, *Westfront 1918* and *All Quiet on the Western Front*. Bernard's nearly newsreel look came not only from location shooting and audacious pyrotechnics, but from the authentic appearance and acting of stars and extras, every one of whom was required to be a veteran. So successful was this recreation that, according to Lenny Borger, the Fox Corporation purchased the North American rights to *Les Croix de bois* at a high price but with no intention of distributing the film, despite its extremely successful runs in many countries. Instead Fox archived it in their "stock shot" collection for later use. Cannibalized, its battle sequences reappeared in the body of war films by John Ford (*The World Moves On*, 1934) and Howard Hawks (*The Road to Glory*, 1936).[35]

Realist in topic and visual design, *Les Croix de bois* employed a dramaturgy owing little to theatrical norms. Less a struggle of wills and language than a dialogue between characters and the hellish surroundings we see from their point of view, *Les Croix de bois* stands in a tradition of "intimate epics" inaugurated in cinema by *Birth of a Nation*. Spectacle underwrites and inflates the

Les Croix de bois: The tradition of intimate epic. CF

sentiments of the characters who draw the audience into a pathetic mise-en-scène. Clearly indebted to novels like those of Victor Hugo, this kind of cinematic realism ratifies the melodramatic through a display of history that is both massive and yet subordinate to the emotions it brings to a few characters and to the millions of spectators identifying with those characters.

Defined as the spectacle of misery, cinematic realism reached an apex in Bernard's next film for Pathé, an adaptation of Hugo's *Les Misérables*. An immense tripartite production lasting over five hours, *Les Misérables* must be considered France's most official film production since Abel Gance's *Napoléon*.

If one can believe the newspapers of the day, so great were the expectations surrounding this film that virtually every French citizen could identify the famous actors incarnating the still more famous characters (Harry Baur as Jean Valjean, Charles Vanel as Javert, Florelle as Fantine, Charles Dullin as Thénardier, and so on). Yet the spectacle of history emerges as the equal of these stars and Bernard deserves the praise he received for balancing intimate sentiments with fabulous longshots of Paris in uproar. Like Griffith and Gance before him, he achieves, through alternating montage, a multiperspectival drama that accelerates to a sublime and transcendent finale.[36]

Despite—or indeed because of—its grandeur, Bernard's *Les Misérables* represents quite an older *optique*, sustaining its putative realism on the grand ideas of justice and history that fill so many of the novel's pages. From the point of view of film history, then, this is the *optique* of Hugo, one explicitly subscribed to by Griffith and Gance, but one that was hardly adequate to the complexities of the contemporary political and social situation or to twentieth-century developments in the novel, photography, and the other arts. Nevertheless, and

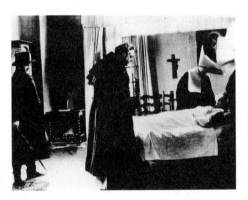 

Les Misérables. BFI   The *optique* of a quainter realism.   *Les Misérables.* CF

symptomatically, the industry (and most critics living off that industry) saluted Bernard for harnessing the cinema to serve Hugo, while at the same moment they were decrying Jean Renoir's misuse of Flaubert in *Madame Bovary*, a film whose material realism (props, tempo, acting) appeared neither uplifting nor spectacular. Almost to confirm their differing sensibilities and ambitions, while Renoir was in the south of France directing unknowns in *Toni*, Bernard had moved on to another favorite novel, Alphonse Daudet's comedy *Tartarin de Tarascon*, where he relished the opportunity to work with France's most famous star, Raimu. Although his 1937 *Le Coupable* would try to disturb France's moral complacency,[37] Bernard apparently considered realism to be merely one genre among many. As far as he was concerned, its importance peaked with the premiere of *Les Misérables*.[38]

By happenstance, however, its premiere brought *Les Misérables* directly into the political arena, despite the wishes of Bernard, who preferred that his film open to a public appreciative of Hugo's timeless ideas and his own careful rendering of these. In fact it opened to a volatile throng stirred up by the Stavisky Affair and ready to use the energy of this or any occasion to mount a political reaction.[39] Alexandre Stavisky had just recently committed suicide (or was it an assassination?) after being exposed for incredible financial embezzlements that directly involved several government agencies. Paris was alive with suspicions and gossip, so much so that a key actor in the Stavisky drama was cheered as he entered the Marignan theater to attend *Les Misérables*. The film itself was cheered when its dialogue brought up the "sickness of the Republic," and when the heroic students of 1832 were shown putting up barricades. Reviews of the film could not resist commenting on its political overtones, even if Bernard had planned none. Two days later on 6 February 1934 the bloodiest riots since the Commune of 1870 erupted in Paris, pitting protofascist vigilantes against leftists who began marching arm in arm in what already looked like a "Popular Front." In its 11 February issue *L'Illustration*, a high-circulation news magazine, followed seven pages of graphic pictures about the public slaughter with four full pages devoted to *Les Misérables*. The textual description of the riots was written by Robert de Beauplan who also reviewed the film, making plain the rapport among social injustice, social upheaval, and the healing powers of forgiveness. But the rapport that interests us is the one linking political events and the movies of the day. Even the entertainment daily *Comoedia* featured a picture of a burning bus at the place de la Concorde on page 1. The back page, however, concerns cinema news of the week and does not mention the riots directly, yet the two main essays, juxtaposed as they are, foretell a new and stronger relation of cinema to realism. Featured on the page is an eloquent essay on *Les Misérables*, presumably *Comoedia*'s last homage to the film that had dominated its back page all week. Entitled "L'Image et l'idée," it praises Bernard for having retained the proper perspective by keeping his photography in check while foregrounding Hugo's sentiments. *Les Misérables*, the piece concludes, "is a film of lofty ideas where the soul of the spectator can meet that of the great poet whose wisdom is still relevant today." And still "salable," the critic could have added.

Just beneath this essay in smaller print and only two inches long hangs a tail strong enough, in my view, to suspend upside down this historic issue of *Comoedia*:

> *La Rue sans nom* will be a film attracting passionate discussion as it opens at the Studio des Ursulines. . . . No Parisian theater is better placed for a film of this sort. For *La Rue sans nom* is an entirely new kind of production, one in which an often audacious realism examines the hidden lives of the inhabitants of those leprous hovels that you sometimes still encounter on the edge of the city.

February 1934. *Les Misérables* is dutifully saluted as a film in the great tradition
of serious ideas and noble sentiments, while out on the streets other sentiments are engaged in a material struggle for power. And in the Studio des
Ursulines (where Buñuel premiered *Un Chien andalou*, and where, one critic
reminds us, *Joyless Street* and *The Tragedy of the Street* had played almost a
decade earlier) another representation of Paris demands attention, not because
of its size or its ideas, not even because of its sentiments. *La Rue sans nom* quite
simply marks the arrival of an *optique* that for the rest of the decade will
struggle to replace literary realism in the grand style.[40] One of its reviewers
declares *La Rue sans nom* to be a new species of film altogether, and names it
"poetic realist." How apt that this film shot in Parisian streets should be saluted
the very days those streets were so contested, and that the birth of poetic
realism should coincide with the birth date of the Popular Front. In a decade
when, generally speaking, cinema can be said to have hidden from politics, we
must remember February 1934. For the anguish of this moment wrenched the
nation's consciousness like nothing else since World War I, and as in so many
other realms, the stakes of art and of cinema were abruptly altered.

THE CINEMA AND MILITANT POLITICS

The twin conception early in 1934 of the Popular Front and poetic realism has
encouraged the belief that a powerful cinema for once participated in developing a social consciousness with consequences in 1936 for politics and for aesthetics alike. Georges Sadoul, deeply involved in both arenas, could only imply
that the maturing of a coalition of workers, students, intellectuals, and the
liberal segment of the middle class should accompany the maturation of a
public hungry for a serious cinema taking on serious issues.

But this appraisal has been undercut by allegations first concerning the size
and popularity of poetic realism and, second, concerning its political indiffer-
ence, even its latent rightism. My study hopes partially to vindicate poetic
realism by developing for it an enlarged cultural context. While certainly not
the cinematic wing of an expanding political will, neither was it isolated from
the issues of its day and the tone those issues cast across an increasingly anxious society. The relation was, in fact, highly nuanced.

Optimism about a heightened political role for the cinema draws breath
from the Popular Front's evident interest in culture. Shortly after it came to
power, the new government instituted the Ministry of Sports and Leisure and
expanded the scope and power of the Ministries of Culture and Education, the
latter under the wunderkind Jean Zay. Largely because the Popular Front is
remembered as "the party of the people's happiness,"[41] its Sports and Leisure
operations, under Léo Lagrange, became the most visible legacy of the era.
Paid vacations, shortened work weeks, offices of tourism, and a playground

of sanctioned outdoor activities were instituted. Cinema's association with it suggests its own vigor. Lagrange divided his office into four committees: Spectacles, Culture, Fresh Air, and Tourism. The latter two committees made fantastic strides in the short period before World War II, whereas Culture and Spectacles, by most accounts,[42] remained areas of largely unfulfilled aspiration, no doubt because these butted up against entrenched commercial industries. Still, the aspirations, at least as professed by Lagrange, were heady:

> Up to the present in France, nothing has been done for the cinema to be used nationally as a social means of transcending class and education. Children, workers, peasants thus absorb without choice and under the most deplorable conditions an irregular assortment of films, many of which are inspired by the basest of sentiments. Therefore the cinema, which could be a marvelous instrument of popular culture if it were used with purpose, must often be considered (what use is there to deny it) as one of the countercurrents against this culture. . . . My wish is that the cinema, this marvelous leisure time activity, become instrumental in the intellectual and moral formation of the masses.[43]

Statements such as these have encouraged historians to view the upgraded status of cinema in 1936 with enthusiasm. Elizabeth Strebel[44] salutes a string of events coinciding with the arrival of the socialist government, including the release of Soviet films in July 1936 (*The Youth of Maxim, Sailors from Kronstadt*), the inauguration of radical newsreels, the victory of the unions over the producers in labor negotiations, and the flurry of feature films deemed populist (by Renoir, Le Chanois, Grémillon, Benoit-Lévy, even Marc Allégret).

But Lagrange's language betrays a patronizing attitude toward the cinema and its audience. Naturally he must express the hope that French cinema would thrive as an industry; just as naturally he must promise to find ways to support serious works of quality. It is clear, however, that cinema would not be treated with the concern the Soviets had given it in the 1920s, for example, or, more to the point, with the care the French authorities continued to display toward the legitimate theater. In Blum's reorganized bureaucracy, cinema was separated from the theater and the other arts, and its status as an adolescent pastime was formalized when it was lodged within the Ministry of Sports and Leisure. Thus the Blum regime, professedly concerned with the cinema, continued to demean it as endemically moronic, even after *Le Crime de Monsieur Lange* and *La Vie est à nous* had played a role in bringing that regime to power. Perhaps militancy in the popular arts is feared no matter who is in power.

Unable or unwilling to initiate major changes directly in an industry that appeared at once large and feeble, the government felt that its most progressive stance was to widen the perpetual rift between producers and production personnel. Their strategy aimed less at fostering new sorts of films than at redressing workers' grievances, which included, by the way, disgruntlement over the excessive sums paid actors. The government took some satisfaction when the film industry was hard hit by the strikes that immediately followed Blum's election. And it did not make special provisions for the cinema sector when the Matignon accords in which these strikes resulted were drawn up, despite the particular onus these would place on filmmaking practice. For example, the new forty-hour work week effectively proscribed a producer's right to schedule production in the most economical way (pushing for the completion of a scene by working overtime or on Sunday, let's say). Meanwhile a governmental commission, headed by Jean-Michel Renaitour, was commissioned to collect information from all sectors of the industry, paying special attention to exhibitors and distributors. To the many filmmakers who had fought for socialism, the Renaitour Report[45] proved that the cinema would be treated not as a cultural resource but like any other industry. They could expect no special government support in their concern to bring about a more socially responsive cinema. In fact sentiments like Lagrange's were powerless to stabilize production or to promote politically relevant movies. For Lagrange's Ministry of Sports and Leisure could not stand up against the Ministry of Finance, which saw the cinema in quite different terms. Gérard Talon goes so far as to describe a virtual conspiracy between the banks and the government during the Popular Front period that kept French cinema in arrears, a conspiracy most visible in the treatment of the bankrupt Gaumont-Films-Aubert, which owed hundreds of millions of francs to one of the government's chief creditors, the Banque nationale du crédit. The fact that Louis Aubert served the opposition party as a member of the National Assembly has not gone unrecognized.[46]

To top it off, the Blum regime, which had come to power with the imprimatur of an unprecedented coalition of leftist artists and intellectuals, horrified many of its most ardent supporters by continuing the policy of censorship that had kept a film like *Zéro de conduite* from reaching the screen.[47] Ironically, Jean Zay, the Popular Front's forward-looking minister of education, upheld the banning of *La Vie est à nous* from commercial distribution. It was alleged that Popular Front censorship of the movies was more stringent than that of the government it had just replaced.[48]

Since the new government evidently treated the medium as immature, no national cinema responding to the new politics of the "Popular" Front was conceivable. Those dedicated to such an ideal needed to persist in the guerrilla tactics of "cinéma engagé." And they did so by exploiting alliances forged since 1934, when the militant fringe of the industry joined forces with the propaganda wings of various leftist organizations to develop an alternative film life.

In the context of French culture as a whole and of the cinema sector in particular, this militant alternative remained pitifully small and inconsequential. Nevertheless, its very existence, together with its impressive roster of participating intellectuals, has lifted its red flag high over the period.[49] This situation duplicates the one we have had to face regarding poetic realism where the magnitude of critical awareness outstrips the number of films made and their popular appeal. In the case of politically engaged films, the issue of popularity must be put aside altogether, since most of the few films made and distributed outside the standard system found their way only to the union halls and *ciné-clubs* of a couple of urban centers. (Adherents to these clubs that sprouted as part of the newly established Maisons de la culture numbered thirty thousand at most.) On the critical front, the communist journal *Ciné-Liberté* lasted less than a year (six issues in toto), scarcely entering the national discourse about the future of cinema.

Even had this journal and these films made their way into the mainstream, however, their potency would necessarily have been diluted. Marginal by choice, they played a role analogous to that of the Parti Communiste during this epoch. Recall that after being instrumental in bringing the Popular Front government to power, the Communists voluntarily withdrew from direct connection with it, refusing to accept positions in the cabinet so that they could militate from the outside, stirring up strikes and furthering the radicalization of the country by remaining an uncompromising bastion of workers' interests.

Ciné-Liberté promised to march back up the mountain of engagement that had been scaled at the end of the 1920s by Les Amis de Spartacus, the *ciné-club* directed by Léon Moussinac and Jean Lods, both members of the Parti Communiste, that counted twenty thousand or more in its Parisian membership, and that showed Soviet films to audiences of a size even greater than that until the nervous police authorities suppressed them altogether.[50] The fall-off from this apex had been precipitous. Partly because of the expense involved in sound technology, as well as the impracticability of distributing sound films to alternative viewing sites, the number of independent radical films dwindled in the first years of the decade. Yves Allégret's 1931 *La Pomme de terre*, with the Prévert brothers playing roles in a Marxist parable, stands as the most memorable.[51] A planned program of such films came about only well after the union of antifascist writers and artists (the AEAR) issued a call for broad and cooperative action following the bloody marches of February 1934, and by this time even Moussinac had largely despaired of the cinema as a primary political organ and had embraced worker's theater and general cultural "animation" instead.

The AEAR and its journal *Commune* (the first founded in 1932, the second in mid-1933) applied the force field that drew together, instigated, and coordinated the cultural activities that shaped the Popular Front. One should expect a large contingent of the film community to have been in this vanguard, but Jean Vigo was the only cinéaste to sign their original appeal for a united Popular Front following the February 1934 riots.[52] And he did so as he went into the hospital to die. Once underway, however, the cultural wing of the Popular

Front movement quickly attracted filmmakers and cinephiles. Within a year the ACI (Alliance du Cinéma Indepéndent) marched alongside numerous fraternal cohorts promulgating resistance to fascism in virtually every realm of culture. At first the ACI limited itself to lobbying for an end to censorship while it developed alternative exhibition venues. Its real goal, though, was the fostering of significant new political films, like the famous one undertaken by the Parti Communiste before the elections in 1936, *La Vie est à nous*. The ACI marked the event of this extraordinary production by adopting the name Ciné-Liberté chosen by the Communist Paul Vaillant-Couturier. Among its active leaders were Renoir, Henri Jeanson, Gaston Modot, Raymond Bussières, and Jean-Paul Le Chanois. A small but complete film center, Ciné-Liberté followed Vaillant-Couturier's successful experiment with Radio-Liberté. On 20 May 1936, that is, in the midst of the governmental takeover by Léon Blum, there appeared the first issue of the journal *Ciné-Liberté*, under the joint editorship of Renoir, Jeanson, and Moussinac, happy to return after two years' absence to the arena of cinema under more auspicious conditions.

Just as no one should overestimate the real consequence of France's leftist film community, neither should one underestimate the political savvy and ambition of *Ciné-Liberté* despite its brief life. Aside from the obligatory editorials against censorship, the bulk of its six pages devote themselves to practical initiatives by announcing debates and screenings and by rendering advice on technical matters of amateur production and on the logistics of running *ciné-clubs*. Over a hundred industry technicians, we are told, have volunteered to answer written questions relating to 16-mm filmmaking. As for the clubs, upon request a print of *La Vie est à nous* would be sent anywhere in the country. Nearly identifying itself with this film, *Ciné-Liberté* invited all new subscribers to a special screening at which Renoir, Jeanson, and Louis Aragon promised to speak.

As its first issue makes plain, the success of *Ciné-Liberté* (the organization and journal alike) was tied to the fame and energy of Jean Renoir, unquestionably the moral gravitational center of the leftist film community. He took responsibility for the magazine's inaugural essay on Chaplin's *Modern Times*. *La Vie est à nous* is reviewed on page 2 in bold print and with bolder praise, just beneath a favorable notice given to *Le Crime de Monsieur Lange*. *Ciné-Liberté* underscored that film's brilliant caustic effect by running several letters from readers commenting on the sophisticated and exuberant reception it received at various Parisian theaters. On 20 June, in a column innocuously entitled "Suggestions," Renoir demands the full nationalization of the industry, eliminating distributors so that filmmakers might reach their audiences directly. His views today sound naive and utopian, but still freshly inspiring. Their effect must have been keen during the strikes that shut down the studios on 8 June. During these heady weeks, Renoir together with Prévert and their friends in the

Groupe Octobre and Ciné-Liberté sensed themselves fighting to radicalize the union and to bring about an utterly new system of filmmaking within the new government.

As we know, the government heeded *Ciné-Liberté* in nothing but their support of the union against producers. After the optimism of the 2 June issue, the lead essay of the third issue, 20 July, rings with disillusion: "We want to see *Zéro de conduite.*" How could this new government from which so much was expected and to whose good sense Renoir had just appealed in the name of art and of the people, persist in banning a legendary film like Vigo's? *La Vie est à nous* was next on the censor's list, triggering Jeanson's most virulent attack on "our beloved and spiritual minister, Jean Zay."

Meanwhile Ciné-Liberté pursued its goals on other fronts. After expanding its circuit of politicized *ciné-clubs* to nearly every arrondissement in Paris and to more than ten cities, it coordinated a "People's Newsreel" to contest the official view of the world promulgated weekly by Pathé news. By autumn, Ciné-Liberté could boast that its production cooperative had graduated from newsreels to short documentaries and that it would embark on small fictional ventures as a prelude to making features. *La Marseillaise* was announced in a special issue of *Ciné-Liberté* early in 1937, although by that time, the fervor of the journal and the group had cooled. Indeed this would be the final appearance of *Ciné-Liberté. La Marseillaise*, advancing more on momentum than on passion, would carry the memory of this journal along with it into the dark days of the Popular Front's demise.[53]

Despite its declamatory rhetoric and its unshakable purpose, Ciné-Liberté never tried to promote a coherent attitude toward film style. Like so many other cultural endeavors of the Popular Front, Ciné-Liberté was more concerned to democratize art than to radicalize it.[54] Hence the interest in clubs and 16-mm production; hence the primary concern over censorship. Only one article in the full run of the journal directly addressed the issue of cinematic style, Jean Cassou's "From Avant-garde to Popular Art," which appeared in November of 1936.[55] Cassou reminds all those who called themselves experimentalists over the past ten years that they should make a social virtue of their intuitive nonconformism. They ought to see in the strictures of capitalist society a perfect target for a cinema that would be formally radical, yet would simultaneously support the people in their quest to break out of the system that keeps them down.

Cassou does not say whether the people absolutely require a radical vision provided by art before they can act politically. Nothing else in the journal would suggest that *Ciné-Liberté* believed this. More likely, in the "extended hand policy" by which the Popular Front and the Parti Communiste sought to recruit as many sympathizers as possible, he was given the task to appeal to disaffected artists in an era that had lost interest in avant-garde experimenta-

tion. Indeed, alongside Cassou's serious discussion appeared a lengthy interview with Carné about *Jenny*, a shamelessly commercial production. Carné's
final word to the *Ciné-Liberté* readership is to ask them to stir up viewers in
theaters, so as to demand of producers films of better quality. Such a strategy
is much more in line with the growth of a film art movement like poetic
realism than with the intervention of a genuinely political cinema. Despite its
gruff tone, *Ciné-Liberté*'s communism was not virulent enough to affect either
the industry or film style. Buchsbaum calculates that this group was ultimately
responsible for nearly a dozen films including a single, "rather ordinary" feature, *La Marseillaise*. One might add to this another dozen shorts produced by
the Socialist Party under Marceau Pivert and a few films made by units associated with the trade unions.

In short, the movement of leftist filmmaking is strident enough to merit the
excellent studies that have sought to savor the potential of each of its completed productions, each of its fragments, and even its unrealized projects.
Still, the movement as a whole must be judged a sidelight in the history of
1930s French film. Most of those who devoted themselves to it (actors like
Gaston Modot, composers like Arthur Honegger, alongside Renoir and Jeanson) did so altruistically while they pursued careers in the mainstream industry. Crossing over to overtly propagandistic works from the acclaimed features
of the time,[56] these men and women must have wrestled with their con-
sciences as they negotiated with the ruling system that fed them and gave
them their fame.

The militant films of the period, then, few though they be, loom as the
conscience of the era and for that reason alone demand the attention they have
been given. But we cannot forget that no more than a few thousand individuals paid attention to the activities of cinema engagé. Seldom were the screenings of such films reported in the mainstream press; never was this rival mentioned by the film industry. Even the government paid it no heed. Yet the
existence of cinema engagé serves as a boundary at the opposite extreme from
the dominant entertainment cinema. Between these two—between pure entertainment and a fully social cinema—poetic realism shot up in the late 1930s.
Its popularity, particularly among foreign and literate audiences, insured widespread attention, while its seriousness tempted critics, historians, and no doubt
a percentage of ordinary spectators to view it as a revealing response to its
epoch. Even Buchsbaum must agree that a general "project of artistic justification has enshrined the admirable works of poetic realism as the signal contribution of French cinema to film history during this period."[57] From his point
of view, and momentarily from ours, however, "these [aesthetic] terms of
analysis have no relevance to an evaluation of the political films produced
during the 1930s, which certainly deserve their place in French film history of
the period even if they call for different critical criteria."

Buchsbaum's criteria, or at least the political conscience that engenders them, must inflect our sense of the value of those "admirable works of poetic realism" that are too often taken to be mere exercises in style. Sharing the confidence of neither traditional nor militant realism, what relation to the contemporary social situation could poetic realism maintain?

POETIC REALISM AND EVERYDAY LIFE AT THE MOVIES

As conceived of by critics, then and now, realism has been a decidedly ethical term for which the word "conscience" might readily substitute. Where was the conscience of French cinema during the depression, the Popular Front, the Spanish civil war, and all the other events preceding the debacle of 1940? The films we have discussed so far, those sporting a traditional realist aesthetic as well as those lobbying for direct political effect, constitute a minuscule percentage of what was made and an even smaller percentage of what was seen. Gérard Talon concludes his bitter overview of the period this way: "It is genuinely regrettable to have to state that in France there was no cinema based on everyday reality between 1936 and 1938."[58] Had there been one, it would have been edged out by distributors who insisted on films that could be sold on the basis of reactionary sentiments. This was the era of themes rather than genres, he aptly notes, and any theme capable of bringing about a knee-jerk reaction in the primarily adult bourgeois sector that dominated the audience in these years would be promoted. No wonder so many military comedies were made, so many films of the Belle Epoque and World War I periods.

Yet to dismiss French cinema collectively because in the main it put its head in the sand with regard to the public issues of the day is both crude and patronizing. Even before the *Annales* School taught us to respect and learn from the practices and products of everyday life, critics and government officials recognized that movies must serve as an important social index, possibly bearing political consequences. Why else did the Daladier and Vichy regimes ban so many works in the poetic realist corpus?

Talon would urge us to calculate the themes that recur with regularity in the period of the Popular Front, and, after recognizing, as we have, how little they have in common with that Front, to decide "according to one's political orientation that the French cinema of the '36–'38 years simply failed to 'reflect' the political and social reality of the moment or on the contrary that the general political desire of the moment was not moving in the direction of the Popular Front."[59] Calculating themes is what François Garçon has also been about in his *De Blum à Pétain*, subtitled *Cinéma et société française (1936–1944)*. Like Talon, he too inculpates French cinema as promoting reactionary and xenophobic values, precisely the values that would be officially instantiated under Vichy. After all, in 1937 97 percent of all French citizens were Catholics and over half of all spectators, according to a survey taken in 1937, practiced their faith.[60] One can hardly expect producers and distributors, all members of the wealthy class, to play up socially revolutionary ideas to an audience of this constitution.

Where Talon scans the films for specific themes related to the questions of politics, Garçon examines a wider swath of ideology, ranged under the headings he borrows from Vichy: "Work, Family, and Country." Both these studies depend on, though never mention, René Prédal's 1972 *La Société française à travers le cinéma*, which sets out to be the prototype for all later "reflection studies."[61] Far more sanguine, perhaps because, working in 1972, he had been able to see fewer films, Prédal notes that few movies made between the wars set out expressly to document the social situation of their times, but that all films reflect their society to some extent and that certain films—those made by strong auteurs—are particularly invaluable indexes.[62] With the help of these auteurs (Vigo, Duvivier, L'Herbier, and preeminently Renoir), all of whom brought a conscience to the diversions their producers paid them to concoct, Prédal races across the demography and the class structure of French society to reassure us that indeed the cinema between the wars does provide an expansive, though poorly framed, portrait. Astutely, he recognizes that most films flatter or satirize the petit bourgeoisie, and that, when taking up workers, French writers and directors cannot avoid fashioning them in the image of the petit bourgeoisie, since this was easily the largest segment of the audience and the one whose values those artists implicitly understood. Garçon underwrites this view when he attributes the tertiary status of the proletariat in French cinema to a dramaturgy committed to the individual hero.[63] He notes that even when a film is set in a working-class milieu (*Gueule d'amour*, for example), the focus on the problems of a single worker (invariably played by Jean Gabin) vitiates a serious description, let alone analysis, of class conditions. Scriptwriters seemed unable to deal with mere workers, thinking of them most often as artisans (Gabin as a typesetter in *Gueule d'amour*). Bernard Eisenschitz accounts for this as a crude displacement by which French filmmakers transferred their putative concern for the working class onto social marginals.[64] No doubt the marginal is a figure every self-respecting writer and director could identify with.

To take the cinema as mirror, then, far from being a natural way to assess both the movies and their period,[65] involves more interestingly the image of those who make cinema. While it is always shocking to be shown how a social group has been misrepresented in the mirror of cinema (Jews, women, North Africans),[66] the greater shock comes from recognizing the face of those for whom such misrepresentations were exactly what fit. With this in mind, poetic realism may be said to tell us less about the unsavory milieus in which its dramas are set than about the movie theaters where French men and women drifted in and out in search of a loose community or a loss of self in nostalgia.

For poetic realist films figure a vague populism or a more vague nostalgia that became a chief function of the very institution of the cinema between the wars. These films are timely even when what they figure in their plots, dialogue, and settings is the "deception of evasion." For what else is a movie than an illusion of evasion,[67] and what else is a movie house than a place for brief encounters, for partial anonymity in a crowd, and for momentary escape—the opposite of what is claimed for the socially sanctioned legitimate theater. Taken self-consciously in this way, the reflection of social conditions that cinema provides to historians need not come down to a flat tallying up of themes whereby every film contributes in some way to a vision of the era that produced it. Taken as an index of the practices and functions of filmmaking and filmgoing, cinema's autoreflection can be seen to vary over the years, not completely in concert with social conditions, but in concert with a cultural tone that ought to belong to any full description of those conditions. Poetic realism marks an important variance in this autoreflection. Reviewers of the time seemed to understand that, and we need to follow their instincts in order to gauge the social consequences of the "evasive" *optique* of poetic realism.

In September 1936, the middle-class weekly *Pour Vous* labeled Julien Duvivier's *La Belle Equipe* "a film of popular atmosphere and social tendency . . . a populist film if this literary term can apply to the cinema."[68] Indeed this term can be, and has been, applied to the cinema, though whether *La Belle Equipe* is a Popular Front allegory is another question, one that *Pour Vous* implied in asking if "Spaak and Duvivier wanted to prove that collective life is only a beautiful illusion, or if they wanted to prove anything at all." In their minds, the film's subject is ambitious enough to merit a comparison with one of the greatest social allegories of the recent past, King Vidor's *Our Daily Bread*. And this view has generally prevailed, as can be verified by the fact that an astute distributor reissued the film in 1980, a few months before the elections that brought a socialist government into power for the first time since 1936.

    La Belle Equipe begs special attention since it addresses the issue of collective life point-blank. *Ciné-Liberté* gave its readers this plot synopsis: "Five buddies who share everything that life brings them . . . win a hundred thousand francs one day in the national lottery. Should they divide the winnings up? This 'belle équipe' decide instead to use the money in common, to purchase a ruined house along the Marne and convert it into a *guinguette du dimanche* [an outdoor café]. They set to work only to have fate descend upon them."[69] Fleshed out, this plot gives critics a chance to recite a litany of Popular Front motifs, including unemployment, Spanish immigration, the national lottery, collective ventures, and the ideology of "fresh air."[70] Moreover, when, after a mediocre initial response, the producer ordered Duvivier to replace the fatal ending with a happy one, he demonstrated for later historians a telling ambivalence in the face of the collective life that is the film's subject. For a time both versions circulated, almost as an emblem of the hesitations of the people's government in power.[71]

One is tempted, on the basis of this key film, to scan the output of the Popular Front period for other potential allegories. Not counting his didactic efforts (*La Vie est à nous* and *La Marseillaise*), from the years 1936–1937 Renoir offers us *Le Crime de Monsieur Lange*, *Les Bas-Fonds*, and *La Grande Illusion*, each of which—particularly the first—sustains ingenious political readings. Films by much lesser directors, for instance Maurice Cloche's *La Vie est magnifique* (1938), might then demand special attention, if they include appropriate topics (in this case one of the Popular Front's signal legacies, "fresh air camping"). This quest for the story of the Popular Front told in the films made during its heyday has frustrated most historians, as we have seen, primarily because of the meager corpus of relevant titles. This is the very reason Jeancolas belittled the output of the entire decade: "an ostrich cinema," he called it, hiding from the issues of the day.[72]

But the literal topicality of its films need not on its own sanctify a national cinema. Who would not recognize the difference between the postwar cinema of Italy, where the contemporary crisis brewed in neorealist movies, and, say, Hollywood's docu-dramas of the same period, or even today's televisual exploitation of current events? The fact that the end of the Third Republic was not documented, or directly reflected, in the films of the day need not disqualify as socially irrelevent the nation's cinematic output.

Even *Ciné-Liberté* understood this when it demeaned the script of *La Belle Equipe* while upholding its mise-en-scène, acting, and dialogue.[73] If a journal like *Ciné-Liberté* was not tempted to amplify a political reading of a scenario with such social overtones, we should all beware. And the director, years later, explains why: "*La Belle Equipe* has no political character whatsoever, unless every film that treats the working class must be considered leftist."[74] Commenting on this remark, Vincendeau is sure that "Duvivier is right, since populist art proposes a spectacle of the proletariat and not an analysis of class conditions."[75] She then undertakes her own analysis of this spectacle, suggesting a number of historical and psychological determinations for the unprecedented attraction Gabin's lower-class and outsider role exerted on a mass audience in a host of films, *La Belle Equipe* above all.

Because it hedges its bets by whispering, yet never quite claiming, political themes, *La Belle Equipe* represents the ambiguous roles film could play in this period, indicating along the way that its social pertinence lies less in such themes than in the authenticity of its particularly engaging "spectacle of the proletariat." Aside from the few genuinely didactic efforts of the political parties, most of the "discussable" films of the 1930s can be understood to waffle more or less in the manner of *La Belle Equipe* between timeless entertainment and quite timely reference or sensibility. A melodramatic vehicle for stars playing characters in the throes of standard moral problems, *La Belle Equipe*

La Belle Equipe:
Populist allegory. BFI

La Belle Equipe:
Or melodramatic star
vehicle. BFI

nevertheless grounds those problems in the specific circumstances of the day, forcing an urgency and directness in tone that even a communist critic like Georges Sadoul found so "realistic," so adult.

Sadoul wanted French cinema to play a mature cultural role. If the plots and themes disappointed him as innocuous or adolescent, he would take seriously the social milieus of the best films of the time. In a truly perceptive overview of the "new school of French realism," prepared for the November 1936 issue of *Commune*, he linked *Le Crime de Monsieur Lange* with *La Belle Equipe* for their "bursting open the sets" and letting their stories develop in locales worth paying attention to.[76] Letting realism stand for style in this way, he could praise a film like Marcel Carné's *Jenny*, despite the fact that its subject was of no real interest to Carné and could even be compared to a piece of froth like *Rigolboche* starring the music hall queen Mistinguett.[77] Carné must have appreciated Sadoul's remark, for he admitted that what he liked best about this, his first feature, were the few shots of the lovers in the poor suburbs of Paris. Carné told *Ciné-Liberté* that he hoped for a chance to do more with this sort of street atmosphere.[78] As we know, *Le Quai des brumes, Hôtel du Nord*, and *Le Jour se lève* were soon to follow.

Although committed to the Parti Communiste, Sadoul never supported a film solely on the basis of its subject matter. For instance, despite a proto-Marxist theme that Sadoul summarizes as "Revolt, the law of the slave," he rates Duvivier's 1935 *Le Golem* as arch, unconvincing, and therefore socially insignificant. Today we would say that it displays itself too gaudily and theatrically—its spectacle, more than its tale, is adolescent. Like Duvivier's life of Christ (*Golgotha*, also 1935), *Le Golem* is a genuine allegory, a genre the French have never comfortably exploited. In contrast, *La Belle Equipe* challenges its ostensible "message" with a nuanced intimacy that involves the spectator in the small details of so many of its episodes.

Prepared to take or leave the possible allegory of its plot, ready to discount its absent or feeble social analysis, I want to follow *Ciné-Liberté*, as well as Sadoul and Vincendeau, in valuing the look and sound of *La Belle Equipe* as "spectacle." Where some historians are disappointed by the film ("The Popular Front is there only as backdrop and for added color, so as to anchor the film in contemporary life. Mere decor," says one),[79] why underestimate the import of decor? Sadoul was to become an early apologist for poetic realism largely because of his confidence in the indirect power of such things as "mere decor" even in films with anodyne or regressive social views. He defended what he calls the "progeny" of Clair's *A nous la liberté* because the admittedly inadequate populist ideas of these films nevertheless urged their directors to develop a new and more intimate rapport with the audience. In a striking review of *Pépé le Moko*, Graham Greene asserts just this:

> In this film we do not forget the real subject in a mass of detail: the freedom-loving human spirit trapped and pulling at the chain. A simple subject, but fiction does not demand complex themes, and the story of a man at liberty to move only in one shabby, alien quarter when his heart is in another place widens out to touch the experience of exile common to everyone . . . we are aware (rare and unexpected delight) of a film which is really trying to translate into dramatic terms the irrelevancies, the grotesque wit, the absurd, passionate tangle of associations which make up the mind. Perhaps there have been pictures as exciting on the "thriller" level as this before . . . but I cannot remember one which has succeeded so admirably in raising the thriller to a poetic level.[80]

Greene is impressed by the palpable details that create constriction in the Casbah environment, details that are first presented in the remarkable documentary prologue as a sign of the film's authenticity. This same attention to detail makes palpable the desire for liberation in the demeanor, costume, and physiognomy of the film's star, Jean Gabin. French cinema has found the secret of realism, he believes, not in its plots, subject matter, or messages, but in the way a simple theme spreads itself across the texture of the work in such detail that the audience can physically experience on the screen what they privately worry over in everyday life.

It is this rapport with the audience that constitutes what I have termed the autoreflective character of poetic realism: virtually all the lionized films of the Popular Front—whether populist (*La Grande Illusion*) or pessimist (*Le Quai des Brumes*)—share the earnest tone Duvivier established in *La Belle Equipe* and *Pépé le Moko*. And most of these films share as well the actor who epitomized that earnestness: Jean Gabin. As easily the most indispensible player in a national cinema that depended unusually on actors,[81] Gabin has been subject to minute scrutiny. Arguably the focus of identification for an entire nation, his roles and his style condense the poetic realist *optique* into a single figure, a body, that moves on the screen.

Among the countless claims made about this figure, those that interest me concern Gabin's reversibility: the male and female attributes he alternately possesses, the confusion of his social status (as simultaneously of the working and the criminal class). For the basic ambivalence of the characters he was asked to play soon came to found, in his way of playing them, the delicious indiscernibility of the world he inhabits and invites us to join (the murkiness of the lighting, the duplicity of his enemies, the restricted vision, the whisperings). What Gabin's immense appeal "reflects," then, is less the sociology of the marginal than the very attraction of marginality, isolation, and authenticity.

In fact, as Vincendeau has shown in the definitive *Jean Gabin, anatomie d'un mythe*, the blurring of worker and criminal is first of all a holdover from nineteenth-century bourgeois class anxiety expressed in the fiction of that century.[82] Second, the increasing popularity of representation in the twentieth century (the industries of song, photography, postcard, radio, magazine, pulp fiction) engendered an aesthetic of the criminal, the worker, and the milieus both inhabit. Ingesting this tradition, Gabin added his specific style—at once laconic and explosive—to the roles and traits he took on, looming as an irresistible yet disturbing presence, whose authenticity and isolation made him morally superior. The better directors of the day learned to use him in any of his guises to invite the audience into a fictional experience of unprecedented density. Graham Greene was responding to precisely this density in his review of *Pépé le Moko*, cited above.

The lure that brings the audience into such intimacy with the characters or situations of these films was established, I have argued, by the persistent representation in this period of the antisocial urban type. In cinema this translated into codes of lighting, camera movement, editing, and acting. Gabin's acting stands, then, as the most powerful instance of the urban iconography that mushroomed during the depression. His remarkable relation to the public owes itself, beyond mere personal talent, to specific strategies of spectacle and performance one finds in the novels of Mac Orlan, the photographs of Brassaï, the "chansons réalistes" of Fréhel. Vincendeau demonstrates how lighting in these films isolates Gabin among his comrades, making his eyes the spiritual source of his body, authenticating, if not justifying, his most antisocial acts. Camera movement and editing then restore this "central" and "centered" being to a context that surrounds it concentrically. Most important to Vincendeau are the sudden performances of song into which Gabin tumbles in so many of his films, in *La Belle Equipe* and *Pépé le Moko*, to take the examples with which we began. These involve diegetic audiences who stare at him and take up the rare exuberance of feeling that gushes from him. Naturally the cinema audience joins the circle of admirers, while also remaining privy to Gabin's silent, inmost being, through identification figured by close-ups. Gabin is taken from margin to center in the course of these films, replicating in the process the social aspirations of the Popular Front that would bring the neglected and alienated lower-class individual into the center of culture. Even when he confronts an inescapable fate, Gabin can thus be seen as a social hero for the age. Vincendeau finds in the lyrics of his songs the major sentiments of the day: fresh air, happiness, and freedom, the imaginary core of the Popular Front. Here she underscores Graham Greene's intuition that *Pépé le Moko* depicts social constriction and the human struggle for liberation in a palpable way. When Greene calls such imaginary dramas "realistic," he crudely preempts Vincendeau's more subtle belief that Gabin is absolutely "relevant" to the tone of the Popular Front, to its particular imaginary.[83]

This symbiosis between (social) subject and (stylistic) treatment in films giving off the outlaw scent of poetic realism has been widened by Nataša Ďurovičová into the specifically French obsession with "crime" and the criminal hero. French cinema, she finds, distinguishes itself from other treatments of this international genre by the attention it accords the individuality, the style, of the criminal. "Crime, the transgression of the laws that regulate this world, is first and foremost a fingerprint, a signature, a sign of style."[84] This explains French pride in François Villon, Baudelaire, and Rimbaud, the unholy saints called upon by the Surrealist poets, and by novelists like Mac Orlan and Carco, in their effort to animate a moribund bourgeois world with the specter of the criminal and his milieus.[85]

With its parentage in photography and melodrama, the cinema inherited the peculiarly nineteenth-century curiosity about criminality. Zola lifted such voyeurism to a kind of respectability, but contemporaneous with him one finds a perverse interest in trials, in melodrama, and in the evidentiary status of photographs. One of the most popular displays at Mme Tussaud's wax museum, at the end of the century, was "The Life and Death of a Criminal." This display served as the basis for one of Pathé's most successful early films directed by Ferdinand Zecca in 1905. We have already seen the excitement generated, some years later, by the urban serials of Louis Feuillade. Apollinaire recognized in *Fantômas* something familiar (the poetics of crime) as well as something new (urban realism). In my view poetic realism follows from the *Fantômas* mania, offering a self-conscious ritual for a community concerned with the romance of criminality.

While such a romance may seem universal, Ďurovičová claims that the element of art gives the French version its specific quality. Not surprisingly, in her account Jean Gabin emerges as a consummate "artisan," set off by this fact from his quite different counterparts in Hollywood. James Cagney and Paul Muni are gangsters who inhabit alternative communities, criminal organizations, that combat the establishment often on equal footing. The twentieth century gave birth to them and to the peculiar dreams of wealth and power that perhaps can only come out of a democracy like that of the United States. Gabin is more traditional: emblem of French film and culture, he is a loner without a gang, in quest of self-determination, not self-aggrandizement. He comes to bad ends, but he comes to them in his own manner, that is, "artistically."

This notion of artisanal crime spilled out of the scripts of the day and into their titles, as in the amiable *Le Crime de Monsieur Lange* whose hero is both a popular artist and an assassin. He is a figure Prévert and Renoir must have identified with, a figure who shows up in many guises in the films both of them made the whole decade long. It is hard to name a Renoir film from the period wherein a loaded gun or open knife does not result in a shattering social and sexual transgression. And look at the murderers in such films: from Maurice Legrand, the painter in *La Chienne*, to Lantier of *La Bête humaine*, a passion that stems from art (a passion for an image of beauty or justice or freedom) causes them to jump the rails on which society glides. The cinema, institution of heightened experience, may tempt one to entertain such passion, to identify with it and with its consequences.

Audiences, then, might be thought to respond to the feedback whereby legitimate artistic daring and illegitimate social behavior amplify one another through the mutually reinforcing strength of authenticity that they invoke and evoke, and that the signature of the criminal and the auteur guarantee. The 360-degree pan by which Renoir renders Lange's assassination of Batala is "notorious" in film history because it boldly transgresses the rules of good filmmaking. Yet in its outlandish visibility, the pan shamelessly beckons the audience to pull the trigger with Lange.

This rapport between art and transgression exhilarated the strong filmmakers of the day who became infected with the ethos of authentic self-projection. Especially within the impersonal entertainment industry of sound film, this veneer of authenticity might go by the name of "the personal," making the artist analogous to the criminal whose personal passion and crime were so dear to the Surrealists, and evidently to a large segment of the public.

Ďurovičová intimates that the French aestheticization of private, "disorganized" antisocial behavior serves to displace the unthinkable: organized antisocial passion that might erupt as revolution or as impersonal mass murder. These latter are the crimes the media will increasingly deal with after the Second World War, when the artisanal pretense of French film has given way to the media industries to which it materially belongs. But during the interwar era, and nostalgically after that (Gabin in *Touchez pas au grisbi* 1953, for example), the French believed that their films, like their criminals, were not subject to any rules at all except those that came passionately from within.

Those critics who at the time doted on the myth of French authenticity were prophets of orthodox auteurism, for they all raised directorial style and worldview above the circumstances of production and reception.[86] Leenhardt could not have been more clear on this: "The output of a cinéaste has value so long as a unity of tone, style, and atmosphere—not to exclude a sense of artistic renewal—convey a particular way of thinking, a personal vision of the world."[87] From Leenhardt and Sadoul through Prédal, the presumption is shared that in France there has been room within the entertainment system for ambition, genius, and the clarifying conscience that transgression brings. The passionate crimes of Jean Gabin mirror not the social conditions of the times so much as the artistic passion of the directors who used him.

Look at Grémillon's *Gueule d'amour*. Although it fails to address any of the serious concerns facing France at the moment the Popular Front was falling apart and Germany was preparing an invasion, it is freighted with "concern" in an abstract sense. As director, Grémillon profits from Gabin's display of social transgression by daring to assault the genre codes French films of the time depended upon. In this way the filmmaker courts his audience as an attractive outlaw himself. *Gueule d'amour* charts the fall of Lucien (Gabin) from pride and glory to self-pity after he leaves the dashing overseas cavalry corps for ordinary life as a typesetter. Lucien's obsession with the elegant but destructive Madeleine (Mireille Balin, playing her old role from *Pépé le Moko*) stems from the imaginary relation to society that the military fosters. His identity is tied to his image as spectacle on parade. Madeleine, whom he first attracts in uniform, remains perpetually beyond him, even if her elegance is as thin as that of a kept woman. Groveling for her, Lucien loses his job and his self-respect, ultimately hiding away in a small bar that he tends near the town of his birth. Out of uniform, he no longer draws anyone's attention. Only his friendship with an old comrade in arms makes life bearable.

To what does the film owe its small claim to realism and relevance: to its survey of social layers, to its displacement of class conflict onto sexual conflict, to its occasional location shots and muted (though symbolic) decor, or to its scarcely hidden sympathy for male friendship that verges on homoeroticism in the devastating conclusion? *Gueule d'amour* is a disturbing, perverse melodrama. Madeleine's sadistic return to seduce Lucien while taunting him with her infidelity to his best friend ignites an outburst that the film has scarcely been able to contain for ninety minutes. Lucien strangles her and then pathetically confesses to his friend who, in the subdued epilogue, helps the nearly catatonic Lucien aboard a train for North Africa. This ending upset right-wing critics for its outright degeneracy, its intimation of homosexuality, and ultimately, I think, for its suggestion (already found in *Pépé le Moko* and other films) that France has become an imaginary realm available only through loss, exile, and nostalgia.

This psychoanalytic reading may not have registered with many critics and viewers. Yet the film's unusual mix of genres (the military farce, the tale of the demimonde, the populist drama) and of textures (Madeleine's gaudy apartment and silk gowns set off against dismal cheap hotels and local cafés) disturbed critics as physically and morally decrepit. Geneviève Sellier argues that *Gueule d'amour* troubles viewers because it troubles the film system, problematically inserting documentary shots, for instance, within the anthology of codified genres it samples.[88] After a completely ethereal night of love in her literally fabulous apartment, the couple walks through the Butte Chaumont park in Paris. Lucien speaks of his need to return to this park as an anchor in his life. The location shots of its famous summit and suspension bridge similarly anchor the film's rather thin melodrama. In the next scene, a camera placed on a rooftop observes workers coming out of a factory at five o'clock. In Sellier's terms, Grémillon thus forces the codes of "realism" to face up to the "real." The shock—nearly ridiculous—of such incongruity is keyed by the dramatic incongruity that has placed the utterly artificial Madeleine (bejeweled, erotic, yet elegantly diffident) beside the unpretentious laborer for whom she serves as fantasy. An affront at once to the cinema, to sexual roles,

Gueule d'amour: In the workplace. MOMA

Gueule d'amour: And, upscale, in the wrong place. MOMA

and to the social system sustaining both, the film fell to the censor's orders even before the Germans breached the frontier.

Grémillon would continue to render psychoanalytically charged melodramas in highly specific social and geographic settings. *L'Etrange M. Victor* plays out its case study along the wharf and market area of Toulon.[89] For *Remorques*, he chose his native Brittany as the backdrop to the legendary adultery between Gabin and Michèle Morgan. My point should be clear: while it demeans the term to claim such films for "social realism," neither should one bury them in the sand as "ostrich" films. Nothing is more revealing than the blindness of their characters to the social circumstances governing their plights, a blindness that a calculated "poetic" style forces us to share. Coming out of the movie theater after *Pépé le Moko*, *Gueule d'amour*, or *L'Etrange M. Victor*, audiences may have attained no clearer vision of France as it approached the end of the Third Republic, but they certainly could now identify—and identify with—an image of the emotional tone of their dying era. It was a tone one could read about in editorials and listen to in songs, but it was a tone that seemed most appropriate in the movie theaters where one treated oneself to deception and occasionally, in those films of conscience, to a spectacle of deception. Graham Greene was not alone in feeling these latter to be, despite their generally juvenile Oedipal tales, the most adult films one could see at the time.

Figures
of the Poetic

A TYPOLOGICAL APPROACH TO POETIC REALISM

When invoking poetic realism, critics and historians have been far more sensitive to the qualifier "poetic" (a term linked to style) than to the substantive "realism" (a term linked to subject matter). For French cinema may have failed to develop any sort of sustained or profound social vision and analysis, but the movies it exported just prior to World War II undeniably contributed to the artistic repertoire of international cinema.

The term *optique* involves a study of elements of style and of genre, but goes beyond these in aiming to distinguish the specific type of experience offered by a set of films to the public. The poetic realist sensibility might provisionally be likened to an artistic reflection on a limited set of motifs. The motifs (elements of genre) have been thought to carry a modest realism, while the meditation (the style) has been lionized as subtly introspective, hence poetic. For instance we shall see how motifs like "Africa" or "the femme fatale" provoke and sustain specific textures of lighting, composition, and so on. No doubt a sociology of the cinema would catalog films according to motif, describing perhaps the place women occupied in French film, or French attitudes toward their colonies. My approach, however, takes up these elements only to the extent that they affect the more historical dimension of the cinematic experience that makes a film worth making or looking at in the first place.

Dwelling on the motifs of these films, or at least on the tone they set, quickly forces a complex of related issues to the fore. Although there are many ways to film any given subject, the choice of subject always carries with it an implicit

OPPOSITE PAGE:
Le Quai des brumes. BFI

understanding of the audience sensibility to be engaged. Thus while poetic realism includes several stylistic variants (usually identified by directorial signatures: Duvivier, Grémillon, Carné) and at least two major topics (the populist and the fatal), the movement coheres in the way that it conceives its audience. Georges Sadoul intuited this when he grouped several films that I have already discussed as precious precursors of poetic realism: "In the desert of mediocrity, 1930–34, the only films that gave a hope in France were all marked by dark pessimism: *La Chienne, La Petite Lise, La Maternelle, Poil de Carotte, Jeunesse, La Rue sans nom.*"[1]

One can quickly distinguish the motifs of these films (abandoned children or vulnerable girls forced to grow up within impoverished milieus), the audience appeal of such subject matter ("dark pessimism," tinged with a large measure of masochism), the aesthetic tone capable of engendering this appeal (an apparently harsh realism redeemed by a certain delicate poetry), and finally the specific stylistic features that embody the aesthetic tone (these vary according to director). Such interdependence of aspects, ruling a number of personal styles and tied to a specific audience appeal at a given moment, is exactly what I have sought to include in the term *optique*.

Poetic realism constitutes an *optique* quite different from that of the theatrical entertainments that numerically dominated the decade. It differs as well from that of the more strident and didactic social films of the time that appeal to us critics and historians today far more than they did to the public that first had the chance to see them. Take Renoir's films made within the umbrella of the Popular Front. They represent a strong, analytic approach, one that poses problems and lays out dramatic solutions bearing potentially political consequences. A certain directness and rationality can be felt even in the wonderfully farfetched *Le Crime de Monsieur Lange* because of the multiple perspectives with which Renoir, like a surveyor, calculates the social world. The classics of poetic realism, on the other hand, are best characterized by their indirection and by their often shameless appeal to the emotions more than to the intelligence of the audience. The heroes of these films are passive characters awaiting their fate rather than choosing it, the way Amédée Lange chose his, or the good citizens represented in *La Marseillaise* chose theirs in 1794, or the working-class characters of the aptly titled *La Vie est à nous* promise and threaten to choose theirs.

While it is dangerous to rely too heavily on binarisms such as active/passive heroes or analytic/emotional styles, two advantages turn this into a worthwhile gambit. First, when we considered types of "realism" in the 1930s that might help distinguish and account for poetic realism, an implicit categorical scheme based on class proved useful. The standard movies that we continue to label "theatrical" or "entertainment" clearly aimed at uneducated mass audiences, while leftist avant-garde films tried to link intellectuals to the more committed wing of the labor unions. In this scheme, the more ambitious narrative films, also thought of as the export or "quality" cinema, were presumably meant to attract a large but discriminating audience, primarily middle-class and educated. In turning now away from realism and to the "poetic" possibilities of cinema in France, we can complicate these categories based on class appeal with those an earlier generation would have based on gender appeal. Whether or not audiences of all classes and both genders actually attended all films indiscriminately, these theoretical categories permit us to imagine various types of appeal and different styles of address that effectively constitute the social range of cinematic experience in the decade.

Largely on account of their inadequacy, these cultural stereotypes require a deeper analysis of the different forms of experience that various films offered. The films that concern us might best be identified as "figural," so as to oppose them to the ostentation of theatrical movies, the clever intrigues of highly plotted dramas, and the moralizing didacticism of the few leftist films one can come up with. The "figural" properties of poetic realism point to the nature of its appeal, though not to the empirical audience that hearkened to that appeal.

Roland Barthes stands behind my use of the term "figure." In *S/Z* he differentiates figure from "person" as an alternative possibility for "character" in narrative fiction.[2] Realist fiction is founded on an interplay of characters who are constructs of a set of conventions he dubs the "semic code," the code that enables us to describe them as rich or on the make, as moral or self-serving, as vulnerable or powerful, and so forth. Interacting with other narrative conventions, the semic code allows characters to develop, become educated, and reach the fullness of their own personhood. It has been said that the notion of the person is the cornerstone of the novel and that its multiple techniques ultimately turn back on establishing, celebrating, or criticizing this unacknowledged God of the modern era. In search of variety in literature and for alternatives in ideology, Barthes called on the "figure" as a force to dislodge the person from fiction, and to depersonalize the literary enterprise. In pre- and postrealist writing (in epics, allegories, and satires, for instance) and occasionally in the realist novel itself, the semic code may construct a figural entity that "biography, psychology, or time" are all incapable of "encompassing." What do we make of this construction?

> As figure, the character can oscillate between two roles, without this oscillation having any meaning, for it occurs outside biographical time (outside chronology); the symbolic structure is completely reversible: it can be read in any direction. . . . As a symbolic ideality, the character . . . is nothing but a site for the passage (and return) of the figure.[3]

With Barthes's vocabulary at hand three avatars of "person" coexist in French films of the 1930s. Because fictional signification in cinema depends on

a prior fiction whereby a living human being incarnates a role, the actor can
be distinguished from the character. When the pretextual status of a particular
(star) actor comes into play in the reading of the film, or when the manner in
which a role is assumed by even an unknown actor somehow disturbs our
involvement in the fiction, then the actor's role in the film is readily legible
alongside the character's role in the plot. This was the thrust of Jean-Louis
Comolli's important essay on the material presence of Pierre Renoir's acting
in *La Marseillaise*, an essay ingeniously titled "A Body Too Much."[4] Next, the
symbolic reach of representation allows character to be separated from figure,
an entity made up of actor and role, but going beyond both to function as a
magnet for a host of values, qualities, and concepts that the reader/viewer
engenders in the course of interchange with the text.

As variations of character, all three become readable through the "semic
code," those textual elements that we recognize as signifying "qualities," generally human ones like jealousy, obsequiousness, virility, and so on. In a film,
the semic makes its appearance via physical traits of the actor and via all the
visible and auditory elements that attach themselves to him or her by association. The latter are very often carried by the mise-en-scène. In fact the manner
by which a film's mise-en-scène is legible in relation to its characters is distinctive enough to distinguish its peculiar *optique*. We can thus rewrite our three
primary categories schematically by attending to the way any character is
constructed in relation to its surroundings. We come up with:

1. theatrical: an actor on a set or stage
2. fictional: a character in a locale
3. poetic: a figure in a milieu

While every film may be read and discussed on all three levels, every film
likewise signals that level on which its most significant work will occur. The
same can be said for genres, styles, periods—or better, for that mix of these I
have designated *optiques*. For instance, and quite obviously, the mass entertainment film based on the theatrical model finds its climax in a powerful
"performance" by an actor (as in the final number sung by Mistinguett in
Rigolboche). It is common to treat such performances as transferable. They
attach themselves to the independently revered body of the star and are directed out to the audiences in a manner scarcely mediated by the text, although the text naturally provides their occasion. The fact that star performers
frequently command the mise-en-scène of the sequences in which they appear
verifies this hierarchy and further identifies the core of this *optique*.

When the actor is forgotten behind the role he or she has helped create, the
audience is obliged to evaluate the mise-en-scène as a field for that character's
action. Here the character may be understood as potentially separate from the
plot's locale, although familiar processes of connotation quickly contaminate
such independence. Even the most rudimentary forms of film criticism point

to the echo of character traits in the physical "characteristics" of the locale, including costume, props, decor, geography, and atmosphere. The priority of plot in such films generally keeps connotations from becoming so dense that they inhibit an understanding of the textual design. Ultimately characters must stand out from one another and from their locales so that the drama of inter-relations that we call plot can unfold. This is particularly true for films labeled "realist," which must relentlessly strive to distinguish entities and their values before ordering them in a moral hierarchy. By and large, Jean Renoir works within this category, at least in the decade of the 1930s. We admire the multi-ple perspectives so carefully separated yet interrelated in *La Grande Illusion* and *Le Règle du jeu*, where Renoir's presentation of a dramatic field of options is taken up differently by diverse characters and the classes they represent.

From this angle, poetic realism is an *optique* that is scarcely realist at all, for in its most signal moments one finds an interpenetration of characters and what is best termed their "milieus." Often to the detriment of plot logic, or even thematic consistency, such films layer their characters with multiple, often contradictory values, signified not just in their verbal and gestural range but in a variety of accompanying imagistic registers. These include lighting, props, composition, and rhythm. Here the mise-en-scène functions in more than a connotative manner; it functions symbolically, with the full force of the figure. And here the film is released from the quest of plot and of understand-ing that orients realist fiction. Figural personages, as opposed to characters, are by definition "achronological" and appeal to the passions rather than the "ac-tions" or quests of the audience. Every element and each succeeding scene contribute not to the progress or retardation of a final view, but to the density of feeling that is diffused in and across the permeable characters of the sym-bolic text.

This intense representation of feelings that are seemingly independent of dramatic purpose must have been what prompted critics to adduce the term "poetic" in relation to such films, for compared to narrative fiction, poetry in our day is considered the genre of passion (with its connotation of "passivity"), lyrical meditation, reaction, and symbolic reading. It is also the genre that is conventionally thought to traffic in the realm of the imaginary (whereas the directness of theatrical performance and the logic of plotted fiction generally keep those genres on a steady keel). Surely a systematic analysis would rapidly deconstruct these distinctions; nevertheless, they served in their day to distin-guish the kinds of effort put out by different films and to that extent they had a historical consequence. Critics identified films of "atmosphere" as appealing to viewers sensitive to the pervasive, undifferentiated tone that in poetic realist works spreads across individual scenes or blankets an entire film.

But atmosphere need not entail softness. The undeniable toughness of po-etic realist themes and images alarmed some critics who insisted that movies should be pleasant to watch and to digest. This bivalence haunts the movement's central star and icon, Jean Gabin. His masculine physique, the strength of his personal code, and his explosive anger were balanced in the symbolic films of poetic realism by his vulnerability, a certain eroticized lethargy, and the general pathos that inevitably led to his self-destruction. Working itself out in different scenarios, his introversion serves as a membrane standing between his dark privacy (including an occluded, traumatic past) and his openness to enter into authentic relations with others. Perhaps more significant, the reversibility of his "figure" infected the production design of Gabin's films, particularly the milieus that served as their settings. Moreover, such a reversible "figure" operated again and again in milieus that came to take on this very reversibility. Even the term "milieu" is reversible, signifying the popular urban *quartiers* of street dances, carnivals, and a grand socialist aspiration, while also signifying *zones* of criminality and the paranoia one can readily feel there. The chiaroscuro that haunts so many of the films of Duvivier, Grémillon, and Carné often expresses this duality within Gabin's world, within his character, and, most important of all, within his appeal to the mass audience hanging on his fate. It would hardly be misleading to label a film like *Le Quai des brumes* a "meditation in chiaroscuro," since its given title readies us for an encounter with a certain troubled figure in a mysterious milieu.

A GENEALOGICAL APPROACH: MELODRAMA AND ROMANTIC POETRY

No matter how clearly the foregoing analysis may have refined an intuitive typology of films and audiences by pointing to the locus of textual work in poetic realism and in neighboring types of films, no typology, no matter how refined, is capable of being so culturally sensitive as to account for the particular power and interest of a set of representations. From the perspective of any typology whatever, poetic realism can only identify for 1930s France one sort of cinematic production and function that surely exists in other places and times—in the silent Swedish classics of Victor Sjöström and Maurice Stiller, for example, or more recently in the films of Terrence Malick. To be of any historical value, a typology must be supplemented by a genealogy that traces the emergence of products and their functions within a tradition.

The genealogy of poetic realism lies right at hand evidently in "melodrama,"[5] and as in the typology just laid out, gender here too plays a key role. So concludes Maureen Turim in a study entitled "French Melodrama: Theory of a Specific History."[6] An outgrowth of a strain of avant-garde silent cinema indebted first to domestic melodrama, and second to the nineteenth-century theatrical sources on which that strain was based, poetic realism displaces "the radically expressive editing styles" of the 1920s onto "a distinctive camera style, heavily marked by the use of crane shots, and atmospheric *mise-en-*

scène."[7] I would add that reduction of plot makes poetic realism a specifically French strain of a genre whose Anglo-American version hinges on thrilling changes of fortune and sudden disclosures. Employing registers of the sound track as well as those of mise-en-scène, poetic realism enlarged the "melos" and reduced the "drama" lodged in the fatality of its themes.

More crucial to Turim than these stylistic distinctions, she finds that in the key poetic realist films of the 1930s "the modernized female protagonist [of the 1920s] is replaced by a working class hero."[8] This marks an important shift, for melodramatic theater, particularly in its French inception with Pixé-récourt, had revolved around females in their struggle to preserve moral or civilized values in a threatening world. Since D. W. Griffith's first shorts, the cinema has never ceased drawing on this reservoir of dramatic possibilities, nor has it ceased appealing to the middle- and lower-class audiences addicted to its formulas. The poetic realist variation with the male hero, a variation that will come under scrutiny in my discussion of *Les Enfants du paradis*, thus distinguished itself not only from Hollywood melodrama but from conventional French fare, so much of which retained a fascination with beleaguered females.

Melodrama carries a proud mien in France, and particularly in the interwar years when most prolific scriptwriters were known principally as authors of stage melodramas, Henry Bernstein foremost among these.[9] They made a living putting female characters through moral hell, and they did so practically as a male club. Whereas scriptwriting had always been open to women in Hollywood, one can scarcely find a female name in the credits of French films (the "générique des années 30").[10] Unfortunately, this is hardly surprising since, with the single exception of Marie Epstein, whose credit as director was always given after that of her collaborator Jean Benoit-Lévy, the French film industry, like most others of the time, was completely patrilineal. There were no women producers, nor any who were permitted to work their way into the *équipes* that formed the creative core of the industry. The only areas open to women lay in traditional female métiers like costuming, where they still had to compete with the likes of Christian Dior.[11] Women with literary and organizational skills could work as "script-girls" and might prove highly influential on and off the set. The extraordinary cases of Denise Tual and Françoise Giroud remind us of that.[12] The fact that these two women used their genius to inflect French cinema from below, however, does not change the structural organization of a system in which effectively they served as secretaries and confidantes for the men who made the movies, who wrote and directed the roles women were made to act out on the screen.

Just how predictable and monotonous those roles are when considered sociologically comes out in Ginette Vincendeau's article on "women's melodrama."[13] Recognizing that there was nothing akin to Hollywood's "woman's

picture" in France at this time,[14] she scans the plots of the decade's twelve
hundred films for those that seriously address women's issues. That she discusses but four titles is already an indication of the slightness of this "genre."
In isolating it from other subgenres featuring women and presumably addressed to them, she mentions costume dramas (*Katia* and *Mayerling*) and light
comedy (*Club de femmes*). She could have added cycles of films about "girls'
schools" (Pabst's *Jeunes Filles en détresse*, Serge de Poligny's *Pauline à l'école*),
about aspiring actresses or singers (*Zouzou*, *Rigolboche*), and so on, but no enu-
meration, no matter how finely broken down, would have satisfactorily accounted for the representation of women in this film industry. Even were
statistics to confirm certain suspicions (for instance, that French cinema focuses on daughters as distinct from the Italian obsession with mothers), this
would only "reflect" demography (in Italy young women remain at home in
large extended families, whereas in France many must—or are permitted to—
live on their own). Cinema may always be counted on to feed cultural commonplaces into its machinery of representation, but what counts for us must
be the impact of those representations, that is, their *production* more than their
reflection of values. How important to the functioning of the movies are the
myriad plots the French devised that isolate young women so as to make them
vulnerable to older men who alternately protect and threaten them?

In featuring male heroes, poetic realism can by no means claim to have
short-circuited the egregious treatment scripted for women in the 1930s. The
"woman" crucial to the poetic realist text becomes a reversible sign serving a
textual function. Like Africa, the free-floating young woman functions in poetic realism as a figure in an ambiguous moral milieu, inflecting the plots and
visual designs of these films. That this makes her a cliché has surprised no
one.[15] In her book that sets out to locate and amplify a specifically female voice
at the margins of the French film industry, Sandy Flitterman-Lewis must begin
by admitting that for the most part the poetic realists elaborated standard
images of women. In films that otherwise legitimately lay claim to important
advances in cinematic representation, she is sorry to note that

> it is precisely this disruptive sexuality which the female represents that forms
> the textual center of the Poetic Realist films. No matter what the individual film
> is ostensibly about, it needs the troubling presence of the woman to generate
> the conflict. . . . This production of femininity across the representational ter-
> rain of the Poetic Realist text tells us much about the conventional function of
> the woman's image within the operations of the cinematic apparatus itself. For,
> in spite of the decidedly "French" tone, the pervasive cultural atmosphere and
> highly visible French alternative to Hollywood production—the female figure
> functions in much the same way in films produced both in Hollywood and in
> France. Always the sexual center, a figure of erotic force, the woman and her
> function are continually and irrevocably defined in masculine terms.[16]

Agreeing no doubt that poetic realist films offer no alternative social role for female characters, Vincendeau like Turim remains struck by the new function male characters assume in *La Bête humaine*, *Le Quai des brumes*, and *Gueule d'amour*. For she concludes her essay by reflecting on the "femininity" of these heroes, their pathos and suffering, even the way they are often "confined to the traditional enclosed spaces of womanhood." In this context she quite rightly scorns those historians who have held up the male heroes of the movement as "tragic" while demeaning their female counterparts as, for example, "lachrymose."[17]

In my view, male and female roles in poetic realism are best understood structurally and figurally, rather than as (insufficient) reflections of actual sociological trends. Thus poetic realism, as an avatar of melodrama, does indeed address itself to a spectator drawn to mute suffering, even though its heroes are male, and whether or not its supporting female characters are strong or weak, thin or complex. For in the most complex poetic realist texts (none scripted, I would add, by the standard melodramatists of the stage), actresses and their roles give rise to the "feminine," a figure that then spreads itself across other characters and the mise-en-scène. Impossible to imagine without melodrama, poetic realism relies on an *optique* more specific than this massive genre.

Melodrama rose to popularity early in the nineteenth century alongside the more noble genre of romantic lyrical poetry. Thanks to its textual concentration, it is this latter that offers especially suggestive material for the incubation of a film movement like poetic realism. Not that scriptwriters and directors foraged in old volumes of Nerval and Lamartine looking for ideas; but the feelings that writers and directors thought it was the province of cinema to arouse, the topics and tone they believed they could profit by introducing into this commercial medium, had been first inculcated in them and in their culture by such poets. This is hardly surprising, for if poetry marches at the avantgarde of the literary arts, then its nineteenth-century sallies might serve the most progressive wing of a twentieth-century popular art like the cinema.[18]

This old-fashioned, sentimental sense of the poetic led to experiments in French cinema as early as 1922, when Léon Poirier explicitly countered the prevailing middle-class studio style by taking his camera to the Alps to shoot a version of Lamartine's *Jocelyn*. But direct adaptations of poetry are not nearly so important in this genealogy as the importation of a poetic function or impulse into what appear otherwise to be standard cinematographic topics. Recall our discussion of *L'Atalante* where complex, poetic figuration depends on characters who offer the audience multiple, often unfathomable, psychological lures. Surrounded by weird objects, innumerable cats, and the shifting French landscape across which they drift, Jean, Juliette, and Père Jules exercise our imagination to the limit.[19] This film's very first and most astute critic, Elie

Faure, immediately noted its aura of nineteenth-century "romantic realism."[20] As an art historian, Faure linked this to Corot; but he might just as well have cited Musset, Baudelaire, Laforgue, and—as would later critics for obvious biographical correspondences—Arthur Rimbaud. In the manner of these illustrious predecessors, Vigo photographed his French landscapes with a delicate play of light meant to trigger the greater play of the imagination, perhaps to let the viewer conjure up foreign lands like those Père Jules recites in the litany of places he has visited: "Shanghai, Singapore, Melbourne . . ."

Although *L'Atalante* addressed a kind of spectator yet to be awakened (performing miserably at the box office even in its compromised version), it gave off an air of being important, so that it was chosen to represent the country at the Venice film festival in 1934.[21] There it joined three other films bearing witness to the germination of a new lyrical sensibility ready to sweep into French cinema: Lacombe's "darkly pessimistic"[22] *Jeunesse*, Ozep's exotic *Amok*, and Feyder's *Le Grand Jeu*. In all four films imagery rivaled plot, a shift most notable in *Le Grand Jeu* because of its immense popular success and because, as a tale of the Foreign Legion, it was supposed to be an action picture. Those few critics who balked at *Le Grand Jeu* recognized that it did not correspond to the "well-shaped dramas in the theatrical mode" they were accustomed to. Feyder was reproached for "working like a novelist, especially in unduly prolonging nondramatic moments."[23] This descriptive prolongation is exactly what gives the film its imagistic density, steering it toward poetic realism and pointing back to the nation's magnificent poetic tradition, which uses Africa and the Orient as a prime inspiration.[24]

To be sure, the French like everyone else had always been drawn to pictures of foreign lands and to strange stories set therein.[25] But in the 1930s *le cinéma colonial* (which had formerly rendered utopic fantasies of expansionism like Feyder's *L'Atlantide*, a 1921 blockbuster) settled onto more homegrown psychological topics. This may have been due to the new technology of sound, to the deteriorating economic and social situation, or to the inevitable entropy associated with the increased familiarity of the French with exotic parts of the world. In any case, the exciting and robust adventure tales of Africa common to the silent screen became transformed into quieter, more desperate films that were closer in tone to an important strain of nineteenth-century poetry. Mediating the social and erotic imagination by evoking foreign scenes, these films rooted the emotional situation of their French characters in the African landscape. In this way they indirectly addressed pressing conundrums and anxieties about identity, sexuality, and "otherness."[26] Although no official mandate was in place, numerous indicators, most unmistakably the International Colonial Exposition of 1931, suggest that Africa had become a necessary construction in France's self-conception. *Le cinéma colonial* traded on the contradictions involved in that self-conception and it did so by summoning up such earlier expressions as Orientalist painting and romantic poetry.

Some of that poetry could readily have found its way straight into French prewar movies. In the 1830s Alfred de Musset seemed to forecast Prévert with lines like:

> Donne-moi tes lèvres, Julie;
> Les folles nuits qui t'ont pâlie
> Ont séché leur corail luisant.
> Parfume-les de ton heleine;
> Donne-les-moi, mon Africaine,
> Tes belles lèvres de pur sang.   ("A Julie")[27]

Or listen to Baudelaire, the poet of perfume:

> La langoureuse Asie et la brûlante Afrique,
> Tout un monde lointain, absent, presque défunt,
> Vit dans tes profondeurs, forêt aromatique!
> Comme d'autres esprits voguent sur la musique,
> Le mien, ô mon amour! nage sur ton parfum.   ("La Chevelure")[28]

In "Parfum exotique" the poet lets an aroma sweep him to an island peopled with frank girls and vigorous young sailors. Elsewhere he would cry out like Pépé le Moko, "Enleve moi, frégate!" ["Carry me off, frigate"], hoping to reach "L'innocent paradis plein des plaisirs furtifs" ["The innocent paradise full of secret pleasures"]. In the end, however, he realizes it is "plus loin que L'inde et que la chine" ["Further away already than India or China"] ("Moesta et Errabunda").

Baudelaire's most uninhibited conjunction of sensuality and North Africa comes in the first stanza of "Les Bijoux":

> La très-chère était nue, et, connaissant mon coeur,
> Elle n'avait gardé que ses bijoux sonores,
> Dont le rich attirail lui donnait l'air vainqueur
> Qu'ont dans leurs jours heureux les esclaves des Mores.[29]

Later in this peerlessly sensual poem, he describes the eyes of his lover as those of a "tigre dompté, d'un air vague et rêveur," adding that "elle essayait des poses, / Et la candeur unie à la lubricité / Donnait un charme neuf à ses métamorphoses."[30]

A century later, censorship, mores, and the requirements of popular narrative would prevent those French films that unquestionably grew out of this same sensibility from going so far in language or in imagery. However, modern prose fiction did flirt with such forbidden zones. Céline, Carco, and Mac Orlan had already plotted the mythographic trajectory that French cinema needed to travel from the outlandish exoticism of the Sahara to the polyglot docks of foreign ports, right into France and the spleen of Paris where poetic realism would find itself most at home.

THE IMAGINARY OF THE INDUSTRY: FEYDER AND DUVIVIER

Poetic realism would become a standard of film art by the end of the decade. Undoubtedly inspired by renegade talents like Vigo and Ozep, its ascendancy depended far more on the influence of industry stalwarts like Feyder and Duvivier to expand the emotional range of that era's dominant theatrical repertoire. For these were surely France's most versatile and professional directors, having successfully taken on assignments in various genres during the silent era. Feyder had even been called to Hollywood where at MGM from 1929 to 1932 he directed among others, Greta Garbo. When in the 1930s he and Duvivier repeatedly brought to the screen the motifs of the exotic and the femme fatale, critics tried to pin down this sensibility using labels like "romantic realism," and "dark pessimism," labels that would only later line up under the master term "poetic realism." Since they inflected their proven styles and themes with this sensibility, these two directors are reliable weathervanes in the shifting winds of the 1930s.

Coming back with the know-how of Hollywood and the adulation of European producers and critics, Feyder was perfectly positioned to lead a change in sound cinema. With a profound understanding of dramatic rhythm, indeed of the workings of many of the arts, his consistency gave him a tremendous head start over his contemporaries, even if it held him back from taking the kinds of chances historians love to recognize in the greatest directors. Never searching for showy cinematic effects, Feyder sought subjects of the proper proportions to which he would devote himself in fleshing out their most promising cinematic contours. No matter how poetic the result, he always started with dramatic structure and would never permit any element of the film, including any star, to unbalance what should be experienced with ease and clarity.

Feyder was primarily a director of actors: his fabled reliance on set design, camera position, and music actually derive from a studied handling of performers. He rehearsed all scenes with the camera out of the room. Though they had been handed a subtly broken-down script, his players were encouraged to improvise their delivery and even their lines. More important to him, they were asked to move about the set in the most natural way possible. If needed, the set could be altered, props added or deleted, or the script amended. Only after the dialogue and blocking were finalized would he dare wheel in his camera and make of it a moralizing narrator.

Virtually all his peers in the industry with equal experience and ambition had gained that experience in the precious, imagistic silent cinema, and most had a difficult time adjusting to the conditions of sound; but Feyder was taken up by Hollywood because of his handling of actors, and because he was the clear master of genres close to American tastes: naturalism (*Thérèse Raquin*), satire (*Les Nouveaux Messieurs, Crainquebille*), and even adventure (*L'Atlantide*). Hence he was well prepared for the turn toward a substantially realist form that world cinema would take after 1930. This is not to say that he became indentured to dialogue. Indeed, Jean Mitry, employing a vocabulary reflected in my typology, suggests that his special talent was one of observation and minute approximation whereby he systematically produced an "authenticity of character in locale."[31]

This would be especially evident in *Pension Mimosas* (1934), a tale of familial strife set in the gambling milieu of Nice. Feyder was the first to note that in this actors' vehicle the work of cinema disappears (in the American manner of apparently effortless pictures), leaving only the characters and their world. What may make this film more obviously French than American is that none of these characters acts freely, each being driven by an obsession, whether gambling, sex, maternal compulsion, or money. But money, because of its abstraction and generality, becomes the master figure of every obsession, just as the frenzied casino contaminates every other setting in this milieu. At the casino the levelheaded father, in his job as overseer of the games, tries to keep the whirling fates from spinning outside onto the streets. But his son's irrational pursuit of a gold-digging girl breaks the balance of the bourgeois household and sends his mother to the gambling tables herself. Although she wins a fortune, by the time she returns home to save her son, he has taken his life. Paper money blows around his body, whipped by the breezes of the Mediterranean.

The unity of tone in *Pension Mimosas* exhibits a maturity rare among domestic melodramas, and Feyder was praised as more than the equal of Hollywood directors working in this mainline Hollywood genre for his sobriety and assuredness. Feyder succeeded in 1934 with exactly the same kind of material that had cost Grémillon so dearly just four years earlier in *La Petite Lise*, indicating the importance of reputation in the industry and perhaps indicating a gradual tilt toward a more mature conception of cinema in French culture. Its relentless fatality makes *Pension Mimosas* an audacious undertaking, one that would lead to equally audacious developments in style when poetic realism would adopt this tone in the period just around the corner.

Feyder had in fact already showed himself prepared to take risks in style a year earlier, with *Le Grand Jeu*. The theme of romantic evasion supported his efforts, for he had to concoct ways of opposing North Africa to the high life of Paris that his hero, Pierre, had led before his financial bankruptcy. In Morocco, Pierre still dreams of the faithless woman for whom he had embezzled company and family funds; and there he literally conjures up her double, a poor amnesiac prostitute who wanders into the cheap hotel where he is staying. To amplify the opposed psychological valences these women stand for, Feyder dared to have a single actress, Marie Bell, play both Florence, the Parisian femme fatale, and Irma, the good-hearted, vulnerable girl in Africa. Simply changing her hair color and dubbing her voice, Feyder pulled off a stunning cinematic trompe l'oeil while figuring obsession in a remarkably new way. Hitchcock would exploit the same tactic to different ends in what is arguably the most densely psychoanalytic of movies, *Vertigo* (1958). It is a tactic that Freud himself celebrated in his analysis of *Gradiva*, one also used by Luigi Pirandello, a favorite author of Feyder.[32]

Le Grand Jeu's overt psychoanalytic foundation (the women representing alternate phases of Pierre's masochism) does not trigger the Germanic photographic feel of *Crime et châtiment* or *Amok*. Hans Eisler's syncopated score, first of all, has nothing of the pathetic about it but drives forward clearly, mercilessly. Merciless also are the Moroccan locations, scrupulously photographed, and carefully blended in with the restrained sets built to represent the seedy outskirts of Marrakesh where most of the action takes place. Feyder's sympathetic but observational stance[33] was in part dictated by circumstances. Refused permission to use legionnaires as extras, Feyder worked out a three-camera newsreel recording of actual military maneuvers, which he then had to meld with equally dispassionate shots of his actors.[34] Moreover, unlike the poetic realist films it must be said to anticipate,[35] *Le Grand Jeu* spreads its focus among several characters, who collectively conjure the ghost of fate as though by triangulation. The hotel owners, Blanche (Francoise Rosay) and Clément (Charles Vanel), suggest alternative ways of coping with the desert, with its dead time, its exposure, and its implacable heat: he through drink, she by mothering the distraught legionnaires who crawl into their shelter. One character, Pierre's Russian cohort, might be said to embody, self-reflexively, the psychoanalytic question the film raises by refusing not only to speak of his past but to listen to the past of anyone he cares about. The Foreign Legion is the locus of amnesia and exhausted passions.

The heat and decay of this milieu eventually wear down every pretense of civilization, producing *le cafard* in one character after another.[36] Clément's ugly lust rises when, full of gin, he finds himself close to Irma's legs as he holds the chair she stands on to change the ceiling flypaper. The dead flies, and the palpability of sweat and gin, motivate the lunge for Irma that pitches Clément off the rotten hotel railing to his death. Feyder alternately asphyxiates his characters in the closed rooms of the filthy Marrakesh bistros and terrifies them with the endless horizon lines surrounding the city. Casual vice diverts most of those condemned to live there, but an essentially metaphysical isolation enervates Pierre. At the film's climax, he relinquishes the chance for rehabilitation when it arrives in the form of an inheritance. He does buy his freedom and Irma's, but at the moment of their embarkment for France, he happens upon Florence, who is passing through Casablanca. Self-destructively, he sends Irma on alone with all his money and with promises of joining her,

Le Grand Jeu: Moroccan days.
BFI

Le Grand Jeu: Moroccan nights.
CF

then chases and once again loses the worthless Florence. Turning away from the harbor and toward the desert, he reenlists in the Legion.

The real tragedy, however, belongs neither to the abandoned Irma nor to the masochist Pierre, but to Blanche. Played with humble majesty by Rosay, Blanche surveys a spreading spectacle of despair in the figures of the tarot cards she repeatedly lays out before her. As Pierre goes out a final time to a Saharan conflict, she turns over the death card and falls to the floor in tears. The camera backs away from her so deliberately that we are left infected by her angst far more than by the romantic mania of the film's catatonic hero. Too discrete to change the course of the drama, but too sensitive not to be devastated by it, she stands as a principle of helpless consciousness facing the empty desert.

By deftly tracking the interwoven lives of multiple characters, and by lodging the consciousness of fate in one of them, Feyder achieved in *Le Grand Jeu* a type of realism much more nuanced than that of the poetic realist films later in the decade. It shares with those films the themes of fate, escape, destructive

Le Grand Jeu. BFI

Torpor and *le cafard* seen
head on.

Le Grand Jeu. BFI

women, a lost hero, and an oppressive atmosphere. But Feyder's narration, unlike that of Duvivier in *Pépé le Moko*, for example, maintains a clarity unaffected by *le cafard*. Only Renoir labored as much as did Feyder to achieve (seemingly without effort) the steady gaze both turned on the torpor and madness of the milieus that afflicted the most serious films of this period.[37]

Feyder was too urbane to share Renoir's (temporary) faith in a rational political vision. Instead it was his commitment to character that kept him from ever tumbling into a fully figurative or poetic approach. But character, he was convinced, could not be served by replicating dramatic theater on the screen. *Le Grand Jeu*, one recent critic argues, falls neatly into the paradigm of the "novelistic," despite the fact that Feyder authored the scenario with Charles Spaak.[38] In its attitude toward decor and character, toward psychology and narration, *Le Grand Jeu* suggests Conrad, Hugo, and especially Balzac. In Feyder, then, more even than in Raymond Bernard who had just adapted *Les Misérables*, the romantic realism of nineteenth-century fiction came to fertilize one of French cinema's main shoots as it sprouted from the frozen ground of the theatrical paradigm covering the entertainment field. With the encouragement of this novelistic aesthetic, that shoot would quickly develop branching motifs such as "the discovery of the city, the criminal class of outsiders . . . [and would offer] a critique of the power of money along with a fascination for it, passionate love stories, and interest in pathetic suffering."[39] In short it would blossom into poetic realism, but only after these motifs that Feyder helped dredge up from the cultural unconscious were given a treatment different from his, a treatment that emanated from the same murky regions, one we keep associating not with nineteenth-century novels but with the lyrical dimension of much contemporaneous French fiction.

Feyder could bring French cinema to the edge of a genuinely different approach because his manner as much as his reputation inspired confidence in producers. And that manner could be said to resemble that of the traditional novelist in that it derives from the facility with which he could organize the disparate elements of his projects. Where the poetic realists and their precursors in the lyrical tradition seemed intoxicated by their subjects, Feyder would stand back more coolly. He professed no special inspiration; sympathetic direction comes from listening to a script and to one's actors. It is a product of intelligence and humility; Feyder would be glad to call it "style."

The fullest study of this filmmaker is fittingly titled *Jacques Feyder: artisan du cinéma*,[40] for the cinema to him was a métier.[41] A powerful talent without an obsessive vision to express, he could wander from the romantic exoticism of *Le Grand Jeu* to the open satire of *La Kermesse héroïque* by dint of the consistently assured technique he brought to each of his projects. In this he serves as bellwether of the industry's most progressive wing. And in this capacity he generally points, in his careful, conservative way, toward the cinema of atmosphere. From his fabled Zola adaptation *Thérèse Raquin* to *Les Gens du voyage* (1937) with its poetic realist motifs (including a Cayenne prison, a fleabag *Hôtel du Nord*, a circus, and a tale of lust and blackmail), Feyder underwrote the ventures of the more self-indulgent members of the "school of poetic realism," including above all his assistant, Marcel Carné.

The other industry regular tempted in the 1930s by the current of dark pessimism was Julien Duvivier. Working in many genres, notably the religious film, he was far more prolific yet far less consistent than Feyder. Unrefined, he disdained the pretensions of the picturesque. Critic André Lang, who wrote the dialogue for *La Bandera* (1935), explicitly preferred him to strong directors like Von Sternberg or Mamoulian because Duvivier "thinks that it must always be the work that imposes its style on the director and not the other way around. Hence, he has but one worry: to bring out the spirit and the character proper to each subject, and, what is more difficult still, to compose its atmosphere."[42] Duvivier's importance for us lies in the way that he labored increasingly to produce that subject's atmosphere. His emergence as a key poetic realist gave respectability to the movement and encouraged producers to stand behind other filmmakers working to the same end.

The case of Duvivier validates our insistence on the term *optique* over that of "style." For during the 1930s Duvivier adopted alternative notions of cinema and its audience function. His half dozen films that are crucial to us share little with the rest of his output, which fall back instead on an earlier *optique*. For example, the heavily promoted *Golgotha* illustrates the final days of Christ in a postcard style, despite the Algerian location where the exteriors were shot, despite its highly mobile camera, and despite its long list of stars (Harry Baur as Herod, Jean Gabin as Pilate, Robert Le Vigan as Jesus). Craggy mountains,

Golgotha: Jean Gabin as Pontius Pilate. BFI

overarched by scudding clouds shot through with sharp streaks of sunlight, emphasize the cosmic miracle at work and render nearly all the performances bombastic. As opposed to the suggestive and unassertive themes Maurice Jaubert composed for poetic realist films, Jacques Ibert's fulsome score is operatic in its sweep. Finally, almost to italicize the literal breadth of Christ's unsurpassed consequence for civilization, Duvivier employs many extreme longshots. The film's few close-ups are reserved for Christ's face, glowing in soft focus, and these seldom show him interacting with other characters. Instead he declaims eternal truth and undergoes eternal passion, while reaction shots show his effect not so much on individuals but on crowds. Evidently we in the audience are meant to sense ourselves part of this great crowd ranged across the rough terrain. Only occasionally does a nervous camera try to animate these static tableaux with whip-pans to unidentified Jews watching the proceedings. Overall, *Golgotha* stands diametrically opposed to the poetic realist *optique* in its cocksure and official presentation of a situation that is already fully developed in the cultural imagination. Herod's entourage, for example, predictably includes a baby leopard in near parody of decadent luxury. Obviously *Golgotha*'s address is to the believing spectator eager for familiar images. Those images come both from popular nineteenth-century religious painting and from movies like Pabst's 1932 *L'Atlantide* whose ancient Saharan court (and leopard) Duvivier might just as well have borrowed whole.

Duvivier plays shamelessly to the spectator, it seems, whenever a traditional subject is at stake. Even during his most strikingly original period (1935–1939) he was content to race through routine remakes of classic silent films: *The Golem* (originally made in Germany in 1922) and *The Phantom Chariot* (made in Sweden in 1920). But amid such facile enterprises came a string of films that insist on a more subtle spectator prepared for a different kind of experience: *David Golder, Poil de Carotte, La Tête d'un homme, Le Paquebot "Tenacity," La Bandera, La Belle Equipe, Pépé le Moko, Un Carnet de bal, Le Fin du jour.*

Unlike the adaptations of legends these films bring no ready-made atmosphere with them and no well-known heroes. Generally concerned with social marginals, the atmosphere for each must be conjured out of the social imaginary. This is why the African films *La Bandera* and *Pépé le Moko* concern us most, since both condense the symbolic properties of a specially charged milieu on alienated figures running away from the urban underworld of France. For in fact these two films, above all others, linked exotic decor and the femme fatale, levering the poetic realist sensibility into an acceptable, desirable goal in the film industry overall.

Duvivier's attraction to marginal characters, to seedy—if not exotic—milieus, and to fatality figured in females is apparent even before the African films. In his 1932 *La Tête d'un homme*, he recognized that to express the ambiguous moral tone of the Georges Simenon novel, the lucid Inspector Maigret (Harry Baur) had to be countered by the spiteful, metaphysically sick émigré who haunts the night scene in Montparnasse. Although Duvivier follows the intricate plot far more scrupulously and with more pleasure than did Renoir when he adapted another Simenon novel a few months earlier, the Dostoievskian killer who makes Duvivier's *policier* interesting pushed him to experiment with what may be called "narration in depth."[43] Instead of merely laying out the scenes before the audience horizontally, so to speak, Duvivier felt compelled to shroud the unrolling events by withholding the motives of Maigret's antagonist.

The impression of depth is built from specific techniques, the most notable involving sound. Key events are accompanied by isolated and disturbing offscreen noises, such as deep human breathing and howling wolves, surrounding the action with a thick and disturbing air. Little unmotivated music knifes through this atmosphere. Instead, the music we do hear is part of the nightclub milieu the characters inhabit. Most memorably it comes through the walls, as the climactic scene begins with the villain trying to rape the woman who has goaded him all along and for whom he has committed "the perfect crime." In the chase that ensues we find our way into the singer's room.

La Tête d'un homme: Damia's lament—"All is fog; all is gray." CF

Played by the famous crooner Damia,[44] a character whom the credits identify only as "la femme lasse" lies surrounded by a band of Montparnasse decadents whom she is taking down to the spiritual depths that her voice was so capable of reaching. Her doleful refrain could aptly cover the entire school of poetic realism: "All is fog; all is gray," she sings.

In France as elsewhere, the inclusion of complete songs delivered on camera was common during the changeover to sound, but Duvivier knew better than anyone how to weave such performances into the fabric of his tales by making sure they shared a common texture. Damia's song in *La Tête d'un homme*, like Fréhel's in *Pépé le Moko*, seems to unhinge the main character and send him to his doom amid wild camerawork. In both these films, the song is not projected out from the screen with us as its target audience, in the manner of a Maurice Chevalier vehicle. In both it reaches us indirectly, infecting first the character who hears it and the mise-en-scène that is attached to his mental collapse. Condensing the tone that the film has been progressively working to express, Damia's lament, like Fréhel's, becomes the pulse of what we experience as a textual body. Employed this way, music becomes the very figure of deep resonance.

Three films and three years after *La Tête d'un homme*, Duvivier found another powerful subject in a different modern novel, Pierre Mac Orlan's *La Bandera*. Its opening sequence could stand as a prologue for poetic realism as a whole: a dark street seen from above; through a second-story window of a cheap hotel, the silhouette of a figure disappears; at gound level now, a tipsy couple careens toward us from the far plane as the camera moves laterally to frame the glistening street, with the hotel standing on one border; the tipsy woman, white-clad, rests against a lamppost in a closer shot that lets us glimpse a man limned in shadow (Jean Gabin); from her perspective we see the man dart out of the doorway; she grabs him in jest, and he pushes her away in hurrying past; when her boyfriend steps over to help, the lamplight reveals bloodstains where her dress was touched by Gabin; the camera slowly tilts to reveal the street sign: rue Saint-Victor.

When a match-dissolve frames a Spanish street sign, the adventure that will lead beyond the Atlas Mountains is underway, an adventure increasingly fraught with outright paranoia. In Barcelona, being held by a police officer and a hotel owner, Pierre Gillieth (Gabin) is unable to follow the intense conversation they carry out in Spanish. "The content of the dialogue means little," one critic admits, "but it permits Duvivier to make use of an effect of malaise created by the incomprehension of the hero (and of the spectator) in an expressionist mise-en-scène accentuated by shadows thrown on the wall by the slatted blinds."[45] Although shadowed and stained by the dark and bloody Parisian prologue, this tale, like that of *Le Grand Jeu*, is bleached of moral nuance in the African sun. *La Bandera* (again like *Le Grand Jeu*) figures Africa as a lawless, anonymous zone, and as a female body whose contours are veiled; but something larger than law, something like fate,[46] traps those who think to race across its sands or hide in its unmappable redoubts. In the absence of markers or of distinguishing features, the Foreign Legion cuts roads into the landscape, tattooing it just as the lovers tattoo themselves to etch a new past for themselves. This mythological, sexualized space nevertheless has a look the French

La Bandera:
Mixing blood with
the African Other
(Gabin and
Annabella). MOMA

were proud to have captured. An article in *Pour Vous* entitled "Le Visage d'Islam, fidèlement refleté par le cinéma français, travesti par Hollywood,"[47] features Annabella in her carefully researched Berber costume.[48] But of course it is Annabella, not a Berber, playing the courtesan. She speaks perfect French, learned, she explains, from all the French men who have moved through her room. Because the French have moved through North Africa, because they have learned to use it and be used in return, otherness has become merely instrumental, not fundamental. When she and Gabin suck each other's blood in a wedding ritual taken from the Foreign Legion, audiences are not shocked by the mixture. The religious and racial difference coded in Annabella's costume and gestures depends on and doubles the ordinary power of sexual difference that is the cornerstone of French and world feature filmmaking. The otherness of North Africa is after all merely a woman to romance and to make one's own.

One might propose that the Moroccan setting of *La Bandera* is incidental to its psychological plot, and that the authenticity of its decor was not really what excited critics. *La Bandera* was praised most for its unity of expression. André Lang writes of the lifeblood flowing through the six hundred cells of its decoupage.[49] Graham Greene writes of the fluid camera that unites atmospheric overview with acute moral drama.[50] In fact the film's driving theme is nothing other than integration, a search for personal wholeness through the device of the Conradian double, a search for social fusion in the Foreign Legion, finally achieved only as the brigade is being decimated. *La Bandera* lashes its mesmerized spectator to its hero, as he is tracked by an implacable fatality from Paris to Barcelona into Morocco and deeper still into the mountains. A common myth of spiritual regeneration in Africa here joins the film's disturbing ideology of brotherhood in the Foreign Legion where pasts are forgotten and the future belongs to those who give the orders.

Proudly displaying its carefully researched costumes and a few Islamic gestures, *La Bandera*'s standard denouement does not in the least concern the area or peoples that serve as backdrop. Its promise of the exotic extends but does not rewrite the usual promise of a hypnotic experience that fiction films have always tendered their audiences. And the African terrain is nothing other than a double of the flesh of the female star. To die in the Sahara is to die in a lover's or a comrade's arms, to die deliciously, picturesquely, and in what must be called cinematographic comfort. *La Bandera* wallows in its fatality. This is why, on its reprise in 1959, Jean Carta could be stricken with the realization that the film is nearly fascist in its sentiment, in its silly patriotism, in its regressive Oedipal scenario, and in its puerile treatment of women.[51]

Feyder's legionnaire film might be thought to mark a realist border to the genre, while Duvivier's marks its most poetic or romantic side. Writing in 1949 when poetic realism was so esteemed by the neorealists, an Italian critic had the perspicacity to invoke Baudelaire as the movement's patron saint.[52] The urban decadence for which Baudelaire is noted was limned with Oriental visions of sensuality and spiritualism. *La Bandera* begins in the former and concludes in the latter. As will be the case with *Pépé le Moko*, its direct heir, the meaning of Paris (la rue Saint-Victor and la place Blanche respectively) is fulfilled only in its African underside. In both cases that underside consists of a homoerotic mythology (the gang, the brigade, the woman that brings the man down) in search of its proper Oedipal trajectory (a healthy return to France). Duvivier celebrates his brigade and its heroic demise without qualification. It may shock us today, but the logic of the film led Mac Orlan to thank Generalissimo Francisco Franco for assisting the production; and it was to Franco that Duvivier unfortunately dedicated the work.[53] Feyder, on the other hand, concludes his film on the figure of the distraught Blanche and on her tragic knowledge. His is by far the more bitter film, one without solutions, certainly without the facile solution offered by the romanticism of the Foreign Legion or of Africa.

According to the research team Lagny-Ropars-Sorlin the importance of Africa for 1930s French cinema peaked in 1936.[54] Astutely, they recognize that the obvious thematic distinctions (including sociological stereotypes of architecture and mores) and the less obvious ideological ploys (the portrayal of Arabs by Caucasian performers, the invisibility of the African enemy, and so on) are not nearly so interesting as the structural rapports that link these two cultural groups textually and psychoanalytically. Standard French film relied on accepted geographical and cultural oppositions to fuel complex dramas about individuals torn by conflicting desires. Sometimes, in the most haunting of these, the carefully delineated distinctions begin to blend.

This is the case for *Pépé le Moko*, Duvivier's astounding international success. It ranked as the top 1937 film in Japan. Hollywood bought the rights and within months had reshot it, scene for scene, as *Algiers*, with Charles Boyer taking the Gabin role.[55] The last adventures of a Parisian dandy hiding out in the Casbah, *Pépé le Moko* gives sweet expression to the bitterness of lost dreams. These mixed or contradictory feelings stem from the doubleness of the character, Pépé, from the way he is paired with a double, Slimane, and from a doubleness at the center of the narration itself.

Its first two sequences render successively the two tones constituting the particular "ratio" that in my mind best defines poetic realism. Staged documentary footage introduces us to the Casbah as an official voice-over identifies the various races and socially marginal types inhabiting the district and spawning the vice that is visibly rampant there. Pépé's entrance then follows in a quiet but dramatic fashion: a close-up of his hand holding a jewel gives way to a tilt to his face when he raises the gem to the light. The sudden arrival of the police forces him to duck into a hideaway. There he is surprised to encounter Gaby, the elegant, bejeweled Frenchwoman, cruising the Casbah for excitement, to soak up its milieu. Pépé's practiced gaze immediately sizes up Gaby's "value" via extreme close-ups of her glittering jewelry that in addition render the stunning charms of Mireille Balin who plays her. In what will develop into

a self-conscious film about filmic desire[56] the audience finds itself caught between the interlocked glances of the two stars it has paid to see together.
Magnified, the shot changes accelerate obscenely until detective Slimane inter-
poses himself as the remote, philosophical, and all-knowing lookout who takes
in the situation as a block. We despise him for his objectivity, and for interrupting our satisfaction and that of the couple.

The remainder of the film will be spent in pursuit of that satisfaction. And
at its end, Slimane will once again wrench Pépé's eyes and our own from
Gaby, when he arrests him on board the ship just inches from her. Pépé's
suicide, like that of the Chinaman in *Broken Blossoms*, offers the spectator a
delicious experience of intimacy and loss, one that Slimane this time is too late
to prevent.

As analyzed by Lagny-Ropars-Sorlin, and confirming my own notion of the
priority of figure over character in poetic realism, the film's specific power is
a function of the dyad formed by the Caucasian outlaw Pépé and the Algerine
policeman Slimane. Only by recognizing the figurative dimension of these
male characters can one credit the power of regret that outweighs the plot
with its legendary nostalgia full of multiple psychoanalytic and sociocultural
implications. Slimane's obsession is to capture Pépé, whom he lures with
Gaby, the ultimate and unattainable jewel. In the scene of their initial meeting,
Slimane does not so much block a heterosexual fusion as triangulate its desire.
He lights the cigarettes they exchange, when Pépé's flesh wound prevents him
from doing it himself. Gaby may slip across national boundaries and violate
the strict segmentation of the city, but she is finally a prisoner of her Parisian
past, a twin of the holed-up gangster. Slimane, on the other hand, is ubiqui-
tous, the *meneur-de-jeu*. He is also Pépé's unacknowledged "other," the subject
of a repressed desire for which the attraction to Gaby is a simple narcissistic
displacement.

Pépé dies at the southern edge of the Mediterranean, as he looks longingly
from Africa toward France, reversing, let us recall, the direction of Marius's
longing in Pagnol's homonymous film. More than a site for conventional romantic feeling, Africa here helps confer a new profundity, metaphysical longing, on French cinema. Increasingly during the decade its geographical "distance" from France expresses the relation of vision to desire as a relation of
vision to pessimism. Vision as "lack" was already incipient in the legionnaire
films I have discussed. In *Pépé le Moko* Africa is a figure for a myopia and
nihilism whose origins lie in France.

This descent toward the fatalism of poetic realism is unmistakable when
Pépé le Moko is compared to a related film, *Justin de Marseille* of 1934. Directed
by Maurice Tourneur, *Justin* is an amiable film like the town it celebrates. Its
easygoing hero, head of the local black market and friend of Chinese dope
dealers, keeps his position through the friendship and respect of all the town's
citizens. Indeed Justin personifies Marseilles, as we are told in a double intro-

Pépé le Moko. BFI

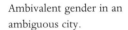

Ambivalent gender in an
ambiguous city.

Pépé le Moko. BFI

duction. First a group of schoolchildren parade through the port area behind
a vagabond pied piper who sings of the city. Then a reporter from Paris in
search of the truth about the city's gangsterism is taken aside by a local truck
driver and told that statistics always lie. The lowlife of Marseilles is also its high
life, he claims. Its gangsters behave with style and Justin is the most stylish
of all.

Parallels with *Pépé le Moko* abound. Both criminals are elegant and associated
with their town. Their compatriots are genial each in his own gruff way,
although both films feature an episode of treachery in which the most beloved
of the gang is killed through the scheme of another unscrupulous member.
Pépé and Justin are equally deliberate and calm in their vengeance, while the
traitor in both cases is shown to be nervous and cowardly, to have no style.
More than these similarities in plot and character, the visual strategies of the
films beg for comparison. Both are careful to include documentary shots of

Justin de Marseille: An untroubled gangster. CF   *Justin de Marseille*: In his amiable town. CF

street life: fishmongers in Marseilles, prostitutes and vendors in the Casbah. Both give us occasional "official" views of the cities and their leading bandits from an outsider's perspective (the French police in *Pépé le Moko*, the reporter in *Justin*). Yet in both cases this objective perspective proves inadequate. The viewer, privileged to share an insider's view, knows more.

The dialogue and settings bring out a poetry in the main characters that constitutes the real source of their power. In a scene that has achieved cult status, Pépé and Gaby recite a litany of Parisian metro stops to culminate their mutual seduction. Similarly Justin, as the film ends, courts his love by running through a list of famous tourist sites of Marseilles. Moreover, both criminals are given one moment when, finding themselves in love, they break into song.

Clearly these two films belong together; just so, their distinct modes of spectatorial address constitute an immense difference. Schematically one might say that *Justin* should be counted a film of presence while *Pépé* would be one of absence. When Justin reels off the place-names of Marseilles, he is standing at the city center, in full control of its upper- and undersides, his arm securely around the girl who had been threatened earlier in the film. By contrast, when Pépé runs through the names of the metro stops, it is a feat of memory, for he is a lifetime distant from Paris. We applaud from the side when Justin uses his knife to dispatch the treacherous Italian. But when Pépé uses his knife on his own belly, we watch through his eyes as Gaby, his dream image of Paris, sails away.

The deep nostalgia of *Pépé le Moko* places it at the official entryway of the poetic realist school. *Justin de Marseille* is a beautifully made film in the French style, but its clear, commanding vision never aims to shake the confidence of the spectator who is invited to look on the display of Marseilles and its colorful inhabitants, spread out as though for its enjoyment. Poetic realism could develop only when the audience was invited deep into the world on the screen, a mysterious world not just to the hero but, it seems, to the narrator and thus the spectator as well. The unfathomable geography of Algiers and the bold but unsettling allure of Gaby have no counterparts in *Justin de Marseille*. Needless to say Justin is not haunted by any psychological specter the way Slimane haunts Pépé. *Pépé le Moko* signals the ascendancy of a new kind of film, serving a new function for a different kind of spectator. It signals the defeat of the lure of Africa by the greater lure of Paris, and the defeat of the strong male (indeed, a bonded male pair) by a glittering female.

In effect, through *Pépé le Moko* French cinema had begun to follow its literary sources back home from across the sea. One of those sources, Francis Carco was born in North Africa and began his literary career there with tales of the exotic. And how can we forget that the next Mac Orlan novel to be adapted after the African *La Bandera* would be *Le Quai des brumes*? These writers learned to evoke the dark, mysterious visage of urban life only after having conjured up the loneliness of the desert or the sea. More important, they made sure that their stories affected the reader like an atmosphere one breathes in walking through it. Whether thick with sand or with fog, the tone of the tale, its breath or spirit, should settle physically on the reader. Once a yeoman director like Duvivier came to realize that such an experience could be achieved through cinema as well, then the possibilities of the whole industry must be said to have matured.

In displacing the sensuality and lawlessness of the desert onto the figure of the female, Duvivier helped arrange everything for the final phase of the movement, since the gritty French milieu could then confer "realism" on the "poetic" image ruled by the erotic enigma of the woman. In this context, Grémillon's *Gueule d'amour* and Chenal's *Maison du Maltais* appear as striking variations to *Pépé le Moko*. Recall that Grémillon's film reunites Gabin and Balin, with the Gabin character having returned to France from the African cavalry corps, where he is undone by a Parisian *mondaine* whom he strangles in the climax. In fact the once vain Lucien is literally out of place in France, making his final deportation to North Africa both a homecoming and a regression to a purer world. The unseen Africa of *Gueule d'amour* is a world without women, a world of male solidarity where women are dreamt of, spoken of, only from afar. It is also a world without center or consequence, a (poetic) vanity that evaporates when it confronts the realities of modern life in France.

La Maison du Maltais audaciously centers on an Arab protagonist, Matteo, played by the Jewish actor Marcel Dalio.[57] A street singer and occasional customs runner, Matteo falls in love with Safia, a beautiful French prostitute (Vivian Romance). Unheard of in thirties films, they conceive an interracial baby, but then are separated when Safia returns to Paris under the care of a wealthy art dealer. In effect taking up at the point of Pépé's suicide, Matteo follows the ship carrying his love to France and to Paris. After years masquerading as a Frenchman and involved with a band of brigands, Matteo meets his former lover in a tawdry hotel. Wanting the best for Safia and his son, disbelieving her love, Matteo dons his ancient Arab robes and kills himself. *La Maison du Maltais* is remarkable for allowing the unplumbed eroticism of Africa to invade a bourgeois *quartier* in Paris. Having allowed us the giddy exhilaration of this dalliance, the Arab becomes once more untouchable, both through his foreign garb and customs (returning in spirit to his father's home, "La Maison" of the title) and through his death. Their son will remain in Paris, raised a law-abiding Frenchman. He will never know that the blood pulsing through his veins carries an erotic fever that brought about his birth. Already in *Pépé le Moko* Africa seemed the feverish vision of the French (with engulfing rear-projections, dazzling jewels); the spectators of *La Maison du Maltais* are left in France with only the memory of the sun and the smells they need never more experience directly. Africa is as distant as a poem by Baudelaire.

LE FANTASTIQUE SOCIAL OF MARCEL CARNÉ

More than a cause of dramatic conflict, the central woman in poetic realism is the abundant source of atmosphere and of a certain meditative rhythm that contributes to an aesthetic of pathos. As in Von Sternberg's films, the presence of a mysterious woman motivates the complete eroticization of the image, often to the point of preciosity and deliberate obfuscation.[58] After 1937 Marcel Carné would receive most credit and most invective for this style that, following Pierre Mac Orlan, he preferred to call *le fantastique social* rather than "poetic realism." Mac Orlan's term has the advantage of eliminating the knotty problem of realism. Perhaps more important, it emphasizes the social—that is to say, populist—element in the formula of such works. Carné's oeuvre has always been treated as the richest vein of poetic realism because it genuinely offers to the spectator a feeling for the populism of the age in conjunction with (and sometimes in opposition to) images of fatalism figured through his pessimistic love stories.

Although he would be branded otherwise, Carné has always claimed to be a social rather than a psychological filmmaker, and with some justification. After all, his career began with the city symphony *Nogent, Eldorado du dimanche* (1929) that bears comparison with Vigo's contemporaneous *A propos de Nice*. He pursued his profession, however, not by climbing the uncertain stairs of amateur productions like *Nogent*, but as assistant to Feyder and to Clair, where it was his job and his pleasure to help establish the palpability of their melodramas. To Carné, detailed texture alone saved Clair and Feyder from the thinness and mawkishness of most melodrama. In an early essay written in the midst of this apprenticeship he chides the standard French cinema for just these vices:

We have probably never felt so weary, as in this 1931–32 season's end, of the talking screen. Wherever we look we see flat vaudeville entertainments, so-called "fantasy films," grinding out the same pretty stories, incessantly repeating the same tired effects. Uniformity again breeds tedium. The cinema lacks freshness, scope, commitment. . . . We resent the cinema for ignoring the profound unrest of our time, the urgent problems at hand, especially when literature and the theater are more and more committed. Some of us feel ashamed that the cinema . . . contents itself with banal, infantile little stories, shopworn entertainments, instead of subjects of real substance that would resonate in our hearts and minds.[59]

In 1932 Carné insisted that those subjects needed to be social in character so as to "invoke the true face of France." A year later, he had not changed his mind, but began to shift emphasis away from "subject" and toward "atmosphere." In the key article I have already cited, "When Will the Cinema Go Down into the Streets," Carné scarcely discusses the genuine life of the streets but talks a great deal about its appearance, mocking the false studio look resulting from cheap solutions to problems posed by sound. In the silent days those "who loved their craft . . . would not hesitate to go down into the street to capture, thanks to the camera lens, a marvelous corner of sky, a little street swarming with movement or life, or the grandeur of a cold, quiet, austere avenue."[60] This is the type of scene for which he would soon become famous. Then, further specifying the method he would adopt, and against his essay's title, Carné insists that, given the new conditions of sound, it is possible and often preferable to bring the city indoors to the camera rather than to take the camera to the street. With reference to Clair he has no doubts:

So subtle are his gifts of observation, that, in a fake milieu [in a studio] . . . he can give us an interpretation of life which is more real than life itself. . . . While sauntering around the city outskirts, we could swear that we had suddenly found ourselves face to face with the streets imagined by Meerson. The dead ends of those construction sites and the dark alley that runs along the rail line of *La Petite Ceinture* in *Sous les toits de Paris*, the street stairs and the little dance hall in *Quatorze juillet*, which we know were constructed as complete sets, move us through their flagrant authenticity.[61]

As a critic Carné made authenticity his chief concern, and authenticity he believed lay in contemporary relevance. This he found principally in the novelists of the day, the ones he hoped to emulate if not adapt.[62] Carné was ideally suited to take a leading role in this struggle for a mature aesthetic within a ramshackle industry, for he combined the implacable adolescent revolt of Vigo, Chenal, and Gréville with the industrial stamp inherited from an apprenticeship under Clair and Feyder. Already in 1930, while working on *Sous les toits de Paris*, he singled out the *policier*, specifically the American films exemplified by Von Sternberg's *Underworld* (1927), as the most exciting hope for new directions in the cinema. His "Elegy for the American *Policier*" predicts not only poetic realism but *film noir*:

> There will be wonderful days ahead for this type of adventure in the cinema. We will see more of this world, so foreign to us now, which we only know through the cinema, a mysterious world, full of weird characters, living in ambiguity, a world swarming with bad guys and with girls who have turned out badly. . . . [The *policier*] gives us the impression of living a new life far from our dull daily existence, far from the monotone workday world. . . . [It] brings a bit of dream and of poetry.[63]

Carné recognized that as much as the French cinema needed the vigorous modern poetry such films exuded, they could not adopt American or German prototypes directly. Attracted though he was to Von Sternberg, Fritz Lang, and Murnau, he expected the Gallic version to respond to Gallic literary forebears, to Francis Carco, and Pierre Mac Orlan as we have seen, and to François Villon, the original creator of marginal malcontents and gutter philosophers.

Carné helped import this hard-boiled tone into French cinema by assisting Feyder on *Le Grand Jeu*, a film he nevertheless denigrated as a rather shallow melodrama.[64] He was itching to launch his own career, to sign his name to a film in which he could believe. Yet Carné was not one to work up sketchy projects on thin resources. Here he differed from the young Vigo, Chenal, and Gréville, who dove into their first projects without thought of how they might land. Carné's years with Clair and Feyder had given him an exceptionally mature sense of all aspects of the French system of filmmaking.

No entrance into that system was better prepared. Given its impressive cast and crew, inherited en bloc from Feyder, *Jenny* (1936) could hardly have failed to take its place on the year's Ten Best lists. Its financing had been secured when, out of friendship, Françoise Rosay agreed to star in the film gratis. In tailoring the script to bring out her peculiar admixture of maturity and sentimentality, Carné fell into a rather conventional scenario concerned with a mother's efforts to hide her dubious profession from her innocent daughter. From their proper middle-class apartment to the fashionable brothel that Rosay runs in the evening, nothing about the decor would seem to suggest the dark themes for which Carné would soon be famous. In fact, despite Carné's resolve, *Jenny* might serve as a fine example of the standard fare offered to the sophisticated French public of 1936: an overt Oedipal drama, spacious enough in its themes to allow for both disturbing implications and overt moralizing, its surface is scrubbed clean. High-key lighting sets off the detailed props, while carefully positioned microphones make the seasoned actors—playing recognizable types—easy to hear.

Two aspects of the film, however, its often perverse dialogue and its occasionally dark ambience, cannot be so readily digested. Here Carné began to

Jenny: High-key melo. CF

Jenny: Low-key "milieu." CF

inflect the norms of the system in ways he would substantiate later on. Sheerly for the sake of atmosphere, he prefaced *Jenny* with a dark and sleazy London sequence, precisely the kind, it must be noted, that Pierre Mac Orlan had created so often in his fiction. This ambience recurs at the plot's turning point, when Jenny's innocent daughter falls in love with a hoodlum from the night-club. As they saunter alongside a picturesque canal, the sincerity of their feelings is confirmed by the working-class milieu.[65] Here the documentary shots of the canal and factories stand up ruggedly against the literally fake glitter of the nightclub and the falsely "proper" apartment. In the film's coda, Jenny, disconsolate but resigned to a life of loneliness, wanders aimlessly across a railway bridge, steam rising from below. These darker moments provide a kind of solid social pedestal atop which the melodrama could play itself out on its flimsy "white telephone" sets. Scarcely motivated by the plot, they indicate something like the filmmaker's path into his kind of movie.

Equally disturbing to the text and the spectator is the film's dialogue, written by Jacques Prévert. Carné claims that until 1936 he was completely unaware of the poet's interest in cinema and thought of him solely as the author of a Groupe Octobre union hall evening he had witnessed a few years earlier. Faced with a maudlin script to adapt, Carné instinctively reached for a writer completely outside the pale of realism.[66] Prévert, he believed, might lighten, streamline, and intensify the film. Their first encounter, which took place at a prescreening of *Le Crime de Monsieur Lange*, was decisive. As we know, for ten years this team would set the course of French and world cinema.

Immediately they recognized in their collaboration a potential that neither could have come up with alone and that would soon lead French cinema toward *le fantastique social*. Self-consciously generic in plot and character, *Jenny* gained from Prévert's pellucid dialogue.[67] This was the "poetry" that Carné, far beyond his mentor Feyder, believed should unmoor the social situations portrayed, letting them float in the imagination. Carné was a prosaic director in search of a remnant of nineteenth-century lyricism. Accordingly Prévert must have seemed to him, despite his satiric side, a sacred font of romantic words and images. All their films are buoyed by small bursts of "transcendence," shamelessly beautiful love duets whose lines Carné instinctively knew how to set off and direct.[68]

Aside from the quality of this dialogue in *Jenny*, Prévert's inventiveness is unmistakable in the hunchback character, Dromadaire (Jean-Louis Barrault). Through this engaging yet repellent misanthrope, Prévert could go so far as to mock even maternal affection. Barrault, and a more scathing misanthropy, would return in the next Carné-Prévert collaboration, the bitterly comic *Drôle de drame* (1937), which I have already described as belonging far more to the writer's sensibility and to the Groupe Octobre than to Carné.[69] It would be in their third production that the legendary Carné-Prévert balance would find its footing, whether going by the label "poetic realism" or *fantastique social*. Fittingly this came as an adaptation of Pierre Mac Orlan's *Le Quai des brumes*. Critics were hard-pressed to isolate the features of the film that made it stand out as so remarkably new, but they intuited that serious movies would be neither made nor seen in quite the same way after it.[70]

Mac Orlan himself was bewitched by the film, despite the quantity of alterations that made it resemble but the husk of his novel. He was proud to have had "influence over a certain atmosphere," praising the film for having the courage to delve into "that misery without end that lingers in the downtrodden sections of cities like an impenetrable fog. Gabin knows the quality of this misery in the violent images of his silence. Michèle Morgan, with neither gowns nor jewelry, without any defense before those who stare at her, offers us the imaginary life, so pure, of a young girl marked by sadness."[71]

The film conjured up its "vie imaginaire" by situating the purity of Nelly (Morgan) and Jean (Gabin) within an "ominous milieu . . . created with great precision, force, and density."[72] Critics were astonished: "Can you recount the story? Was there a story? It's a cruel game . . . a tragic poem that smells of the debauchery of the blood,"[73] a film that "has re-created the veiled atmosphere, gray and nostalgic, of Pierre Mac Orlan, our great poet of the dream state."[74] The moral dimension Carné sculpted in the film's heavy atmosphere surrounds Prévert's script, which goes a step further toward the dream state than even Mac Orlan had dared. One critic praised Prévert for contorting Mac Orlan's novel into a series of evocative incidents that unroll in a single, undifferentiated day. Some found the script too "literary"; others defended just this aspect: "I don't find Prévert's scripts too literary. I find in them the honest accent of exactitude; still (you can feel it in the songs he wrote for Marianne Oswald), Prévert knows how to make 'realism' in poetry. If this is literary, then that's too bad. I say, 'Long live literature.'"[75]

Literature's life was generally conceived as very long indeed. In France "literature" has always meant serious ideas and feelings, and it has meant attention to images more than to intrigue. So the respect that had been attained by

novelists like Mac Orlan, Francis Carco, or Roland Dorgelès (and that explicitly devolved on *Le Quai des brumes* in reviews that mentioned these authors)
was due to their "poetic"—that is, heavily imagistic—styles. Curiously, "painterly" atmosphere became the criterion for "literary" cinema. More curiously
still, such cinema was justified by its deep and dense expression of "reality."

This whirlpool of terminology symptomizes a scarcely understood shift in
the general perception of the role of cinema. Such a shift one can attribute first
to the Popular Front mentality that brought an anarchist poet like Prévert to
settle into a narrative form, and second to a critical community that had
shown itself increasingly prepared to listen rather seriously to a novelist like
Mac Orlan. We have seen that it can also be attributed to the influence of
German expatriates working in Paris since Hitler. Marianne Oswald, for example, brought "German expressionism into the French song" via her work with
Prévert and Joseph Kosma,[76] and cameraman Eugen Schüfftan, who shot *Le
Quai des brumes*, relied on a visual tradition that Carné cited as his own, the
tradition of Murnau and the *Kammerspielfilm*.

No matter what its source, this serious and widespread acceptance of popular "poetic" material in all the arts finds its cinematic apotheosis in *Le Quai des
brumes*. That Prévert's script was deemed "literary" points not to the fact that
a poet had sought to lift up an urchin art form, but that his script expressively
transformed lower-class values and issues as they were simultaneously being
transformed in song (Brecht, Weill, Marianne Oswald), in photography (Cartier-Bresson, Brassaï, Schüfftan), and in fiction (Mac Orlan, Carco). "Literary"
refers, in either a patronizing or a sanctifying way, to this panartistic aspiration. After all, the indisputable literary revelation of the decade was that
image-poet of the destitute, Louis-Ferdinand Céline.

Le Quai des brumes topped all French competition at the box office in 1938,
scoring heavily abroad as well. At the Venice Film Festival, Carné was honored with the prize for best direction, though his film was vilified for its decadent moral vision. An anonymous Italian critic expressed the amazement and
ambivalence it caused at Venice in what is, I believe, the most evocative review written for this or any other poetic realist film, a review given here in
extenso:

> For some time French cinema has fallen into the rhetoric of the representation
> of evil. People in decline, diseased in spirit and body, drunks and delinquents
> have been the protagonists of many films in which the lens with enormous
> clarity has magnified the details of vice, the wrinkle of sin, the stamp of moral
> decay, of a swarm of people adrift in society. Rough, violent and pitiless studies
> are the order of the day in French film production. Even French critics are
> rushing to demand an end to this flood of films whose documentary value is no
> credit to the country. From the visual angle of these films, France appears to
> have fallen prey to an anarchy of the spirit that it would like to pass off as

liberty; it appears bound to the lowest form of material life, to disorder and to violence; logically many who have a sense of dignity and pride will rise against this trend.

In films of the underworld, there is a conventional way to proceed, using contrast to strengthen the effect. When the darkness of the milieu seems to have snuffed out every hope of light, exactly then a faint torch is lit to restore the fertility of motivation according to the usual curve of dramatic rhythm, only to be shattered at the end in a dramatic crash. Similarly, in the mud flats of evil, a pool of water will reflect the sky, even a sky covered over with thick clouds. Or close by the desolation of a soul will always be found some spark of goodness and trust; in this way a dialectic lifts the film onto the level of poetry.

In *Le Quai des brumes* immorality is converted into sheer pessimism; through a delicacy of visual touches and of dramatic compositions, where an overall succession of gray shots slide quietly one after another in a cold and nerve-wracking sequence of bitter actions. Characters, coming out of nothingness, move as specters before falling again into nothingness. . . . A suicide and a de-serter, men who kill and are killed, these are the protagonists. Subjects who ought to be studied by criminal pathology turn out in this film to characterize frozen humanity in general. Certain psychological features, unusual for their acuteness in a film whose topic is so exhausted and abnormal, reach virtuosity in their expression; but it is a pity, I must immediately add, that such directorial talent is wasted on a project that is already feverish with the symptoms of consumption. . . . On the thread of its delicate introspective narrative, the film sometimes loses its balance, though more often excelling in its skillful direction.

With the excellent interweaving of gestures and actions to clarify the love of the two young people, the deserter and the pure girl . . . [Carné sheds] a zone of light in the middle of the darkness of so many errors and crimes. Jean Gabin and Michèle Morgan, the perfect couple, make tangible their delicate feelings through a network of glances and words that slowly and inexorably come to weave around them a destiny even stronger than themselves. These two lovers have hope; indeed they are the only ones who believe in and attain the strength to struggle in this pack of weak-willed people. The weaving of their union has the fineness of a sumptuous embroidery, bringing together the most beautiful shades of the entire story.

With this film the young director of *Le Quai des brumes*, Marcel Carné, be-comes one of the best of film directors. . . . In him one finds an assimilation of techniques so complete that one never notices the welding of the pieces, the linking of the scenes, or within any single scene the kind of mechanical compo-sition one usually sees in French film. The photography, by that old and clever Eugen Schüfftan, is marvelous. The shades of black and white, softened by filters, achieve a balance of the masses of dark and light that precisely follow the sense and the value of the film's poetic intention.

Le Quai des brumes: "Characters, coming out of nothingness, move as specters . . ." BFI

> We should call *Le Quai des brumes* the sad song of the underworld because of
> its form and content, so profound in its tone of truth. But for the sake of the
> spirit of these filmmakers and of their civilization we would prefer that the
> French should abandon, after this film, the representation of a world that is
> closed, oppressive, tormented with desperation and misery. Why cover this
> world over in slime only to seek a few shoots of wheat one might sow, when
> vast cultivated fields already exist?[77]

It is not just any atmosphere that this astute critic is describing from his healthy
Umbrian fields. It is a dark miasma that carries disease, or at least unease, and
that, while driving the cinema toward new depths of "introspective narration,"
responds to, and inadvertently produces, a degenerate society. Such moral
arguments are familiar. They form the foundation of Siegfried Kracauer's *From
Caligari to Hitler*. Within a year they would be leveled not only at *Le Quai des
brumes*, but at a score of French films, by the short-lived Daladier regime and
then again by Vichy. One might begin an inventory of poetic realist titles by
looking at the list of those films banned in 1939 as "demoralizing."

   It is never pleasant to dredge up Jean Renoir's cruel attack on *Le Quai des
brumes*, an attack so vicious it must surely have arisen from pressures it is best

not to contemplate. Like our Italian critic, and like the right-wing French, Renoir accused the film of decadence. What had he in mind when he went so far as to call it fascist? True, all the decent characters live on the penumbra of the town at Panama's bar, literally a last refuge. It never occurs to them to try to change their fate. Renoir, whose optimistic version of French citizenry, *La Marseillaise*, was shot and distributed at virtually the same time as *Le Quai des brumes*, found Carné's film repulsive in its lack of moral authority and in the passivity of its victims. Suicide, desertion, flight, alcoholism, and a low-key *amour fou* provide the only options for characters who wait to be oppressed. As our Italian critic pointed out, these specters come out of nothingness and fade again into it, never forming a community that might sustain better values. Every person struggles alone. This Renoir could not abide, but why term the film "fascist"? After all, Carné and Jacques Prévert certainly did not deserve even the suspicion of fascist leanings. Carné claims to have been tabbed before Renoir to oversee *La Vie est à nous* for the Parti Communiste in 1936. And, in any case, his are among the very few films that involve working-class concerns.

Renoir was perhaps cringing at the film's disturbing representation of contemporary life on the margins, at the petty thugs who run virtually unchecked through Le Havre while serving Zabel, Nelly's respectable, cultured, but sexually perverse "protector." Even before Renoir's hasty response was printed, Louis Chavance had seen to the bottom of Carné's social pessimism. In comparing *Le Quai des brumes* to Fritz Lang's *Fury* (1936), just released in Paris, he said, "Where the American film is tragic in the rebound of its action, the tragedy of *Le Quai des brumes* takes the form of inevitable steps toward a grandiose necessity, rather like some iron restraint exercised by the social body on the personality."[78] Chavance sees a great gain in the quiet, personal tragedy of the French film over the vengeful muscle of Lang's *Fury*. But Renoir reads such apathy as an invitation to fascism, indeed as protofascist in its sentiments about human frailty, the need for authority, and the relation of sexual decadence to violent behavior.[79] He might have pointed to the fairground scene where, let loose in their bumper cars, the wild id-figure incarnated by Pierre Brasseur crashes into the other "social units" careering around the floor. When he runs into Jean Gabin, however, the adolescent is slapped down and sent sniveling home. Edward Turk calls this a "primal scene" and an allegory of France's breakdown just before the war.[80] He also underscores the sexual anxiety of the punk Lucien (Brasseur), the suggested anti-Semitism in Michel Simon's portrayal, and the androgynous depiction of Nelly. Read psychoanalytically, these and other signs point to Carné's own anxieties; read sociologically, the film "is a very exact expression of prewar France."[81]

Given the reaction it stirred, one is tempted to say that *Le Quai des brumes* speaks the unconscious of a nation. The fairground scene, the bludgeoning of the father figure in the cellar, and the oneiric effect of the fog that blends such

Le Quai des brumes: The primal scene of social disorder. BFI

scenes together are crowned by the sinister discourse on art and on the loneliness of the artist spouted by the painter (Le Vigan) before his suicide. Jean will repeat this aesthetic as he seeks his own passage out to sea. *Le Quai des brumes* is an introspective narrative in the extreme. It advances a wholly personal moral code, one in which Chavance sees the personality blocked by the social body. And it came out the year of Sartre's *La Nausée*.

Of course Sartre would quickly come to stand for the engagé existentialist, committed to leftist political action. But in the days before the German onslaught, the tone he set, a tone Carné's film follows in its own way, whimpered with an overweening pessimism. Social retribution does not lead Jean to bludgeon Zabel to death, but rather something akin to personal disgust, anger at a grotesque world that contaminates an innocent like Nelly. Two years earlier there had been social fury when the same actor crushed another ugly miser in Renoir's *Les Bas-Fonds*. In that film Gabin's Pépel was cheered and then protected by the populist community around him. In *Le Quai des brumes* he acts alone and then wanders obliviously into the street to be gunned down. Dying in Nelly's arms, he hears the doleful horn of the ship leaving without him for Venezuela.

The purity of its morose expression distinguishes *Le Quai des brumes* from the dark atmospheric films that led the way to poetic realism proper. Jean

Gabin's helpless death at the end of *Pépé le Moko*, in sight of a ship leaving without him that blasts its horn and carries off his dreams, begs comparison with the Carné-Prévert classic. Where the exotic Casbah keeps Pépé from returning to France, and from the bejeweled enigma of Gaby, Jean dies on the very edge of France cradled by the plain, forlorn Nelly. Pépé's tragedy is one of lost opportunity, of nostalgia for a bright Parisian world that lies across the sea and back in years. Jean, on the other hand, is precisely a Parisian deserting his bleak country. In both films Jean Gabin, that archetypal "regular guy,"[82] dies on the margins of the marginal world he inhabits. And what of France? In the earlier film Fréhel sang of its centrality to all values, but in *Le Quai des brumes* it has faded into the general gloom.

More telling than the hopeless theme of *Le Quai des brumes* is its wistful dramatic construction. The entire tale unrolls within twenty-four hours across a series of vaguely linked locations. The streets, gray in the day, fog-enshrouded at dusk, take us ineluctably from one locale to the next where characters who are attracted to, or repelled by, one another develop the film's values through their laconic dialogue and seemingly futile gestures. By contrast *Pépé le Moko*, though primarily confined to the Casbah, manages to take us to a dozen locations through vigorous cuts. Pépé may be fated from the outset, but he maintains the illusion of controlling his destiny, an illusion the film's narrator perpetuates right up to the final scene. To calculate its difference from *Le Quai des brumes* one need only listen to the musical partition that amplifies Pépé's hopes and his danger; whereas Maurice Jaubert composed two quiet but relentless themes that correspond to no action whatsoever but act on the body of the film continually and chemically, not unlike the dominant gray of its lighting. Editing provides another measure of comparison. Count the large number of scene shifts and shot changes in *Pépé le Moko. Le Quai des brumes* contains fewer than two hundred shots, less than half the norm for French films of the period.[83] Only in its finale does Carné at last knot together through editing several of Prévert's most telling symbols: the departing boat, the escaping dog, the dying deserter, the drunkard sleeping soundly between white sheets. This coda is meant to bring out the inevitable interrelation of locations that might be thought of as pale pools of light diffusely spread about this crepuscular city set beside a darkling sea.

One can ridicule or rhapsodize the insistent sentiment *Le Quai des brumes* expresses; what counts for us is its manner of expression. In this context the atmosphere that dominates poetic realist films is interesting less for its meaning or tone than for its function as a medium blending characters with the worlds they inhabit. Atmosphere as an effect of cinematic texture, as a pervasive overtone emanating variously from cinematography, set design, sound, music, script, and acting, is also a figure. It speaks of sublimation (mists of feeling rising from a plot), of envelopment (where the spectator is suffused in the same light and sound as the character), and of figuration itself (where the visual and aural milieu embodies the character's way of being, *becomes* that being).

Through atmosphere poetic realism takes up the silent screen's project of cinematic impressionism, though without optical distortions and without the conceits whereby mental states were cinematically mimed. The label "poetic realism" suggests a blending of inner and outer states, not unlike that sought by the impressionist filmmakers. But Carné and his peers hoped to achieve something like a popular impressionism, one where the central consciousness of each film would not be precious and refined but would be "average," belonging prototypically to Jean Gabin. Gabin's unassuming discretion—his sincerity—invited mass audiences to adopt his limited view of a still more limited and inexplicable world, the world just as easily called *la fantastique social*.

A PERVASIVE PESSIMISM

Lest this characterization of poetic realism turn too insistently on the work of a single auteur or team (Carné-Prévert), rather than on the more general *optique* that had become available, indeed prevalent, in 1937, I would like to conclude by mentioning one more film of that year, *Le Puritain*. The inaugural feature by the forgotten Jeff Musso, *Le Puritain* arose to immediate, though temporary, prominence on the strength of its tone and its address. Adapted from a novel by Liam O'Flaherty (an Irish writer compared by some to Mac Orlan), it consciously sought an atmospheric style in the manner of another famous O'Flaherty adaptation, John Ford's *The Informer* (1935).[84]

Le Puritain has most in common with Chenal's *Crime et châtiment*, perhaps because O'Flaherty wrote the novel after visiting the Soviet Union where he had consciously sought to locate and digest the spirit of Dostoievsky. Like Raskolnikov, Francis Ferriter (Jean-Louis Barrault) is an impoverished, feverish intellectual whose ideas lead him to commit murder. Like Raskolnikov he is hounded by a police inspector (Pierre Fresnay) obsessed with both the crime and the criminal. Most important, like the Chenal film, *Le Puritain* unrolls in an oppressively dark and claustrophobic milieu that can be taken as the psyche of the central figure.

The credits roll over a bleak cul-de-sac reminiscent of *La Rue sans nom*. The camera repeatedly follows Ferriter through the low archways and up the winding stairs to a small garret where his bed is trapped in a corner. Doors and corridors dominate the film more than does its action. Even the murder of the young prostitute Molly seems anticlimactic after the approach to the threshold of her room. The spectator is thrust into the role of spy in this paranoid world that comes to rest only as a final door is closed, that of Ferriter's prison cell.

Signs of poetic realist decadence are abundant. Once again Fréhel, more forsaken than ever, sings of better days. Once again two men lock themselves

Le Puritain: A pervasive darkness. BFI

in a psychological drama that literally takes place over the body of a young woman. Once again the plot's moral (that prudery and rectitude harbor an unhealthy fascination with vice) sinks into ambiguity in the general atmosphere of the film's pictorial design. Like Grémillon, Musso was a professional musician and composed his own score for a film that works to equalize the registers of expression.

Banned in New York and many other states and countries, *Le Puritain* promised a serious and mature experience hardly conceivable early in the decade. Critics compared the film to Kirsanov's *Rapt* and to Mac Orlan's novels. They wrote time and again of its atmosphere. And they went on to award it Le Prix Louis Delluc, in a narrow vote over Renoir's *La Grande Illusion*. The astounding box-office and critical success of *Le Puritain* is the best evidence available to certify the triumph of a new kind of film, filling a different sort of audience expectation in France before the war. O'Flaherty "declared significantly that it could only have been made in France."[85]

In its palpable expression of a disturbed moral state, *Le Puritain*, like *Le Quai des brumes* and other poetic realist films, approaches in a popular mode the most sophisticated fiction of the time; it approaches both Sartre's *La Nausée*, with its spongy climate and alienated hero, and Georges Bernanos's *Le Journal d'un curé de campagne*, a novel written from within the soul of its central figure and set in the dank gray milieu of northern France.

Jean Renoir: Adaptation, Institution, Auteur

THERE are good reasons for treating Jean Renoir as an independent force orbiting French cinema from the lofty space to which he was launched by his prestigious family connections and his enormous talent. But Renoir can just as easily serve to illuminate the national cinema he contributed to. Never an average or representative filmmaker, Renoir was still faced with the same kinds of aesthetic, social, and business problems and options as his colleagues during the 1930s. He made enough films, and under a sufficiently diverse set of circumstances, that he can claim to have belonged to this period as much as any industry hack. And we can examine those films to stage in summary fashion our own representation of that period.

This need to scan the work of an acclaimed director may amount to a concession to auteurism, but it is motivated by an effort to gauge the general prospects for filmmaking and film viewing as these changed in the years preceding World War II. Can we not take Renoir as a kind of institution set within the larger institution of the film industry? Can we not treat him as a force and a resource as we do a host of other institutions (theater, criticism, labor unions, government cultural agencies)? Like these, Renoir's impact may have varied from case to case and year to year, but he stood out prominently and consistently enough to be in the way of whatever trajectories French cinema might think to take.

Renoir's talent (or "genius," as auteurists would call it) may argue for his special status, but surely he was by no means the only brilliant director of the epoch and more surely his talent required cultivation. Up until the Popular Front in

1936, he was scarcely noticed outside his homeland; and in France he was thought something of an "amateur" whose wealth and family fame permitted him to experiment now in one direction, now in another. But from *La Grande Illusion* in 1937 until the war, no one made films that were more ambitious, more costly, or more prestigious. It is not only because he became a giant in these years that I devote a chapter to his work; Renoir's consistent attitude toward the medium and his peculiarly independent status make him a quantity impossible to avoid. The same could be said, perhaps, of Marcel Pagnol (or even Sacha Guitry). We take up Renoir, however, because unlike these veritable auteurs who never strayed from their peculiar principles in carrying out their ideas about cinema, Renoir's consistency included his way of adapting to, or rather negotiating with, the shifting aesthetic norms and sociopolitical conditions of his times. Where Pagnol sequestered himself in southern France with his troupe and produced a unique species of movie that thrived in this period, Renoir's rapport with French cinema was more dialectical. Only after he returned to France in the 1950s can we begin to invoke something like Renoir's autonomous "world," the way critics from the beginning wrote of "le petit monde de Marcel Pagnol."[1] During the period that concerns us, Renoir's world was the public one of politics and entertainment, a very large world to which he needed to adapt.

Most of Renoir's films in the 1930s, especially the earlier ones, are literally adaptations, begging the question of authorship. Unlike other giants such as Sergei Eisenstein or Charlie Chaplin, Renoir was at home with material already shaped to the requirements of another medium. Does this inclination or this historical circumstance reduce claims about his stature? Those who believe he came into his own only with *La Grande Illusion* and *Le Règle du jeu*, based on original scripts, must feel this way. Yet, as we shall see, Renoir was forever adapting to whatever was around him. If his early efforts in the 1930s ransack literary sources, why not see this as in tune with industry practice, a practice that diminished in the second half of the decade? Renoir's authorship, in short, is bound to the practice of "adapting," taking that notion in its largest sense. Beyond his frequent reliance on literary works, Renoir adapted himself to industry conditions, to ideas and causes, and to methods that he intuited to be important. Walter Benjamin celebrated this sort of genius in his wonderful essays (written, by the way, at exactly this moment) "The Translator" and "The Storyteller."[2] Presumed to be mere middlemen in the commerce of culture, the translator and the storyteller are actually more appropriate to our age than authorial giants who belong rather more aptly to the nineteenth century. In keeping one eye on their own language and their own public, they strive to bring culturally relevant texts to life in contemporary history. The storyteller—and Renoir was proud to call himself one[3]—is at once an adaptor, an institution, and an author. In our century and in the cinema this is hardly paradoxical.

ADAPTATION: THE FIRST YEARS OF SOUND

Renoir may have had a privileged upbringing, but he sauntered into the 1930s like everyone else connected with the French film industry, searching for an appropriate response to sound technology and to American cinematic imperialism. Salvation seemed to lie in her literary patrimony, but which patrimony? At first, her prestigious theatrical tradition seemed the best hope for autonomy. Given the theatrical background of French producers, it was natural for them to ask playwrights to be the first to leap into the empty crater that the explosion of sound had made in the entertainment complex. Uncertain about this new hybrid, they could at least count on characters and sets that had been pre-tested on stage.

As we saw in detail with Grémillon's *La Petite Lise*, alternatives to this theatrical orientation frightened most producers who were wary of the expense and unpredictability original scripts always imply, particularly since they customarily could allot only a quarter the amount of money per film that Hollywood expended. Renoir could see that a respected and ingenious director like Grémillon would never receive the budgets or the distribution his films required and deserved. Even such stars of the silent era as Marcel L'Herbier and Abel Gance were suspect, while a rising force like Raymond Bernard was saluted by the industry precisely for his "caution."

Because of the dearth of soundstages, initially the new technology restricted production and gave producers far more authority than they had exercised only a few years before. Renoir, we have seen, forded the technological river of 1930 on the back of his friend Pierre Braunberger, who had decided to barter a reputation as promoter of the avant-garde for exciting commercial ventures with the entertainment entrepreneur Roger Richebé. It was the businessman Richebé who insisted that Renoir turn out the farce *On purge bébé* before entrusting to him La Fouchardière's riskier novel *La Chienne*.[4] And Renoir was happy to follow suit. In other words, although Renoir may have developed important new stylistic options in his early sound films, he did so while turning out theatrical comedies, including *Boudu sauvé des eaux* and *Chotard et Cie.*, just like everyone else.

This impasse, wherein strong directors were needed to counteract the inherent theatricality of French cinema, yet where such directors were distrusted, characterizes a petty industry hounded by taxation and fierce international competitors. Soon frustrated by his experiences getting work at the studios and then working there, Renoir sought financing outside the industry. His fabled exuberance helped him clinch precarious deals that had as collateral little more than his family name to which he could add the reputation of the novels the projects were based on: Georges Simenon's *La Nuit du carrefour* (1932) and Flaubert's *Madame Bovary* (1933). Renoir surely anticipated that

Chotard et Cie.: Light comedy genre. CB   *La Nuit du carrefour*: Dark *policier*. CB

both films would be looked at suspiciously by the industry. Unfortunately, however, both were also bruised by the critics and expired for lack of distribution. They are important for us, however, because they broke two paths (the prestige adaptation and the *film noir*) that French cinema has followed in its quest for distinction. Equally important was their artisanal mode of production, Renoir overseeing as "patron" what evidently were family projects carried out with the kind of verve, inventiveness, and coordination that would characterize the strongest films of the decade.

Out of his admiration for the genre, Renoir was the first to adapt a Georges Simenon *policier* to the screen. He was able to secure independent financing for *La Nuit du carrefour* because of the reasonable success he had just scored with *La Chienne* and because of the growing reputation of Simenon, who was a personal friend glad to authorize the project. Simenon would go on record as preferring the spontaneous improvisation of a filmmaker who plays with a novel to weighty adaptations that try to force the classics of Dostoievsky and Pirandello into some rigid conception of high cinematic art.[5] In Renoir he found exactly the sort of unpretentious approach he approved, and this satisfied the already-friendly producer. Moreover, Renoir could point to the current popularity of the actor he had in mind for Inspector Maigret, his brother Pierre, who was having a marvelous year on the Parisian stage.[6] Since this particular project arose among friends at the end of an exuberant dinner party, *La Nuit du carrefour* would have to be called an "amateur" production, although at this time such "one-shot" ventures were the norm. Between 1932 and 1934 close to two hundred production companies went bankrupt, most having tried to launch but a single movie. Unusual opportunities existed in a business climate that saw so many films under way and so many companies going under.

Perhaps because of its casual origin, its very modest budget, and its brief appearance on the screen, *La Nuit du carrefour* has been treated by later generations almost as a home movie that carelessly lost the thread of its complicated

plot, a film where friends and relatives adopted gangsterish poses amid makeshift sets or on evocative locations.[7] Renoir no doubt provoked this reception
by calling attention to the film's "féerique" tone, as compared to solidly plotted and acted gangster pictures like *Scarface* (1932), which it in fact cites.[8]
Critics have always been fascinated and audiences consternated by the central
role given over to atmosphere. Georges Altman in his *L'Humanité* review
described the dark and foggy effects of several scenes, adding that this visual
sadness harmonized "with the slang that from time to time bursts from the lips
of one of the characters," sinking us into a world much deeper than the plot.
Altman almost baptizes "poetic realism" as he struggles to define the film's
appeal.

> One could reproach the film for its languorous tempo, but this is just what
> removes it from an ordinary *policier*, bringing something brand new to the
> genre. Here one finds the impression of a mysterious duration that is so rare in
> the cinema. [The actors] play out this film just as they should: with more
> concern for its interior sensibility than for its dialogue and gestures. In truth, a
> curious film since it brings to its tale of murder a kind of new poetry, like a song
> full of foreboding in the night.[9]

A half century later Alexander Sesonske can only add detail to Altman's clairvoyant passage:

> Though over three-fourths of the film occurs in well-lighted interiors, it is not
> these moments that stay with us. Rather, our impressions of the gray highway,
> of darkness, rain, and fog in long vistas of the night, an obscure figure by a wall
> or under the trees, headlights brightening a small area of the dark road, seem
> to overwhelm these bright interiors and create the dominant tone of the film.
> A traveling shot past trees along the highway—the sharp black verticals of the
> trees receding to emphasize the deep diagonal perspective of the road—leads
> us into the film and holds us there. A shot of three work horses plodding slowly
> down a rain-swept road becomes charged with mystery and meaning.
>   The highway sounds that prevail through much of the film help give these
> exteriors their dominance ... the two sounds we hear most are the growl
> and whine of the highway, harsh, heavy, and insistent, and the light melody
> of the tango Maigret sets spinning on Else's phonograph.... This popular
> dance tune, wholly incongruous with the situation, has a rhythm that catches
> the movement and cutting of the scene and impels it forward as the mystery
> does indeed unravel itself.[10]

The very year that *La Nuit du carrefour* was shot, Pierre Mac Orlan characterized his poetic realist approach to fiction by providing an example that might
have come directly from Renoir's film: "I have no imagination. I rarely speak
about anything except what I have passionately observed. But what I have
seen generally bears with it such an air of mystery that I must seek out (as

reporters are always saying) supplementary information. Such information is often fortuitous and disconcerting. An accordion melody put next to a murder would produce a total effect of something that must be termed an enigma."[11] Sesonske too speaks of enigmas in this film greater than those of plot, enigmas that "create an atmosphere of the bizarre, the unpredictable, which join with the rain and dark and fog to form the most vivid impression we carry away from La Nuit du carrefour, an impression whose persistence erases the flow of incident and action from the center of our awareness."[12]

Ever since Victorin Jasset's Zigomar series (1911) the gangster and the mystery film have thrived by maintaining a careful ratio of plot, violence, and ambience. In tipping the ratio toward ambience, Renoir followed French taste, at least as it can be gleaned from the few memorable films made in that country in the silent era.[13] When the French did edge up to such subjects, as in Feyder's Thérèse Raquin, plot was subordinated to "the sordid, oppressive atmosphere" that turned into "a strange black and white symphony" of suffering and doomed intrigue.[14] The same could be said for Jean Epstein's supernatural films and for Grémillon's Tour au large (1927) and Gardiens de phare (1929), all of which use mystery and suspense as a pretext to explore the psychological valences of atmosphere.

Renoir may have banked on this tradition, and perhaps more on the popularity Von Sternberg had found in Paris with his Underworld and Docks of New York.[15] But in fact La Nuit du carrefour lost badly in competition with another sort of mystery film, the puzzler, best represented at this time by Marcel L'Herbier's visually straightforward adaptation of the classic "whodunit" Le Mystère de la chambre jaune (1930). Like La Petite Lise before it, La Nuit du carrefour was quickly plowed under and reduced to fertilizer for the atmospheric cinema that would take root after 1934. Renoir had guessed right about where the cinema was heading, even if he had gotten there too soon to profit from his investment. Mystery writers like Simenon—indeed, Simenon himself[16]—would be a crucial source not only for the tone of poetic realism but later on for American film noir.

With its minuscule publicity budget and short theatrical run, no one paid much attention to La Nuit du carrefour. Madame Bovary, on the other hand, put Renoir in the limelight for close to a year, even though it can just as readily lay claim to amateur status. It too was a pet project taken on by people outside the industry; it too was based on a novel, or should we say, the novel. The audacious plan to adapt Flaubert was taken up by publishing magnate Gaston Gallimard, who intended to test the cinema market for literary masterpieces. Rich and well-connected, he was able to muster uncommon resources, for example, commissioning a score from the famous composer Darius Milhaud. Yet Gallimard's commitment to the cinema remains in question. Robert Aron, one of his prolific authors, actually served as production administrator for *Madame Bovary*, which turned out to be Gallimard's only completed feature. Was it just an enormously expensive gift for his mistress, the celebrated stage actress Valentine Tessier? Gallimard insisted that she incarnate the most famous French character of all.[17]

At first Jacques Feyder was sought to direct a script to be written by the illustrious novelist Roger Martin du Gard. When Feyder refused, feeling ill at ease with the leading actress, Martin du Gard also pulled out. Undaunted, Gallimard approached Robert Siodmak and finally Jean Renoir, whose father had been close to his own father years before. A longtime acquaintance of Valentine Tessier, Renoir was glad to be able to direct her in a film, especially since alongside her he quickly cast his brother and the legendary actor Max Dearly. Paradoxically, in his view *Madame Bovary* offered a challenge to the resources of cinematic theatricality rather than narration.

> What finally attracted me, the great reason for this film, is that it was an experiment with people from the theater. Valentine Tessier and my brother Pierre were essentially people of the theater, and around them we had a troupe composed of many actors from the stage. Max Dearly was above all a man of the theater. And I was very happy to make a film, to write a scenario for these actors, with dialogue that I thought ought to be well spoken by people from the theater.[18]

Renoir's fascination with screen acting has little to do with that theatricality we have characterized as the zero degree of standard French film style. The latter derives from the boulevard stage with its "mots d'auteur," and its contrived discoveries and peripeties, whereas *Madame Bovary* presented Renoir with "les mots de Flaubert" and a sequence of actions that could surprise no one. Instead of the swiftness and brilliance sought by French producers and audiences, Renoir's languorous *Madame Bovary*, especially at its scripted length, was calculated to be monotonous, the "bovaristic" dialogue falling intentionally flat in the tedious interiors and moist countryside of Normandy. Renoir shot the exteriors in such a way as to emphasize their "cultivation." Fences and roadways organize the fields into predictable patterns that reduce the visual horizon. Sesonske calls this Renoir's darkest film, the one offering the fewest contrasts. Its style remains cool and objective, casting the romantic desires of its title character in a classical mold.[19] Renoir would return to this problematic in *La Règle du jeu* where a romantic aviator is constricted by a society and a geography laid out in advance. In both films, spontaneity being impossible, the romantic is doomed to die, leaving the suffocating structure intact.

Madame Bovary illuminates for this period the complex ecology involving subject, style, production practice, and reception. Having chosen this novel for its distinction, Gallimard could hardly refuse to accord it special treatment. For instance, he authorized an extraordinary amount of location shooting since Flaubert virtually demands it. This in turn could only stretch the technical acumen of an industry that otherwise was content to perpetuate old studio habits. Time and again, set designer Georges Wakhevitch was challenged to link the decor of a Parisian studio set with that of a location in Rouen. In one case this included a rainy exterior seen by Bovary through his office window. The solution to this problem, he claims, was more complex than fabricating the gargantuan sets he later designed for La Marseillaise.[20]

In another instance Renoir was determined to track from the hotel set where Emma Bovary lies beside her lover, past the room's tawdry decor, then out the window to catch the dreary facades of houses, before continuing along the little channel that carries away the city's rainwater and sewerage. Renoir was adamant that an organ-grinder in the street should play a nostalgic tune throughout the scene. The studio personnel despaired of pulling off such a complicated tracking shot, let alone trying to match the texture, light, and movement between the Parisian set where the actual filming had to begin and the Rouen location where it had to conclude. Renoir persisted and Wakhevitch, relatively new to film design, avidly worked against all advice. We know how important the success of such an effort was to Renoir who repeated similar camera movements in his remaining films; and Wakhevitch testifies amply to the learning experience this proved to be for him and for the rest of the technical personnel. One can scarcely overestimate the impact of this search for realism and ambience on those who form the artisanal corps of the film industry. Under the often preposterous aesthetic demands of a Renoir and the ingenuity of émigrés like Wakhevitch, the French cinema would learn to create remarkable effects on a reasonable budget.[21]

The adventure of shooting Madame Bovary might be said to outstrip the ultimate importance of the movie that resulted, for it was a remarkable event that had every chance to cause a public stir and to inflect the larger culture in a serious way. According to his biographer, Gallimard, with his entourage, hovered around the shooting both in Paris and for many weeks in Normandy, where he did not seem to mind paying for the leisurely production that was characteristically full of camaraderie and long sumptuous dinners. ("The ecstasy of intimacy," Renoir called it.)[22] As a publisher of great literature and a major benefactor of the theater, Gallimard had more right than most producers to hope to shape French cinema with a major work. Searching through the credits of French films of the 1930s one can occasionally locate other well-placed figures who tried their hands at prestigious film production. For instance, André Malraux's close friend, the dashing aviator Edouard Corniglion-Molinier, would finance Siodmak's Mollenard, Carné's Drôle de drame, and Malraux's own Espoir toward the decade's end. We have already encountered the most influential of such productions in *Lac aux dames*, which Philippe de Rothschild undertook at the very same time that Gallimard was assembling *Madame Bovary*.

Culturally prominent productions like these were meant, among other things, to regain for cinema the flagging attention of the educated class,[23] but equally they could serve as diversions for their producers. And in fact, this seems to have been the fate of *Madame Bovary* when Gallimard lost interest in what was never for him a genuine commitment to cinema. In fact, according to industry gossip,[24] his enthusiasm for the project was so linked to his commitment to Tessier that it waned when he fell out with his leading lady just as the film was being completed. Allegedly he threatened to burn the negative.[25] In any case he was in no mood to wager additional money on this sideline and inadvertently shunted the film onto insensitive distributors so as to have done with worrying about it. Unprotected, *Madame Bovary* was now in the hands of businessmen who thought nothing of shearing to under two hours what may have been a film over four hours long, one that might perhaps have been exhibited in two parts. Those who saw the director's cut (including Bertolt Brecht) were very enthusiastic.[26] But such are the dangers of independent production.

Madame Bovary's lack of dramatic high points and its generally depressing tone arrested any box-office advantage that the names of its stars may have initially provided and that Gallimard's authors tried to sustain through their generous criticism.[27] The *Pour Vous* critic summed up popular opinion in regretting a film so "monotonous on occasion—like the book, like life."[28] It is tempting to assume that Renoir ignored the public so as to directly confront the cultural elite of France, tempting to think that this was a major experiment in cinematic dramaturgy. Was this not Gallimard's mission in sponsoring the film in the first place: to enlarge the cinema through a serious novel, seriously acted? Had it received proper distribution, might *Madame Bovary* have shaken the foundations of the French system, or was its indifferent reception an inevitable result of its aesthetic ambition, as would be the case with *La Règle du jeu*?

It would be wrong, however, to think of Renoir as a renegade or prophet. He spent the first half of the 1930s scanning his cards and playing his hand from the little corner of the table he occupied. By and large he accepted the game, raising the stakes in many of the genres of the day: the staged comedy, the atmospheric *policier*, and the prestige literary adaptation. Those who look closely at his films will surely find an indicative tension in his handling of these genres. For us Renoir simply needs to stand as the most intelligent player of the day, leading us to the action—to realism, atmosphere, social topics, and a personal rather than industrial approach to production. The time when these qualities would flourish would soon arrive.

INSTITUTION: RENOIR AND THE POPULAR FRONT

Even before his connection with Ciné-Liberté, there could be no question that Renoir was *the* cinéaste of the populist movement. The production of *Toni*, something Renoir had taken on personally and without any pressure, certified his instinctively leftist sympathies and made him an independent force waiting to be drafted for the proper political enterprise. His first sound film without a literary source, his first to be shot fully on location, with neither stars to coddle nor producers to mollify, *Toni* can be taken to represent, in as pure a form as the cinema ever permits, its director's interests, concerns, and attitudes. What we earlier discussed in terms of Renoir's commitment to an exceptional "realism"[29] we might now think of as "social concern." What to do with that concern would consume and trouble Renoir's mind for the next three years as he moved into and out of association with the Groupe Octobre, the Parti Communiste Français, and the Popular Front. His political disaffection would come in 1938, as it did for so many other intellectuals. After that he obscured his biography, playing down his earlier involvement in communist causes and leading most historians to question, erroneously in my view, his commitment to the Popular Front.

Toni is rightly taken to be Renoir's first politically alert film, though it was hardly an astute intervention. While his genuinely politicized friends and colleagues were casting about for organized reactions to the events of 6 February, while the AEAR (an association of left-leaning artists and intellectuals) was mobilizing antifascist resistance through meetings, manifestos, and rallies, Renoir retreated to the south of France. So it would not be wrong to suggest that Renoir backed into film history by leaving the capital to make *Toni* at a particularly difficult moment in Parisian politics and in the film industry. Historians may argue over this film's import as a source for neorealism and hence a source for modern cinema *tout court*, but Renoir had nothing special in mind in making it other than the chance to exercise his métier in peace and quiet.

As for his political orientation, Renoir remained embarrassed by his privileged origins yet incapable of giving himself over to a movement.[30] On the other hand, the subject and style of *Toni* gave Renoir a definite cachet among leftists and should have raised their expectations for his next project, *Le Crime de Monsieur Lange*, particularly since this one was the inspiration of Jean Castanier, an occasional member of the Groupe Octobre.

Today, *Le Crime de Monsieur Lange* appears to have been written with the politics of the day directly in mind. Historians[31] treat it as either a significant or a disappointingly naive tale of socialist aspirations, as though Renoir designated it to play a strategic role just prior to the elections that would bring the Popular Front to power. In fact, it began like most other projects, with an idea tossed out, sketched into a scenario, sold to a producer, and developed for production. True, Jean Castanier's work with the Groupe Octobre may have tinged his original idea a bit red, and the eventual involvement of the Groupe in the production surely added to the relevance of its satire, but no party or individual monitored the film's usefulness. Jacques Becker, originally slated to direct the venture, was replaced by Renoir on strictly commercial grounds. And Jacques Prévert came aboard to rework the script because of its dramatic, not its ideological, clumsiness. If the result seems potent today, why was it taken so lightly by the leftist press in 1936?

Not that it was badly received. Indeed everyone agreed it was remarkably entertaining with no hint of theater about it. Its swiftness, and what François Truffaut later identified as its "spontaneity" and "grace,"[32] saved it from didacticism and pretension. But at first no one wanted to detonate its social charge. Roger Leenhardt of *Esprit* loved the film but apologized for its anticlerical jests, as if the cinema were no place for trenchant social satire.[33] Sadoul and Pierre Bost, as different as were their politics, agreed that the film's impact lay in its style, not its theme. "It's not the subject that makes the spectator applaud in front of *Le Crime de M. Lange*," argued Sadoul, "but the realism evident in each episode."[34] Bost said straight out that while "the film remains vivid, briskly conducted, and well supported by numerous genuine characters and a solid decor, I do not believe this story of a bad boss has any great social significance; nor does the character of the false priest have great satirical significance. But it's a fine film, firm and incisive."[35]

Keith Reader has traced the gradually emerging awareness of the politics of the film's style by sampling reactions to the famous 360-degree pan at the moment of Batala's assassination. In 1936 Leenhardt deemed it whimsical and superfluous. In the fifties Bazin came up with the brilliant intuition that the shot physically wrapped the whole collective into a single moral entity. Finally, in the late seventies, Daniel Serceau politicized Bazin's notion by tying the circling shot to the film's flashback structure, so that the audience becomes included in both the murder and its judgment.[36] The pan shot figures the dissemination of the film's Popular Front message from the courtyard to the borders of France and in this way embodies the élan of a social movement whose ideology has been best described less in terms of doctrine than of "movement":

This cultural élan [of the Popular Front] had repercussions on the distribution of culture as well as on artistic production, and even transformed models of behavior of social groups or individuals, shaping collective sensibilities. Jean Lacouture's expression for characterizing this historic moment, "a brief and fervent encounter between People and Culture," expresses this general effervescence and defines, at the same time, the consensus which cemented the active forces of the Popular Front: People in the place of proletariat; Culture with a capital C, a sole indivisible patrimony, instead of class cultures. . . .

We know that such a consensus was made possible ... by the profound reshaping of the political strategy of the PCF which passed from the slogan of "class against class" to one of rallying all democrats against fascism, of the union of French people against the 200 families. From 1935 onwards, the effects of this decisive transformation began to be felt, little by little, in all sectors of ideology and culture.[37]

Le Crime de Monsieur Lange must have been one of the first places this transformation was felt, for it not only preaches the doctrine of collectivity against the bosses, the clergy, and other vested interests, but it preaches as well the virtues of popular art in the age of mechanical reproduction. Lange's fervid imagination finds its way into the back pages of a tawdry magazine, then spreads across the city, proliferating in deluxe editions, posters, and even a movie version. A populist film about the worth of the "popular," *Le Crime de Monsieur Lange* promotes a genuine political alternative with verve and imagination. Amedée Lange "entertains" an audience and a social ideal; he entertains in the precise etymological sense of the term: "to hold between," "to keep up," "to keep going." This is the politics of representation on which the Popular Front ran, the charisma of a pentecost, a sending forth of the message. At this heady moment, publishing and filmmaking were more than businesses; they were, or must become, sacred commissions and holy institutions.

Le Crime de Monsieur Lange: Showdown of the stars. CB

Le Crime de Monsieur Lange: Cooperative "Groupe" venture. CB

Just back from Moscow, the Groupe Octobre felt very sure of their "anarchic gaiety" and wild improvisation. Reviewing *Le Crime de Monsieur Lange*, *Pour Vous* lauded Renoir for tying Prévert down to earth, making him stick to a serious line of thought, while Prévert, they claim, lent Renoir an inventiveness that gets to the truth by "flogging reality."[38] The friendship of the workers, the execution of the tyrant, the flight of the lovers, the anticlericalism—all this bubbles out of the spirit of the Groupe, lucid and enthusiastic, holding fast to a single maxim: "There are the bastards and then there are the others."[39]

As *Pour Vous* enjoyed pointing out, the film's irrepressible spirit flows from the spontaneity and improvisation on Castanier's modern Parisian set, whereas across the way, at the same studio, French cinema proceeded in its usual, heavy-handed manner: massive Harry Baur could be seen parading around a grotesque mock-up of a Russian town, barking out stilted lines as the eponymous Tarass Boulba. But "on [Renoir's] courtyard," *Pour Vous* continued, "we are all at the 'Editions Batala, Imprimerie, Livres et Périodiques, ateliers fermés de douze à quatorze heures.' Let's open the door."[40]

We have already walked through that door onto the inventive set Renoir animated with his tracking camera and deep-focus lens. The courtyard, laid out as a patterned array of individual but interlocking bricks, can be seen as the key metaphor for the social collective.[41] The diversity of characters and ambitions coexists in front of a camera that can peer across its limited expanse, observing foreground and distant activities. The film's central inspiration, the courtyard necessarily organizes the other spaces brought into play. The city of Paris is shown as a fan of streets, a potentially giant courtyard, united by bicycles, magazines, and the aroma of fresh laundry. The blending of location scenes in Paris with realistic studio sets is matched on the other side by the play of cardboard on the fictional set of Arizona Jim, something one of the characters explicitly notes ("It's not natural; it looks like a movie set"). Thus Renoir's film, like Castanier's set, explicitly inserts itself between fantasy and reality as a truly imaginative representation of the possibilities of social life. What kind of streets do we walk on, the film asks? What kinds of spaces join and divide us?

Le Crime de Monsieur Lange mythologizes the politics of the day, but in such a way as to make those politics seem within reach. The film takes its cue from its title character, for Amedée Lange is a writer whose tales of a far-off land inevitably become filled with local references. Lange's own creation, "Arizona Jim," may be a crudely projected ego ideal, but that character then fashions Lange into an effective hero himself, who can use a gun to right a wrong and then disappear across the border. Fiction, in short, creates images necessary for any politics worth the effort. And fiction, though conceived in the imagination, is born in the media industries, in the publishing industry foremost, but also in posters, photographs, and even in motion pictures. Once born, the images of fiction grow almost in spite of their author. The people demand "Arizona Jim" in new adventures and formats, all produced by the collective in what is truly a dream factory. Unlike Hollywood, however, this factory is itself based on a dream, that of shared social and economic relations.

And so before constituting an allegory about the morality of revolution, of individual acts of violence benefiting the social group, *Le Crime de Monsieur Lange* stages a prior allegory about the power and uses of representation. When the cunning entrepreneur Batala, disguised as a priest, asks at a newsstand for a copy of the right-wing tabloid *L'Echo de Paris*, he is overrun by throngs of poor children screaming for the newest installment of "Arizona Jim," hot off the press. Here the film questions not only the politics of publishing houses but their organization as well. In the 1930s one would have to think of Gallimard Press, where an inherent hierarchy and elitism nevertheless traded on leftist visions of social cohesion. Going further than this, *Le Crime de Monsieur Lange* questions the established hierarchy of the arts, which holds literature above popular fiction and writing above images.

"Arizona Jim" must outduel *L'Echo de Paris* for the hearts of the citizens of a renewed France, before Lange can gun down Batala in the corner of the courtyard. The people, popular culture, and the imagination must work together, in a giant spiritual and material collective, to protect the young baby that Estelle and Charles will produce, to protect the ideas incubating in the heads of other Langes, to protect the collective. As befits a good "western," they must do so without the protection of established social institutions like police and government. Justice is meted out by ordinary citizens who listen to Valentine's apology in a café. The people judge Lange innocent, as do we who eavesdrop on the proceedings by watching Renoir's movie. Thus Valentine tests the truth of socialism in the story she so exuberantly tells, and the movie we watch comes ringed with the warm glow of a "natural community" of enthralled but judicious auditors. In the mythology of the Popular Front, publishing, radio, and filmmaking amplify but do not alter this fundamental mise-en-scène of storytelling.

Le Crime de Monsieur Lange makes us confident in the media when these are properly—that is, humanly—employed. In 1936 Jacques Prévert and Jean Renoir inspired such confidence, committed as they were to small-scale human virtues like simplicity and wit. The stories they told, the one in language, the other on the screen, take flight from a wonderful gift they shared, a gift that innumerable witnesses have elaborately reported: both found their greatest joy in entertaining friends around the café table with provocative, penetrating, and always amusing anecdotes. *Le Crime de Monsieur Lange* celebrates the lightness of that gift and somehow makes it weighty.

Seen beside the rather turgid naturalism of *La Chienne* and *Madame Bovary*, *Le Crime de Monsieur Lange* dances through the often disturbing issues it raises (class exploitation, abortion, and assassination, just for instance). Riding atop the material forces of history, the little community in the courtyard takes on a buoyancy that makes the film rise all the higher, the more Renoir's tactile approach presses it down. Just after the cooperative has been proposed and declared, the camera describes (in the geometric sense of the term) an exquisite figure of liberation. Outside the printing shop it moves laterally to track Lange as he skips happily to Pierrot to tell him the news. Deftly it dips as he descends the stairs (anticipating the famous 360-degree climactic pan) and then reframes the boarded windows of Pierrot's room on which have been plastered grotesque ads for Batala's series *Javert*. Crowbars come from out of frame

Le Crime de Monsieur Lange: Love across the courtyard. BFI

to peel away the posters and the boards, letting the sunlight break onto Pierrot's sickbed. A reverse shot now lets Pierrot see just as far as he likes across the courtyard. There right in front of him are his friends, tools in hand, asking after his health. And there in the most distant plane is Estelle, being lifted (floating it seems) out the laundry window to run to him across the diameter of the courtyard. The space, the sunlight, and the bright anticipation of young lovers charges with feeling whatever the abstract notion of "cooperative" may have held for us.

Le Crime de Monsieur Lange may have started like any other project, flowing naturally onto the screen in 1936, but it would have been inconceivable in 1930. The stakes of what was possible in cinema had been raised. Even if the press, including the leftist press, had not understood this, some viewers got the picture. A letter to the editor of *Ciné-Liberté* provides this rare testimony: "I saw *Le Crime de Monsieur Lange* in a theater composed of proletarians and petit-bourgeois. They applauded and always at the most characteristic passages with a sureness of judgment that would stun 'the elite' if these would ever condescend to mix with the people. They were especially raucous at the moment when Jules Berry disguises himself as a priest and says: 'With this costume you can go anywhere and people give you money to boot.'"[42]

Read as the first of a series of social allegories, *Le Crime de Monsieur Lange* exuberantly expresses the optimism of prerevolutionary passion. Self-confident, its style, like the community whose song it sings, exults in youthful power, a power to playfully bash in the wooden boards that block a view of the courtyard of life and that keep us from seeing the horizon of history. After such a film, Renoir was expected to bring social consequence to all his work. Not that he held a coherent or sophisticated political viewpoint. He had to be convinced to accept the offer the Parti Communiste made that he oversee *La Vie est à nous*. He never joined the Party, and one account suggests his relationship with it ought to be recognized as blatant and mutual opportunism, even claiming that he accepted the offer only after Pierre Braunberger assured him it would give him what he desperately needed, a loyal following and a core audience.[43] Yet even were this so, once he started work with his friends on *La Vie est à nous*, Renoir dedicated himself seriously to the politics it preached.

And he was rewarded for it. In December 1936 the Prix Louis Delluc was bestowed on him—by a self-constituted jury of "those under forty years old"— ostensibly for his most recent effort, *Les Bas-Fonds*. Curiously no one was willing to stand up for that film itself, about which critical reaction was mixed. In fact, Renoir was being honored for his general service to the Popular Front across three daring films none of which had been a commercial success. *Comoedia* went so far as to suggest that the prize was actually a belated honor to the wonderful and underappreciated *Le Crime de Monsieur Lange*.[44] The honor was tainted by gossip surrounding the voting. Evidently numerous ballotings were required, and Renoir came in as a compromise winner, to offset the recipient of the more official Grand Prix du Cinéma Français, which went to Léon Poirier, whose *L'Appel du silence* represented the other end of the political spectrum, having been produced with funds raised by the Catholic Church.

Les Bas-Fonds was certainly taken in the spirit of the Popular Front. Renoir's greatest antagonist, the fascist critic François Vinneuil, had no doubts that "M. Jean Renoir only chose this subject, of course, because he saw in it a symbol of the class struggle . . . a depressing film, treated with all the usual pissoir atmosphere of naturalism and with a stupendous sense of futility."[45] Other critics were flabbergasted that Renoir could utterly deracinate this Russian tale. Yet this was what he stipulated to Alexandre Kamenka, the émigré head of Les Films Albatros who had approached him to direct. Renoir was lured to adapt Gorki out of a solidarity with the Soviet Union, but he could not imagine adapting himself and his actors to Russian garb, mores, and gestures, making a sort of lower-class *Tarass Boulba*. Better to adapt the play to French circumstances, or to a no-man's-land that his French actors could populate. Gorky readily gave him his imprimatur, though he had renounced his own play several years earlier as out of tune with the new social realism of the day.[46]

Kamenka had chosen Renoir on the advice of Eugène Lourié, the Russian set designer who would replace Castanier and work with Renoir for the rest of his career in France and the United States. Lourié had happened on the set of *Madame Bovary* in 1934, where Renoir's way of handling actors had impressed him. He convinced Kamenka that Renoir's version would be more up-to-date, and more accessible to a contemporary audience than a version done by a Russian director like Victor Tourjansky, which was bound to be nostalgic.[47] For his part, Renoir recognized in the mix of Gorki's characters the chance to play out his favorite dramatic device, that of having a member of one class pass into another. Here the Baron (Louis Jouvet) descends from the heights of nobility to the lowest rung, while Pépel (Gabin) rises from the criminal ranks to take on a social role as unelected moral leader of the tene-

Les Bas-Fonds: The baron, downwardly mobile. BFI

ment's motley inhabitants. Prostitutes, alcoholics, failed artists, and brigands give Renoir a spectrum of types and personalities varied enough to hint at a populist union of interests. This is confirmed by Pépel's spontaneous murder of the evil landlord, ratified by the crowd that surrounds him, in a scene that must be taken as a reprise of Lange's assassination of Batala.

The minor argument surrounding Renoir's adaptation of Gorki coalesced on its setting. Opponents were angered not just that a Russian play should be ripped away from its Slavic home but that such a materialist play should be acted out in limbo. Renoir, however, was not concerned to flagellate the Russian social system of 1904, the date of the play's composition, or to take on any particular political institutions. For him, *Les Bas-Fonds* focuses on the more universal, prepolitical interplay between social classes and social groupings, no matter what the geography.[48] He stages this interplay on three different sorts of locales. At the bottom we find the zone of the play's title, the tenements and the prison. At the top we have the Baron's manor, the casino, and the military headquarters. Pépel's surreptitious invasion of the manor during his burglary symmetrically inverts the Baron's invasion of the doss house. Their dramatic encounters lead them to the banks of the river, typical of the film's third locale. Here and at the riverside café we can imagine middle-class Frenchmen concerned with neither aristocracy nor destitution. Indicative of Renoir's interests, these open spaces provide the background for the film's most famous dialogues and for its incongruously upbeat conclusion, Pépel and his girl jauntily going down the road à la Charlie Chaplin, Boudu, and the heroes of *A nous la liberté*.

Les Bas-Fonds carries contradictory, perhaps incoherent social ideas, but it is true to a good many Popular Front themes. The same may be said for *La Grande Illusion*, easily Renoir's most successful film. This time the military serves as gathering point for men of different classes, different nationalities, religions, and races. The matrix comprises both national solidarity (all the French work toward the success of the escape) and class solidarity (Boildieu and Rauffenstein show mutual respect, German and French common soldiers fraternize). The decline of the aristocracy, sentimentally symbolized by the cut carnation, is balanced by the rise of a wealthy class of bankers represented by the Jew, Rosenthal. The thematic richness of this film seems inexhaustible.

Yet it is less for his socially complex themes than for their ingenious presentation on the screen that Renoir is celebrated as the decade's greatest filmmaker. He was the populist director par excellence because, as Henri Langlois put it at the time, he displayed a "naturalistic talent . . . which works through externalization: in the look of a decor, in the seductiveness of a costume, in a character's attitude and gestures."[49] While several other directors may have employed social issues as provocative background for the stories they told, Renoir put the clash of classes into direct visual and dramatic play. The deep-focus photography he championed, the shooting through doorways and windows, the long tracking shots, and the seemingly casual but always indicative blocking of actors turn the spectator into both sympathetic witness and judge. Renoir's humanism derives less from the sentiments his characters express than from a style that maintains contradictory elements in a single field, and from the themes suggested by such coexistence.

Whether hovering around his themes or his style, dozens of studies have credited Renoir's humanism as the triumph of a brilliant worldview expressed over and over in the great films of this period. But from the point of view of the period, the credit may lie elsewhere, as Christopher Faulkner heretically suggests in relation to Renoir's most beloved film, *La Grande Illusion*: "Qualities for which Renoir the man is generally praised in this film—his much celebrated fraternity and internationalism—were produced by the Popular Front. In fact, there is no useful evidence that these are qualities of character at all; rather, they are themes, themes authored by history. They are not 'natural' to Renoir or inherent in his personality."[50] Faulkner shocks us with the realization that while fashioning this masterpiece of cinematic art—while perfecting an aesthetic to express timeless human values—Renoir was paradoxically caught up in and by his times. He devoted his evenings, for instance, to the often virulent political tracts he dashed off for *Regards*, *Commune*, and *Ciné-Liberté*. History, even more than genius, ran through his camera and his pen.

To read Renoir's later interviews or the judgment of critics, one would never suspect that *La Marseillaise* was thought at the time a far more impressive and consequential undertaking than its predecessor *La Grande Illusion*. Its failure at the box office and with the press quickly deflated the balloon of hopes that this would be a great and totally relevant film. From the moment of its disappointing premiere, the politics associated with *La Marseillaise* have distressed both cinephiles and politically conscious critics alike. The former confide that politics contaminates Renoir's aesthetic just then attaining its most glorious heights; the latter accuse that very aesthetic (based on the ethical premise that "everyone has his reasons") of establishing a conciliatory tone that disarms the violently successful Revolution of 1792 it treats and the rather pathetic one of 1936 that it purportedly wants to resuscitate.

La Marseillaise was never tacit about its parti pris. This is the French Revolution as seen by the Popular Front. The question is: in what ways can or must a film made about a revolution—equally a film made for a revolution—be itself revolutionary? Its sheer size, instead of lifting hopes about its social and aesthetic consequence, raised doubts about its effectiveness as a mass market strategy. To leftist historians of later generations, the very idea of pandering to the masses via entertainment is at odds with the mission of contestation common to all truly political films. In Buchsbaum's view, *La Vie est à nous* far outscores *La Marseillaise* just on the audacity and novelty of its genre, the political essay.[51] Renoir could not but compromise his art and his politics in trying to couch a significant allegory within the tired form of the historical epic.

Indeed the question of form displaces and restates the film's own question of political revolution: how can a radical vision held by a few grow to infect the throngs of those who make up a society? How can the beliefs about a populist cinema, promulgated by an elite at *Ciné-Liberté* and in *La Vie est à nous*, break out into the commercial cinema so as to revolutionize it? Or again, how can the Popular Front take command without compromising the aggressive ideas that were articulated by the intellectual cadres responsible for its organization?

The extent of disappointment over *La Marseillaise* may be, as Buchsbaum insists, "directly proportional to the inflated hopes with which the project had been inaugurated,"[52] but I take those hopes to be tied less to the politics of the project than to the expectations set up by the very genre of the historical epic. In the anxiety of 1938, even politically astute critics were unable to put aside their conventional notions of what a national historical film ought to look like. From this perspective we might even say that the failure of *La Marseillaise* testifies to its challenging, not its compromised, form. Reworking a tired genre in unexpected ways, it lay undigested in the public's belly, just as *La Règle du jeu* would eighteen months later.

With the film's genre in mind, Renoir seems hardly ingratiating. Had he truly wanted to rally the French at all costs, he would have used the movie stars of the day to play the heroes of yesteryear. Instead he rendered an anonymous history with anonymous players and, except for the crucial instance of the storming of the Tuileries, he filmed a history that might be called "eventless." Rummaging in archives he located names of unknown characters to portray scenes of marginal use to his plot and of less use to the plotting we usually think of as history. Small scenes such as that in which the conscripts are taught to load and shoot muskets risk showing off his erudition.[53] More germane sequences, as when the patriots are taunted by the Royalists on the Champs-Elysées, question revolutionary heroism altogether by dint of their clumsiness. Soldiers seldom march in *La Marseillaise*; they saunter jovially with girls on their arms. Even at the film's climax, Renoir deliberately focuses on children playing marbles in the street before craning up to show the people gathering to storm the Tuileries. He would seem to be a prophet of the new historiography that was taking root in the 1930s. As he later put it, "History with a capital *H* is fabricated by historians. But in a film one can try to make comprehensible the 'côté haché,' the irregular unforeseeable current of life as it is led even during the great moments."[54]

Renoir went out of his way to insinuate his camera comfortably into the lives and habits of characters who generally receive little screen time in historical films. When Bomier's mother acquiesces in selling some property, allow-

La Marseillaise. BFI   The history of everyday life.   *La Marseillaise.* BFI

ing him to enlist in the Fédérés, he skips jauntily out the door. Every principle of filmmaking requires Renoir to follow Bomier, to make use of his energy and his direction, and to join the band that will be the focus of the narrative. Instead Renoir tracks from the sobbing mother along the wall of the modest home, where it notes a pitcher, a platter, a coffee grinder, and a pile of potatoes, en route to the window where his sister looks out in silhouette. As she shutters the window, we can glimpse a group of men roofing the building across the way. Incidentally we catch sight of Bomier cavorting through the streets below. "More than the jumps and jolts of history, [Renoir] has chosen the *longue durée* that makes the small people into conquerors. This sense of history brings with it . . . an approach to mankind by means of the quotidian."[55]

Two sequences seem designed to highlight the popular aesthetic *La Marseillaise* is out to promote. The first replicates in miniature Renoir's project: when Bomier takes his girlfriend to a shadow play, they watch a political allegory on a white screen just as we do in the movie theater. Their laughter forms a community meant to spill from the eighteenth-century theater to the one in which we sit. Moments later, the popular press—the *Ciné-Liberté* of its day— begins turning out broadsides to alert all citizens to the state of history and of their part in it.

La Marseillaise asserts the ascendancy of these popular forms of representation as the means to the ascendancy of a new body politic in France, a body with a new voice bellowing its allegiance to nation rather than to the deteriorating person of the king. Yet the common citizens of 1938, many of whom had contributed to the film through their trade union, wanted to see Danton, Robespierre, and Marat and wanted to see them played by the kings and queens of the fan magazines. Nonetheless, Renoir dealt out of his film the great actors of the day who had offered their services when it was first announced. Louis Jouvet survives, but neither Jean Gabin nor Erich Von Stroheim nor Maurice Chevalier. Instead little-known actors from the south take on the roles of the equally little-known patriots. Curiously, even these were replaceable. The role of Bomier, destined for Blavette, was given to Ardisson during shooting. One can still glimpse Blavette's Bomier in the background of certain sequences,[56] a "mistake" that makes a point: Bomier is a function, not a person, and each of us might take up that function if called upon. Renoir's film meant to make such a call.

But reviews indicate the call went unheeded, for the scenes with the courtiers, portrayed by Comédie-Française thespians, were universally preferred to those of the ragged patriots. The infuriated fascist press clamored for a return to Abel Gance and his treatment of *Napoléon*, while many leftist critics felt let down too, not buying the argument that Renoir had assassinated History on behalf of its formerly anonymous subjects, just as those subjects did away with the king in the great story of the Revolution.

The Left particularly deplored Renoir's gentility in filming the émigré nobles. Their quotidian stupidity, their obsessions with concepts we no longer understand, and their recourse to elegance let nostalgia seep into and contaminate Renoir's satire. In this *La Marseillaise* is the direct forerunner of *La Règle du jeu*. Not only do all have their reasons, but each possesses them in a manner worthy of attention. Renoir's analysis of class interests requires a sympathetic treatment of both sides of the dialectic. He refuses to merely applaud patriotic sentiments at the expense of Royalist views, for all ideas—even those on the way out—are signs of their times.

Yet Renoir's position is not quiescent. Political history, like the history of artistic styles, depends on forcibly grabbing power at the moment a disintegrating institution can no longer wield it with authority. *La Marseillaise* provides a particularly shiny emblem of this position. After Moissan has delivered an impassioned order to seize the forts surrounding Marseilles, Renoir cuts logically to a tower standing out against the ocean. But then he lets all tension slip as his camera glides along the shoreline below the fort to give us a fresco of men lounging easily at the beach. This is a shot that could have come out of *Une Partie de campagne*, precisely the kind of lax, directionless shot for which he was criticized in his handling of *Les Bas-Fonds*. In the context of the French Revolution, such leisurely observation seems completely inappropriate. The camera finally rests on a jovial man, a painter and stand-in for the director, who bemusedly denigrates sentimental art as he draws smoke from a pipe into his large belly. "Most dawns are dull and gray," he says, "though a look at paintings would never tell you so." The pan continues: behind the painter and to his left stands Arnaud intently looking at his pocket watch. He gives the signal that it is time to begin. Without changing demeanor, our painter rises to become a militant patriot, helping bringing down the fort by a ruse and by the camouflage of his perpetual good humor. In refusing to divide the landscape and the action with even a single cut, Renoir joins geological timelessness ("most dawns") with eventful history ("It's time to begin"). Arnaud can sense when "most dawns" must be supplanted by the "new dawn of history" that Goethe announced after Valmy, and with which the film concludes.

Put this way *La Marseillaise* lives up to its understated subtitle: "A Chronicle of Some Happenings That Contributed to the Fall of the Monarchy." Put this way it is no wonder that its most illustrious original collaborators, Marcel Achard and Henri Jeanson, should so excoriate it upon its release. Achard found it utterly boring. "Not a scene, not a speech, not even an image in its whole first hour is worthy of a remark."[57] Naturally Achard attributes this to its ill-conceived script and its "stringy, ragged dialogue." Clearly he would have preferred a script featuring a clash of great men, where spectators participate in the birth of the Republic through identification with leaders who struggle to the death almost in a ritual of sacrifice. Renoir demanded more of the cinema and more of his audience.

To summarize, current judgments about the worth of *La Marseillaise* either decry its weakling political stance or they applaud it for digging beneath the public events of the official revolution, that is, for representing the scarcely discernible movement of ordinary people that pushed the revolution up through the cracks in the marble floors of the royal palace. In the first case, the film's box-office and critical failure measures its timidity. In the second case, its failure, like that of *La Règle du jeu*, should be taken as an index to the enormous strain it put on a complacent public, a public unprepared to take responsibility for its own history and loath to make the effort demanded of a cinematic experience in which everything has not been predetermined by stars and by plot.

From my perspective *La Marseillaise* deserves neither condemnation nor canonization. It deserves in fact the fate of the Popular Front that spawned it. Its generosity of tone was meant to fuse together the multiple coexisting incidents that make up the history of everyday life in the same way that the national anthem is meant in the film to join quite different people in the common pursuit of justice. Did the architects of the Popular Front or of this film ever believe in the possibility of such democratic harmony? How could Renoir offer a Revolution at once amiable and effective, spontaneous and historically directed? A potential for bad faith lies here, in the way Renoir has structured his film so as to provide the illusion of a lack of structure. The narrator both harbors the proper perspective on history and yet feigns to be a mere citizen, standing modestly in the crowd as one of the people.[58]

This is hardly Renoir's problem alone or one confined to filmmaking. The Popular Front would never have succeeded had not anarchists and malcontents found themselves conscripted by history and by political savants, so that they could march enough in step to swing an election. Free play may be the goal of social change, but it is hardly the means. To make an effective film while avoiding dramatic plotting and control is just as contradictory as hoping a new order will arise without the discipline of politics or the sacrifices of violence. No one should be more aware of this than a film director responsible for coordinating the vast resources that go into a monumental production like *La Marseillaise*.

Renoir's harmony with the Popular Front arose because of the generous conciliatory tone both preached.[59] "For a short time," Renoir wrote, "the French really believed that they could love one another. One felt oneself borne on a wave of warm-heartedness."[60] Even before the politically inspired *La Marseillaise*, the coordinated understandings among rich and poor, Jew and Catholic, even Frenchman and German had been the subjects of *Les Bas-Fonds* and *La Grande Illusion*. Diversity coordinated under a "unity of conception" is the way Renoir defined his approach to filmmaking and his style while working on *La Marseillaise*, a film carrying the tone of the Jacobin meetings it depicts where many have their say, where everyone reacts enthusiastically and idiosyncratically, and where a single anthem miraculously emerges, sung in various registers but sung by everyone together.

The very "warm-heartedness" of such a vision of art and of politics is enough to put it under suspicion. But it is a vision that held sway in those suspended months of the Popular Front. Sharing it, Renoir was led to relinquish absolute control over his film so as to respond spontaneously to the action and the actors he had set in motion. Avoiding the patronizing bombast of crude propaganda and the puerility of mere entertainment, he sought a middle zone, where he and his film could profit from the tension between his viewpoint and that of his co-creators, between the vitality of the parts and the intelligibility of the whole, between history (both past and present) as accomplished fact and history as still unknown. It has been one of my chief goals to pay attention to those films that mined this middle zone. If locating it there defuses the revolutionary pretensions of *La Marseillaise*, we can at least credit Renoir with an uncanny understanding of the social responsibility of style. From this understanding comes his status as an artist at once popular and elite, amiable and difficult. He was exactly the right director for the Front he marched with in these years.

Auteur: Renoir and Naturalist Fiction

Although Renoir lent himself to the leftist causes of the late 1930s (and later regretted having done so), he always believed himself independent of every movement, cultural and aesthetic, including poetic realism. An early auteurist, he believed style and subject matter to come out of the biography and biology of the director and he loathed being grouped with other artists. He is known to have denigrated Vigo and vilified Carné. He caused a scandal when he lashed out at *Le Quai des brumes*, which he retitled *Le Cul des brêmes* ("the whore's ass").[61] He could have pointed to a dozen aspects that he abhorred: its sniveling fatalism, its sparse and tidy sets, its reduction of characters, its focus on a single character at the expense of social context, its brooding tone, and so on. Although many of these characteristics belong equally to *La Bête humaine*,[62] Renoir can be tied to poetic realism only against his wishes and perhaps momentarily. For the poetic realist sensibility appears timid and death-obsessed when set alongside the expansive, life-enthralled, bon-vivant image that we know he cultivated. Roger Leenhardt insisted on the literally corporeal foundation of this opposition, seeing Carné as fundamentally a loner and Renoir as garrulous and gregarious by nature:

> I distinguish a fat and a lean France. Lean Racine, Diderot, Mérimée, Anatole France, Valéry. But fat Rabelais, Hugo, Balzac, Zola, Claudel. Renoir is a fat Frenchman who loves to surround himself with a team of solid eaters and drinkers, merry people full of flesh, just as his father loved to paint his carnations and his bathers bursting with health.[63]

And so as much as modern scholarship might like to gauge Renoir's films and activities from 1935 to the war with reference to the prevailing social conditions and political ideology,[64] the eight magnificent and varied films he fashioned, one after another, in these short years have compelled most critics on the contrary to gauge the period with reference to him. His staggering output spreads far beyond the contours of the dominant social and aesthetic movements of the day: the Popular Front and poetic realism. This is what I mean in suggesting that Renoir can himself stand as an institution. If he lent himself to other institutions from 1935 to 1938, he also built himself into a supremely confident auteur at the same time, planning and executing projects of immense consequence for the history of cinema.

Renoir's self-fashioning has its own history. He may have adopted the social concerns of the Parti Communiste in 1936, but he came to this period with a way of understanding the world and art that was as personal as his own extraordinary biography. By disposition and background, for example, he identified himself as born and bred a "naturalist," and a certain brand of naturalism is what, among other things, he determined to bring to French cinema. Even after his approach began at last to mesh successfully with the norms of the industry, his films continued to convey the sense that they derived from a source independent of the industry, that they came from an auteur standing in relation to, but not utterly assimilated by, his troubled era.

Not only does this perspective return Renoir to his customary status, the topic of directorial independence comes to rest on poetic realism, seen this time as a set of strong films cut off from social institutions. The intersection of Renoir with poetic realism, approached already in *La Chienne*, takes place at last in *La Bête humaine*, a film set on the hither side of the Popular Front, a film in fact set beyond the support of the social institutions it involves and peripherally analyzes. In his singular way, Renoir condensed the unspoken project of poetic realism by giving birth to a film that is as private and as dark as could be imagined at that time. *La Bête humaine*, I plan to show, takes Renoir away from the staging of social dramas to the writing of an intensely intimate novel, and it does so because of the tradition of naturalism that he had carried with him even in his most theatrical productions. *La Bête humaine* is prefaced by a full-screen photograph of Emile Zola, whose solemn mien darkens the entire film, reminding us that society is ultimately made up of isolated individuals the mystery of whose complexes it is the job of the novel, and of a certain cinema, to represent.

Because of *La Bête humaine* Renoir appears today as the filmmaker in whom the contradictory tendencies of the period are most visible. In him the optimism of the Popular Front meets the pessimism of poetic realism, and the sociality expressed in the subject matter and the form of theater stands alongside the alienation of the novel and the isolation of every reader of fiction.

Renoir is usually associated with the theater. By some accounts his very choice of vocation grew out of his love of actors and of staging them. His first film of the 1930s, *On purge bébé*, derived from the playwright Feydeau while his last, *La Règle du jeu*, was made explicitly in the manner of Alfred de Musset with Beaumarchais and Marivaux also in mind.[65] In between one finds other films taken from plays (*Chotard et Cie.*, *Boudu sauvé des eaux*, *Les Bas-Fonds*) as well as films that flaunt a theatrical style. *La Chienne*, for example, though drawn from a novel, opens with the pulling back of a stage curtain.[66] It should have surprised no one that in the last phase of his career he would concentrate on the very subject of theater (*La Carosse d'or*, 1953; *French CanCan*, 1955). And, as if to seal that career with a label valid forever after, he titled his final work *Le Petit Théâtre de Jean Renoir* (1970).

The prestige of this oeuvre demands that we reconsider what "theatricality" might mean in the cinema and what it did mean in 1930s France. Except in a few cases, we have taken it as a sign of artistic lethargy, of smugness even. The strutting of actors schooled in familiar roles seems antithetical to cinematic ambition. The standard theater of the day, the theater that influenced film producers, reaffirmed rather than questioned the values constituting the fabric of culture. Given the calamitous political climate of world depression and preparation for war, the genial sociality of the theater at the end of the Third Republic crumbles in the face of the private, often desperate search of novelists like Céline, Bernanos, Sartre, and even Mac Orlan.[67]

One need not go back to the Renaissance or classical antiquity to realize the immense cultural role that theater can play. Leo Braudy convincingly demonstrates that nothing about Renoir's use of theater should be termed smug or unquestioning. The theater provided him a literal and metaphorical frame that always stood in tension with the shifting complexities of a fluctuating, recalcitrant world. For the epigraph to his chapter "The Freedom of Theater,"

Braudy cites Renoir: "I like films or books which give me the feeling of a frame too narrow for the content."[68] Perhaps that is why he opened *La Chienne* with a Grand Guignol puppet play. Through this device Renoir "wryly mocks the order of art that is so totally separate from human anguish while at the same time he enhances the striving for art that constitutes a kind of salvation by perspective."[69] *La Chienne* constricts within such an artificial frame "the naturalistic observation of milieu and the Zolaesque plot of illicit romance and murder."[70]

Renoir's great films are all propelled by this tension between the clarifying artifice of theater and the murky biologism of naturalist literature. His genius may stem less from aesthetic innovation than from the savvy combination of the traditions that his biography thrust upon him. Through his brother he was in continual contact with the latest developments and theories coming from the Parisian stage. Through his father he inherited not just a taste for the fleshy materiality of life, but a set of acquaintances professing the "naturalist impressionist" creed. With close family ties to Zola and the Cezannes, as a youth Renoir aspired to become an author in the naturalist mold. When it came to developing a narrative cinema that would be social, realist, popular, and artistically innovative, he unhesitatingly turned to Zola as source and model, selling some of his father's canvases to make *Nana*. Leenhardt recognized that Renoir's tie to "naturalist impressionism" qualified his caricature that I quoted above of the roly-poly *meneur-de-jeu*, who loved the social side of theater and film. "The health, the powerful vigor and taste for life that bursts forth in Renoir's oeuvre . . . carries within it the germ of tragedy, a point of subversion. . . . His splendid materialism is often counterposed to a bitter pessimism."[71]

Renoir scarcely hides these "counterposed" tendencies in his treatment of actors. He shows himself quite prepared to lampoon the whole cast of *Une Partie de campagne*, including himself as the innkeeper, yet only so as to point up more strongly the deep mystery within the simple adolescent played by Sylvia Bataille. The close-up of her tear after the seduction on the island is not meant to tell us how she feels, but rather to confront us with her sudden awareness of herself as animal, an awareness we feel all the more because it is set off against the playacting of the older couple as Pan and nymph. Renoir pushed this tension to the limit in *La Règle du jeu* by locking a whole cast of social stereotypes in the tight and artificial dramatic structure of a classical play. The actors must supply the energy of this film, which they do in part because most of them are thought to be miscast. Improvising in quite unfamiliar roles, they provided Renoir's catlike camera opportunities to document the genuine feelings that resulted as they move in and out of phase with the fiction they enact.[72]

Renoir's legendary camera movements take us into the volume of a space these actors and these characters make use of but never exhaust. Even the static shots include unused diegetic material on the periphery or in the background of the action. Such dramatic refuse becomes a theme in La Règle du jeu, where the efforts of the society to stage their power (the hunt, the evening skits, the hierarchic layout of the château) are undermined by secret trysts, costume changes, and the wily snooping of poachers. The climax begins on a stage that becomes peripheral to the multiple erotic dramas that crisscross through the rooms and verandas of the château. Shots are fired while the camera races to catch up with action that always seems to be elsewhere. Renoir, playing Octave, a failed son of a famous orchestra conductor, can scarcely follow what is going on and must be pulled from the dancing-bear costume that fits him all too well.

Renoir imagined La Règle du jeu during the shooting of La Bête humaine, confessing that he had finally exhausted his obsession with naturalism and could not wait to work in a more measured way and with a very different sensibility. "I was entering a period of my life when my daily companions were Couperin, Rameau, and every composer from Lully to Gréty."[73] But if my view is right, only the naturalist appetite for overbrimming passion and suffocating material detail could provide the pressure needed to disturb the rigid social and dramatic organization of the later film. La Règle du jeu, dealing as it does with the refined classes, with "the people who danced to that music," may be the classical version of the romantic and proletarian La Bête humaine.

Leenhardt called naturalism the "disquieting source . . . without which [Renoir's vigorous films] would scarcely be art." But Leenhardt understood that in the 1930s one could not simply adopt a nineteenth-century formula for "inquietude." Although Renoir twice adapted Zola and shared his social and aesthetic concerns, Leenhardt attributed Renoir's naturalism more to what he curiously terms "American poetic realism, that of [Erskine] Caldwell and [William] Faulkner." No doubt these American authors, so much the rage in Europe at the time, learned a great deal from Maupassant and French nineteenth-century naturalism.[74]

Naturalism, then, is best thought of as an impulse rather than as a codified literary movement, an impulse that proved crucial to the cinema from its earliest years. Renoir came right out and said, "I believe that the so-called realist film is a child of the naturalist school."[75] Zola and his followers engaged in what they felt was a scientific sociology, one for which photography and later the cinema were ideal tools. The voyeurism built directly into the cinematic apparatus matched perfectly the interest they had already excited among a large readership eager to peer into the life of the downtrodden, the power mongers, the addicted, and the obsessed. A veneer in two layers, one of science and one of art, gave a sheen to this dubious project in the new entertainment industry of the movies. Already by 1902 one finds an adaptation of L'Assommoir by Ferdinand Zecca, trading both on Zola's name and on his forbidden subject. Actually this was an adaptation of an adaptation, since the novel was in its second life as a popular stage play. D. W. Griffith used the same material seven years later. More than sixty versions of novels by Zola followed.[76]

Given the common currency of such adaptations, how can naturalism retain for Renoir or for anyone its power to disturb? Griffith and Zecca, both religious, conservative men, could hardly have held to the radically atheist social Darwinism of Zola and his followers. Nor can the sentimental melodramas they filmed stand up to the literary aspirations of naturalist fiction. What they shared with Zola was a large middle-class audience with an interest in cultivating forbidden experiences. The fact that these filmmakers could so quickly reverse the tone of the novels they adapted by appending moralizing conclusions to their tales only illustrates how close Zola may have been to the Victorianism he was intent to overturn. Naturalism sits rather comfortably within the secure circle of middlebrow entertainment, even as it provocatively raises the banner of the scandalous. Like the cinema in general, it advertises more risks than it takes.

This should hardly surprise us; the laws of cultural economy predict the dilution of radical theories like Zola's as they filter first into his own novels and then spread via imitation and adaptation. Yet this does not undermine the impulse driving the formulation of such theories, or the genuine way they have been resurrected by those wanting to change culture. Zola's treatise on the theater, for example, directly challenges the Parisian stage I have caricatured as overly congenial.[77] Rather than aiming for proportion, balance, wit, and pleasure, Zola argues that a play should assume the shape of its subject matter, promoting the detached observation of the social world, not the essentially narcissistic replication of cultural values. He demands that playwrights take on the diversity of social life and its contradictory struggles by juggling a full range of characters chosen for their typicality, not their idiosyncrasies. No matter how spectacular and contrived his fiction may seem today, Zola insisted on a dedramatized theater in which the veracity of individual scenes, rather than a clever plot, would hold audience interest. He likewise championed a natural decor promoting the kind of interplay between character and environment found on the streets. Significantly for us, Gorki's *Lower Depths* (1904) stands out as among the most important examples of the sort of theater Zola envisioned. If Renoir's adaptation mollified Gorki's fierceness one can blame the soft spirit of the Popular Front, but one can equally credit Renoir's belief in the essential "poetry" of naturalism. Listen to him: "One usually takes Zola as a purely realist author . . . but what interests me in Zola is his poetry."[78] Roger Leenhardt was certain that Renoir had achieved a proper cinematic naturalism by producing a kind of "carnal poetry." Such poetry, Leenhardt goes on, is neither lyrical nor artificial: "On the screen authentic poetry can only come as a natural emanation of the image, of the most precise and naked image."[79]

La Bête humaine is full of supremely naked images that beg to be taken as both poetry and realism. In the name of Emile Zola, whose photograph looks out at us till the locomotive bursts through it onto the screen, this is a film meant to combat the idealism and sophistication of the flatulent theatrical cinema that Renoir, even when most taken by theater, never condoned. *La Bête humaine* demonstrates the surge that a particular kind of novel could give to the now fully developed cinema of atmosphere. Shall we call it a "poetic realist" work? Certainly its director never edged closer to that *optique*.

LA BÊTE HUMAINE AND THE APOGEE OF POETIC REALISM

To assess Renoir's connection to the cinema of his day and to measure that cinema in return, it seems best to avoid *La Grande Illusion* and *La Règle du jeu*, his two most famous films. Even by industry standards, these were exceptional works. Deriving from original scripts, they each radiated an ambition to alter the very nature of cinema. Both required lengthy preparation and production scheduling. As projects they were utterly self-conscious; as finished products they were remarkable and remarked upon. Squeezed between these giants in 1938, *La Bête humaine* gives us access to a more unconscious Renoir, the film-maker working by reflex and certainly for money. Like the majority of films shot in 1938 *La Bête humaine* was prepared and filmed in relative haste,[80] its producers advertising it crudely as a passionate tale of love and murder from France's greatest novelist by way of its most respected director. Its stars, particularly Gabin, led a promotion that secured for it excellent first-run theaters in all cities and a favorable distribution outside of France. Like *Mayerling* and *Pépé le Moko* it may not have topped the French box-office statistics, but its combined national and export showing has to be termed exceptional, as was its critical appraisal everywhere.

To be so well received, *La Bête humaine* must have adopted, consciously or not, many of the cinematic and cultural standards of its day, specifically a "Popular Frontist" tone on the one hand and the era's "poetic realism" on the other. Although its populism has been questioned,[81] in spite of its pessimism *La Bête humaine* provides a sympathetic and nearly ethnographic view of the conditions of a working man. Not only are Jean Gabin's costume, makeup, and gestures natural, he is surrounded by comrades whose daily chores keep the trains running on time. We see them in the roundhouse, in the mess, and at the *bal des cheminots*. When Pecqueux (Julien Carette) offers to mix his eggs with the ham Jacques Lantier (Gabin) contributes to their breakfast in the workers' canteen, we are beyond friendship and enter the sacramental rituals of Renoir's socialism. He would write of this film, and against most later views, that it was a tragedy of class, unthinkable among those with money in the bank.[82] Friendship, competence, and comrades quietly surround Lantier. If they fail to save him, if the *bal des cheminots* appears tawdry when set against the convivial dinner celebration of *Le Crime de Monsieur Lange*, it is due to the cold machinery of an *optique* Renoir may have disliked but seemingly could not avoid, that of poetic realism. Renoir fought the clean studio look of poetic realism in countless ways. You can see the difference in so small a detail as costuming. Compare Gabin's dirty engineer's overalls, casually worn, to his garb in Carné's *Le Jour se lève*. In the latter film, he is clearly marked as the "archetypal worker" to contrast with the young girl of the flowers in a most symbolic way.

Renoir generally avoided turning his characters into types, his props into symbols, and his plots into allegories; still, for this novel, and at this particularly grim moment of history, he declared that he was ready to "throw himself toward the poetic side of things," implicitly accepting Carné and Prévert's central aesthetic tenet, that of "unity of action."[83] Unlike his other films of the decade, *La Bête humaine* contains only a few characters, though we feel many others lurking at the edge of the frame, ready to be explored if time permitted. But time does not permit; the film runs on schedule, ticks off its dramatic measure on Grandmorin's gold watch and along the narrow rail line that allows no room for extras. Although he would bristle at the comparison, Renoir pursued Gabin's character along those rails until he leaped from the tracks to his death just as Carné had pursued Gabin to his violent end in the morning fog of *Le Quai des brumes*. The fatal circumstances governing both films are only vaguely comprehended by the character and the audience alike. We are buckled to the character's restricted view and acquiesce in his ultimate demise.

La Bête humaine bathes us in more atmosphere than any Renoir film since *La Nuit du carrefour*. Renoir shamelessly gave himself over to the poetic milieu of railyards and the glorious symbol of the train. He was glad to let them stand out broadly without being shaped into a coherent view of human action. Renoir seems deliberately to have excised from the novel every glimpse of wide perspective, and certainly each of the Olympian moments of clarity Zola permitted himself. Renoir accompanies a character blind to the reason or consequence of his role, strangely beleaguered from within.

Five years earlier, when Roger Martin du Gard had developed a scenario for the very same novel, he declared that he hoped to lead the feeble French film in the direction of that tortuous, slow, and dark cinema of the German silents, especially the *Kammerspielen*.[84] With German cameraman Curt Courant, Renoir may have shared this hope, but he could not square it with Martin du Gard's simultaneous desire to retain Zola's psychological analysis through a panoply of cinematic techniques like superimpositions and dream sequences.[85] Martin du Gard proposed to crosscut between life in the railyards and life in the centers of business, and between Roubaud's trial and events leading up to

World War I. In this he evidently thought to bring to the film the same sort of Olympian historical perspective that Zola commanded, and that he took for granted in his Nobel Prize–winning series of novels, *Les Thibault*.

Renoir found this script "too literary" when he received it through the agency of Synops.[86] In scrapping its mobile and broad perspective for his own myopic one, Renoir subscribed momentarily to the dominant poetic realist way of experiencing and expressing life. Compare its obsessive concentration to the expanse of his other films. Compare *La Bête humaine* to the just completed *La Marseillaise* with its enormous cast deployed across France. Or recall that in *Les Bas-Fonds* and *La Grande Illusion* he had gladly bartered the intensity of focusing on single characters in favor of a complex analysis of class achieved through a constantly shifting focus. Class difference was his subject (as it would be again in *Le Règle du jeu*), expressed through the destabilizing aesthetic of shifting styles, running from comedy to bathos in a single film. The clarity and understanding achieved by this approach through parallax lent political optimism to even tragic films like *Toni*. However *La Bête humaine* seems to have capitulated to the blind fatalism of the hour.

In sum, *La Bête humaine* marks the convergence of two aesthetic impulses: the poetic realism that had catapulted French cinema to international acclaim, and the naturalism Renoir had been tinkering with since *Nana*. Mid-1938 sadly brought the political erosion that channeled such a convergence. It was impossible to avoid pessimism in one's daily contacts. In Paris during final studio shots and editing, Renoir and his company witnessed Daladier returning from the Munich agreement. Before that in Le Havre,

> the air was charged with the tension of impending war. . . . Madrid was besieged by General Franco's forces, and the German Luftwaffe, helping Franco, bombed and obliterated the small Basque town of Guernica. In front of our hotel we often saw groups of stowaways being led from arriving steamers to police stations. . . . Le Havre, one of the largest seaports in Europe, was the hub of shipments to Spain. The city was nervously aware of war rumors and full of secret agents working for or against Franco.[87]

There was no escape from the brewing international cataclysm, not even in the peaceful countryside location where the sequence with Flore was shot. There Renoir ran into André Gide, who during lunch at his country home volubly expressed his disillusionment with Soviet communism, Gide who had led droves of intellectuals toward the Popular Front just a few years before. Resignation now seemed the proper sentiment after the hoopla of brotherhood in *La Marseillaise* had produced such a hollow echo. While working on that film Renoir had signed a plea for recognition of the Spanish problem and of workers' rights. It was co-signed by Aragon, Malraux, Nizan, Ortega, and many other intellectuals. Yet during the filming of *La Bête humaine*, only a few months later, he ceased his contributions to *Regards*, *Ce Soir*, and other leftist journals. The Popular Front was over; that much was clear. Indeed it officially capitulated three weeks before the film premiered. The image of an open and progressive polis gave way to the closed, regressive determinism of the human beast hurtling to its dark future.

La Bête humaine is the most tenacious film Renoir ever made. It drives forward with the mad pulse of Lantier's blood. And it relentlessly proceeds with the inevitability of Grandmorin's gold timepiece, ticking away under the floor, keeping the trains on schedule and the classes in place. Humorlessly, Renoir follows to its conclusion the prophecy lodged in his epigraph, that Lantier is doomed to the fate of the chromosomes passed down to him from generations of twisted lives.

The film's blind advance may stir us to rebel against its authority, but, caught up in the tale, we are more likely to be disgruntled at those moments or scenes that stammer and trip us up as we follow down its passage to darkening death. While the film as a whole glides deftly around corners and barrels down its converging rails, four obstinate scenes screech loud with the friction of their difference, endangering the whole feeling the film conveys by exposing it. These are, first, the words and photograph of Zola; second, the episode with Flore; third, Séverine's visit to Grandmorin's mansion; and, last, the interrogation of Cabuche.

The first comes right away in the laborious epigraph that initially appears like an apology tacked on by a timid producer. But then a portrait appears to face us, underscored by crashing music and underwritten by an authentic and authenticating signature. Emile Zola addresses us through this film. His visage wants to hover over the movie, spelling doom for its characters, and for the Third Republic that received its tainted start at the close of his novel. Now at the end of 1938 the prophecy of that novel's end seems more apt than ever: France like the railyards at night is inhabited by furtive characters darting amid the rubble while waiting for the train of history to depart.

With the scream of a whistle the train pulls away from its credits and its putative father, involving us instantly in the destiny of its flight. From the hellish fire of its boiler Renoir pulls back to expose the sooted machine-men who keep this massive train on line and bring her into shelter. This magnificent overture sings the awesome power of full-throttle technology in counterpoint to the warm solidarity men find in shared physical labor. The muscular grandeur of this sequence, the hurtling of an immense locomotive through the shifting, often stroboscopic, light of towns, countryside, and girded bridges, bears us into a world ruled by power and sensuality. From the outset the characters are shown to have adapted to motion and to force, just as the actors have had to commit to second nature their labor and their gestures on board this monster. Such an opening sequence immediately announces Renoir's intention to deliver the physicality the novel achieves in its inflated diction. Zola conjured up his drama in the quiet of his study, whereas Renoir felt that drama arise aboard the very train that is its setting and central symbol. This is why Renoir insisted on so much location shooting and why Gabin literally earned an apprenticeship in engineering. More than mere trappings of realism, these measures validate the premise of the novel, for they insist on the priority of the instincts, of the physical, over our understanding of them. And so the inarticulate power of these first eight minutes wrests the story from Zola and his wise portrait, placing it where he would surely have wanted, in the searing boiler of the engine and the equally searing heart of the engineer.

The film runs smoothly now, self-propelled, until Séverine reaches the mansion of her godfather. Here, for the only time, we leave the world of the railroad with its mix of lower- and middle-class life to enter instead the traditional site of French cinema, the gussied-up domain of the upper bourgeoisie.[88] The inauthenticity of this brief scene can be attributed to Simone Simon's too familiar gait, her nonchalance in the presence of great wealth. The feather in her hat has no place in the world of *La Bête humaine*, as even those who worked on the film have pointed out,[89] though she might readily have worn it to the set on the morning of the shoot. As a highly paid actress, she blends familiarly into this *haut bourgeois* decor, confirming that the character she portrays is fully a child of Grandmorin's decadent social class, literally at home there as its daughter and mistress. Yet the scene's formal distance sours the growing intimacy of the narration and hampers the growth of our sympathy for her. In fact this scene might be said to come straight from the world of the producer and his studio. Almost a parody of the standard decor in Italian white-telephone films or Paramount "Continental" features, the setting overwhelms the small action that takes place there.[90] This scene is marked by the discourse of the producer: a language of parquet floors, ornate divans, curtains, and framed paintings, of lovely actresses decked out fashionably and escorted from room to room by gracious tuxedoed servants. This is the respectful discourse of the movies as every country knew them in the 1930s. Yet this discourse is false to the panting of *La Bête humaine*, and its aberration in tone helps us to differentiate Renoir's project from Zola's, for the novelist quite comfortably mixed scenes in the railyard with those in the salons of captains of industry and politics. In this novel, as in the whole structure of the Rougon-Macquart saga of which it forms a part, Zola sought to represent opposed characters and social classes so they could simultaneously be kept in view. Shall we say that Renoir's is a lesser project because, aside from this scene, he found himself unable to turn away from the railroad and its denizens? It is in any case a different view from Zola's naturalism, one inflected by the poetic realist sensibility ("concentration") that formed the particular style of melodrama at the end of the Third Republic.

If the scene at Grandmorin's mansion seems isolated from the film, the interrogation of Cabuche in the magistrate's office is equally cut off from the dominant tone, belonging, it is easy to imagine, to Renoir as director. Placing

La Bête Humaine:
Renoir (Cabuche) in direct
address. CB

himself before the camera, Renoir confesses directly to us. The innocence of
his presentation condemns him in the intricate world of law. Vulnerable and
expressive, the director would address us directly just as he allowed Zola to
speak at the outset. In a single setup lit undramatically by common daylight,
he tells of being ostracized, of his blameless affection for nature and for another young girl ruined by Grandmorin. Unable to hide his feelings—having
nothing to hide—he is caught and accused. For a time it appears that his
predicament may twist the intricate plot of deception, for Lantier will not see
his innocent friend unjustly punished. But in the cobwebs of dark desire, of
concealed booty and caresses, Cabuche is completely forgotten, left to hang
for the stabbing of Grandmorin, an example of what the lowest class may
expect when the higher are disturbed.

One further scene, the encounter with Flore, resists the film's blind movement because it is contested. Renoir and Zola wrestle to control its thrust. The
tableau that first presents Flore derives from Renoir's pictorial heritage. Two
arches of a bridge cross a sinuous river, the bridge supporting a steaming
locomotive, the river holding in its midst a rowboat in which the girl washes
her bare legs. The contrast of rail and river, one flowing through the countryside in leisure and grace, the other brutally cutting a gash to the city—these are
common subjects in Renoir. The virgin Flore, ogled by the local boys, brings
back the budding girl of *Une Partie de campagne*, rowed toward a sexuality
she half wants, half resists. Both girls submit not just to the insistent virility of
their earnest men, but to their own vaguely understood physical desires. In
the earlier film, Henriette Dufour (Sylvia Bataille), resting her head on her
mother's shoulder, speaks poetically of the life she feels in the grass and in her
breast. She floats toward an isle and a rendezvous with nature and her own
physical nature. Flore's rendezvous is more sinister as she steps out of the
stream to mount the embankment with Lantier. Only the mighty screeching
of a passing train keeps her from the fatal consequence of this encounter. What
has happened to Renoir and to France in just two years? His naturalism, we
cannot deny, is double-sided. The all-embracing, all-ingesting, all-forgiving

Une partie de campagne: Rowing toward nature.
CB

Une partie de campagne: Realizing her nature.

CB

picture of natural love inherited from his father is backed by another canvas picturing love and nature quite differently; he titled this one *La Bête humaine*.

So startling is this sudden violence, so cynically does it arise from the gentle impressionist landscape, and so final is the cutting of the train through this landscape and through this scene that the film requires another start and an explanation of its motivation. Later Renoir would claim to regret Zola's primitive psychobiology, but twice in the film he shows it to be the source of the wild cascades of desire that spill over the plot. Zola's personal appearance at the outset of the film may be said to recur here in the person of Lantier as he tries to explain his temptation to violence. The monologue is an absurd patch to keep the dramatic pressure from leaking out all at once. But it fits somehow, even today, whereas that photo of Zola no longer commands respect. In both cases the theory and its bombastic expression are of another era, and Renoir knew it. "It is not particularly beautiful," he said, speaking of this speech. "But if a man as handsome as Gabin said it . . . in open air, with a good deal of horizon behind him, and perhaps some wind, it would take on a certain quality."[91] Gabin does recite his speech like Lincoln or Jesus with a vast moving sky behind his head, shot heroically from below. But he is no leader and has no vision. A shrieking train calls him back to the narrow rails of his life.

Flore now disappears from the film, as will poor Cabuche soon enough. Both represented alternatives to the industrial network, to the psychosocial economy that governs all the other characters and the film as a whole. That economy is at work in a style that now brooks no opposition. These four "deviant" scenes can be brushed aside as extraneous. We are left without the comfort of Zola's knowledge, of Renoir's innocent belief in nature, or of the usual look and discourse of the cinema. We are left alone with this film, with the guttural tone rising from its throat. Let us listen to the way it speaks and to what it says.

La Bête Humaine: Burying guilt. CB

La Bête Humaine: Emerging mania. CB

It all begins innocuously enough, in a stray event on the quay: a middle-class woman complains about a wealthy voyager's dog. This is the origin of a fatal series of gifts and aggressions, up and down the ladder of the sexual and social system. Roubaud, the station master, does his job, which is to guard the orderliness of schedules and behavior, a job he believes in but one he got through the railroad king Grandmorin because he married his adopted daughter. Now that job stands in jeopardy from the irate and powerful voyager, and Roubaud must offer his wife to Grandmorin so as to protect himself. When Grandmorin has been exposed as a lecher, Roubaud recognizes the rot on which his own decency as well as Grandmorin's has been based. Almost resignedly he murders the railroad king, then wanders pathetically through the remainder of the film in a stupor, burying the old man's watch and money underneath the floor, and burying himself in cards and absinthe. He never entertained a vision of life beyond a cloying respectability.

Séverine, in contrast, learned early to use but not believe in social position. In her first scene she perches on a windowsill, waiting the return of her man. Roubaud imagines her his canary, filling his room with song. But windows look outward as well, down onto the steaming railyards where her future lies. When Roubaud drives the knife into the old man, Séverine stands guard in the first-class cabin, watching. In the corridor leading from the murder she crosses Lantier returning home on the train after his near murder of Flore. In a crude joke, Renoir positions him before a sign bearing the word "fumeurs" as he removes a cinder from his eye. This is the man who was first seen wearing goggles against the wind and who last was heard to confess that smoke comes to cloud his vision in times of stress. Did he see the murder? No matter, he has seen Séverine and made a pact with her eyes. Renoir insists on this at the trainside inquest by a camera that cuts from his eyes and tracks to hers. Later Jacques will say, "You asked me with your eyes."

Now the film turns from a trajectory of object exchanges (knife, ring, letter, money, watch) to one of glances. Knowledge, solidarity, and suspicion are exchanged in ways the cinema has grown to master. Desire turns eyes prehensile and follows a biological instinct of looking. Earlier this instinct was directed at Flore by the local men and then by Lantier until Flore drove him mad by looking back. In his awful frenzy his eyes had dropped first to her neck, then rolled up into some inner haze that literally made him blind to his actions. Passion can short-circuit vision and arc lethally behind his eyes. Now Lantier finds in the murderous Séverine the one woman with whom he can exchange looks. Deprived of social affection—the one for reasons of genetics, the other from a trauma of upbringing—they find in the mirror of each other's eyes a self-love that degradation cannot corrode. They pursue this love to its apotheosis outside the toolshed, as they gaze together at the moon. Here subject and object, image and reflection, are joined on the great mirror of the screen for us to contemplate.

Renoir is in awe of this elemental union. He tracks it, takes on its heaving motion. His insinuating camera takes a most figural turn when it slides away from the bodies that slink down into murky sex so as to frame a bucket overbrimming with rainwater from a gushing downspout. The music soars to cover their animal ecstasy. A dissolve finds the bucket now still, while the camera pans back to the shed to mark one pair of muddy shoes emerging. At last the other pair emerges and the camera tilts to frame from below two translucent faces pressed together in the night, hands clutching at one another's oilskin coats. Should we expect these lovers to notice the sharp shadow cutting across their transported faces and their blighted future?

In this scene the orchestration of feeling, light, music, and movement outstandingly exemplifies that singleness of purpose which, outside the four exceptions already noted, courses through the body of the film. Each successive scene contributes to and modulates an invariant, dark tone. Renoir encouraged his cameraman Courant to fashion and poeticize this tone by perfecting a gauze filter that reduced the ambient illumination while letting selective light sources (headlights, for instance) come through cutouts in the gauze.[92]

La Bête Humaine:
Whispers of love
and murder. CB

The future of the lovers must be clouded by this darkness and by the suffocating decor that daringly matches the train compartment of the bloody murder with the toolshed. These are the spaces of unconscious urgings that the camera stands back from and will not enter. In both cases a resolute couple literally falls upon a passion. From the outside the thrusts of love and those of murder seem the same. And from the inside too, as an exhausted Séverine afterwards whispers of the murder, "I lived my whole life in that instant."

Compartments, small rooms, a railyard are the sets on which entire lives are led. And throughout, the hulking presence of trains. Designer Eugène Lourié struggled to include an engine in every scene. He even had a replica of a window wall in the studio set constructed on a high platform above the railyard, so Séverine and Roubaud's discussions, filmed in the studio, could resonate with the breathing of real engines. The "corridors" of public life and transaction are no less confining. Public spaces in Renoir films generally encourage a change of perspective, even a relaxation. But here the workers' canteen and dormitory are cramped; their smoky café gives out onto the railyard. Even the dance hall is dingy and depressing, dominated by the absurd cutout of a golden locomotive in front of which servants dance in a joyless rite.

As for the sound track, Renoir planned to fill the theater with train noises from first to last. Whistles, chugs, and the exhalation of steam surround the characters and the audience. There is no escape from this dramatic boiler with its relentlessly building pressure. If *La Bête humaine* needs to be seen within the heritage of poetic realism, then we must emphasize that Renoir here adds something quite new to that particular dialect. The sound tracks of poetic realist films are spare. Dialogue is paramount, particularly in those films scripted by Prévert. At most ambience may be evoked through musical leitmotifs and carefully chosen aural details (Arab chanting in *Pépé le Moko*, a foghorn in *Le Quai des brumes*). In comparison *La Bête humaine*'s sound track is uncommonly rich. We hear overlapping conversations of railway men, music filtering in from nearby rooms, and most of all, indeed ceaselessly, the various sounds of trains. The ubiquity of train noises shifts them from the realist to the poetic side of the balance, as they establish the tone and rhythm of the film in the prelude and then maintain its pulse throughout.

La Bête humaine's most signal innovation may paradoxically lie in the muffled tone of its recited dialogue. This understatement of passion contrasts with, or results from, the shrill trains that literally run over human lives. Fernand Ledoux's restraint in portraying Roubaud is most remarkable, trained as he was in a stentorian theatrical tradition. Here he tempers his voice and even when angered mumbles morosely. Gabin and Simon were already stars of a new generation of acting. They project a secret urgency in their hushed bedroom conversation when she tells of her sordid youth and of the murder, and when he laments the sudden waves of sadness that wash over him. Graham Greene knew he was in the presence of something remarkable in this scene, reviewing it at its London premiere.[93] The whispers fit well with the darkness, to be sure, but primarily they figure a fatalism that oozes from the mouths of the characters. Unlike the dialogue of Prévert's films, nothing is to be expected from the words exhaled in *La Bête humaine*. No flourishes, surprises, or reversals; rather the slow spelling out of what seems obvious to the inner self of each character and to the overriding structure of the world they exist within.

The film's most dramatic moment, the failed assassination of Roubaud in the railyard, is scarcely audible. In silent complicity Séverine and Lantier skulk through the debris until they hear Roubaud approach. The phallic pipe is found and grasped. Lantier, mesmerized by the intensity of Séverine's stare, looks out with her to track the shadow of her husband. Willpower more than courage then fails him, as he drops the useless pipe and impotently buries his face in his arm. Séverine scarcely reproves him, accepting this weakness as a state of nature. Her quiet disappointment sounds almost understanding. Whether passionate or despairing, these mumblings of wayward human beings become lost under the churning wheels of the locomotive.

And this was the plan of the film, that everywhere the inhuman pressure of schedules and the unnatural noise of huge machines should palpably overwhelm all pious thoughts of "nature." Exhilarating in its first rush, the engine *La Lison* fatigues us in the end as she does her doomed driver. Yet she is the only woman capable of satisfying him, as he literally rides her, spending his expertise and power. *La Lison* is destiny incarnate; on board she offers a utopian perspective, a utopia not just of the union of man and machine, but the utopia of satisfying movement, of a thrilling surge that connects countryside, city, and small town. The timelessness of this ecstasy is that of orgasm and of death. Lantier tells Séverine that while streaking across the land he can nevertheless pick out all the flowers and even discern individual rabbits running between them. But once the ride is over, once the thick engine lies sleeping and snorting in the railyard, Lantier becomes dull, his senses somehow detached. Renoir has built two time schemes into this film, that of passion and that of passion spent. The latter must necessarily absorb and dissipate the energy of the former.

Exhaustion in the face of limitless spent energy characterizes the tone of *La Bête humaine*, a film told from the final effects its drama provokes. This explains the haunting denouement, in which Renoir crosscuts Séverine's death with a cute *chanson* sung at the dingy *bal des cheminots*. No suspense attends this murder, only the playing out of a tune about popular love, one we are likely to hum on our way home from the movie theater. Nor is any frenzy left in Lantier. When he stares at himself fully in the mirror, he has reached the feeling that controls the film, a feeling Roubaud expresses in another register when he slouches to the entrance of the room and spies his wife's body on the floor. The camera, in a redundant but apt figure, reapproaches the doorway, closing in on him and then on the gold watch dangling from his side. His hunched shoulders and pathetic sobs mark the end of a wretched story, the end of desire and of *La Bête humaine*.

Zola's theme of exhausted hope aboard an ungovernable train seems designed for a nation where socialist aspirations have just foundered and where a numbed populace braces for the imminent catastrophe of war. In expressing these feelings so directly Renoir has opened himself to criticism: how is socialism possible, if its most insightful proponents so quickly lose their perseverance to wallow instead in pessimism?[94] The murder of the corrupt Grandmorin, a captain of the country's economy, by the bureaucrat Roubaud has none of the clarity of Lange's gunning down Batala in the communal courtyard three years earlier, or Pépel's braining the slumlord of *Les Bas-Fonds*. Roubaud acts for a woman already corrupted by the aristocracy. Without social vision, his explicitly Oedipal murder of the father links Roubaud to the tormented victims of German expressionist films, rather than to the clearheaded populist heroes of Soviet revolutionary epics or French Popular Front dramas. His violence like Lantier's runs berserk.[95] Its source is not the French Revolution so gloriously sung in *La Marseillaise* earlier in 1938, but the industrial revolution that stupefied generations of the lower classes. How could anyone have expected a healthy Popular Front to be engendered from a legacy of sexual abuse, incest, and alcoholism, the inevitable fruits of a system that exploited workers sixteen hours a day in cramped quarters? *La Bête humaine* tells of the repressed violence of the underclasses, its hero, played by an incorruptible Jean Gabin, tainted by the complicity of silence he shares with Roubaud that permits furtive sex in the toolshed while Cabuche suffers unjustly for the crime.

And yet Renoir does not despise these characters, nor does he feel superior to them. Rather he stands in awe of the blind forces that erupt in their hearts and of that greater but equally blind force of history whose modern image is still, as it was for Zola, the runaway locomotive. Renoir emphasizes blindness and instinct more than did Zola who allowed himself to ruminate on the plight his plot details. Renoir instead moves in and in for the close-up examination of what is essentially animal behavior. The film goes beyond its source in adopting the approach then dominating American fiction, where behaviorism and sociology are rendered by minute description. With such narrow focus, a rail tie wide, Renoir abandons Zola's Olympian vision so as to give us a film as maniacal as its characters and its age. We are its direct descendants.

In 1938 a whole culture had to face Renoir's vision of personal and social decadence, had to see in it the representation of the berserk violence rolling over entire populations. Had Marc Allégret been able to film Martin du Gard's version in 1934 as was proposed, or Marcel L'Herbier been able to act on the option to the same script in 1935, we would have had a film of a different feel altogether. We would have looked in at the fatal love of Lantier and Séverine from a knowing perspective. Clever references to World War I in the concluding scenes would have instructively tied social history to personal morality.[96] Renoir's version, on the contrary, instructs us in nothing, but makes us dive into hell with Lantier from its first shot of the flaming boiler. The discourse of his film is one of sheer body language, a language cruder and yet more fundamental than that of the romantic, though indispensable, Zola, more authentic than that of the codified genres of proletarian, populist, and social realist fiction. Renoir gives us a worker's world he neither patronizes nor inflates, one he makes us confront without the guideposts of religion or politics. His triumph is that, despite his own visible presence in the film as well as that of Zola, he makes us confront it without the guiding judgment of the artist either. La Bête humaine looks force directly in the face. And this force is palpable, beyond concept, beyond artistic control.

Naturally we prefer the humane and winsome La Grande Illusion and the sage, though bitter, La Règle du jeu. But La Bête humaine will not rest submerged underneath these masterworks. With the beauty of an animal gesture, the cinematic reflex of La Bête humaine testifies to the instinctive way poetic realism could reach for its audience in 1938. Because it flowed so effortlessly and so assuredly from Renoir as he relinquished with relief his allegiance to the institutions of the Popular Front, La Bête humaine seems written in the dominant key of its era. It satisfied audiences then as now like the return of a piano composition to the tonic scale at the end of a complicated sonata movement. Perhaps a "weak link" in his social cinema,[97] it was right in tune with Renoir's sensibility and evidently with a broad social sensibility as well.

Poetic realism seems to have caught Jean Renoir unawares as he turned away from his discouraging political affiliations and returned to the gutty naturalism he believed to be his personal source. In falling back on what he thought of as himself, Renoir was hardly prone to fall back on some outdated way of treating a story, or treating actors, or treating an audience. He was determined to bring Zola's story into the 1930s and so he adapted his style to an *optique* absolutely right for that moment, an *optique* that validated a subject, a style, a tone, and a murmured address to a public that knew how to cock its ear and listen to it groaning.

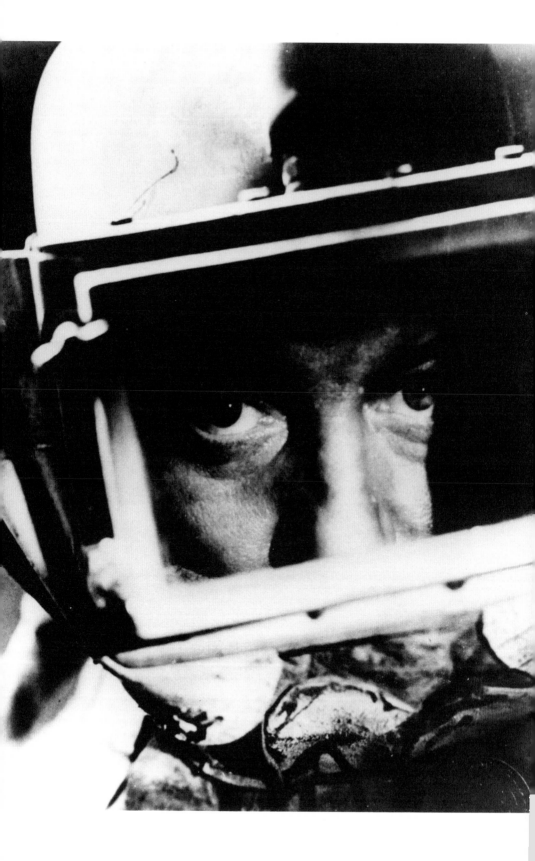

10

The Myth of Poetic Realism

AT LEAST every decade the French conduct a poll of industry personnel, critics, theater owners, or filmgoers, in an effort to determine the greatest French films of all time. Invariably *Les Enfants du paradis* (1945) comes out on top.[1] As the longest, most expensive, and most star-studded film the French had yet made, its proportions match the romantic myth it recounts. Edward Turk calls it "a film for all time," the summit of Marcel Carné's career, indeed the summit of French cinema. *"Les Enfants du paradis* marks the culmination of France's Golden Age of moviemaking . . . [it] will always retain a privileged position among film masterworks."[2] Jean-Pierre Jeancolas is still more explicit: *"Les Enfants du paradis* is an ageless film, one that concentrates, sums up, and crowns fifteen years of French cinema."[3] How can we avoid examining it?

What could it mean for a movie to be "for all time"? Perhaps that its sensual appeal is so immediate, so biological, that history cannot attenuate the effect of its chemistry on every human organism it comes in contact with. Viewing *Les Enfants du paradis* today we would have to imagine our experience completely congruent with that of its Parisian audiences in 1945. Its perennial appearance not just on *ciné-club* programs but at revival houses would go to confirm this. Evidently *Les Enfants du paradis* satisfies humans the way bread and sleep do, or the sounds of a nursery rhyme, all of which are equally "for all time."

And yet by lifting itself to the timeless heights where masterpieces perdure, how can *Les Enfants du paradis* be said to partake of the poetic realism it crowns? If poetic realism is, as I claim, more than a catalog of stylistic elements, if as an *optique* it involves a dialogue with the culture it addresses, no film can stand back from history to epitomize it. The term *optique* has been deployed so as to account for the rapport every film sets up with its culture. This means that we have every right to examine masterpieces of cinema, even to relish their aesthetic achievement, so long as we examine them either as quite timely or as culturally impertinent.

My study of poetic realism, indebted to cultural history as much as to aesthetics, must culminate, then, in this paradox wherein a film can be shown to crown a particularly valuable way of making movies but, by doing so, must be excluded from the group it crowns. The most famous of French films, *Les Enfants du paradis* can stand as a distillation of poetic realism that clarifies its style and that at the same time allows us to understand what it is in poetic realism that goes beyond style to involve the life of an age that is so murky it can never be distilled.

In part because he participated in the shifting historical circumstances of their production and reception, André Bazin could sense in Carné's films the cultural surplus that flowed beyond a simple notion of film style and that made each film appropriate or untimely. With characteristic lucidity he wrote:

> A work should not be defined only in relation to itself and without reference to its time. It would be pure abstraction to place Carné's talent on one side, the sensibility of the public on the other, and to note their accord around 1938, since this accord is not a simple passive connection but one of the indirect creative components of the work. In other words, Carné's inspiration, his work as an artist, participated in the period; it answered its questions, but the questions determined the direction of the responses. Now by responses I do not mean an objective content, but the expression given to this content, that is to say, a style. The perfect inner equilibrium, the happy arrangment of all the elements of *Le Jour se lève*, which give it the strength of myth . . . correspond to a sociological maturity of the themes that guided his genius.[4]

Bazin hints here that *Les Enfants du paradis* (and *Les Portes de la nuit*, which followed it in 1946) may share with *Le Jour se lève* a team of creative personnel (share particularly Prévert's pellucid dialogue), and share the theme of the impossibility of the survival of pure love; nevertheless, they spoke to an audience seeking quite different experiences at the cinema, and consequently they spoke in altogether different manners.[5] The later films, we might say, are calculated to evoke admiration through a display of artistry, whereas *Le Jour se lève* aims to provide an experience so immediate that the spectator never thinks to admire the expression that touches him or her to the bone. Applicable here is the distinction Friedrich Schiller proposed two centuries ago between "naive and sentimental poetry." Naive writing seems at one with nature; it is simple and instinctive. At a later, more sophisticated time a poetry of calculated effects comes to take its place, a sign perhaps "of the exhaustion of genres, of a growing self-consciousness, or of an increasingly complicated life generally."[6] Bazin would use different terms to suggest the trajectory of Carné's career, calling the 1930s work "classical" (meaning both natural and realist) in relation to a more and more "baroque" direction taken later on where an "equilibrium" of elements is replaced by striking effects.[7] Poetic realism developed naturally in the 1930s, but in the hothouse of the Occupation it recognized its nature and became codified and citable. Hence *Les Enfants du paradis* and *Les Portes de la nuit* stand paradoxically outside poetic realism by summoning it up, then by summing it up and trying to crown it. They bear its heritage, magnificently in the first case, unsuccessfully in the second, to another cultural moment inhabited by another kind of spectator.

We have seen in detail that the heritage of poetic realism did not originate with the Popular Front but reaches back to certain prophetic films of the early sound years, to the *photogénie* of the 1920s, to Feuillade, and even to trends in nineteenth-century fiction and drama usually thought of under the rubric "melodrama." Melodrama supplies the continuity felt among all Carné-Prévert films, whether pre- or postwar, save of course the satiric *Drôle de drame*. *Le Quai des brumes* and *Les Portes de la nuit* alike rework serious literary motifs on the scale of the everyday, striving to portray moral dramas within a preternaturally symbolic world. As did the plays of Pixérécourt after the French Revolution, poetic realist films stretch nonverbal registers (set design, props, portentous acting, music) in an effort to express the inexpressible and to bring to a large audience the uplifting power of art previously reserved for the elite.[8] Carné, Prévert, and their extraordinary team (Alexandre Trauner and Joseph Kosma especially) could legitimately believe themselves to be expanding the reach of cinema just as Hugo, Dickens, and Balzac had expanded fiction when they turned toward melodramatic writing a century earlier.

No film sets out more directly to recall the strategies and atmosphere of melodrama than *Les Enfants du paradis*. Perhaps its veneer of timelessness results from the fact that melodrama is itself the film's primary referent. Its action opens in the 1820s, on the very boulevard du Crime where melodrama flourished in its heyday. We follow Garance in the crowd as she haphazardly encounters, one after the other, the three heroes who anchor the film both in melodrama and in history: the celebrated actors Baptiste Deburau and Frédérick Lemaître, and the Napoleon of crime, Lacenaire. The historical Lemaître got his start in the popular theater and became such a powerful figure on the Parisian stage that melodramas were literally rewritten to make use of his immense talent. Like Prévert who reinvented him for the film, Lemaître loved to mix genres and felt no shame in playing Shakespeare in repertory with sentimental crowd pleasers.[9] Naturally the Shakespeare he first turned to was *Othello*.

Deburau, as the most famous mime of all time, brings to *Les Enfants du paradis* the theme of muteness, singled out by Peter Brooks as one of the essential elements of melodrama.[10] In the 1840s he turned his private life into melodrama when he found himself charged in one of the most sensational murder trials of the era. All Paris, we are told, flocked to the courtroom as the darling of the mime shows revealed to the public for the first time the sound of his voice. Baudelaire wrote of this incident and he wrote as well of Lacenaire, the dandy who transformed his malfeasance into romantic poems and ultimately into a spiteful book of reminiscences written in his prison cell. He did not disappoint the huge crowd assembled at his execution, dramatically flinging himself upon the guillotine.

Carné and Prévert chose these colorful characters and chose the world of melodrama in general with no hint of condescension. "The greatest creators of cinema—and Carné is certainly among these—don't hesitate to make melodramas since that's where the real popular essence of their art lies."[11] Every strategy of expression at their command they mobilized to inflate the sentiments of the characters whose lives are tied together by threads crisscrossed in an ultimately fatal and suffocating pattern. Each character, prop, and speech stands out as significant by its very inclusion in the film as well as by its hieratic treatment. Baptiste's primary nemesis, for instance, is a ragpicker named Jericho who wanders among the characters crying out doom, reciting his lines in litany. Primordial objects like the moon, mirrors, and flowers are sanctified by their calculated recurrence and by the words "lune," "miroir," and "fleur" so carefully pronounced by characters who weigh their import. The "simplicity and exaggeration"[12] of such objects and words issue from a morally and aesthetically superior world, where everything turns on a phrase, on the color of a gown, on the presence or absence of the moon.

Generations of critics have described *Les Enfants du paradis* as an immense tapestry, woven of multiple plots, predestined coincidences, duels, class conflicts, and absolute moral choices,[13] and representing not the nineteenth century so much as the fictions of that era.[14] Boldly Carné exploits the role and metaphor of theatricality, dividing the film into two distinct acts, each bracketed by curtains that mark them open and closed. He convinces us that "the total articulation of the grandiose moral terms of the drama"[15] belongs not just to theater but to life as it was lived a century ago. This deft and marvelous transformation of life into art and back again challenges the audience to enlarge itself. In speaking of *Les Enfants du paradis*, Marcel Oms declared that "the ethical function of cinematic melodrama consists in proving to the spectator that this other world is within him, proving it to him by making him experience it."[16] To its first audiences who stepped out of the film not only onto the streets represented in it but onto streets still full of the intrigues of the Nazi Occupation (the maquis, the black market), Prévert's diction (replete with absolutes like "evil" and "purity") and Kosma's dramatic score may not have sounded unusual at all. We who live out a more banal epoch are hypnotized by this film, finding in it the measure of life as we feel it should be led.

Les Enfants du paradis takes hypnotic representation as its theme. Baptiste puts a silent spell over all who watch him, over the crowd at the Funambules, over us in the movie theater, and most critically over Garance who represents everything that art desires. Garance, introduced as the spectacle of "truth it-self," naked except for her beauty, holds a mirror that keeps her to herself even while leering males ogle her. They dream of possessing not so much her beauty as her diffident self-possession. But this she offers only to Baptiste, like her an unassuming silent voice of the people.

The purity of their attraction to one another forecloses the realization of their union. Baptiste stages an allegory of unfulfilled love in a self-reflexive skit that features all the characters of his life. Dreaming beside the statue of Phoebe for whom he pines (played by Garance) Baptiste does not notice Harlequin (Frédérick Lemaître) entering to steal her away. As the laundress enters (played by Nathalie, faithful to Baptiste to the end) we catch with her a glimpse in close-up of his real, not his represented, despair. Baptiste and Pierrot, actor and character, become an indistinguishable unit that looks not at Nathalie but offstage where in the wings Frédérick whispers flirtatiously into the delighted ear of Garance.

More than a tiny allegory of jealousy, this skit stages a crucial opposition between the silent mime who loses the only audience he cares for to the loquacious actor. When next we see Frédérick, his bravura, sophistication, and the reassuring sonority of his deep voice have won not just Garance but the

Les Enfants du paradis: Loquacious actor, silent mime. BFI

heart of Paris. In a tour de force, he whimsically toys with his assigned role in a new play, outraging the authors, until the audience cheers his victory over the drama written for him. If Baptiste stands for the "naive," nearly religious function theater assumed after the French Revolution and Lemaître for the "sentimental" revival of sophistication on the stage, then Baptiste may also represent the cult of the silent cinema losing its audience to the urbane, promiscuous talkie. Edward Turk reminds us that the initial inspiration for the entire project came after Barrault saw Charlie Chaplin, cinema's most famous mime, in his first speaking role in *The Great Dictator* (1940).[17]

Les Enfants du paradis invites one to multiply its allegorical applications. Garance can be the purity of the French soul during the Occupation or the elusive vision of all those weighed down by domestic burdens and the demands of a corrupting reality. But before standing for any of these, she embodies the concept of the perfect audience whose unbroken and marvelous stare in the face of a mime's pure hypnotic performance is returned by him until together they look out at the moon, the purest and most distant of screens on which they project their dreams and we ours.

In this sense, *Les Enfants du paradis* is indeed a film for all times, for it represents above all the magic of films and the dreams every great film inspires. In this it might be compared to Cukor's *A Star Is Born*, which takes the musical as its intertext. Both follow a common pattern in the sociology of art whereby early examples of a genre reach outside themselves for the material they reshape. The musical originally drew on vaudeville, for example. Much later that genre would begin to feed on itself, explicitly reshaping its own cinematic form.[18] Like *A Star Is Born*, *Les Enfants du paradis* is such a second-degree movie, modeling the world of cinematic melodrama, constructing an allegory of it.

If *Les Enfants du paradis* allegorizes the power of melodrama, can it provide audiences with a genuine melodramatic experience?[19] Its nostalgia for a better form of representation indicates, perhaps against its wishes, that such bare experience belongs to the past. That past may have been chaotic and ungoverned, but in its plight prewar French society could look to the movies for evidence of the values it might count on and share. Jean Gabin never reassured them, demonstrating instead a tight-lipped style of suffering they understood and introjected. His fidelity to himself and to the authenticity of his isolation outlasted the movies that inevitably brought him to a bad end. By turns silent and explosive, Gabin was an "everyman" (indistinguishable in his anonymous costume)[20] at odds with a corrupt system he was unable to fathom and had to face alone. Fatherless and marginal, he paradoxically became the central protean figure in the vague milieu poetic realism represented again and again.

The creators of the most important films of the 1940s may well have wanted to evoke the same values that the Gabin figure had pursued film after film through his hopelessly private quest (uncompromising honesty, pure love);

only now those values had to be represented as cultural, not individual, achievements. There could be no orphans in a society under the care of Maréchal Pétain and dominated by innumerable fathers. And the cinema could no longer serve as the secret site where alienated auteurs, figures, and spectators might furtively meet.

While not always purveying the ideology of "Travail, Famille, Patrie," under Vichy the cinema accentuated its public and cultural role. One imagines prewar spectators arriving singly at the theater, putting all obstructions from their minds, and virtually climbing through the screen to join the figure of Gabin as he groped through his poetic realist films. Audiences during the Occupation, the argument goes, attended films in couples or groups, asking to be fascinated by a spectacle that benevolently looked down on them. No matter that Fate and Destiny so often remained the dramatic motor in the Occupation films as they had been in the prewar works; there was now something reassuring about the (allegorical and spectacular) way such themes were dressed and displayed. Fate does not haunt the no-man's-land of contemporary urban life in *Les Visiteurs du soir* and *Les Enfants du paradis* the way it does in *Le Quai des brumes*. The duc de Berry sets of the *Les Visiteurs du soir* in fact were specifically meant to look like illuminated miniatures, that is, like models. Watching *Le Jour se lève* or *Le Quai des brumes*, on the other hand, had been like watching life itself with no model to go by, for Gabin seemed to have wrested narrative authority from the filmmakers whose "culture" and "paternal care" never inserted itself between spectator and text. No historical references, no showcasing of sets or stars, came to deliver that spectator who was left alone in what I have prematurely been calling the "existential" situation of melodrama.

These distinctions can help explain the disastrous reception accorded the next Carné-Prévert film, *Les Portes de la nuit* (1946). Nearly all commentators, including the most recent and sophisticated, have attributed the failure of this film to its untimely pessimism, particularly to the way in which it relentlessly evokes such daily realities as "blackouts, black markets, the famine, and the last metro" at a moment when the French wanted and needed a vision of the new future that lay before them. "Film audiences were not ready to confront images of themselves so aggressively condemnatory as *Les Portes de la nuit*'s."[21] Can it be this simple? Can we calculate the success rate of films according to the degree to which the topics they treat are in public favor? Everything we have discovered about the complex interplay of culture and representation in the 1930s leads us beyond such a "reflection theory," leads us in fact to the category of *optique*.

From this perspective, and despite its contemporary setting, *Les Portes de la nuit* must be classified as allegory alongside the historical films that preceded it. Conceived in the same stentorian style as *Les Enfants du paradis*, with a character this time literally named "Destin" spouting Prévert's poetry across the enormous stretch of another of Trauner's elaborate sets, *Les Portes de la nuit* traces the vicissitudes of pure love in the black-market world of the Liberation. The audiences that had responded to the directness of the prewar melodramas, and had then been enthralled by Carné's allegory about melodrama in the nineteenth century, scorned allegory as a way of treating the complexities of the postwar period that surrounded them. Its clarity and fussy style, self-consciously arty, could never recover the immediacy of the Gabin films, to which *Les Portes de la nuit* purportedly harked back. Edward Turk points out:

> Through metaphor and allegory [*Les Visiteurs du soir* and *Les Enfants du paradis*] captured the spirit of their times. *Les Portes de la nuit*, on the contrary, aimed to furnish a social document. With the Occupation ended, Carné and Prévert no longer had to confine themselves to subjects set in the Middle Ages or the nineteenth century; they could again give expression to the temper of their age. Their miscalculation lay in the inherent incompatability between the newer, more direct realism they strove for and the *poésie* they could not abandon.[22]

What Turk calls "newer, more direct realism" seems nothing other than topicality of subject matter, and what he terms "*poésie*" is in fact allegorical style. Neither of these terms brings us back to the conditions of "poetic realism" or to melodrama proper, which always involves the fundamental relation a film establishes and maintains with a contemporaneous audience, a relation, to be specific, that fosters immediacy, recognition, and identification. These qualities are missing from *Les Portes de la nuit*, a film constructed with just as much skill and seriousness as its predecessors.

The opposition between "immediacy" and "model" shows itself unmistakably in differences of acting. The forthright portrayal of "Absolute Goodness" and "Absolute Evil" in *Les Portes de la nuit*[23] rings false both because it is set in modern Paris and because the central actors (Yves Montand in his first key role, Nathalie Nattier in her last) carried neither the authenticity of Gabin (immediacy) nor the professional finesse of Barrault, Arletty, Pierre Brasseur, and Marcel Herrand (model). It is the astounding skill of these latter that so enlivens *Les Enfants du paradis*, a film that, played poorly, would have been stiff or quaint. James Agee affirmed that never before Barrault had a film actor been able truly to portray artistic genius on the screen.[24] José Ferrer is merely a signifier for Toulouse-Lautrec in *Moulin Rouge* (1952); Harry Baur is a ludicrous shadow of Beethoven in Gance's 1936 biographical film; but Jean-Louis Barrault stuns us in exactly the way Baptiste Deburau stunned the audiences of the Funambules a century ago until we are led to wonder if those audiences would not have preferred Barrault. Yet Barrault and his supporting actors play with stentorian clarity to the camera or at least to its wishes. Even the pantomiming could not be more articulate, nor could the chaos of the finale be more clear. Thus the acting of *Les Enfants du paradis*, like its retreat to the

Les Enfants du paradis: Climax at the theater of Life. BFI

safety of another century and its wonderful evocation of the life of the theater, protected it from direct confrontation with the authorities and buffered its popular reception too, making it easy to digest. An enormous mime show, it playacted scenes and sentiments that seemed to belong literally to the films and the era of the 1930s. When Baptiste dramatically crosses his image off a mirror with a streak of makeup, crying, "That's the end of Baptiste," he echoes Gabin who, just after shattering the mirror in *Le Jour se lève*, rails at the crowd below, "François is through; there's no more François." In *Le Quai des brumes* Gabin need not even speak, for he has lost his identity by adopting that of a suicide who leaves him his clothes and passport.

All three heroes suffer from the impossible reach of their longings,[25] but while Gabin internalizes his emotion, Baptiste suffers exquisitely and artistically, modeling rather than replicating the immediacy of feeling that belonged innately to Gabin, who developed a rapport with the critics and public of France that has never been equaled in that country. Invariably cast in contemporary working-class roles, invariably suicidal at the end, Gabin became the self-conception of an entire generation. It is with good reason that his name was virtually synonymous with poetic realism, a style that suited him and

Le Jour se lève: The destiny of Jean Gabin. BFI

suited the era, a fully expressive style designed to bring out what Bazin would call "le destin de Jean Gabin." Listen to Bazin:

> It remains for the sociologists and moralists . . . to reflect on the profound meaning of a mythology in which, through the popularity of an actor like Gabin, millions of our contemporaries rediscover themselves. Perhaps a world without God becomes a world of the gods and the fates they dispense.[26]

From this standpoint *Les Enfants du paradis* is at once the apotheosis of poetic realism and a betrayal, through contrivance and theatricality, of its innocence and vulnerability. It asks first for admiration from its audience rather than for unthinking involvement in the world portrayed. *Le Jour se lève* aims to provide the experience of fusion that *Les Enfants du paradis* merely represents. On the eve of the Nazi takeover, a sizable audience begged to be inundated completely in Gabin's destiny, which they took on without the compensations of the dignity of art or the pride of history. Unlike *Les Enfants du paradis*, which relies on a Hugoesque narrator to guide us through the complex, often hidden relationships and the multiple threads of subplots stretching across years, the paternity of *Le Jour se lève* lies in question from its first moment. Who has narrative authority when the initial credit reads: "Jean Gabin / dans un film de Marcel Carné" and when Carné apparently surrenders control to Gabin and his memories?[27] We are soon trapped not only in François's garret, surrounded by the police; we are trapped as well within his mind. The alarm clock that winds down throughout the film belongs equally to Carné's sense of dramatic fatality and to François's own psychic time bomb. And François shoots himself only seconds before Carné (in the guise of a policeman) detonates the tear gas grenade to thud the conclusion of the film.

This contested narration allows *Le Jour se lève* to reach its dramatic high point. Just after François has recalled the decisive episode in Clara's room during which he learned of Françoise's liaison with Valentin, a fade-in takes us from his memory to render his optical vision: the wardrobe blocking his door. In the reverse shot he is shown still sitting on his bed staring thoughtfully. Carné's camera responds to every flicker of his eye and mind. A shift of his eyes occasions a cut to a close-up insert of the telltale brooch lying on the mantel. Then returning to him, the camera follows as he leaps out of bed to grab the brooch and hurl it against the wall. Now Jaubert's music begins its quiet but incessant drive as François lights a cigarette. He paces and we track with him until he crosses before the mirror. Glancing at himself, he continues out of frame, while we hold on the mirror. The music and the camera next conspire to bring him to a final realization of both his past and his future. We glimpse him in the mirror again, just as he hurls a chair to shatter his image. This stops the music, but only momentarily. A second later it starts its drone again while the camera tracks outside to frame him through the bullet-ridden window, a visual cousin of the broken mirror. François comes forward and looks out. The shot that follows, a cityscape in the first glimmerings of dawn, serves to take the narration definitively from François. Technically a depiction of what he sees, this shot is a prompt card spelling "Doom." François has become a spectacle, first to himself in the mirror, then to Carné who snared him in a dramatic trap, and finally to the crowd below whom we join in a final series of shots. The workers of the *quartier* cry, "We'll stand by you," looking up with us to their cohort hanging on the gibbet of his tenement.

In this scene, editing, camera, and music have linked François to the crowd, the crowd to Carné, and Carné to us in a complex relay of identification: alongside the crowd we are spectators to the plight of someone who is one of us, but one of us raised—because portrayed by Jean Gabin—to the purest essence of ourselves. From film audience to street audience to sympathetic camera in his room, we are carried deeper still as the film fuses itself to the movement of his eyes and mind. Importantly, that movement is itself one of identification, for François will rest only if he can join himself to his double, Françoise. More than the engine driving the film, identification becomes its central focus as early as their meeting at the factory where they recognize that they bear one another's name and childhood history. In the following scene in Françoise's bedroom, photos, simulacra, and reflections multiply to render *en abyme* a tunnel of identification we are meant to tumble into. Gabin is

François, and before her mirror Françoise and he are one; together they stare at themselves and at the teddy bear he holds, "Bolop," with whom she, motherless, has slept throughout her life. Bolop resembles him, Françoise declares, with a sad eye and a bright one. They gaze as well at the little strip of photos of François stuck on the mirror as though it were a picture frame (a strip of photos of her is tacked to his wardrobe). This embedded structure of symmetries and identities comes to us in François's memory image that unrolls through another strip of photos, 35-mm wide, to which we attend stupefied.

Orphans, François and Françoise imagine themselves alone on earth, a primal couple who have found in one other that "original other" that each as a child had been deprived of. By portraying identification as an imaginary drive toward fusion that refuses to recognize the difference of the "other," *Le Jour se lève* explicitly interrogates our own relation to Gabin, whom we watch with one sad eye and one bright. We would feel what he feels, see only what he sees. Such is the lure held out by melodrama and by the hypnosis of the "imaginary signifier" of the cinema.

But movies are never truly hypnotic and spectators never unrecoverably locked within a character. Although the bulk of the film comes to us through Gabin/François in flashback, we share with the blind man at the opening and with the crowd at the end a terror that stems as much from incomprehension as it does from sympathy. François's longing and ordeal are seen and judged in the larger social world. He is not us but our representative, and we join ourselves not to the "figure" of François, which self-destructs before our eyes, but to the interpretation of the world made possible by this figure. We are the ones who must live on in the day that has so mercilessly dawned. This is to say, we are invited to go through Gabin, and even through François as played by Gabin, to the nameless values and anxieties that reverberate across the representation as a whole. Our identification with a character's perspective allows us, in Paul Ricoeur's crucial formulation, to complete the world the character leaves in death, to appropriate it in a fully imaginative act of interpretation. And so a proper (ex)change takes place in the movie theater when the spectator is himself as Gabin, "soi-même comme un autre."[28]

Poetic realism names this particular transaction at the movies, and its specific form of cinematic address comes into relief when examined beside neighboring *optiques*. When Gérard Philipe appeared as the Gabin of the postwar years in such films as *Le Diable au corps* and *Une si jolie petite plage*, he was acclaimed for the intelligence of his performances, for the minute correctness with which he portrayed characters like François, alienated to the point of suicide, but forthright and honest. Gabin's prewar performances were never termed intelligent. He is treated by critics and the public as always and only himself: volatile, absolute, unassuming. Gérard Philipe, on the other hand, is the star of a style of film justly labeled "psychological"—not "poetic"—

realism. Though recovering the prewar marginal hero and placing him in an atmosphere full of mystery and intrigue, these postwar films made famous by Yves Allégret and Claude Autant-Lara are incisive and bitter in a way foreign to poetic realism. Studied elaborations of the situation that *Le Jour se lève* embodies, they promote the pleasures of knowledge more than those of experience.

This is not to say that poetic realism is a literally immediate style of filmmaking, that it is a model of nothing but itself. Rather, what it models is the fact of identification, our drive to identify. Other modes of cinematic discourse use this drive (*Les Enfants du paradis* does so allegorically; psychological realism does so naturalistically); but the classic poetic realist texts take identification as both means and end. Edward Turk approaches this realization through a psychoanalysis of Carné for whom fusion with the film screen replaced a broken rapport with his mother.[29] *Les Enfants du paradis* represents that lost woman through the character Garance, carted away from Baptiste in the final carnival. The most brilliant artistry has come to replace her as a kind of fetish, the artistry of mime, music, design, and acting that represent Carné's and Baptiste's displaced desire for her in a film as beautiful as that one. But it is *Le Jour se lève* that affords the experience, not the representation, of such fusion.

Ever since the war, a rather crude social psychology has tried to account for the ritual sacrifice of the alienated individual that the cinema provided French culture at the end of the Third Republic, by suggesting that the blind fatalism of the movies responded directly to general moral collapse in the face of the Nazi machine. The orphan hero of these films spoke to a populace that must have felt betrayed by the fathers of the Republic (scandals and mismanagement ever since World War I). Where could they turn? Surrounded by fascist fathers in Spain, Italy, and Germany, and recently betrayed again by the self-proclaimed father of international communism, Joseph Stalin, the French had also been disillusioned by the brief brotherhood of the Popular Front. Their moral situation indeed seems aptly expressed by the grim finales of *Le Quai des brumes* and *Le Jour se lève*.

To remain attuned to those years, one need not espouse a reflection theory whereby art finds its significance by referring, even obliquely or symbolically, to social history. Ricoeur urges us to scuttle "reference" altogether in favor of "applicability," where fiction and even historical reconstruction take on the burden of proving significant for those who need to appropriate it.[30] In his view, "appropriation" occurs only when the reader or spectator understands the appropriate questions to which the artwork stands as a response. Poetic realism was taken into a culture that understood questions of moral isolation as had few other generations.

This indirect relation among producer, context, work, and audience that Ricoeur characterizes as one of question and response is exactly what inter-

ested Bazin when he sought to explain the waning of Carné's relevance after
the war. To repeat his observation, "Carné's . . . work as an artist participated
in the period; it answered its questions," questions, I am suggesting, about
where to put one's faith. The films do not reflect their period so much as
respond imaginatively to it. And "the [period's] questions determine the direction of the responses. Now by responses I do not mean an objective content,
but the expression given to this content, that is to say, a style." That style, we
have seen in case after case, turns inward to the solitary, orphaned self, to
private morality based on private memory and experience, and to a solidarity
among the downtrodden based on the intimacy of identification. When a response like this is appropriate to key questions of the age, then, both through
and beyond its style, a film finds itself appropriated by a culture. This results
in what Bazin calls that "perfect inner equilibrium, the happy arrangement of
all the elements of Le Jour se lève, which gives it the strength of myth" and
which takes the film beyond the director because it "corresponds to a sociological maturity of the themes."[31]

Le Jour se lève, Bazin implies, was not alone when, in responding to the
question of where to put one's faith, it turned inward to the solitary, orphaned
self. Aside from the full catalog of poetic realist films, we can locate in French
culture of the late 1930s innumerable expressions up and down the ladder that
share its attitude. At the lowest rung, the "chansons realistes" (Fréhel, Piaf) as
well as the joyful Charles Trenet tunes so popular at this time are an index to
the nation's focus on personal sentiments and sentimentality. Like Le Jour se
lève these songs scarcely hint at the social or domestic framework surrounding
private experience, and when they do, it is in the key of nostalgia. The same
myopia, this time strategically employed, shapes the insights of the developing
philosophy and literature of existentialism, the most famous contemporaneous example of which is Sartre's La Nausée. Heightened expressions of personal
honesty in the face of social and cultural isolation abound; later on they would
seem inappropriate, indecent, or at least maudlin. Bazin ends his essay on the
diminishing impact of Carné this way: "The director of Le Quai des brumes is
not wrong in being unfaithful to his past, but only in trying to prolong it
beyond that situation where the meeting of a style, a time, and his themes
made perfection possible. The time has changed, the style has evolved, the
themes have remained the same, and we discover that they are no longer
myths."[32] Myths may be ageless; but films only appear to be myths. In fact, as
I hope to have shown, they are thoroughly cultural and historical phenomena,
even when what they express repudiates culture and history.

Epilogue:
Le Temps des cerises
and the Fruit
of Regret

THE PERSISTENCE OF POETIC REALISM

Seen as the condensation of what is always most
characteristic about French cinema, poetic realism
begins to lose historical importance, for it dissolves into a general impulse like "intimate melodrama." As mere melodrama, even especially effective melodrama, poetic realism can hardly be
said to offer world cinema anything particularly
noteworthy. Indeed in its very name poetic realism takes into itself the tension that, ubiquitously
from Lumière and Méliès to our own day, defines
cinema at its most vigorous. Its urge to uplift—to
sublimate—the everyday is so common to most
photographic theories that its reappearance in
1930s France, even in a powerful form, is significant but unremarkable.

Perhaps for this reason historians have progressively downgraded what I would term the
"power coefficient" of poetic realism. From the
veritable hurricane that it was for Sadoul and
Mitry, poetic realism seems more like a tropical
storm to Jeancolas and measures as a mere low
pressure weather system (exaggerated, perhaps,
because of identifiable historical "radar echoes")
for Vincendeau and Buchsbaum. Its force is dissipated by those who spread it toward the past into
the silent era or who allow it to bleed through the
membrane of the decade into the Occupation and
postwar years.[1]

Essentially an issue of historical scale, the import (indeed the identity) of poetic realism depends on the type of meshing that the historian
employs to filter significant objects and relations
from the indefinite amount of information available. Our rather fine mesh has turned up qualities (such as multiple acting styles) and relations

(between, say, the photographers Kertesz and Brassaï, the novelist Mac Orlan, and the director Carné) that were scarcely visible to the first audiences of these films. Sifted by scholars equipped with coarser mesh, designed to capture larger phenomena, poetic realism slips through the decade of the 1930s and adheres to the cinema of the Occupation, or to the cinema of quality, or (at the furthest remove) to cinematic melodrama in general.

But it has been my contention that on close inspection there is no such thing as "cinematic melodrama in general," only varieties of films that in specific historical circumstances took up certain potentials of melodrama to "respond to the questions of their day." Under the interrogation called cultural history, which tries to hear again the questions and responses that make up culture in the first place, poetic realism assumes a ghostly form that later eras, beginning with the Occupation and Liberation, recognized and were moved by, sometimes even moved to emulate for their own purposes.

When poetic realism is said to persist in French cinema beyond 1940, it is mainly under the sign of nostalgia or regret, the movement's chief emotional register. Whether recruited by a timely political opening (as when the Popular Front was called upon during François Mitterrand's successful election campaign in 1981) or dredged up for the inevitable fiftieth anniversary celebration as it was in 1986, poetic realism both constitutes and stands for a past that shimmers attractively at a distance.

To ask the uses of regret is to ask the purpose of this book and of the films it treats: regret for a cinema of genuine intimacy, regret for a popular yet serious audience, regret for a relation between movies and viewers that is human in scale. A mirage projected at a distance of over half a century, poetic realism today names a function that movies putatively served and a tone they sounded. In sounding the same tone, later filmmakers have sought to reform a modern, more jaded, audience by comparing our times as well as our movies to those of another era, an era that appears more authentic than ours because its movies went so desperately in search of authenticity.

I have searched for this search mainly in the "address" of movies to audiences. And I have dramatized a conflict of *optiques* (taken as major alternatives of address, ambition, style, function) on the stage of the screen, so to speak. In the first years of sound, French cinema by and large displayed its theatrical verve to the nation and the world, showing off acting, design, dialogue, and music in abundant adaptations from plays and even in films written directly for the talking picture. Among the few alternatives to this dominant *optique* there developed a quieter, more intimate address that gradually provoked critical and then popular approval and enthusiasm. Poetic realism buttonholed critics around the world with an unmistakable tone of sincerity. It gave spectators not just sincere characters to identify with, but a limited, situated camera perspective from which to peer out on an indistinct world with those characters. It made a virtue of myopia. Renoir called this virtue into question in a number of brilliant films, most radically in *La Règle du jeu*, by developing his own *optique*, a highly sophisticated brand of theatricality that worked by the parallax of multiple perspectives. To use Lionel Trilling's distinction, if poetic realism sought sincerity, then Renoir can be said to have reached for, and achieved, authenticity of expression.[2]

These distinctions, and their implied development or progress, correspond to a sociological commonplace about the decade. In its first five years, French sound films resonate with the deep bass voices of father figures played by powerful stage actors like Raimu, Harry Baur, Gabriel Gabro, and Pierre Alcover. Whether wise and all-knowing, troubled, or failed, these mature men present themselves forthrightly and forcefully in their families or social groups. And they present themselves the same way to the audience paying to applaud the strength of their expression. Because poetic realism always conjures up the image of its most famous actor, Jean Gabin, its break with the earlier form is striking. For Gabin is no father; indeed he does not even have a father he can identify. His sincerity can be called "adolescent" in its naïveté and righteousness, giving him a new sort of strength, that of the determined underling who has no family and small tradition to rely on in his response to the drama that consumes him. His inarticulate mumblings as well as his outbursts full of argot spoke directly to an anxious audience about anxiety. This is one basis for speculation that poetic realism predicts or guides American *film noir* a few years down the road.

To say that fathers and adolescent sons struggle for survival in these films, and do so with the fate of vulnerable young women in their hands, may open up a crude sociology of the period. Uncomfortable in viewing films as direct reflections of social conditions, I take these repeated dramatic concerns rather as "topoi" (traditional "subjects" in art history or "commonplaces" in rhetoric); they provide filmmakers with opportunities to explore intriguing yet tested material to represent in a new fashion. In the same way that the baptism of Christ by John in the desert gave painters across the centuries opportunities to play with techniques to solve problems of perspective, of picturing the flow and transparency of water, of constructing a moral landscape, and so on, French tales of fathers and then of troubled adolescents permitted, indeed demanded, attention to possibilities in the medium ranging from the technical to the aesthetic to the moral.

Sociology creeps back into this picture whenever we think we can identify the values at stake for a culture in one or another type of representation, one or another problem it explores and exploits. But if a culture can be identified by its specific rhetoric of question and response, as Paul Ricoeur has led me to suggest,[3] no first cause need be posited. Filmmakers did not, or did not only, attend to the social issues of the day before shaping stories whose tone was appropriate to those issues; filmmakers equally articulated particular styles of anxiety or satisfaction and produced pictures of intriguing states of affairs that

raised the level of cultural concern over issues that may not have been otherwise expressed as "concerns." I have tried to treat poetic realist films as eloquent answers to murky, inchoate problems.

While the issues to which the words "sincerity" and "authenticity" ring out
as replies have been with us, Lionel Trilling notes, since Hamlet[4] (whom
Gabin could readily have played in 1938), they take on a specific shape in
France after World War I. The Surrealists mocked the kind of romantic sincerity based on individual genius and on "the blood of a poet," including self-
styled film poets like Cocteau or Abel Gance. Calling on Freud, the Surrealists
favored a dispersed subjectivity that nevertheless could result in the authentic
expression of automatic writing, unmediated collective dreamwork, and the
forcible abolition of cultural constraints. Poetic realism looks far less confident
than Surrealism even when it butts up against the same constraints. Compare
Gaston Modot's direct bludgeoning of social convention in pursuit of Lya Lys
in L'Age d'or of 1930 to Gabin's literal bludgeoning of the corrupt shopkeeper,
Nelly's protector, eight years later in Le Quai des brumes. We applaud Modot
as the urgent figure (without interior) of an authentic erotic impulse destined,
once released, to succeed in its quest; whereas Gabin we identify with in the
sincerity of his subjectivity. He constitutes a volume of perceptions, memories, and values that refuses to let mendacity have its usual way; he crushes it,
then dies unheralded as a result.

The differences between 1930 Surrealism and 1938 poetic realism should
tempt us to introduce for comparison related expressions from later moments
in French culture. The postwar films of psychological realism have already
been characterized as disingenuous. Their distraught heroes, like their spectators, are dominated by a superior and calculating narration whose tone of
address Truffaut believed to be supercilious, not sincere.[5] Ten years later still,
Truffaut's sincerity would break through this veneer of good taste in Les
Quatre Cents Coups, a film "signed Rapidity. Art. Novelty. Cinematograph.
Originality. Impertinence. Seriousness. Tragedy. Renovation. Ubu-Roi. Fantasy. Ferocity. Affection. Universality. Tenderness," as Godard declared in his
ecstatic review.[6] Godard's own A bout de souffle, made the next year, tested the
limits of "authenticity" beyond Truffaut's potentially sentimental sincerity.
Significantly for us, reviewers caught echoes both of Sartre and of Le Quai des
brumes in the crudely direct behavior they variously attributed to Jean-Paul
Belmondo's character, Michel Poiccard, and to Godard's abrasive style.[7]

It would require a thick cultural history to understand the appropriateness
of, say, Sartre's thinking for those living in France from 1938 through 1960, or
the appropriateness of the New Wave as a response to cultural problems that
brought on the Fifth Republic. The mention of postwar films should remind
us of the great cultural shifts that must ever keep poetic realism at a certain
remove even from the French who look back with fondness on it. Like any
style or school of art that deeply impressed its own era, poetic realism would

continue to impress later periods, but necessarily in the mode of critique, or more often nostalgia. Filmmakers of the 1950s, of the 1970s, or of today might dredge up old styles and old concerns whose impertinent, clumsy fit with the discourse of these later cultural moments can stand as a rebuke to, or evasion of, contemporary concerns.

The Bygone Days of *Casque d'or*

The first great film to cite poetic realism in just this nostalgic way, I have argued, is *Les Enfants du paradis*. Six years later another masterwork, *Casque d'or*, summoned up, in a more regretful mood, the same cinema of regret.[8] Actually, *Casque d'or* might be thought of as a genuine poetic realist project, for it was first envisaged in 1939. Renoir purportedly looked at Henri Jeanson's scenario of the subject, and Julien Duvivier was in preproduction when World War II forced Robert Hakim, the producer, to scuttle this along with his other films.[9] Hakim then failed to mount it two years later in Hollywood with Jean Gabin in the male lead. As a project, then, *Casque d'or* came through the Occupation and Liberation protected by its poetic realist veneer. Someone was sure to take it on. That someone would be Jacques Becker.

More curious for us, the tale it tells, taken from lurid newspaper accounts of the lives and deaths of romantic urban outlaws (*apaches*) at the turn of the century, calls up *Les Enfants du paradis*, which also romanticizes the Parisian demimonde of a bygone era. As would be the case for *Casque d'or*, a woman stands at the center of the multilayered Oedipal struggle Carné and Prévert invented, the mysterious Garance, flower of the underworld, whose welcoming glance at the mime Baptiste precipitates the longing, the intrigues, and the disasters that carry the film across its marvelous three hours.

Jacques Becker began to work on *Casque d'or* in 1946, just after the triumph of *Les Enfants du paradis*. It would take him five years to find his Arletty in Simone Signoret, five years to pare down and refashion a scenario that, like *Les Enfants*, had grown larded with subplots, thrillingly contorted coincidences, and flowery language. Following his instincts as a clean craftsman of the cinema, Becker refused to inflate poetic realism the way Carné had done during the Occupation. Instead he returned to the straightforwardness of the prewar model, mercilessly slashing scenes, characters, and dialogue so as to stage more purely and directly its mythic theme of doomed love. Manda (Serge Reggiani) takes Marie (Signoret) from Leca, the leader of a ruthless Parisian gang. When Leca responds by framing Manda's old buddy, Raymond, and after Raymond dies in a prison escape that Manda has engineered, Manda tracks Leca down and kills him in the presence of the police where the coward had run for protection. In the last scene, Marie looks on as the guillotine falls on Manda's neck.

Like Manda (and like Baptiste in *Les Enfants du paradis*) the film is modest, reticent, yet full of unrestrained longing. In its lengthiest, most ebullient love scene, a promenade in the forest covered in ten lyrical shots, Marie utters but two brief sentences, while Manda utters none. Indeed, in the full ninety-six minutes of this movie, Manda has a total of only seventy-eight lines, surely fewer than any other hero in French sound cinema, excepting of course M. Hulot.[10] Language is the privilege of fathers and pretenders, of the eloquent Lacenaire, the strident Frédérick Lemaître, and, in Becker's film, the dandy Leca. Language controls and seduces. The mime Baptiste, the taciturn Manda, distrust it; so does Jacques Becker. His directness and sincerity cut through the overwrought, loquacious cinema of quality whose frothy costumes and sets, and whose flowery language, tried often and vainly in the 1950s to replicate the Carné-Prévert masterpiece.

Casque d'or was singled out by François Truffaut, himself an enfant terrible, as standing up boldly to the stodgy *cinéma du Papa*.[11] Its production like its plot can be read as an Oedipal drama, Becker wrestling the cinema of quality to the ground in his need to achieve something fresh. Simone Signoret bitterly recalls how the film was "murdered by the critics and at the box office," as though this were the revenge of the father. Yet the production was graced by good fortune, by good will, and by the supreme effort of all concerned.[12] It was, she declared, her greatest role, as the British critics and public would finally be able to convince the French.[13] Her Marie, like Arletty's Garance, is the very image of freshness and grace. A popular goddess who rows up to the napping hero and bestows herself upon him, she is both the ideal of beauty French cinema has flirted with all century long, and the fickle public for whose favors—for whose attention and gaze—filmmakers have betrayed one another. She is the mythical destiny of popular romance over whom father and son will lose their lives. Becker was devoted to her.

Preparing the film, Becker was inspired by a representation of the world he wanted to bring to life: Auguste Renoir's 1881 *Le Déjeuner des canotiers*.[14] Early on he provides us this painting as a *tableau vivant*, staging at an airy riverside *guinguette* the buoyant dancing, drinking, and fighting that Renoir's shimmering colors and decentered composition suggest. If he felt capable of mimicking Renoir's lusty yet social painting, it was because he had imbibed that spirit when he was assistant to the great painter's son during the flourishing cinema of the Popular Front. It was Becker, we must not forget, who pushed *Le Crime de Monsieur Lange* into production. And so Becker's is an earned nostalgia, neither vague nor sentimental. In *Casque d'or* he forthrightly displays for his generation exactly what that generation lacked in its cinema as well as in its life: professionalism and sincerity. Today we experience this lack at a double remove, for Becker's own period, as compromised as it may have been, seems vastly more professional and sincere than does our own. Hence the aroma exuded by *Casque d'or* is more luxuriant for us; not the solemn aura of incense dispelled by Walter Benjamin in his famous essay on the work of art, but the tobacco flavor of a bygone populism where solid craftsmanship stands above fine art.

As professionalism, forthrightness, and sincerity decline, the sheer surface appeal of *Casque d'or* must necessarily increase each year, and with it the nostalgia and regret the film thematizes. Jacques Becker surely traded on nostalgia in imaging the decor, the gestures, and the codes of the Belle Epoque. In France's postwar crisis of values where "ambiguity" clouded personal and political motives and acts, the apparently limpid moral codes of 1900 seemed a tonic, a restorative rebuke. For this was an era that knew what it wanted out of life and pressed unapologetically to attain it. The sureness of Manda's strokes as he planes fine boards in the cabinet shop defines his ability and his determination; it defines the competence of an era for a later, degenerate era at the brink of losing its skill in carpentry and in living.

Becker was not naive. He knew that the historical Manda was a dangerous thug who broke with Leca to lead a splinter gang, precipitating the violent jealousy over a beautiful woman that truly ended in murder and execution.[15] But he chose to make his Manda a laborer who, because of a troubled past, is quite at ease in the underworld. Manda proudly wears the worker's casquette that Leca's middle-class pretension scorns.[16] In this way Becker brings us closer to a certain cinema of the 1930s than to the historical reality of the turn

Casque d'or: A laconic hero, with no apologies. BFI

of the century. *Casque d'or* mimics the most classic of poetic realist films, *Le Jour se lève*, whose hero—like Manda a worker and an orphan[17]—stands up to, then shoots to death, the dandy who has corrupted the woman he loves. In Carné's classic, François (Jean Gabin) disdains excuses, choosing to die cornered on the top floor of his tenement, while a crowd looks on from the street. In a reverse image of this scene, Manda is guillotined in the street, while Marie looks down from a top-floor room that might as well be François's. Becker seals the reference by quoting Carné's famous "vertigo shot" down the building's spiral stairwell.

The purity of characters and motives in *Casque d'or* is of a piece with the modesty and stylistic rectitude that Bazin attributed to poetic realism in its classic phase. Manda, as portrayed by Reggiani, inherits his silent integrity as well as the *casquette* from Gabin. He belongs to the 1930s, belongs with the old carpenter Danard and with his prison buddy Raymond, particularly as played by Gaston Modot and Raymond Bussières, respectively. These actors carry the 1930s in their blood, having worked with Buñuel, with Prévert, and above all with Renoir. As actors they stand for the brotherhood of the workers' theater tradition.[18] As characters they serve as tokens of the tough but good old times, particularly the times Raymond shared with Manda before prison and before Manda went straight. Those times are gone, he warns his friend; gangsters like Leca no longer honor the codes of their profession. And filmmakers like Delannoy, Truffaut would add, no longer respect their profession and their audience.

Casque d'or would return us to those legendary times by involving us in a legendary love, the sort of oblivious love glorified by poetic realism. As were the audiences of those films, we are drawn into fusion with *Casque d'or*, following the lead of Manda and Marie. Like Manda lying on the grass, we cannot but lose perspective, as beams of reflected light fall to us from the screen; the film presses up to our eyes and lips and asks us to embrace it. But like Manda again, we wake from our delicious dream of fusion. *Casque d'or* fades as we watch it. In the final shot, the couple literally twirls into a future that has already been cut short, fading away under the melody of "Le Temps des cerises."

"Le Temps des cerises" expresses the delicious fatality of poetic realism, played out this time by Manda and Marie, but it evokes simultaneously the warmth of the Popular Front that the mature friendship of Manda and Raymond represents. Genuine friendship, where workers implicitly count on each other, stands opposed to the image of the gang that Becker seems to take from Carné's *Le Quai des brumes* with its popular psychological version of the fascist sensibility. In that film Michel Simon played a respectable but depraved shopkeeper whose wealth comes from a group of thieves led by the sniveling Lucien (Pierre Brasseur). Gabin's quiet strength erupts to slap down Lucien and to bash in the head of his boss in quite the same way that Manda without

Casque d'or: Undemanding
love and brotherhood. BFI

Casque d'or: Adolescent
dependency. BFI

regret puts an end to Fredo and to Leca. Leca's good taste and impeccable costume scarcely mask the duplicitous and sadistic behavior of this chief of the *apaches*. His followers, like Lucien in the Carné film, exhibit symptoms of arrested adolescence and fixation on father figures. When caught stealing by Leca, for example, Fredo not only whimpers as he takes his punishment, but then meekly goes out to buy his boss cigars. Instead of rebelling or standing up for himself, Fredo introjects this father, mistreating Marie and bullying his mates. Leca recognizes a miniature of himself in Fredo, promoting him to right-hand man.

Leca's strength, like that of Fredo, is sheer facade; it crumbles when tested: "Don't shoot, Manda. Don't shoot," he pleads when cornered. Manda not only shoots; he empties his gun into Leca. But even before this, we learned that Leca's power rests on that of the commissioner of police, who in turn jokingly admits that he takes orders from his wife, a woman Leca buys off with gifts of port wine. In this world of slaps and favors, no one is on top. To belong to the system is to kneel before someone else, weakly, begging permission to exercise power over someone weaker still.

Raymond, the oldest member of the group, refuses this narcissistic syndrome and breaks from the gang when it threatens Manda. He insists on the difference of a kind of friendship that "doesn't happen very often," an undemanding affection the film upholds as an alternative to both oblivious heterosexual passion and infantile dependency with homosexual overtones. This difference is that of a chosen brotherhood, a Popular Front. Where the gang can be seen to represent the "scoutism" of the 1930s, with its reverence for authority and its implicit misogyny, Manda and Raymond are shown to be men of the Popular Front, standing shoulder to shoulder in respect and in equality.

In the theme song, "Le Temps des cerises," itself legendary, Becker evoked the goodness of the Popular Front. Composed in 1866 by Jean-Baptiste Clément, it sings the sentiments of passion and regret that let it aptly underscore one of French cinema's greatest love stories.[19] Yet immediately there accrued to it explicitly revolutionary overtones when Clément published it along with other songs in his *Chansons révolutionnaires* in 1868.[20] Overtaking France during the end of the Belle Epoque, performed by Montéhus, the famous crooner of the world of the *apaches*, this now utterly political anthem would persist into the 1930s when it was sung along with the "Internationale" as an antidote to the right-wing "La Marseillaise."

The political thrust in Becker's adoption of this song as the leitmotif of *Casque d'or* comes clear when we note that in 1937, as Jean Renoir was seeking to wrest the national anthem from the right wing, his co-director at Ciné-Liberté, Jean-Paul Le Chanois, was simultaneously in production with a much more radical film, one completely financed by the Parti Communiste, the title of which is in fact *Le Temps des cerises*. Becker had worked with Le Chanois on Renoir's *La Vie est à nous* in 1936, a film edited by *Casque d'or*'s editor Marguerite Renoir. As in *Casque d'or*, the action of *Le Temps des cerises* begins at the turn of the century. Moreover, it features Gaston Modot playing a carpenter, the role Becker would have him repeat fifteen years later.

Named after such a song, Le Chanois's *Le Temps des cerises* cannot help but be sentimental.[21] But in contrast to the fatalistic *Casque d'or*, it rallies nostalgia, gathering the radical past of the Commune as a weapon to wield in the politics of the present. Although the film's first episode is set in the Belle Epoque as the Eiffel Tower is being completed, its finale could not be more contemporary. Under the same Eiffel Tower we see the pavilions being constructed for the International Exposition of 1937. Two lovers huddle beneath the cold shoulder of the recently constructed Palais de Chaillot, ostentatious emblem of progress. An old man approaches wistfully singing "Le Temps des cerises" while the young man tells his fiancée about his father's death in a construction accident that occurred while he helped complete the famous tower. From here the lovers (and the film) become resolute in demanding better treatment for the old. An impassioned seven-minute off-camera speech calls upon all citizens of conscience to form a Popular Front to lead a society where people, not monuments, are respected and invested in. Intellectuals, workers, and artists are pulled together in a final sequence that toasts such a future, one that is bound to come and bound to be theirs.

At the outset of the 1950s *Casque d'or* points to no such future, to no future at all. Jacques Becker was led to confess, "I have a horror of my own generation,"[22] as he openly looked back to a better one, the generation of the Popular Front. Today *Casque d'or* has itself become for us an image of a better era—and of a better cinema too—one based on solid craft and direct sentiment, a real time of cherries. The genius of the film is that it predicted, understood, and thematized this inevitable process of decay and nostalgia. It made of it a legend.

POETIC REALISM WILL BE SIXTY-FIVE IN THE YEAR 2000

In 1975 the strains of "Le Temps des cerises" once more wafted from a French film, or more precisely a Swiss-French one, *Jonas qui aura 25 ans en l'an 2000*. This time it is sung by the inmates of an old-age home, where one of the nine principal characters of *Jonas*, Marco Perli, has taken a job, as though answering the call Le Chanois's film had put out in 1937. Sitting at the piano he leads the community who follow the famous lyrics with their sheet music. To affirm his film's populist pedigree, Alain Tanner chose Raymond Bussières, by then a septuagenarian, for the role of the retired train engineer, Charles. Bussières had played Raymond in *Casque d'or* and, before that, had helped found the Groupe Octobre. At a key moment he assures Marco Perli, and through him all the disillusioned veterans of 1968 who populate Tanner's movie, that life was better in 1936.

But as its title suggests, *Jonas qui aura 25 ans en l'an 2000* does not bury itself in memories of '68 or '36; rather it projects these pasts tentatively toward a millennial vision. Old men and old women may sing "Le Temps des cerises," but *Jonas qui aura 25 ans en l'an 2000* dedicates itself to the young, even to the unborn. That dedication takes its cue from Jean-Jacques Rousseau, the film's patron saint, whose statue looks down approvingly on Marco the radical teacher and on Matthieu whose quest for an even more radical form of education leads him to quit his job and devote himself full-time to the commune's children in the open classroom he fashions in a literal greenhouse.

Harmonizing a concern for the old and the young, harmonizing the competing impulses of nostalgia and of revolution, is the classroom subject that Marco professes, history. History forms the core, he tells us, of all education. In an inspiring lecture to his lycée students, Marco explains—with the aid of

Jonas qui aura 25 ans en l'an 2000: The old (Raymond Bussières). CF

Jonas qui aura 25 ans en l'an 2000: The young. CF

a metronome, a butcher knife, and a length of blood sausage—that history can be sliced up in many ways, but only when it is seen from the right perspective can one peer through its holes to the past and then prophetically into the future. He promises to help each student find this liberating perspective.

But it is Charles who speaks best about perspective. In a speech that might serve as the epigraph for any book on politically engaged cinema, Charles explains to Marco, who listens reverently:

> I'll tell you something, travelling by train and driving a train are two completely different things. Because of the rails. Do you still sometimes travel by train? What do you see? The countryside going by, like in the movies. Myself, I don't go to the movies anymore. But in the locomotive engine, the countryside doesn't go by. You travel inside. Always: inside, inside, inside. It's like a kind of music. You go in front of yourself, right to the horizon, and then it goes on, right to the place where the rails come together. And they never come together.[23]

Charles (or rather Bussières) invites us to rethink our usual passive spectatorship at the movies, but he might just as well have been speaking about our relation to education or to history: the old historiography is lateral, spatial, and sedentary. Revolutionary history puts us inside time, driving forward to a point we will never reach but that must always be our goal. History ought to emulate music, not movies, which is why Marco brings his class to a close by having the students clap in rhythm in order to measure time, accelerating until the interval "disappears in total synthesis," like Charles's converging rails.

Such an ideal mission for education—where past, present, and future line up meaningfully, and where differences are harmonized by an action whose rhythm everyone shares—returns us to Jean Renoir and to the Popular Front.[24] The glorious dinner that brings together nearly all the characters and stories of *Jonas*, the dinner at which Jonah receives his name in utero, is a reprise of the celebration of the collective at the end of *Le Crime de Monsieur*

Le Crime de Monsieur Lange: A toast to cooperative life and art. CB

Lange. Here Tanner most recognizably inherits Renoir's spontaneity with actors, his relaxed digressions into the ordinary rituals of meals and conversation, and, to realize all this, his use of long take, mobile camera, deep focus, and overlapping dialogue. Both dinner parties approach the sanctity of utopia. Tanner's camera slowly circles the group as each in turn ventures a name for the baby that Mathilde will soon deliver. Despite their differences and despite the absence of Marie and Charles, Tanner buckles them in the round of a gentle musical theme that gradually is shaped into the title song of the movie. The group partakes of this communion and Jonah receives his name.

Structured on the partially overlapping lives and concerns of its separate characters, all remnants of May 1968, *Jonas qui aura 25 ans en l'an 2000* strives for that "equilibrium" that Renoir's narrative prowess achieved in the 1930s,[25] a democratic aesthetic he most pointedly put to work in *La Marseillaise* and *La Règle du jeu*, where multiple characters and incidents play across a dramatic field that could never be represented as a "plot line." Emulating this approach to narrative,[26] Tanner seems to relinquish the power of "directing" all the technology and all the actors at his command in favor of balancing the multiple goals, events, styles, and personalities who contribute to the loose community that takes shape during the course of the film. The musical theme that emerges in the film expresses that balance; never guiding our attention, it encourages us to reflect sympathetically on what we see and hear, and to partake of its spirit.

We have already recognized and questioned the attractive politics of this "hands-off" directorial pose in relation to *La Marseillaise*, where Renoir had hoped to propagate the spirit of the Popular Front through a modest history lesson. With *Jonas* in mind, we now can add an implicit pedagogy to that film's innovations in historiography and style. For the harmless plot Renoir devised to humanize his little "chronicle of events leading to the fall of the monarchy" involves precisely the learning of a song. As the diverse individuals who make up the citizens in action meander north, Bomier is progressively taught to accept a certain rhythm in the air and to add his voice to the chorus that is singing—in countless different registers—the future of the country.

In combating the notion of history as a sequence of causal events like some highway to the present, *La Marseillaise* might serve to illustrate Marco Perli's lecture:

> Capitalism supplies the idea of time-as-highway. Highway of the sun, the highway of progress . . . during the 19th century the fear of the past was transformed rationally into scientific law. Time then became a road without curves. . . . And their roads had boundaries. Absolutely regular. Millions of years divided into eras, into dates, into days and into hours of work to punch in on the time-clock. Like sausage.[27]

Renoir and Alain Tanner promise a history of the land, not the highway, one that accounts for biology and leisure (for food, love, talk, and play) before calculating the effects of progress, technology, and regulated work. And why not? The Popular Front had put in question the ideology of labor. The Matignon Accords of 1936 had limited work to forty hours a week. In 1937 vacations became a right, not a reward. The country declared life to be larger than production, and Renoir responded by representing French history as more interesting and varied than a straight line.

In aiming to teach all French citizens the power, rights, and responsibilities of belonging to a nation wrested from the nobility in 1792 and from the "200 families" in 1936, *La Marseillaise* participated in the pedagogical mission of the Popular Front. The new government's minister of education, Jean Zay, explicitly called on the cinema to be a means of extended popular education. The very week that he ceremoniously announced the project for *La Marseillaise* to an overflow crowd at the Salle Huyghens, he proclaimed the ratification of his reforms to national education. The fact that Zay is remembered as a visionary public servant, a saint in the arena of modern education, strengthens the links among film style, pedagogy, and historiography, for Zay in fact was responsible for the film's title and even for the outline of its script.[28]

Yet we know that the optimism of *La Marseillaise* rang hollow, just as Zay's educational reforms today seem minimal first steps to liberate students from an oppressive paternalism that his ministry itself represented. Such are the contradictions of any Popular Front that proclaims freedom but requires concerted action, that encourages everyone to whistle any tune whatever just so long as all voices form a chorus when the time comes to chant a revolutionary anthem.

Versions of this contradiction necessarily arise in the script John Berger wrote for Tanner. While Marco professes a history of the land and of leisure, a history that is not laid out as a highway, Charles argues more convincingly that history takes place not on the land but on the rails. The popular revolution about which he wistfully reminisces requires that the people take their place in the engine of history; yet the revolution Marco demands would uproot those rails altogether, destroy the highway, and return the fields to geological time. The broken hopes of 1968 have given birth to a nostalgia for a rural utopia he shares with his friends on the farm; whereas Charles's Popular Front was ever and always a progressive, urban phenomenon for which the railroad remains an apt symbol.

Jonas qui aura 25 ans en l'an 2000 is a more sober film than *La Marseillaise* in part because, coming later, it has learned the immediate fate of the engine of history. After the glorious finale that concludes *La Marseillaise*, Renoir's very next image was taken literally from Charles's engine cab, an exhilarating but self-destructive image of Jacques Lantier at the throttle of *La Bête humaine* as it streaks above the rails. Those rails converged not on a socialist future but on murder and suicide, and figuratively on the inevitable catastrophe of world war.

In sight of such a wreck, our relation to the utopia of the Popular Front can only be nostalgic, and in this it takes on the sensibility of poetic realism, though at one remove. *Jonas* does not in the least resemble the narrative concentration of poetic realist films; and it strives to distance rather than to absorb the audience. But like poetic realism, it exudes what has been called "a nostalgia for the present." This at least is the feeling engendered by *Pépé le Moko*, *Le Quai des brumes*, *Gueule d'amour*, and *La Bête humaine*. Because the pleasure of nostalgia compensates for the absence of what is truly desired, it is a sensibility that can easily be maligned as passive, indolent, and evasive, particularly during the heady days of revolutionary fervor.

But nostalgia, like other states of the soul, may function in multiple ways. True, a great many French films of the 1930s slipped into reveries about strong fathers and about the Belle Epoque as a way to avoid recognizing the bleak orphanhood of contemporary life. Poetic realism, on the other hand, spoke to the questions of its time. It was an *optique* suited to the Popular Front, in that it forced viewers out of their habitual roles as passive spectators who watch while images of the landscape of history roll by. It thrust them onto the screen alongside the solitary heroes with whom they identified; in comparison with the theatrical model of representation, poetic realism strove to involve the individual in a serious, fatally serious, way. But how could such attention to individual experience ever produce the coordinated social vision on which the Popular Front depended? Even in 1936 these films were nostalgic for a present they could not come into contact with.

Later generations would be jealous even of the pain and longing expressed in poetic realism, for it signals a vivacity that the cinema enjoyed before the war, a vivacity that has evaporated since. To the makers of *Casque d'or* and of *Jonas qui aura 25 ans en l'an 2000*, this was "le temps des cerises," a time of authentic, though paralyzed, cultural response to the social plight. In calling up the era of the Popular Front, Becker and Tanner are not out to evade their own times but to recruit the values of the past as a tonic to help us survive the malaria of our own culture and the malarial dreams of our cinema. In the spiritually stricken 1970s, nostalgia for such things as the fertile earth, the caring village, and the politics of camaraderie unites those who are tossed out of the centrifuge of modern society epitomized by Geneva, the city of banks. In their shared disillusionment, Tanner's remnant admits a certain kind of defeat, yet builds a spiritual nest for those who will follow them—for Jonah.

In writing this book, I hope to join such a remnant. Wistfully or proudly, one can proclaim poetic realism naive in the high-tech world of today's films and criticism. Yet this is all the more reason to regret it. And regret is precisely what brings us close to its sensibility. Indeed regret may be the most noble, most honest lesson passed on to us from the 1930s, a lesson we can take with us as we too look ahead with Jonah to the year 2000.

Appendix
Chronology of French Films Mentioned

_____

DATES used are those of first screenings, including press screenings. English titles correspond wherever possible with those Alan Williams employs in *Republic of Images*. American release titles are sometimes given either alone or as the second English title. No English equivalent is provided for titles that are proper names or cognates.

1902
  Assommoir, L' (The Dram Shop, Zecca)

1911
  Zigomar series (Zigomar, Jasset)

1913–1914
  Fantômas series (Fantomas, Feuillade)

1915–1916
  Mystères de New-York, Les series (The Mysteries of New York, Pathé Frères)
  Vampires, Les series (The Vampires, Feuillade)

1917
  Coupable, Le (The Culprit, Antoine)
  Judex series (Judex, Feuillade)

1919
  Tih-Minh series (Tih Minh, Feuillade)

1920
  Barrabas series (Barrabas, Feuillade)
  Hirondelle et la mésange, L' (Antoine)

1921
  Atlantide, L' (Atlantis, Feyder)
  Deux Gamines, Les (Two Urchins, Feuillade)
  Fièvre (Fever, Delluc)
  Terre, La (The Earth, Antoine)
  Trois Mousquetaires, Les (The Three Musketeers, Diamant-Berger)

1922
  Jocelyn (Poirier)

1923

Crainquebille (Feyder)
Souriante Madame Beudet, La (The Smiling Madame Beudet, Dulac)

1924

Belle Nivernaise, La (Epstein)
Entr'acte (Intermission, Clair)
Fille de l'eau, La (Whirlpool of Fate, Renoir)
Inhumaine, L' (The New Enchantment, L'Herbier)
Miracle des loups, Le (Miracle of the Wolves, Bernard)
Paris qui dort (The Crazy Ray, Clair)

1925

Feu Mathias Pascal (The Late Mathias Pascal, L'Herbier)
Photogénie mécanique, La (Grémillon)
Poil de Carotte (Carrot Head, Duvivier)

1926

Croisière noire, La (Expedition to Darkness, Poirier)
Joueur d'échecs, Le (The Chess Player, Bernard)
Ménilmontant (Kirsanov)
Misérables, Les (Fescourt)
Nana (Renoir)
Rien que les heures (Only the Hours, Cavalcanti)

1927

Coquille et le clergyman, La (The Seashell and the Clergyman, Dulac)
Glace à trois faces, La (The Three-Paneled Mirror, Epstein)
Napoléon vu par Abel Gance (Napoleon as seen by Abel Gance, Gance)
Tour au large (A Sea Journey, Grémillon)
Voyage au Congo (Congo Journey, Allégret)

1928

Argent, L' (Money, L'Herbier)
Chapeau de paille d'Italie, Un (An Italian Straw Hat, Clair)
Chute de la Maison Usher, La (The Fall of the House of Usher, Epstein)
Nouveaux Messieurs, Les (The New Gentlemen, Feyder)
Passion de Jeanne d'Arc, La (The Passion of Joan of Arc, Dreyer)
Thérèse Raquin (Feyder)

1929

Chien andalou, Un (An Andalusian Dog, Buñuel)
Gardiens de phare (The Lighthouse Keepers, Grémillon)
Nogent, Eldorado du dimanche (Nogent, Eldorado on Sunday, Carné)
Peau de Pêche (Peach Skin, Marie Epstein / Benoit-Lévy)

Route est belle, La (The Road is Beautiful, Florey)
Trois Masques, Les (The Three Masks, Hugon)

1930

Age d'or, L' (The Age of Gold, Buñuel)
Amour chante, L' (Love Sings, Florey)
A propos de Nice (On the Subject of Nice, Vigo)
Chiqué (Colombier)
David Golder (Duvivier)
Enfant de l'amour, L' (The Child of Love, L'Herbier)
Mystère de la chambre jaune, Le (The Mystery of the Yellow Room, L'Herbier)
Paris la nuit (Paris at Night, Diamant-Berger)
Petit Café, Le (The Little Cafe, Berger)
Petite Lise, La (Little Lisa, Grémillon)
Prix de beauté (Beauty Prize, Genina)
Roi des resquilleurs, Le (The King of Freeloaders, Colombier)
Sous les toits de Paris (Under the Roofs of Paris, Clair)

1931

A nous la liberté (Give Us Liberty, Clair)
Blanc et le noir, Le (The White and the Black, Florey)
Chance, La (Luck, Guissart)
Chienne, La (The Bitch, Renoir)
Coeur de lilas (Heart of the Lillies, Litvak)
Croix de bois, Les (The Wooden Crosses, Bernard)
Faubourg-Montmartre (Bernard)
Jean de la lune (Jean of the Moon, Choux)
Mam'zelle Nitouche (Allégret)
Marius (Pagnol)
Million, Le (The Million, Clair)
Mistrigi (Lachmann)
On purge bébé (Baby Gets a Laxative, Renoir)
Opéra de quat'sous, L' (The Threepenny Opera, Pabst)
Paris-Béguin (Genina)
Pomme de terre, La (The Potato, Yves Allégret)
Roi du cirage, Le (The Shoeshine King, Colombier)
Train des suicidés, Le (Train of Suicides, Gréville)
Tumultes (Siodmak)

1932

Affaire est dans le sac, L' (The Deal Is in the Bag, Pierre Prévert)
Atlantide, L' (Pabst)
Boudu sauvé des eaux (Boudu Saved from Drowning, Renoir)
Chien jaune, Le (The Yellow Dog, Tarride)

Chotard et Cie. (Chotard & Co., Renoir)
Don Quichotte (Don Quixote, Pabst)
Fanny (Allégret)
Fantômas (Fejos)
Femme en homme, La (The Woman as Man, Genina)
Hurdes, Las (Buñuel)
Mater Dolorosa (The Torture of Silence, Gance)
Nuit du carrefour, La (Night of the Crossroads, Renoir)
Poil de Carotte (Carrot Head, Duvivier)
Quatorze juillet (Bastille Day, Clair)
Sang d'un poète, Le (Blood of a Poet, Cocteau)
Tête d'un homme, La (A Man's Head, Duvivier)

1933

Amok (Amuck, Ozep)
Cette vieille canaille (That Old Scoundrel, Litvak)
Ciboulette (Autant-Lara)
Dans les rues (In the Streets, Trivas)
Epervier, L' (The Sparrow-hawk, L'Herbier)
Grand Jeu, Le (The Great Game, Feyder)
Jofroi (Pagnol)
Knock, ou le triomphe de la médecine (The Triumph of Medicine, Jouvet/
   Goupillières)
Madame Bovary (Renoir)
Misérables, Les (Bernard)
Rue sans nom, La (Street without a Name, Chenal)
Topaze (Gasnier)
Zéro de conduite (Zero for Conduct, Vigo)

1934

Angèle (Heartbeat, Pagnol)
Atalante, L' (Vigo)
Dame aux camélias, La (Lady of the Camelias, Gance)
Dernier Milliardaire, Le (The Last Billionaire, Clair)
Hôtel du Libre Echange, L' (Free-Trade Hotel, Allégret)
Jeunesse (Youth, Lacombe)
Justin de Marseille (Justin of Marseilles, Tourneur)
Lac aux dames (Lake of the Ladies, Allégret)
Maternelle, La (The Nursery School, Marie Epstein/Benoit-Lévy)
Paquebot "Tenacity," Le (The Steamship "Tenacity," Duvivier)
Pension Mimosas (Hotel Mimosa, Feyder)
Poliche (Gance)
Précieuses ridicules, Les (Perret)
Rapt (The Mystic Mountain, Kirsanov)

Remous (Whirlpool, Gréville)
Scandale, Le (The Scandal, L'Herbier)
Tartarin de Tarascon (Tartarin of Tarascon, Bernard)
Zouzou (Allégret)

1935

Bandera, La (The Brigade/Escape from Yesterday, Duvivier)
Bonheur, Le (Happiness, L'Herbier)
Commissaire est bon enfant, Le (The Police Chief Is a Good Kid, Becker)
Crime et châtiment (Crime and Punishment, Chenal)
Golem, Le (Duvivier)
Golgotha (Duvivier)
Kermesse héroïque, La (Carnival in Flanders, Feyder)
Napoléon Bonaparte (Gance)
Toni (Renoir)

1936

Appel du silence, L' (The Call of Silence, Poirier)
Bas-Fonds, Les (The Lower Depths, Renoir)
Belle Equipe, La (They Were Five, Duvivier)
César (Pagnol)
Chemin de Rio, Le (The Road from Rio, Siodmak)
Club de femmes (Ladies Club, Deval)
Crime de Monsieur Lange, Le (The Crime of Monsieur Lange, Renoir)
Grand Amour de Beethoven, Un (Beethoven's Great Love, Gance)
Hélène (Marie Epstein/Benoit-Lévy)
Homme de nulle part, L' (Man from Nowhere, Chenal)
Jenny (Carné)
Mademoiselle Docteur (Salonika/Nest of Spies, Pabst)
Mayerling (Litvak)
Messieurs les ronds de cuir (The Bureaucrats, Mirande)
Mister Flow (Siodmak)
Partie de campagne, Une (1945 release, A Day in the Country, Renoir)
Rigolboche (Christian-Jacque)
Roi, Le (The King, Colombier)
Roman d'un tricheur, Le (The Story of a Cheat, Guitry)
Sous les yeux d'Occident (Under Western Eyes/Razumov, Allégret)
Tarass Boulba (Granowsky)
Un de la Légion (A Legionnaire, Christian-Jacque)
Vie est à nous, La (Life Is Ours/People of France, Renoir)

1937

Affaire du courrier de Lyon, L' (The Courier of Lyon, Lehmann)
Affaire Lafarge, L' (The Lafarge Affair, Chenal)

Alibi, L' (Alibi, Chenal)
Carnet de bal, Un (A Dance Card, Duvivier)
Choc en retour (Backfire, Monca)
Coupable, Le (The Culprit, Bernard)
Drôle de drame (Bizarre, Bizarre, Carné)
Entrée des artistes (Stagedoor, Allégret)
Etrange M. Victor, L' (Strange Mr. Victor, Grémillon)
Faisons un rêve (Let's Create a Dream, Guitry)
Gens du voyage, Les (The Travelers, Feyder)
Grande Illusion, La (Grand Illusion, Renoir)
Gribouille (Heart of Paris, Allégret)
Gueule d'amour (Love Face, Grémillon)
Ignace (Colombier)
Marseillaise, La (Renoir)
Messager, Le (The Messenger, Rouleau)
Mollenard (Siodmak)
Orage (Thunderstorm, Allégret)
Pauline à l'école (Pauline at School, de Poligny)
Pépé le Moko (Duvivier)
Perles de la couronne, Les (The Pearls of the Crown, Guitry)
Puritain, Le (The Puritain, Musso)
Regain (Harvest, Pagnol)
Temps des cerises, Le (The Time of Cherries, Le Chanois)

1938

Alerte en Méditerranée (Alert on the Mediterranean, Joannon)
Bête humaine, La (The Human Beast, Renoir)
Café de Paris (Mirande)
Circonstances atténuantes (Extenuating Circumstances, Boyer)
Drame de Shanghai, Le (Shanghai Drama, Pabst)
Entraîneuse, L' (Cocktail Hostess, Valentin)
Femme du boulanger, La (The Baker's Wife, Pagnol)
Fin du jour, La (The End of Day, Duvivier)
Hôtel du Nord (Carné)
J'accuse (I Accuse, Gance)
Katia (Tourneur)
Maison du Maltais, La (The House of the Maltesian, Chenal)
Monsieur Coccinelle (Bernard-Deschamps)
Or dans le montagne, L' (The Gold in the Mountain, Haufler)
Prisons de femmes (Female Prisons, Richebé)
Quai des brumes, Le (Port of Shadows, Carné)
Remontons les Champs-Elysées (Let's Go Up the Champs-Elysées, Guitry)
Tarakanova (Ozep)
Vie est magnifique, La (Life Is Wonderful, Cloche)

1939

Charrette fantôme, La (The Phantom Chariot, Duvivier)
Dernière Jeunesse (End of Adolescence, Musso)
Dernier Tournant, Le (The Final Twist/The Postman Always Rings Twice, Chenal)
Duel, Le (The Duel, Fresnay)
Espoir (Man's Hope, Malraux)
Ils étaient neuf célibataires (Once There Were Nine Bachelors, Guitry)
Jeunes Filles en détresse (Girls in Distress, Pabst)
Jour se lève, Le (Daybreak, Carné)
Paradis perdu (Paradise Lost, Gance)
Quartier sans soleil (Town without Sun, Kirsanov)
Règle du jeu, La (The Rules of the Game, Renoir)

1940–1941

Remorques (Stormy Waters, Grémillon)

1943

Adieu Léonard (Farewell, Leonard, Pierre Prévert)
Visiteurs du soir, Les (The Night Visitors/The Devil's Envoys, Carné)

1945

Belle et la bête, La (Beauty and the Beast, Cocteau)
Enfants du paradis, Les (Children of Paradise, Carné)

1946

Portes de la nuit, Les (The Gates of Night, Carné)

1947

Diable au corps, Le (Devil in the Flesh, Yves Allégret)
Une si jolie petite plage (Such a Pretty Little Beach, Yves Allégret)

1949

Orphée (Orpheus, Cocteau)

1951

Casque d'or (Golden Headpiece/Golden Marie, Becker)
Juliette ou le clef des songes (Juliette or the Dream Book, Carné)

1953

Carosse d'or, La (The Golden Coach, Renoir)
Touchez pas au grisbi (Don't Touch the Dough, Becker)

1955

French CanCan (Renoir)

1958

Amants, Les (The Lovers, Malle)
Orfeu negro (Black Orpheus, Camus)

1959

Quatre Cents Coups, Les (400 Blows, Truffaut)

1960

A bout de souffle (Breathless, Godard)

1961

Jules et Jim (Truffaut)

1967

Vieil Homme et l'enfant, Le (The Old Man and the Child, Berri)

1970

Petit Théâtre de Jean Renoir, Le (The Little Theater of Jean Renoir, Renoir)

1975

Jonas qui aura 25 ans en l'an 2000 (Jonah Who Will Be 25 in the Year 2000, Tanner)

Notes

THROUGHOUT this text, translations from the French, where uncredited to a published source, are my own.

PREFACE

1. André Bazin, *"Le Jour se lève . . . Poetic Realism,"* in *Le Jour se lève* (New York: Simon and Shuster, 1970), 8–9.

2. André Bazin, "The Virtues and Limitations of Montage," in *What Is Cinema?* vol. 1 (Berkeley and Los Angeles: University of California Press, 1967), 41–53, and "A propos de Jean Painlevé," in *Qu'est-ce que le cinéma?* vol. 1 (Paris: Cerf, 1958), 37–40.

3. André Bazin, "The Myth of Total Cinema," in *What Is Cinema?* 1:17–18.

4. Bazin, *"Le Jour se lève,"* in Jacques Chevailler, *Regards neufs sur le cinéma* (Paris: Seuil, 1953).

5. For detailed information on the French film industry, see Colin Crisp, *The Classic French Cinema, 1930–1960*. This well-researched book was published just after my own manuscript went to the press, and so I was unable to incorporate its findings.

6. For an encyclopedia, I continue to turn to Raymond Chirat's *Catalogue des films français de long métrage: films sonores de fiction 1929–1939*.

CHAPTER 1
INTRODUCTION: A COMPASS IN THE MIST OF POETIC REALISM

1. Alexandre Arnoux, "Vers un style français du cinéma," *Pour Vous* 7 (Jan. 1929): 3.

2. This remark is also attributed to Léon Moussinac. See Richard Abel, *French Cinema: The First Wave, 1915–1919*, 260. In his *French Film Theory and Criticism: A History/Anthology, 1907–1939* Abel details Delluc's populist vision of the art. See 1:101.

3. For details on such measures see Paul Leglise's two volumes, *Histoire de la politique du cinéma français*.

4. *La Cinématographie française* began to chart the number of spectators attending the cinema as compared with other entertainment forms in the second half of the decade. Film-by-film rankings were not available, however, until the industry was put under a national organization, a process that was only beginning when the Nazis invaded.

5. Jean Mitry, *Histoire du cinéma* (4:325), rightly attributes this review to Michel Gorel but mistakes the date. Gorel's review came out in *Cinémonde* 277 (8 Feb. 1934), not in October of the previous year. Gorel had interviewed Chenal in August 1933 (*Cinémonde* 250) where the novel's mixture of the "real and the irreal" had come up and the term "merveilleux social" rather than "réalisme poétique" had been mentioned.

6. Georges Sadoul, "A propos de quelques films recents," *Commune* 39 (Nov. 1936). Reprinted in his *Chroniques du cinéma français*, 1:14 and translated in *French Film Theory and Criticism*, ed. Abel, 2:218–23.

7. Marcel Carné, *La Vie à belles dents*, 117.

8. Jack C. Ellis, *A History of Film* (Englewood Cliffs, N.J.: Prentice-Hall, 1985), 167.

9. *La Cinématographie française* (3 Mar. 1939) notes that in 1938 the top three foreign box-office titles to have played in the United States were French.

10. One hundred of the 170 films are strongly praised, while about 30 are panned. The remaining 40 films receive mixed ratings.

11. *New York Times*, 1 May 1936, 3 May 1939, and 22 Dec. 1939, respectively.

12. Sadoul is credited with this attribution in *L'Enyclopédie du cinéma*, ed. Boussinot (Paris: Bordas, 1967–1970), 1255. The initial reference to poetic realism in his *Histoire du cinéma mondial* (first published by Flammarion in 1948; 273 in the 1963 Flammarion edition), though, is a citation from the British critic Roger Manvell. Manvell wrote of "the famous French school that one could call Poetic Realist" in a 1945 article appearing in the short-lived British journal *Film*.

13. Paul Rotha, *The Film Till Now: A Survey of World Cinema* (London: Vision, 1949), 530. Rotha may well have relied on the opinion expressed by Emile Vuillermoz in a 1938 article called "A Case of Conscience," translated in *French Film Theory and Criticism*, ed. Abel, 2:250.

14. Ibid., 539.

15. See for instance *Le Grand Histoire illustré du 7eme art* (Paris: Atlas, 1982), 62–63.

16. See Robert Chazal, *Marcel Carné*, 65.

17. Adam Garbicz and J. Klinowski. *Cinema, the Magic Vehicle: A Guide to Its Achievement* (Metuchen, N.J.: Scarecrow, 1975), 288. Virtually every general history of film devotes a section to poetic realism, with Ellis (*A History of Film*) giving it special attention.

18. M. Bex in *Volunté*, 10 Dec. 1930.

19. Alan Williams, *Republic of Images: A History of French Filmmaking*, 232.

20. Mitry, *Histoire du cinéma*, 4:293–316. Carné mentions Von Sternberg, Murnau, and Lang as influences. See Edward Baron Turk, *Child of Paradise: Marcel Carné and the Golden Age of French Cinema*, 41.

21. Mitry, *Histoire du cinéma*, 4:292.

22. Poetic realism is discussed in volume 4 of his seven-volume opus.

23. Pierre Mac Orlan, *Le Quai des brumes* (Paris: Gallimard, 1927). References to the film adaptation of this work often suppress the definite article in its title.

24. Pierre Mac Orlan, *Masques sur mésure, essais*, 13–15.

25. This is how Jean-Pierre Jeancolas groups them in *15 Ans d'années trente: le cinéma des français 1929–1944*, 268

26. The full title of Vincendeau's dissertation is "French Cinema in the 1930s: Social Text and Context of a Popular Entertainment Medium."

27. Jeancolas, "French Cinema of the 1930s and Its Sociological Handicaps," in *La Vie est à Nous*, ed. Ginette Vincendeau and Keith Reader, 72. Jonathan Buchsbaum in *Cinema Engagé: Film in the Popular Front*, however, unearths the politically savvy films made by the unions and the left-wing parties.

28. Even Renoir has been challenged on these grounds, specifically for his most "poetic realist" film, *La Bête humaine*. See François Poulle, *Renoir 1938 ou Jean Renoir pour rien*, 62–69. Buchsbaum, *Cinema Engagé*, 175n.87, similarly dismisses the politics of the bulk of films made by directors like Renoir and Carné.

29. Geneviève Sellier, "Ces singuliers héretiers du cinéma français des années trente," *Cinéma* 268 (1981): 4–26.

30. Buchsbaum treats another canon in *Cinema Engagé*, a small set of rigorous films bearing an equally rigorous social message.

31. Concerned though she is with the social aspects of cinema, Sellier went on to write an excellent monograph, *Jean Grémillon: le Cinéma est à vous*, the focus of which must put her in the auteurist camp.

32. Michèle Lagny, Marie-Claire Ropars, and Pierre Sorlin, *Générique des années 30*, 13.

33. Roland Barthes, *Writing Degree Zero*, trans. Annette Lavers and Colin Smith (New York: Hill and Wang, 1968). Originally published in 1953 (Paris: Seuil).

CHAPTER 2
IMPRESSIONISM AND SURREALISM: THE ORIGINS OF AN *OPTIQUE*

1. Alain Resnais, "The Serpents and the Caduceus," in *Rediscovering French Film*, ed. Mary Lea Bandy, 37–38.

2. Francis Lacassin establishes Resnais's ties to Feuillade, mentioning that his first film, shot in 8-mm in 1936, was an episode of *Fantômas*. See Lacassin, *Pour une contre-histoire du cinéma*, 207–12.

3. Cited in Marcel Oms, "Le Retour du patron," *Cahiers de la cinémathèque* 48 (1988): 54.

4. Rudolf E. Kuenzli, Introduction to *Dada and Surrealist Film*, ed. Rudolf E. Kuenzli, 8.

5. Colette, *Colette at the Movies*, 4 and 30.

6. Richard Abel, *French Cinema: The First Wave, 1915–1929*.

7. Cited in Roger Icart, "Louis Feuillade et la 'Nouvelle Vague' des années vingt," *Cahiers de la cinémathèque* 48 (1988): 47–48.

8. The show was broadcast on major radio stations throughout Europe on 3 Nov. 1933 as part of a *Fantômas* retrospective produced by Paul de Herme. Kurt Weill composed the accompanying music. Desnos's poem was printed in his *Choix de poèmes* (Paris: Minuit, 1946).

9. Robert Desnos in *Le Soir*, 26 Feb. 1927. Reprinted in *French Film Theory and Criticism: A History/Anthology 1907–1939*, ed. Richard Abel, 1:398–400.

10. André Breton and Louis Aragon, Prologue to *Trésor des jésuites* (Paris: Variétés, 1929). Cited in Oms, "Le Retour du patron," 58.

11. Oms, "Le Retour du patron," 56.

12. René Clair, *Cinema Yesterday and Today*, 22.

13. This famous fire of 7 May 1897 is best recounted in Jacques Deslandes, *Histoire comparée du cinéma* (Paris: Casterman, 1968), 2:22–26.

14. André Bazin, *What Is Cinema?* vol. 1 (Berkeley and Los Angeles: University of California Press, 1967), 59.

15. Georges Franju, "Feuillade, l'unique," *L'Avant-Scène du cinéma* 271/272 (July 1981). A Georges Champreux essay in this issue bears a title I am happy to underscore: "Louis Feuillade, poète de la realité." See also Jonathan Rosenbaum, "Birth of a Notion," *Chicago Reader* 17, no. 3 (9 Oct. 1987).

16. Louis Delluc, "Antoine at Work," a 1917 essay reprinted in *French Film Theory and Criticism*, ed. Abel, 1:140–41. Antoine's anger at the pretentiousness of Delluc and his friends is discussed by Abel in the same volume, 201.

17. Other barge films of the time include Jean Epstein's *La Belle Nivernaise* (1924) and Renoir's *La Fille de l'eau* (1924). Of course, there is also *L'Atalante*.

18. See Delluc, "Antoine at Work," in *French Film Theory and Criticism*, ed. Abel, 1:140. In a November 1989 presentation on Antoine given at the University of Iowa, Glenn Myrent of the Cinémathèque française noted Delluc's similar style, particularly in regards to *L'Hirondelle et la mésange*. This film was shelved after shooting, so Delluc could not have seen it. The print circulating today was reconstituted by Henri Colpi in 1983. Antoine's other films, especially *La Terre* (1921) and *Le Coupable* (1917), were financial successes. Myrent showed that *L'Hirondelle et la mésange* is the epitome of their incipient aesthetic, and not really out of step with much of impressionist film theory.

19. Léon Moussinac, "Cinema: *Fièvre, L'Atlantide, El Dorado*, in *French Film Theory and Criticism*, ed. Abel, 1:253.

20. See the essay "*Broken Blossoms*, the Vulnerable Text and the Marketing of Masochism," in my *Film in the Aura of Art*, 16–27.

21. Jean Grémillon (Unpublished address delivered at the Maison des Centreaux, 1926), 3–8. Typescript in the personal archives of Mme Christiane Grémillon.

22. Ibid., 2–3.

23. Ibid., 3.

24. Ibid., 9.

25. Ibid., 10.

26. Ibid., 12–13.

27. Ibid., 13.

28. Ibid., 11.

29. Léon Moussinac, "*Broken Blossoms*," in *French Film Theory and Criticism*, ed. Abel, 1:233.

30. Cited in Sacha Guitry, "For the Theater and against the Cinema," in *French Film Theory and Criticism*, ed. Abel, 2:98.

31. Moussinac, "Cinema: *Fièvre*," 251.

32. Andrew, "*Broken Blossoms*," 24–27.

33. Alexandre Arnoux, "Vers un style français du cinéma," *Pour Vous* 7 (Jan. 1929): 3.

34. Walter Benjamin, "The Work of Art in the Age of Mechanical Reproduction," in his *Illuminations*, ed. and trans. Hannah Arendt (New York: Schocken, 1969).

35. Abel, *French Cinema: The First Wave*, 395.

36. For a discussion of Delluc's "populism," see *French Film Theory and Criticism*, ed. Abel, 1:98–106. Also in that volume, see Delluc, "The Crowd," 59–64.

37. Jean Goudal, "Surréalism et cinéma," in *The Shadow and Its Shadow*, trans. Paul Hammond (London: British Film Institute, 1978), 49–57.

38. "Entretien avec Philippe Soupault," *Etudes cinématographiques* 38–39 (1965): 31.

39. Luis Buñuel, *My Last Sigh*, 92.

40. James Clifford, "On Ethnographic Surrealism," *Comparative Studies in Society and History* 23, no. 4 (Winter 1981): 539–64.

41. Buñuel, *My Last Sigh*, 107.

42. Linda Williams, *Figures of Desire: A Theory and Analysis of Surrealist Film*, esp. 150.

43. Buñuel mentions Magritte several times in *My Last Sigh*, 95.

44. Ibid., 118.

45. These incidents are often recounted. See, for instance, André Thirion, *Revolutionaries without Revolution*, 256–58.

46. In 1930 Maurice Bessy predicted the decline of *ciné-clubs*, their loss of audience, and their increasing reliance on standard films. See *Ciné-Magazine* 1930 (Paris: L'Avant-Scène Cinéma, 1983), 143.

47. André Breton and Philippe Soupault, *Les Champs magnétiques* (Paris: Gallimard, 1967). The date of the first publication (three hundred copies) is 1919.

48. Philippe Soupault, *Ecrits de cinéma, 1918–1931*, 170–72 and 210–13.

49. Ibid., 30–37.

50. Breton for his part prepared a script from Barbey d'Aurevilly's famous tale *Le Rideau Crimoisie*.

51. Ado Kyrou, *Le Surréalisme au cinéma*, 153–55.

52. Walter Benjamin, "Surrealism: The Last Snapshot of the European Intelligentsia," originally published in *Literarische Welt* 5 (1929), translated in *One-Way Street and Other Essays* (New York: Harcourt Brace Jovanovich, 1979) and in *Reflections: Essays, Aphorisms, Autobiographical Writings* (New York: Harcourt Brace Jovanovich, 1978).

53. Benjamin's term in "Surrealism," 227.

54. Allen Thiher, *The Cinematic Muse: Critical Studies in the History of French Cinema*, 49.

55. Alain and Odette Virmaux, *Les Surréalistes et le cinéma*, 90.

56. Guillaume Apollinaire, "L'Esprit nouveau et les poètes," *Mercure de France*, 1 Dec. 1918. Cited in Virmaux, *Les Surréalistes et le cinéma*, 17.

CHAPTER 3
ADOLESCENTS IN AN ADOLESCENT INDUSTRY

1. By 1935 the Gaumont syndicate was in bankruptcy and the head of the Pathé syndicate, Bernard Natan, was in prison.

2. Tobis Klangfilm produced sixteen films in five years, all but three directed by major talents like Clair, Feyder, Pabst, Genina, and Duvivier.

3. Georges Sadoul, *French Film*, 58 (my emphasis).

4. Maurice Bardèche and Robert Brasillach, *The History of Motion Pictures*, trans. Iris Barry (New York: Museum of Modern Art, 1938), 327–28.

5. Sadoul, *French Film*, 58–59.

6. Leonardo Quaresima, "Voci," in *Francia anni '30: cinema, cultura, storia*, ed. Patrizia Dogliani et al., 70.

7. Olivier Barrot establishes this throughout *René Clair, ou le temps mesuré*.

8. Marcia Butzel, *Illuminating Movements: The Choreographic Aspect of Cinema*.

9. René Clair, *Cinema Yesterday and Today*, 69.

10. This was the wonderful phrase of Walter Benjamin in his essay "Surrealism: The Last Snapshot of the European Intelligentsia," in *Reflections: Essays, Aphorisms, Autobiographical Writings*, trans. Edward Jephcott (New York: Harcourt, 1978), 178.

11. Clair, *Cinema Yesterday and Today*, 83–88.

12. Jean-Pierre Jeancolas, *15 Ans d'années trente: le cinéma des français 1929–1944*, 74.

13. Luis Buñuel recounts Breton's reaction in *My Last Sigh*, 112.

14. See Allen Thiher, *The Cinematic Muse: Critical Studies in the History of French Cinema*, 69–77.

15. Gilles Deleuze, *Cinema 1: The Movement-Image*, trans. Hugh Tomlinson and Barbara Habbercam (Minneapolis: University of Minnesota Press, 1986), 41–42.

16. André Bazin noted years ago (see his *Jean Renoir*, 85) that in the final sequences of *Boudu sauvé des eaux*, Renoir's focus shifts to the actor, Michel Simon, to his outrageously expansive movements, and particularly to the idiosyncratic grace of his playful swimming down the Marne. The future he represents, I might add, will be taken up by many characters: by Amédée Lange who is expunged from the collective he has built and disappears across the border, by Pépel who escapes the horror and the community of *Les Bas-Fonds*, by Maréchal crossing borders again in *La Grande Illusion*, and most significantly by Jean Renoir playing Octave, setting out grimly from the death-trap estate in *La Règle du jeu*.

17. Genina's professional experience and personal elegance allowed him to imitate Clair, as in *La Femme en homme* (1932). He even replaced Clair on a project, the stunning *Prix de beauté* (1930).

18. Another film that opens with the camera tracking in on a street singer is Anatole Litvak's *Cette vieille canaille* (1933). An adaptation from a stage play, this film exhibits realist touches and an attempt to evoke a lower-class milieu.

19. Bardèche and Brasillach, *Histoire du cinéma* (Givors: A. Martel, 1953), 2:52.

20. Ibid.

21. Vigo's ties to anarchism are summarized by Alan Williams in *Republic of Images: A History of French Filmmaking*, 218–22.

22. Donald Crafton, "Shooting Vigo's Films: An Interview with Boris Kaufman," *Yale Film Quarterly*, Spring 1984. See also P. E. Salles Gomes, *Jean Vigo*, 55.

23. Jean Vigo, "Toward a Social Cinema," translated in *French Film Theory and Criticism: A History/Anthology 1907–1939*, ed. Richard Abel, 2:60–63. Vigo's term "document" alludes to the journal *Documents* started the year before by Georges Bataille and Michel Leiris, the most important source of what James Clifford has called "Ethnographic Surrealism." See Clifford, *Predicaments of Culture* (Cambridge: Harvard University Press, 1988).

24. See, for example Valéry Jahier's review of *L'Atalante* in *Esprit* 26 (Nov. 1934), translated in *French Film Theory and Criticism*, ed. Abel, 2:186.

25. Elizabeth Grottle Strebel, *French Social Cinema of the Nineteen Thirties: A Cinematographic Expression of Popular Front Consciousness*, 32.

26. For a detailed discussion of this point see my essay "The Fever of an Infectious Film: *L'Atalante* and the Aesthetics of Spontaneity," in *Film in the Aura of Art*, 59–77.

27. Ado Kyrou, *Le Surréalisme au cinéma*, 158.

28. Buñuel, *My Last Sigh*, 124. In full Buñuel says here, "More than the innovations or the refinements of my tastes and ideas, the aspect of surrealism that has remained a part of me all these years is a clear and inviolate moral exigency."

29. François Truffaut, "The Fever of Jean Vigo," in *The Films of My Life* (New York: Harcourt, 1978).

30. Deleuze, *Cinema 1*, 79.

31. Ibid.

32. *L'Age du cinéma* 4–5 (Aug. 1951).

33. Alain Virmaux, "*L'Atalante*: l'univers surréaliste," *Etudes cinématographiques* 51–52 (1966): 31–41.

34. Kyrou, *Le Surréalisme au cinéma*, 157–59.

35. Virmaux, "*L'Atalante*," 40.

36. Bruno Voglino, "Un Realisme poètique," *Jean Vigo*, Premier Plan 19 (Nov. 1961): 102–4. Originally published in Italian in *Centrofilm*, 1961.

37. Voglino, "Un Realisme poètique," 104.

38. Gomes, *Jean Vigo*, 216.

39. Breton quoted Prévert's aphorism this way, "Un pied sur la rive droite, un pied sur la rive gauche, et le troisième aux derrières des imbéciles," in the catalog *A la rencontre de Jacques Prévert*, 24.

40. Guy Jacob, "Situation de Jacques Prévert," *Jacques Prévert*, Prémier Plan 14 (Nov. 1960): 5.

41. Ibid., 10.

42. See *A la rencontre de Jacques Prévert*, as well as Michel Rachline, *Jacques Prévert: drôle de vie*.

43. For a full treatment of Prévert's milieu, see Claire Blakeway, *Jacques Prévert: Popular French Theatre and Cinema*, and Michel Fauré, *Le Groupe Octobre*.

44. Cited in *A la rencontre de Jacques Prévert*, 24.

45. Pablo Picasso, from *Conversations avec Picasso* by Brassaï, cited in *A la rencontre de Jacques Prévert*, 25.

46. See his interview in *Ciné-Magazine* 1930, reprinted by L'Avant-Scène Cinéma (Paris, 1983): 126.

47. Denise Tual, *Au coeur du temps*, 115. For detailed information about Prévert's early life, see, in addition to Tual, Blakeway and Fauré (cited in n. 43 above) as well as René Gilson, *Jacques Prévert* (Paris: Belfond, 1990), and André Thirion, *Revolutionaries without Revolution*. Emile Natan headed production while his brother Bernard ran Pathé-Natan.

48. Fauré, *Le Groupe Octobre*, 186.

49. Denise Batcheff and her husband Roland Tual, another Surrealist, would become instrumental as producers during the poetic realist years, whenever possible employing the Préverts and their friends. See chap. 6 below.

50. Information on Autant-Lara comes from the Collection Rondel at the Bibliothèque de l'Arsenal in Paris and his autobiographical works, *La Rage dans le coeur* and *Les Fourgons du malheur: mes années avec Jacques Prévert*.

51. *Pour Vous* 282 (12 Apr. 1934).

52. Guy Jacob, *Jacques Prévert*, Premier Plan 14 (Nov. 1960): 32.

53. For more details on the production see Christopher Faulkner, *Jean Renoir: A Guide to References and Resources*, 89–92, and Alexander Sesonske, *Jean Renoir: The French Films, 1924–1939*, 186–190. Sesonske recounts the difficulty Renoir and his producer had in making the lazy Prévert maintain a good pace. They locked him in a room, letting him out only for meals and only after he had slid a sufficient number of pages under the door.

54. Roger Leenhardt, "L'Esthetique de Jacques Prévert," *Fontaine* 42 (May 1945): 259–64.

55. Both these films were produced by Roland Tual. Surrealist seeds bore fruit years later.

56. Jean-Louis Barrault, Preface to *Drôle de drame* (Paris: Bibliothèque des classiques du cinéma, 1973), 7. Denise Tual discusses her disappointment at length in *Le Temps dévoré*, 156–57.

57. Edward Baron Turk, *Child of Paradise: Marcel Carné and the Golden Age of French Cinema*, 89–95.

58. Ibid., chap. 2.

59. This amounts to a theatrical solution to the general problem interwar writers faced in integrating spoken language and literary genres, a problem directly, though variously, addressed by Louis Aragon, Michel Leiris, Jean Paulhan, Brice Parrain, and Maurice Blanchot.

60. Maurice Valency, Introduction to *Five Plays* by Jean Giraudoux (New York: Random House, 1972), 15.

61. The rivalry between these stars and their acting styles is fabled, yet it evidently worked to the advantage of the stage and screen performances that put them together. See Turk, *Child of Paradise*, 83.

62. Kyrou, *Le Surréalisme au cinéma*, 153–54.

63. Thirion, *Révolutionaires sans révolution*, translated as *Revolutionaries without Revolution*.

CHAPTER 4
FRENCH CINEMA AND THE SONIC BOOM

1. *La Cinématographie française* 973 (25 June 1937).

2. At Venice in 1937 *Un Carnet de bal* took honors for best foreign film, *La Grande Illusion* was cited for best acting, and Sacha Guitry won the award for best script (*Les Perles de la couronne*). *La Cinématographie française* 979 (6 Aug. 1937).

3. *La Kermesse héroïque* (1936), *Pépé le Moko* (1937), *La Grande Illusion* (1938), *La Femme du boulanger* (1939).

4. *La Cinématographie française* 986 (24 Sept. 1937): 92.

5. *La Cinématographie française* 986 (24 Sept. 1937).

6. *La Cinématographie française* 979 (6 Aug. 1937).

7. *La Cinématographie française* 986 (24 Sept. 1937): 89.

8. Marcel L'Herbier in *Cinémonde*, 3 Jan. 1929, traces the decline from its premier status in 1914 to second in 1919, third in 1923, fourth in 1927, and fifth in 1929.

9. See for example Roger Metzger (head of French film export after the war), "Le Film français et le marché mondial," in *Le Livre d'or du cinéma français*, ed. René Jeanne and Charles Ford (Paris: Agence d'Information Cinégraphique, 1946), 183–84. A more contemporaneous report, written in the 25 Mar. 1937 issue of *La Cinématographie française*, insists that in 1937 France became the world's number two exporter, behind Hollywood. Between 30 and 40 of its 120 films were listed as being of export quality. And *Le Journal* (4 Mar. 1938) bragged that French cinema was putting British films out of business. Not only were audiences in London flocking to French pictures, the British banks had turned away from their own nation's films to produce French films. Indeed this report claims that 75 percent of all French films are financed out of London.

10. See the items in the bibliography listed under Paul Leglise, Francis Courtade, Jean-Michel Renaitour, and Ginette Vincendeau.

11. Henri Fescourt, *La Foi et les montagnes, ou le septième art au passé*, 401.

12. Louis Cheronnet, *Beaux Arts*, 17 Sept. 1937.

13. This was the Renaitour committee whose findings in meetings held at the end of 1937 were made public in the book *Où va le cinéma français?*, ed. Jean-Michel Renaitour.

14. Roger Leenhardt, "Le Cinéma, art national," *Esprit* 65 (Feb. 1938), reprinted in Leenhardt, *Chroniques de cinéma*, 57–60.

15. Leenhardt, *Chroniques de cinéma*, 58.

16. Henri Diamant-Berger, *Il était une fois le cinéma*, 213.

17. Ibid., 206. See also 187.

18. See Gérard Talon, "1936–38: trois années qui ébranlèrent la France," *Cinéma 75* 194 (Jan. 1975): 43.

19. Valéry Jahier, "La Saison de cinéma 1937–38 vue de Paris," *Esprit* 73 (Oct. 1938): 110–11.

20. *Variety*, 23 Apr. 1930.

21. *Film Mercury*, Mar. 1930.

22. See his acerbic autobiographical volumes *La Rage dans le coeur* and *Hollywood Cake-Walk* (Paris: H. Veyrier, 1985).

23. Luis Buñuel, *My Last Sigh*; see especially 127–36.

24. Yves Mirande, *Souvenirs*, 139. Mirande's autobiography contains over forty pages of reminiscences concerning the position of the screenwriter in the early days of the talkies, both in Paris and in Hollywood.

25. "Paramount: Oscar for Profits," *Fortune* 35, no. 6 (June 1947): 89–97.

26. *Variety*, 30 Apr. 1930.

27. Diamant-Berger, *Il était une fois*, 177.

28. Ginette Vincendeau and Nataša Ďurovičová are both currently at work studying these films.

29. Paramount was battered by the depression more than any other studio, going from profits of $18 million in 1930 to deficits of $15 million in 1932. In 1932 they cut production from sixty-five to fifty-two features, and in 1933 they halved their production budget. Joinville was a casualty of this. See *Fortune* 35, no. 6 (June 1947): 89–97.

30. Paul Tabori, *Alexander Korda* (London: Oldbourne, 1959), 100–117.

31. *Variety*, 10 Dec. 1930.

32. *Variety*, 14 Jan. 1931 and 31 May 1932.

33. Roger Icart, "L'Avenement du film parlant," *Cahiers de la cinémathèque* 13–15 (1974): 124–41.

34. The past decade has seen a celebration of these films and of the popular entertainment program of which they form a part. Ginette Vincendeau's dissertation, frequently cited above, is consecrated to just such a reevaluation.

35. Icart, "L'Avenement du film parlant," 51–52.

36. No less a figure than André Gide helped form a short-lived company called La Société d'études et de réalisation pour le film parlant. Its brief history is discussed in chap. 6.

37. Pierre Braunberger, *Cinémamémoire*, 52–54 and 61. See also Richard Abel, *French Cinema: The First Wave, 1915–1929*, 271. A second such distributor was Robert Aron, a young editor at Gallimard Press who helped launch *La Revue du cinéma*.

38. Braunberger is proud to recall that André Gide hovered around the set of *Fanny* and (unknown even to most experts) can be glimpsed as an extra. See *Cinémamémoire*, 100.

39. Roger Richebé, *Au-delà de l'écran: 70 ans de la vie d'un cinéaste*, 48–50.

40. Ibid., 70–71.

41. Brian Taves, *Robert Florey: The French Expressionist*, 121–24.

42. Braunberger, *Cinémamémoire*, 79.

43. Jean Renoir, *My Life and My Films*, 103–7.

44. André Bazin, *Jean Renoir*, 22.

45. Ibid., 102.

46. Renoir, *My Life and My Films*, 105.

47. Geneviève Sellier, *Jean Grémillon: le cinéma est à vous*, 85.

48. Jean-Georges Auriol, "La Chienne," *La Revue du cinéma* 28 (Nov. 1931). Reprinted in *French Film Theory and Criticism: A History/Anthology 1907–1939*, ed. Richard Abel, 2:87.

49. *Variety*, 12 Jan. 1932.

50. Henri Agel, *Jean Grémillon*, 33.

51. Jean-Georges Auriol, *"La Petite Lise,"* *La Revue du cinéma* (Jan. 1931): 57–58.

52. Sellier, *Jean Grémillon*, 69–90.

53. Ibid., 74.

54. Marcel Lapierre, *Les Cent Visages du cinéma*, 212.

55. Henri Langlois, *Les Lettres françaises* 801 (3 Dec. 1959).

56. Sellier, *Jean Grémillon*, 74–75.

57. Pierre Henry, cited by Langlois in *Les Lettres françaises*.

58. See my *"Broken Blossoms*: The Vulnerable Text and the Marketing of Masochism," in *Film in the Aura of Art*, 16–27.

59. Natan had been jailed in the twenties for trafficking in obscene films.

60. Jacques Cleynan, "La Politique du cinéma français: stratégies et réalisations 1929–1935" (Unpublished thesis manuscript: Ecole des hautes études en sciences sociales, 1985). MS held at the library of the Institut des hautes études cinématographiques, Paris.

61. Jean Dréville, *"La Petite Lise* de Jean Grémillon marquera une étape," *Comoedia*, 11 Nov. 1930.

CHAPTER 5
THEATRICAL MODELS FOR FRENCH FILMS

1. René Clair, Preface to *Entr'acte* and *A nous la liberté* (New York: Simon and Schuster, 1970).

2. *The 1934 Motion Picture Almanac* (New York: Quigley Publications), 1012.

3. See especially Michèle Lagny, Marie-Claire Ropars, and Pierre Sorlin, *Générique des années 30*, chap. 6.

4. Charles Wolfe has traced the heritage of performance into the very first sound films. See his "On the Track of the Vitaphone Shorts," in *The Dawn of Sound*, ed. Mary Lea Bandy (New York: Catalogue of the Museum of Modern Art, 1989), 35–41.

5. See chap. 4 above.

6. Thomas Elsaesser elaborates this point in comparing France to Germany in his "Pathos and Leave-taking: The German Emigrés in Paris during the 1930s," *Sight and Sound* 53, no. 4 (Autumn 1984): 278–83.

7. Ginette Vincendeau, "French Cinema in the 1930s: Social Text and Context of a Popular Entertainment Medium," chaps. 2 and 4.

8. Cited in Edmond T. Gréville, *Mes Années dans le jungle du cinéma* (Paris: Revue Internationale de l'histoire du cinéma, 1979).

9. Vincendeau, "French Cinema in the 1930s," 84.

10. Valéry Jahier, "Préface à un cinéma," *Esprit* 25 (Oct. 1934): 73–78, translated in *French Film Theory and Criticism: A History/Anthology 1907–1939*, ed. Richard Abel, 2:182–86.

11. Léon Moussinac, *L'Age ingrat du cinéma*, 334–50, translated in *French Film Theory and Criticism*, ed. Abel, 2:105–11.

12. In fact the effects of the depression hit France only after 1933, though some analysts recognize a decline beginning at the start of the decade.

13. I treat this issue at length in "Family Diversions: Live Entertainment and the Popular French Cinema," in *Popular European Cinema*, ed. Ginette Vincendeau and Richard Dyer (London: Routledge, 1992).

14. Vincendeau ("French Cinema in the 1930s") effectively divides the theatrical origins

of the film industry into five categories (which I give with representative actors in parentheses): Classic Parisian boulevard stage (Jules Berry, Sacha Guitry, Elvira Popesco), Music Hall (Milton, Bach, Maurice Chevalier, Mistinguett), Marseillais (Raimu, Fernandel, Andrex, Charpin), noble styles of the Odéon and La Comédie-Française (Louis Jouvet, Pierre Renoir, Pierre Fresnay, Marie Bell), and Surrealist/Anarchist groups (Raymonde Bussières, Jacques-B. Brunius).

15. Of Pathé's first fifty-two sound films, only twelve left their homeland, and these were sent to Belgium and Canada. No Pathé films were dubbed; hence they were restricted to francophone communities. It should also be noted that in this period French mores (or at least their tradition of representing such subjects as prostitution and adultery) created problems for censors in these other countries.

16. Jacques Cleynan, "La Politique du cinéma français: stratégies et réalisations 1929–1935" (Unpublished thesis: Ecole des hautes études en sciences sociales, 1985), 135–36. MS held at the library of the Institut des hautes études cinématographiques, Paris.

17. See Vincendeau, "French Cinema in the 1930s," chap. 2.

18. Vincendeau can cite in the same regard *Pépé le Moko*, *La Grande Illusion*, and other topnotch films.

19. Naturally counterexamples abound. See my discussion of Mistinguett in "Family Diversions." Vincendeau has isolated a small set of films centered on women in her essay "Daddy's Girl: Oedipal Narratives in French Cinema of the 1930s," *Iris* 8 (Jan. 1989): 71–81.

20. André-Paul Antoine, "Marcel Pagnol, Marcel Achard, Henri Jeanson," *Revue de deux mondes* (May–June 1962): 528–29.

21. See Yves Mirande's autobiography, *Souvenirs*, as well as Claude Beylie's "Un Prince de la comédie mondaine: Yves Mirande," in *Cinématographe* (Sept. 1984): 56–65.

22. I noted in the last chapter that MGM even recruited him for a year's stay in Hollywood to gain his help with French versions of their films and to keep him out of competition.

23. A winning apology for boulevard comedy was written by the future director Bertrand Tavernier, "Le Cinéma français des années 30, essai d'anthropologie sociale," *Positif* 117 (1970).

24. Vincendeau ("French Cinema in the 1930s") argues convincingly that the very plots of many French films had to be fitted to conform to the age of the key actors of the twenties who moved into premier position in the thirties (Raimu, Baur, Larquey, Vanel, Simon), making this a cinema dominated by father figures.

25. Marcel L'Herbier, *La Tête qui tourne*, 204.

26. Alfred Savoir in the Gallimard periodical *Marianne*, 29 Nov. 1933.

27. His response to *La Petite Lise* and *La Chienne* is discussed in chap. 4 above.

28. See chap. 3 above.

29. Claude Beylie, *L'Avant-Scène Cinéma* 209 (June 1978): 28, calls this film the most perfect melodrama of the early sound period.

30. *Un Grand Amour de Beethoven* was among the five finalists for the first Louis Delluc award in 1936.

31. The latter film was done while he was setting up a three-part film on Christopher Columbus, El Cid, and Ignatius Loyola. See Norman King, *Abel Gance: A Politics of Spectacle*, 169.

32. Marcel Achard interviewed in *L'Intransigent*, 16 Apr. 1937.

33. See chap. 1 above.

34. Cited in René Clair, *Cinema Yesterday and Today*, 151. Pagnol's pronouncements were

published first in *Le Journal* (1932) and then in his own *Les Cahiers du film*. See especially his broadside essay, "La Cinématurgie de Paris," in the 15 Dec. 1933 issue. This essay is translated in *French Film Theory and Criticism*, ed. Abel, 2:129–35.

35. For additional discussion of the production of *Marius* see chap. 4 above.

36. The corporation would be rechristened Le Société des films Marcel Pagnol the next year.

37. André Lang, *Tiers de siècle*, 70–77.

38. Benjamin Fondane, *Ecrits pour le cinéma*. Also see John K. Hyde, *Benjamin Fondane: A Presentation of His Life and Work* (Geneva: Droz, 1971); and Peter Christensen, "Benjamin Fondane's 'Scenarii Intournables,'" *Dada/Surrealism* 15 (1987): 72–85.

39. Fondane's remarks crop up in an interview he gave to *Aujourd'hui*, 24 Feb. 1934.

40. Martin Esslin, *Antonin Artaud*, 31.

41. Denise Tual who edited the film recounted this "near miss" in an interview conducted by Sylvie Blum-Reid in Paris, March 1986.

42. For instance, only one Comédie-Française actor could appear in any given film.

43. Bettina Knapp, *Louis Jouvet: Man of the Theater*.

44. Gaston Baty was a proponent of "total theater" and emphasized the physicality of the plays he produced so as to rebalance what he claimed was a serious verbal Cartesianism in French theater. But he in no way eliminated or distorted language the way Artaud did.

45. John Edward Van Meter, "The Theater of Louis Jouvet" (Ph.D. diss., University of Florida, 1959), 43-45.

CHAPTER 6

THE LITERARY AND ARTISTIC SOURCES OF POETIC REALISM

1. Alexandre Arnoux, *Pour Vous* 343 (13 June 1935).

2. *La Cinématographie française* 973 (25 June 1937): 161–67.

3. Gabin did appear in two adaptations from plays in this period: Renoir's *Les Bas-Fonds* from Gorki, and *Le Messager* from Henry Bernstein.

4. See chap. 5 of the *Catalogue exposition Roger Martin du Gard* (9 Oct. 1981), a copy of which I consulted at the Bibliothèque de l'Arsenal in Paris.

5. Léon Poirier had once headed Gaumont's production. His *La Croisière noire* (1925) is a classic ethnographic film that brought him to Gide's attention just before the latter left for the Congo journey. See Poirier, *24 Images à la second* (Paris: Mame, 1953), 93–94. For details about Gide's journey, see Marc Allégret, *Carnets du Congo* (Paris: Presses du C.N.R.S., 1987).

6. *Variety*, 13 Mar. 1929.

7. The N.S.F (Nouvelle Société de Films), an offshoot of the N.R.F., was first under the direction of Paul Morand. See *Pour Vous* 249 (24 Aug. 1933). This would evolve quickly into Synops. See below.

8. See the last section of this chapter for details concerning the production of *Lac aux dames*.

9. Gide's relation to the cinema is detailed by Claude Sicard, "Gide et le cinéma," in *Annales de l'Université de Toulouse le Mirant* 16 (1980): 75–92. As for the Zola adaptation, only Jean Gabin could bring into existence a project that had kicked around for five years. By that time Martin du Gard had given up on the cinema, ceding his script to Renoir. By happenstance, while shooting this film Renoir spent time with Gide, whose country home in Normandy lay near the tracks on which so much of the film takes place.

10. Denise Tual, *Le Temps dévoré*, 116–17.

11. Interview by author with Chenal, August 1988.

12. "Edmond T. Gréville et Pierre Chenal: deux cinéastes méconnus," in *Le Cinéma français 1930–1960*, ed. Philippe de Comes and Michel Marmin, 64.

13. François Vinneuil, in *Action française*, 24 Mar. 1935, and Georges Champreux in *Gringoire*, 22 Mar. 1935.

14. Anonymous critique cited by Gréville in his "35 Ans dans le jungle du cinéma," *Revue internationale de l'histoire du cinéma* (microfiche) 29 (1978): 109.

15. The influence of Soviet montage and camerawork on *Remous* is noted in *Le Cinéma français 1930–1960*, ed. de Comes and Marmin, 67.

16. Marcel Carné, "When Will the Camera Go Down into the Streets?" in *French Film Theory and Criticism: A History/Anthology 1907–1939*, ed. Richard Abel, 2:127–29. Originally published in *Cinémagazine* 13 (Nov. 1933).

17. Dabit and Martin du Gard correspondence, Bibliothèque nationale, Paris.

18. André Lang, *Tiers de siècle*, 233.

19. Brassaï, Introduction to *The Secret Paris of the Thirties*, trans. Richard Miller (New York: Pantheon, 1976), 9.

20. *Paris by Night* is the title of his most famous collection of photographs, published in 1933. For more information on Brassaï see Marja Warehime, *Images of Culture and the Surrealist Observer: Brassaï* (Baton Rouge: Louisiana State University Press, 1994). The photographer André Kertesz also needs mention. Like Brassaï he had come to Paris from eastern Europe in the mid-twenties and immediately encountered the Prévert brothers and Mac Orlan, whom he photographed. In the thirties he illustrated articles that Mac Orlan, Francis Carco, and Colette wrote for the journal *Arts et Médecine*.

21. Denis de Rougement, Introduction to Charles-Ferdinand Ramuz, *The End of All Men*, trans. Allan Ross MacDougall (New York: Pantheon, 1944), xv.

22. J. E. Flower, *Literature and the Left in France* (London: Methuen, 1983), 79.

23. De Rougement, Introduction, xvi.

24. Ibid., xvi.

25. Fondane claims to have worked on over a hundred scripts at Paramount without taking credit for any. See chap. 5 above.

26. *Aujourd'hui*, 24 Feb. 1934.

27. A review from an uncited source, found in the *Rapt* file of the Fond Rondel at the Bibliothèque de l'Arsenal.

28. *L'Indépendent belge*, 27 Apr. 1934.

29. Valéry Jahier in *Esprit* 31 (Apr. 1935).

30. Roger Regent in a review (newspaper unknown) in the clipping file for *Rapt* (Rk 7904) at the Bibliothèque de l'Arsenal, Paris.

31. See especially Jahier in *Esprit* 31 (Apr. 1935): 117.

32. Pierre Chenal, *Souvenirs du cinéaste*, 55.

33. Michel Gorel, *Cinémonde* 277 (8 Feb. 1934).

34. Claude Vermorel, "Zola à l'écran," *Pour Vous* 313 (15 Nov. 1934).

35. Aymé had involvements with only two other films in the decade, one of which was helping Chenal adapt Jack London's *The Mutineers of Elsinore* in 1936.

36. Chenal, *Souvenirs*, 66–67.

37. Ibid., 69.

38. Henri Jeanson explicitly honored him with this title in *Le Canard enchaîné*, cited in Chenal, *Souvenirs*, 69. And Roger Leenhardt said, "Of all the films of newcomers in last

year's season, *Crime et châtiment* is by far the most significant." See his review of the film in his *Chroniques de cinéma*, 74. His review originally appeared in *Esprit* 33 (June 1935).

39. Chenal, interviewed in *Technique cinématographique* 54 (June 1935).

40. Chenal, *Souvenirs*, 72.

41. Chenal, in *Technique cinématographique* 54 (June 1935).

42. Chenal, in *Pour Vous* 341 (30 May 1935).

43. According to Chenal in an interview with the author, June 1988.

44. Chenal, interview with the author, June 1988.

45. Louis Cheronnet in *L'Humanité*, 29 July 1937, explicitly called it an "atmosphere film" rather than a *policier*.

46. Leenhardt, who praises Chenal on most counts, faults his decoupage. See his *Chroniques de cinéma*, 74.

47. Claude Beylie, *Écran 76* 53 (15 Dec. 1976).

48. Chenal, interview with the author, June 1988.

49. André Bazin, "An Aesthetic of Reality: Cinematic Realism and the Italian School of the Liberation," in *What Is Cinema?* (Berkeley and Los Angeles: University of California Press, 1971), 2:31, 38–40.

50. Review of *Amok* in *Ciné-Miroir* 495 (28 Sept. 1934).

51. The director Maurice Tourneur speaks of it in a short article he wrote for *Pour Vous* 315 (29 Nov. 1934).

52. *Pour Vous* 385 (2 Apr. 1936).

53. Elie Faure in *Pour Vous* 283 (31 May 1934).

54. Claude Vermorel, *Pour Vous* 281 (31 May 1934).

55. All three of these critics expounded on *L'Atalante* in *Pour Vous*, numbers 289, 263, and 305, respectively.

56. If I insist on this bizarre comparison between Vigo, an extreme leftist, and Céline, an extreme rightist, it is only because critics from both camps suggested it at the time. See particularly Maurice Bardèche and Robert Brasillach, *The History of Motion Pictures*, trans. Iris Barry (New York: Museum of Modern Art, 1938), 56.

57. *Pour Vous* 292 (21 June 1934).

58. Claude Vermorel, *Pour Vous* 263 (1 Dec. 1933).

59. Henri Fescourt, *La Foi et les montagnes, ou le septième art au passé*, 401.

60. Ibid.

61. Pierre Mac Orlan, "Présence de l'obsession dans les films," *Ciné pour tous*, 2 Feb. 1951.

62. *Variety*, 24 Oct. 1928, 9 and 16 Apr. 1930, details some agreements set up between French and German companies. Richard Abel, in *French Cinema: The First Wave, 1915–1929*, 27–33, details the French presence in Germany during the twenties.

63. Dossier in the Fond Rondel of the Bibliothèque de l'Arsenal in Paris.

64. Joseph Kessel, in *Matin de Paris*, Apr. 1932.

65. Kessel, *Pour Vous* 180 (28 Apr. 1932).

66. Thomas Elsaesser, "Pathos and Leave-taking: The German Emigrés in Paris during the 1930s," *Sight and Sound* 53, no. 4 (Autumn 1984): 279–80.

67. Interviewed in *Cinémonde*, 8 June 1933.

68. See Marcel Achard's review of *Mister Flow* in *Marianne*, 11 Nov. 1936.

69. Hervé Dumont, *Robert Siodmak, le maître du film noir*, 108.

70. See Ginette Vincendeau, "Les cinéastes allemands en France pendant les années trente," *Positif* 323 (Jan. 1988): 45–49. Vincendeau suggests that the varied backgrounds of those working on these films encouraged a heterogenous product, but so also did the

standard, not the poetic realist, French film of the day. The average French film, unlike German and American pictures, routinely drew on multiple styles, banking little on the strict tradition of genres.

71. Dumont, *Robert Siodmak*, 126.

72. Ginette Vincendeau, "French Cinema in the 1930s: Social Text and Context of a Popular Entertainment Medium," 103–4. Also see her article in *Positif* cited above, n. 70.

73. Elsaesser, "Pathos and Leave-taking," 282.

74. Edward Baron Turk, *Child of Paradise: Marcel Carné and the Golden Age of French Cinema*.

75. *Cinéopse*, 1 Mar. 1934.

76. *Ciné-Miroir*, 6 Oct. 1933.

77. See "Les Chefs opérateurs étrangers dans le cinéma français des années trente," *Positif* 323 (Jan. 1988). This dossier renders the filmography of fifteen émigré cameramen.

78. Jacques Colombier, "Pour un style français," *Le Film français* 1 (1945). This was the first issue to appear after the war.

79. See Lenny Borger and Catherine Morel, "L'Angoissante aventure: l'apport russe de l'entre-deux-guerres," *Positif* 323 (Jan. 1988): 38–41.

80. This number includes productions of Ermolieff-Films and of Les Films Albatros. One could add to these the five films of the Westi Consortium (Ciné-France-Films), which was a splinter group, primarily Slav in personnel.

81. My calculations concerning the number and types of films involving Russia and Russian émigrés is largely confirmed by the exhaustive research Genya Gindilis of New York University reported on at the October 1994 Ohio Film Conference.

82. Léon Barsacq, *Caligari's Cabinet and Other Grand Illusions*. Barsacq, a Russian émigré, could be said to belong to the third wave of émigrés, following those of 1919 and those of 1926.

83. André Bazin, we must remember, refused to see 1927 as a Red Sea. In his "Evolution of the Language of Cinema," in *What Is Cinema?* 1:24–28, he argues that some aesthetic impulses managed to traverse sound without serious concession. He mentions the realism of Renoir, and I would add the incipient poetic realism of Grémillon, Chenal, and the handful of others we have examined, as relying on a subtle relation of space to character and to fiction that sustained much silent work, including Renoir's.

84. Lucie Dérain, "Décors et décorateurs dans le cinéma français," *La Revue du cinéma* 27 (Oct. 1931): 26–31.

85. Donald Albrecht, *Designing Dreams: Modern Architecture in the Movies*, 43 and following.

86. See chap. 3 above.

87. Paul Monaco, *Cinema and Society: France and Germany in the Twenties* (New York: Elsevier, 1976).

88. Lazaare Meerson, "Une Harmonie," *Cinémagazine* 21 (Jan. 1927), reprinted in the French edition of Barsacq, *Le Décor de film*, 191. Mallet-Stevens's work in cinema is thoroughly treated by Albrecht, *Designing Dreams*, 44–52.

89. Alexandre Trauner, in Michel Ciment and Isabell Jordan, "Entretien avec Alexandre Trauner," *Positif* 223 (Oct. 1979): 11.

90. Albrecht, *Designing Dreams*, 56–58.

91. Barsacq, *Caligari's Cabinet*, 78.

92. Germain Bazin, "Degas et l'objectif," *L'Amour de l'art* 38–39 (July 1931).

93. See Hélène Chardavonne, "Evolution du décors du cinéma français" (Mémoire de

Maîtrise, directed by Jean Mitry, The Sorbonne, 1973). On file at the Bibliothèque de L'IDHEC.

94. He had it built in concrete where it still exists.

95. Barsacq, *Caligari's Cabinet*, 78.

96. Mallet-Stevens had published an influential monograph entitled *Le Décors moderne au cinéma* (Paris: Charles Massin, 1928).

97. Quoted in Barsacq, *Caligari's Cabinet*, 84.

98. Ibid.

99. Ibid., 80.

100. See chap. 4 above.

101. Jean Epstein, "The Cinema Continues," from *Cinéa-Ciné* 1 (Nov. 1930), translated in *French Film Theory and Criticism*, ed. Abel, 2:66–68. Abel notes that although Epstein shot "several personal films set in Brittany," his commercial failure forced him against his will back into the studio and into theatrical projects he abhorred.

102. Barsacq, *Caligari's Cabinet*, 78–80.

103. André Bazin must be credited with starting this discussion in an essay that appears in English as the preface to the screenplay of *Le Jour se lève* (New York: Simon and Schuster, 1971). Hélène Chardavonne writes at length about Trauner in her thesis, "Evolution du décors du cinéma," and Trauner himself contributed a substantial essay on decor to *L'Ecran français* (11 Sept. 1946).

104. Trauner compares the two versions in the interview in *Positif* 223 (Oct. 1979): 12–14.

105. Italo Calvino, "Autobiographie d'un spectateur," *Positif* 181 (May 1975): 17.

106. Trauner's importance in this era has received much recent attention. See especially Marcel Carné, *La Vie à belles dents*, and Alexandre Trauner, *Cinquante Ans de cinéma*.

107. The terms "figure" and "milieu" will be discussed in chap. 8.

108. Joan Littlewood, *Milady Vine: The Autobiography of Ph. de Rothschild* (London: Jonathan Cape, 1984), 104–7.

109. Alain and Odette Virmaux, "Colette and *Lac aux dames*," *L'Avant-Scène Cinéma* 284 (Feb. 1982): 7.

110. Aumont's amusing anecdote includes the spectacle of him stripping to his underwear to show off his physique to Rothschild, Gide, and Allégret. This occurred when Johnny Weissmuller was unavailable. See Jean-Pierre Aumont, *Sun and Shadow*, 30–31.

111. Allégret in *Pour Vous* 242 (6 July 1933) also mentioned that his next project would be *La Bête humaine* and would require even more time.

112. Tual, *Au coeur du temps*, 135–39.

113. *Excelsior*, 8 June 1934.

CHAPTER 7
DEMANDS OF REALISM

1. André Bazin, "The Myth of Total Cinema," in *What Is Cinema?* vol. 1 (Berkeley and Los Angeles: University of California Press, 1967).

2. I discuss this rapport in my essay in *"East of Suez": Orientalism in Film*, ed. Matthew Bernstein and G. Studlar (New Brunswick: Rutgers University Press, forthcoming).

3. René Lehmann, review of *La Chienne*, *Pour Vous* 158 (26 Nov. 1931).

4. Jean Grémillon, "French Realism," in *Rediscovering French Film*, trans. Catherine A. Surowiec (New York: Museum of Modern Art, 1983), 113.

5. André Bazin, *Jean Renoir*, 90.

6. Louis Delluc, *Photogénie*. Marcel Tariol explicitly places Delluc at the fountainhead of poetic realism in his *Louis Delluc* (Paris: Seghers, 1965), 61–62.

7. See chap. 2 above.

8. This term, like the others I am discussing here, is analyzed in *French Film Theory and Criticism: A History/Anthology, 1907–1939*, ed. Richard Abel, 1:199–213.

9. See chap. 1 above.

10. Claude Vermorel, "Zola à l'écran," *Pour Vous* 313 (15 Nov. 1934).

11. See especially *What Is Cinema?* vol. 2, where Bazin's essays on Italian neorealism endorse that movement's relation to the American novel but also claim that it has nothing in common with traditional literary realism.

12. Paul Monaco examines this genre in detail in his *Film and Society* (New York: Elsevier, 1976).

13. *The 1934–1935 Motion Picture Almanac*, ed. Terry Ramsaye (New York: Quigley Publishing Co., 1935), 1013.

14. *Pour Vous* 276–278 (1, 7, and 14 Mar. 1934).

15. Although this was not Madeleine Renaud's first role on the screen, as Sandy Flitterman-Lewis states (*To Desire Differently: Feminism and the French Cinema*, 189), most of the parts she had played before *La Maternelle* came straight from the stage, as for example in the 1931 hit *Jean de la lune*, from Marcel Achard's famous play.

16. Flitterman-Lewis, *To Desire Differently*, 179. See her entire section on Marie Epstein, 141–214.

17. See *New York Times*, 15 Oct. 1935; Maurice Bardèche and Robert Brasillach, *The History of Motion Pictures*, trans. Iris Barry (New York: Museum of Modern Art, 1938), 338–40; Henri Fescourt, *La Foi et les montagnes, ou le septième art au passé*, 402–18.

18. Flitterman-Lewis effectively describes the strenuous research that permitted Epstein and Benoit-Lévy to create an unusually authentic ambience in the studio. *To Desire Differently*, 181–83.

19. Erich Auerbach, *Mimesis* (Princeton: Princeton University Press, 1953).

20. See Flitterman-Lewis's fine chapters on Marie Epstein in her *To Desire Differently* (chaps. 5 and 6).

21. Ibid., 193.

22. Christopher Faulkner, *Jean Renoir: A Guide to References and Resources*, 88. See also Valéry Jahier's review of the film in *Esprit* 31 (Apr. 1935), translated in *French Film Theory and Criticism*, ed. Abel, 2:187–88. Jahier concludes, "In short, everything in this work contrasts sharply with the artificial world conjured up most of the time by the products of our studios." During the period, a minuscule percentage of French features were shot on location, somewhere between 2 and 5 percent. See François Garçon, *De Blum à Pétain: cinéma et société française (1936–1944)*, 16.

23. Léon Moussinac immediately intuited the film's break with convention in a contemporaneous review reprinted in *Jean Renoir*, Premier Plan 22–24 (May 1962): 158.

24. Jean Renoir, "Toni et le classicisme," *Cahiers du cinéma* 60 (June 1956).

25. Léon Moussinac, *L'Humanité*, 3 Aug. 1935, reprinted in *Jean Renoir*, Premier Plan 22–24 (May 1962): 160.

26. Bazin, *Jean Renoir*, 38.

27. Renoir, *"Toni* et le classicisme."

28. Jean Renoir, "How I Give Life to My Characters," from *Pour Vous* 242 (6 July 1933), translated in *French Film Theory and Criticism*, ed. Abel, 2:125-26.

29. Buñuel implies that he was always ready to make ethnographic cinema, claiming that he had been invited to document the Dakar-Djibouti expedition in 1931, and that he was responsible for Michel Leiris's being chosen secretary. He turned down the chance, he implies, because his ethnographic interests have always and only been with the places he himself has inhabited.

30. Renoir in *Jean Renoir*, Premier Plan 22-24 (May 1962): 155. Also, Faulkner, *Jean Renoir*, 89.

31. Renoir chided the censors, saying they "permitted only old noble corpses, killed without blood in duels." Renoir, in *Jean Renoir*, Premier Plan 22-24 (May 1962): 155.

32. Christopher Faulkner, *The Social Cinema of Jean Renoir*, 50, borrows this phrase from Eric Rhode and opposes it, quite rightly I believe, to Bazin's view (in *Jean Renoir*, 39) that the setting is predominantly "moral" rather than social.

33. "Raymond Bernard, un directeur à l'américaine" is the title of the essay Geneviève Sellier consecrated to Raymond Bernard in *Cinéma 83*, no. 294 (June 1983): 67-70.

34. For details concerning the production and distribution of *Les Croix de bois* see Lenny Borger's essay on the film in *Cinématographe* 91 (July–Aug. 1983): 30-35.

35. Ibid.

36. See Sellier, "Raymond Bernard, un directeur à l'américaine."

37. See François de la Bretèque, *"Le Coupable,"* in *Les Cahiers de la cinémathèque* 18-19 (Spring 1976): 78.

38. Interviewed just before the premiere, Bernard evinced much more interest in his upcoming film with Raimu than in the social consequences of *Les Misérables*. See *Comoedia*, 2 and 3 Feb. 1934.

39. I discuss the part played by Bernard's film in the turbulent moment of the Stavisky Affair in an article written in collaboration with Steven Ungar: "Presse/Première: *Stavisky* ... et le mise-en-page de l'histoire," *Hors cadre* 10 (1992): 99-114.

40. *Pour Vous* 273 (8 Feb. 1934). This review of *La Rue sans nom* goes so far as to claim that this film can genuinely change French cinema, although it will not appeal to "anyone looking for an hour of distraction or dream life at the movies." In the same issue *Les Misérables* is described in idealist terms: "One feels not so much the hand of the master [Raymond Bernard] but the breath of the greater master [Victor Hugo]" in the charged atmosphere of this film.

41. Jean-Louis Bory, *Le Nouvel Observateur*, 3-9 Sept. 1969, quoted by Keith Reader in "Renoir's Popular Front Films: Texts in Context," in *La Vie est à Nous*, ed. Ginette Vincendeau and Keith Reader, 51.

42. Juliette Pary, "Le Temps des loisirs, une grande enquête-reportage," *Regards*, 14 Oct. 1937.

43. Léo Lagrange, "Le Cinéma es les loisirs," *La Critique cinématographique*, 5 Dec. 1936, as cited by Elizabeth Grottle Strebel, *French Social Cinema of the Nineteen Thirties: A Cinematographic Expression of Popular Front Consciousness*, 128.

44. Strebel, for example, believes that the government did not have the time to implement its desired reforms in the cinema sector, implying that those reforms would have come about had the government lasted. See her *French Social Cinema*, 127-29.

45. Published as *Où va le cinéma français?* (Paris: Baudinière, 1937).

46. See Gérard Talon, "Regards critiques sur la production et la réalisation des films au temps du Front Populaire!" *Cinéma 75* 194 (Jan. 1975): 38.

47. Jean Vigo was the only cinéaste on record as an original member of the Comité de vigilance, formed as a response to the right-wing demonstrations of 6 Feb. 1934.

48. Strebel documents the relaxation of censorship from 1934 to 1936, allowing for the success of such Russian films as *Sailors from Kronstadt* and *The Youth of Maxim*. See her *French Social Cinema*, 107–12.

49. Five prodigiously researched studies, crowned by Jonathan Buchsbaum's *Cinema Engagé: Film in the Popular Front*, have chronicled the doomed but heroic effort of the era's leftist filmmakers. See G. Fofi, "The Cinema of the Popular Front in France (1934–38)," translated in *Screen* 13 (Winter 1972–1973); Strebel, *French Social Cinema*; Talon, "Regards critiques"; Pascal Ory, "De 'Ciné-Liberté' à 'La Marseillaise,' Hopes and Limitations of a Liberated Cinema," translated in *La Vie est à nous*, ed. Ginette Vincendeau and Keith Reader, 5–37.

50. Bernard Eisenschitz supplies this perhaps exaggerated estimate of the club's size in "Histoire de l'histoire," in *Défense du cinéma* (St. Denis: La Maison de la culture de la Seine, 1975). For more information on the political fate of this club and others like it see Buchsbaum, *Cinema Engagé*, 25–26; Abel, *French Cinema: The First Wave*, 264–66; and Strebel, *French Social Cinema*, 26–35.

51. Buchsbaum, *Cinema Engagé*, 43–46.

52. P. E. Salles Gomes, *Jean Vigo*, 216.

53. See Ory's definitive essay on this period, in *La Vie est à Nous*, ed. Vincendeau and Reader, 5–37.

54. See Julian Jackson, *The Popular Front in France*, chap. 4. Ory mentions that this strategy was criticized by the orthodox Marxist Jacques Duclos, who found such watering down of programs in the name of widening leftist culture to be repeating the errors of 1848. See Ory's "De 'Ciné-Liberté' à 'La Marseillaise,'" 9.

55. *Ciné-Liberté* 5 (1 Nov. 1936), translated in *French Film Theory and Criticism*, ed. Abel, 2:217–18.

56. Strebel graphs this correspondence through the bilateral work of members of the Groupe Octobre in her *French Social Cinema*, 170–73.

57. Buchsbaum, *Cinema Engagé*, 176.

58. Talon, "Regards critiques," 56.

59. Ibid., 52.

60. *La Cinématographie française* 977 (23 July 1937).

61. A typical and unabashed reflection study is that by Rémy Pithon, "Le Cinéma français et la montée des périls: analyse spectrale de la production 1938–39," *Cahiers de la cinémathèque* 18–19 (Spring 1976): 93–105.

62. René Prédal, *La Société française (1914–1945) à travers le cinéma*, 8–14.

63. Garçon, *De Blum à Pétain*, 58.

64. Eisenschitz, "Histoire de l'histoire."

65. "Cinéma-miroir" is the title Prédal gives to one of the sections of *La Société française*. On 208 he lists films from the Popular Front era that evoke the agenda of that government, such as old-age benefits and paid vacations.

66. See, respectively, Pierre Sorlin, "Jewish Images in French Cinema of the Thirties," *Historical Journal of Film, Radio, and TV* 1, no. 2 (1981): 140–49; Flitterman-Lewis, *To Desire Differently*; and David Slavin, "Native Sons? White Blindspots, Male Fantasies, and Imperial

Myths in French *Cinéma Colonial* of the 1930s," in *Identity Papers: Scenes of Contested Nation-hood in Twentieth Century France*, ed. S. Ungar and T. Conley (Minneapolis: University of Minnesota Press, 1995).

67. Strebel makes this point in *French Social Cinema*, 267, perhaps drawing on remarks about poetic realism included in Prédal's *La Société française*, 91.

68. *Pour Vous* 409 (17 Sept. 1936).

69. *Ciné-Liberté* 5 (Nov. 1936).

70. See, for example, Raymond Chirat, *Le Cinéma français des années 30*, 52, or *Julien Duvivier*, Premier Plan 50 (1969): 105–6.

71. In the new version that circulated in the second-run theaters and in the provinces, the femme fatale (Vivian Romance) is repudiated by the two men she comes between (played by Gabin and Charles Vanel) who shove her away and dance through the night. In the original version, the one Duvivier preferred, the perfume of Vivian Romance ultimately drives Gabin to shoot his friend, whereupon he is dragged off by the police. The lovely *guinguette*, christened "Chez Nous" (as though a refrain from *La Vie est à nous*), lies abandoned. The place of sexuality within community will be addressed by Renoir in *La Marseillaise* when the four exiles on the mountaintop (the priest, the peasant, the artisan, and the lawyer), after singing the utopia of a future based on their brotherhood, are reminded by the peasant that harmony exists just until the moment when a woman joins the group.

72. Jean-Pierre Jeancolas, "French Cinema of the 1930s and Its Sociological Handicaps," in *La Vie est à Nous*, ed. Vincendeau and Reader, 70.

73. *Ciné-Liberté* 5 (Nov. 1936).

74. *Cinémonde*, 15 Sept. 1959.

75. Ginette Vincendeau and Claude Gauteur, *Jean Gabin: anatomie d'un mythe* (Paris: Nathan, 1993), 162.

76. Georges Sadoul, "A Propos Several Recent Films," *Commune* 39 (Nov. 1936), translated in *French Film Theory and Criticism*, ed. Abel, 2:218–23.

77. Curiously *Ciné-Liberté* (Oct. 1936) reviewed *Rigolboche* in a witty, even delirious, way, making fun of the young boys and old men who should be banned from gazing too long at "Miss." Also, see my chapter comparing *Rigolboche* to *Le Crime de Monsieur Lange*, in *Popular European Cinema*, ed. Ginette Vincendeau and Richard Dyer (London: Routledge, 1991).

78. *Ciné-Liberté* 5 (Nov. 1936).

79. Jean-Pierre Jeancolas, *15 Ans d'années trente: le cinéma des français 1929–1944*, 209.

80. Graham Greene in *The Spectator*, 23 Apr. 1937.

81. The belief that French film of the thirties was dominated by actors, more even than the cinema of Hollywood, is expressed in the title and concluding chapter of *Générique des années 30* by Michèle Lagny, Marie-Claire Ropars, and Pierre Sorlin.

82. Vincendeau and Gauteur, *Jean Gabin*, 147.

83. Most of these points can be found in ibid., chap. 5, a chapter significantly entitled "Un Français." Vincendeau pioneered these ideas in her article "Community, Nostalgia, and the Spectacle of Masculinity," *Screen* 26, no. 6 (Nov.–Dec. 1985): 18–38.

84. Nataša Ďurovičová, "Disorganized Crime: Aesthetics of Transgression in French Films of the Thirties" (Unpublished paper delivered at the Society for Cinema Studies Conference, Montreal, May 1987).

85. In 1945 Pierre Mac Orlan brought out a feature film entitled *François Villon*, and directed by Renoir's longtime collaborator André Zwoboda. Mac Orlan published the screenplay and several articles about Villon at the time. See *Mac Orlan et le cinéma*.

86. Graham Greene shows his respect for French realism in many places, but most importantly in a review of *Alerte en Méditerranée*, in his collected film criticism, *Graham Greene on Film: Collected Film Criticism 1935–1940*, 205.

87. Roger Leenhardt, in *Esprit* 38 (Nov. 1935): 332. Leenhardt goes on to deny to Duvivier the status of "cinéaste" that he bestows on Clair, Feyder, Renoir, and even Chenal. Without a proper signature, without a passionate transgressive style, Duvivier is deemed only an "honest craftsman." These are the very terms under which Truffaut in France and Andrew Sarris in the United States will develop auteurism.

88. Geneviève Sellier, *Jean Grémillon: le cinéma est à vous*, 24–38.

89. Raimu plays the town's upright mayor who has a terrible secret: he sent another man to prison for his own crime. The latter escapes and returns, hiding out in the mayor's home where he falls in love with the mayor's wife.

CHAPTER 8
FIGURES OF THE POETIC

1. Georges Sadoul, *Histoire du cinéma mondial des origines à nos jours*, 271.

2. This application of ideas from Barthes's *S/Z* to poetic realism was the inspiration of Phil Beck who wrote a brilliant, unpublished paper, "Figures in Milieux," for a seminar I gave on French cinema in 1979. I owe an immense amount to Beck, since this insight is fundamental to my entire view of the period.

3. Barthes, *S/Z* (Boston: Hill and Wang, 1974), 68.

4. Jean-Louis Comolli, "Historical Fiction: A Body Too Much," *Screen* 19, no. 2 (1978): 41–53.

5. Although increasingly melodrama seems applicable to virtually the whole of cinema. See Jacques Goimard, "Le Mélodrame: le mot et la chose," *Cahiers de la cinémathèque* 28 (1979): 17–66, for a discussion of the omnipresence of melodrama in cinema. I will return to this issue in chap. 10.

6. Maureen Turim, "French Melodrama: Theory of a Specific History," *Theater Journal*, Oct. 1987, 327.

7. Ibid.

8. Ibid.

9. One of Bernstein's most famous plays, adapted to the screen, was titled simply *Melo*. Alain Resnais remade this play in 1985.

10. Colette's name stands out on the few scripts she signed, most of them "women-oriented" projects. Her most significant script was the adaptation of Vicki Baum's *Lac aux dames*. She likewise scripted the adaptation of her own novel *La Vagabonde*, which, as I have noted, was one of the very few films directed by a woman, Solange Bussi. Another of her fictions, *L'Envers de music-hall* she developed for a screen version by Max Ophuls in 1935.

11. Curiously the French were far ahead of Hollywood and most countries in turning editing over to women, presumably because in its conditions and function it was thought to resemble sewing. Colin Crisp makes this observation in his essay "The Rediscovery of Editing in French Cinema 1930–1945," in *History on and in Film*, ed. Tom O'Regan and Brian Shoesmith (Perth, 1987), 62.

12. The most notable example of a powerful "script-girl" is Françoise Giroud who, after starting out with her family friend, Marc Allégret, went on to become assistant director on

a dozen features, always under the pseudonym France Gourdji. See her autobiography, *Si je mens* . . . .

13. Ginette Vincendeau, "Melodramatic Realism: On Some French Women's Films in the 1930s," *Screen* 30 (Summer 1989): 51–65. This essay analyzes four films: *Jenny* (Carné, 1936), *Angèle* (Pagnol, 1934), *Hélène* (Epstein/Benoit-Lévy, 1936), *L'Entraîneuse* (Valentin, 1938).

14. Actually the woman's picture did not exist in Hollywood either until the forties.

15. Michèle Lagny, Marie-Claire Ropars, and Pierre Sorlin, *Générique des années 30*, do not even bother to deal with the Gaby character in *Pépé le Moko*, finding her no doubt a predictable tool for use in the construction of the truly fascinating bonded male figures, Pépé and Slimane.

16. Sandy Flitterman-Lewis, *To Desire Differently: Feminism and the French Cinema*, 185.

17. Vincendeau, "Melodramatic Realism," 65.

18. The popular chanson of the thirties also owes a tremendous debt to romantic poetry. See Lucienne Cantaloube-Ferrieu, *Chanson et poésie des années 30 aux années 60* (Paris: A. G. Nizet, 1981), chap. 2. Importantly, Jacques Prévert wrote material for both cinema and song, as these media supported one another by creating a tone and a repertoire of images that spoke to their period.

19. See my essay on *L'Atalante* in *Film in the Aura of Art*.

20. Elie Faure on *L'Atalante* in *Pour Vous* 283 (31 May 1934).

21. In fact, for reasons I have not been able to determine, despite its selection it failed to be screened in Venice.

22. Recall that this characterization comes directly from Sadoul, *Histoire du cinéma mondial*, 271.

23. Victor Bachy, *Jacques Feyder: artisan du cinéma, 1885–1948*, 122.

24. Christopher Miller, *Blank Darkness: Africanist Discourse in French Literature* (Chicago: University of Chicago Press, 1985).

25. See David Slavin's comprehensive essay, "Native Sons? White Blindspots, Male Fantasies, and Imperial Myths in French *Cinéma Colonial* of the 1930s," in *Identity Papers: Scenes of Contested Nationhood in Twentieth Century France*, ed. S. Ungar and T. Conley (Minneapolis: University of Minnesota Press, 1995). Also, see Deborah Root, "Sacred Landscapes/ Colonial Dreams: The Desert as Escape," *Lusitania* 1, no. 4 (1993): 25–34.

26. See my essay in *"East of Suez": Orientalism in Film*, ed. Matthew Bernstein and G. Studlar (New Brunswick: Rutgers University Press, forthcoming).

27. "Give me your lips, Julie; the wild nights that made you pale have dried their shining coral. Perfume them with your breath; give them me, my Barbary, your lovely lips of pure blood stock." "To Julie," in *The Penguin Book of French Verse 3: The Nineteenth Century*, ed. Anthony Hartley (London: Penguin Books, 1967), 109.

28. "Languorous Asia and burning Africa, the whole of a distant world far away, nearly defunct, lives in your depths, aromatic forest! As other spirits drift upon music, mine, O my love! floats upon your perfume." "The Hair," in ibid., 153.

29. "The darling was naked, and, knowing my heart, she had only kept on her sonorous jewels, whose rich accoutrement gave her the conquering air that Moorish slaves have in their happy days." "The Jewels," in ibid., 162.

30. " . . . a tamed tiger with a vague dreamy air, she tried various positions, and ingenuousness joined to lubricity gave a new charm to her metamorphoses."

31. Jean Mitry, *Histoire du cinéma*, 4:279.

32. Adam Garbicz and Jacek Klinowski refer to both Hitchcock and Pirandello in their

entry on *Le Grand Jeu* in *Cinema, the Magic Vehicle: A Guide to Its Achievement* (Metuchen, N.J.: Scarecrow Press, 1975), 216. Peter Christensen discusses Pirandello in a dense study of *Le Grand Jeu* appearing in *Film Criticism* 12, no. 2 (Winter 1987–1988): 4.

33. This stance seems to me very similar to the one that reached its apogee in Kenji Mizoguchi. See my chapter on the Japanese master in *Film in the Aura of Art*.

34. The Foreign Legion was purportedly tired of assisting film producers gratis. They liked neither the distortions to which Hollywood routinely subjected them, nor the very different tone Feyder proposed. See Bachy's aptly titled *Jacques Feyder: artisan du cinéma*, 121.

35. Garbicz and Klinowski, *Cinema, the Magic Vehicle*, 216.

36. Slavin glosses this supposed disease as a special form of homesickness produced by the desert. See his "Native Sons?"

37. Mitry, *Histoire du cinéma*, 4:436.

38. Christensen, "*Le Grand Jeu*."

39. Ibid.

40. Bachy, *Jacques Feyder: artisan du cinéma*.

41. Feyder and his wife Françoise Rosay entitled their joint autobiography *Le Cinéma, notre métier* (Geneva: Skira, 1946).

42. André Lang, *Pour Vous* 357 (19 Sept. 1935).

43. Raymond Chirat, *Julien Duvivier*, Premier Plan 50 (Dec. 1968): 45.

44. Damia and Fréhel were the two most famous "chanteuses réalistes" before Edith Piaf. Damia in fact had been taught to sing by Fréhel's first husband. See C. Brunschwig, L.-J. Calvet, and J.-C. Klein, *Cent Ans de chanson française* (Paris: Seuil, 1981), 115–16.

45. Geneviève Sellier, "Charles Spaak, ou le réalisme français des années 30–45," *Cinéma* (Paris) 299 (1983): 24.

46. In the physical, moral, and sexual extremes of the desert, the sleazy detective tracking the hero runs up against the limits of law, in the unconcern, indeed disdain, shown him by the captain of the brigade when he reports on Pierre's past. This is what leads to his profound conversion. Renouncing his role as policeman, he accepts his role in the brigade and achieves heroism. The last to hold the fort before its rescue, he taps the collective spirit of the slain around him and proclaims his allegiance to the Legion. He has become a slave of freedom.

47. "The look of Islam, faithfully reflected by French cinema, burlesqued by Hollywood."

48. *Pour Vous* 494 (4 May 1938).

49. Lang, in *Pour Vous* 357 (19 Sept. 1935).

50. Graham Greene, review of *La Bandera*, in *The Spectator*, 6 Dec. 1935.

51. Jean Carta in *Témoinage chrétien*, 17 July 1959.

52. Roberto Paolella, "La poesia simbolista e il cinema francese," *Bianco e Nero* 16 (May 1949): 132–35.

53. In *Excelsior*, 26 June 1935, where Mac Orlan also attributes the power of the movie to the authentic suffering of cast and crew during its production. Goffredo Fofi has accused Mac Orlan of attending numerous pro-Franco demonstrations during the thirties, perhaps providing a motive for Renoir's attack on *Le Quai des brumes*. See Goffredo Fofi, "The Cinema of the Popular Front in France (1934–38)," *Screen* 13 (Winter 1972–1973): 40.

54. Lagny, Ropars, and Sorlin, *Générique des années 30*, chap. 4, "L'Afrique de l'Autre."

55. Anatole Litvak directed this remake. The changed ending (Hollywood unable to permit the suicide of a hero) is cause for comparative sociological speculation.

56. I am indebted to Simon Dixon who argues this point in a seminar paper written at the University of Iowa, Dec. 1992.

57. Dalio was to have incarnated Slimane in *Pépé le Moko*, but a stage engagement forced him to accept the lesser role of Arbi. Imagining him as Slimane gives extra force to the comparison between Duvivier's film and Chenal's.

58. Also, as with Von Sternberg some would find this aesthetic "effete" and "decadent," perhaps because its style expressed what today could be characterized as a "gay sensibility." Edward Baron Turk engages the question of cinematic style and Carné's homosexuality throughout *Child of Paradise: Marcel Carné and the Golden Age of French Cinema*. See 51 and 393 especially. While he notes that it was "supporters of Pétain and Laval" who called *Le Quai des brumes* "effete" and "decadent" (114), even Renoir's distaste for the film may have had homophobic origins.

59. Marcel Carné, "Cinema and the World," *Cinémagazine* 12 (Nov. 1932), reproduced in *French Film Theory and Criticism: A History/Anthology 1907–1939*, ed. Richard Abel, 2:102–3.

60. Carné, "When Will the Cinema Go Down into the Street?" *Cinémagazine* 13 (Nov. 1933), reprinted in *French Film Theory and Criticism*, ed. Abel, 2:127.

61. Carné, "When Will the Cinema Go Down into the Street?" 128.

62. See chap. 6 above.

63. Carné, "Eloge du film policier américain," *Cinémagazine* 6 (June 1930).

64. Carné, *La Vie à belles dents*, 49.

65. André Heinrich glosses this topos in his introductory notes to the script of *Jenny* (Paris: Gallimard, 1988), 16–17.

66. Carné, *La Vie à belles dents*, 73–75.

67. Two recent books emphasize this. Turk's *Child of Paradise*, 66, and Claire Blakeway's *Jacques Prévert: Popular French Theatre and Cinema*, 100–104.

68. Turk finds that the more labored and mundane tone of *Hôtel du Nord* suffers from an absence of such scenes. Henri Jeanson's writing style was far too worldly and witty. See his *Child of Paradise*, 150.

69. See chap. 3 above.

70. A long string of contemporaneous reviews are included in André Heinrich's Preface to the screenplay for *Le Quai des brumes* (Paris: Gallimard, 1988).

71. Pierre Mac Orlan, "A propos de *Quai des brumes*," *Le Figaro*, 18 May 1938, reprinted in part in André Heinrich's Preface to the filmscripts by Prévert, *Jenny/Quai des brumes*, 155.

72. Claude Briac in *Ce Soir*, 20 May 1938, links this film to John Ford's *The Informer*, a film that played in Paris at the end of 1935, one that came from a novel by Liam O'Flaherty. O'Flaherty was important to poetic realism for the adaptation of his novel *The Puritain* in 1937.

73. Paul Gignac in *La Patrie humaine*, 20 May 1938.

74. Pierre Nord in *Le Prestige*, 1 Sept. 1938.

75. Marcel Lapierre in *Le Peuple*, 27 May 1938. Marianne Oswald was a cabaret singer who left the Berlin of Brecht and Weill when Hitler came to power and was exceptionally popular in Paris where Prévert wrote nostalgic laments for her raspy interpretation.

76. C. Brunschwig, L.-J. Calvet, and J.-C. Klein, *Cent Ans de chanson française* (Paris: Seuil, 1981), 292.

77. Review of *Le Quai des brumes* in *Bianco e Nero* 2, no. 9 (Sept. 1938).

78. Louis Chavance in *Toute l'Edition*, 7 May 1938.

79. For a summary of Renoir's article and the debate it caused, see Jean-Pierre Jeancolas, *15 Ans d'années trente: le cinéma des français, 1929–1944*, 270–73.

80. Turk, *Child of Paradise*, 115–18.

81. Ibid., 120 and 126.

82. Ibid., 120.

83. See Crisp, "The Rediscovery of Editing in French Cinema."

84. Liam O'Flaherty was a relative of John Ford's and worked on the sets of several films, including *Le Puritain*.

85. Cited by Roger Leenhardt, "Le Cinéma, art national," *Esprit* (Feb. 1938), reprinted in *Chronique de cinéma*, 57–60.

CHAPTER 9
JEAN RENOIR: ADAPTATION, INSTITUTION, AUTEUR

1. See chap. 5 above for a discussion of Pagnol's world and worldview. "Le Petit Monde de Marcel Pagnol" is the title of a diorama on permanent display in the center of the city of Aubagne (Bouches-du-Rhône).

2. Walter Benjamin, *Illuminations* (New York: Harcourt, Brace, 1968).

3. In his first published essay he insists on his orientation as storyteller. Renoir, "How I Give Life to My Characters," *Pour Vous* 242 (6 July 1933), translated in *French Film Theory and Criticism: A History/Anthology 1907–1939*, ed. Richard Abel, 2:125.

4. See chap. 4 above.

5. Georges Simenon, "Le Cinéma est un nouveau riche," *Le Figaro*, 4 July 1938.

6. Alexander Sesonske, *Jean Renoir: The French Films, 1924–1939*, 102.

7. Christopher Faulkner, *Jean Renoir: A Guide to References and Resources*, 81, perpetuates the sense of the plot's incompleteness by retelling and correcting the notorious anecdote concerning the loss during production of two reels of film by Jean Mitry. Chardère, on the other hand, claims that a perusal of a dozen contemporaneous reviews reveals no anxiety about plot. See *Jean Renoir*, ed. Bernard Chardère, Premier Plan 22–24 (May 1962): 132.

8. Faulkner, *Jean Renoir*, 80–81, and Sesonske, *Jean Renoir*, 105. It is Sesonske who has noted, on this same page, the *Scarface* reference.

9. Cited in *Jean Renoir*, ed. Chardère, Premier Plan 22–24 (May 1962): 134.

10. Sesonske, *Jean Renoir*, 104–5.

11. Pierre Mac Orlan, interviewed by André Lang in *Tiers de siècle*, 237.

12. Sesonske, *Jean Renoir*, 105. Raymond Durgnat writes even more eloquently about the film's haunting beauty and its indistinct subject. See his *Jean Renoir*, 76–84.

13. Richard Abel, *French Cinema, The First Wave, 1915–1929*, 134–35. Abel counts very few films in the 1920s that hinge on surprising plot twists or on violence.

14. Ibid.

15. See Jean Mitry who cites the importance of these late silent films in his *Histoire du cinéma*, 3:429–39.

16. Georges Simenon's novels were the basis of only two other films in the 1930s, Jean Taride's *Le Chien jaune* and Duvivier's extremely important *La Tête d'un homme*, both made in 1932.

17. Pierre Assouline, *Gaston Gallimard* (New York: Harcourt, Brace, 1988), 186.

18. *Cahiers du cinéma* 79 (Dec. 1957): 31, cited in Sesonske, *Jean Renoir*, 144.

19. For an elaboration of this style see Sesonske, *Jean Renoir*, 145–47.

20. Georges Wakhevitch, *L'Envers des décors*, 75.

21. Ibid., 76.

22. Renoir, quoted by Assouline, *Gaston Gallimard*, 187.

23. *Madame Bovary* was featured as a prestige export, the first of Renoir's films since *Nana* to play in New York.

24. Pierre Braunberger, *Cinémamémoire*, 90.

25. Assouline mentions nothing about this, claiming that Gallimard stayed by Renoir's side during the excruciating period of the film's poor premiere and poorer reviews, but Célia Bertin, in her *Jean Renoir: A Life in Pictures*, 103–5 goes so far as to identify Pierre Renoir as the one who stole Tessier from Gallimard, provoking the latter to deep anger over the whole film project.

26. Wakhevitch, *L'Envers des décors*, 75. Faulkner indicates that the original was 3 hours 20 minutes, cut to 2 hours in France, 102 minutes for the English version. See his *Jean Renoir*, 86. Sesonske, *Jean Renoir*, 146, calculates the aesthetic cost of these cuts.

27. André Beucler wrote a lengthy appreciation in *Marianne*, 17 Jan. 1934, and Eugène Dabit did his best several weeks later in the *Nouvelle Revue française*, both company organs of Gallimard.

28. *Pour Vous* 252 (14 Sept. 1933).

29. See chap. 7 above.

30. Bertin, *Jean Renoir*, 106.

31. And I must include myself in such a list. See my chapter "Family Diversions" in *European Popular Cinema*, ed. Ginette Vincendeau and Richard Dyer (London: Routledge, 1992). Christopher Faulkner, in *The Social Cinema of Jean Renoir*, develops the most thorough political reading of this film.

32. Truffaut in André Bazin, *Jean Renoir* (French edition), 232–33.

33. *Esprit* 43 (1 Mar. 1936).

34. Georges Sadoul, *Commune* (Nov. 1936), translated in *French Film Theory and Criticism*, ed. Abel, 2:218–20.

35. Pierre Bost, *Vendredi*, 31 Jan. 1936, translated in *French Film Theory and Criticism*, ed. Abel, 2:205–6.

36. See Keith Reader, "Renoir's Popular Front Films, Texts in Context," in *La Vie est à Nous*, ed. Ginette Vincendeau and Keith Reader, 43–48.

37. Pierre Gaudibert, "The Popular Front and the Arts," in *Communication and Class Struggle*, ed. Armand Mattelart and S. Siegelaub (New York: International General, 1983), 2:182.

38. Jean Wahl in *Pour Vous* 282 (Apr. 1934) and *Pour Vous* 375 (Jan. 1936).

39. *Jean Renoir*, Premier Plan 22–24 (May 1962): 165–66.

40. *Pour Vous* 363 (31 Oct. 1935). At the time of this report, the film was still known by its original title, "Sur la cour."

41. Tom Conley, "A Pan of Bricks, McDonald, Renoir, Truffaut," *Enclitic* 1 (Spring 1979): 27–36.

42. *Ciné-Liberté* 4 (20 Aug. 1936).

43. Bertin, *Jean Renoir*, 117.

44. *Comoedia*, 23 Dec. 1936.

45. François Vinneuil, in *French Film Theory and Criticism*, ed. Abel, 2:228. Originally published in *Action française*, 25 Dec. 1936.

46. Gorki would die shortly before the film was completed.

47. Eugène Lourié, *My Work in Films*, 9–10.

48. See ibid., 10.

49. Henri Langlois in *French Film Theory and Criticism*, ed. Abel, 2:229. This piece originally appeared in *Cinéma-tographe* 1 (Mar. 1937).

50. Faulkner, *The Social Cinema of Jean Renoir*, 86.

51. Jonathan Buchsbaum, *Cinéma Engagé: Film in the Popular Front*, 279–80.

52. Ibid., 259–61.

53. Célia Bertin reports in *Jean Renoir* that Renoir had been chastised in a letter from a spectator for undermining the verisimilitude of *La Grande Illusion* when it came to the pistol Rauffenstein uses to bring down Bouldieu. Enchanted by the letter, Renoir enlisted this spectator as a firearms expert for *La Marseillaise*.

54. Renoir in *Cahiers du cinéma* 196 (Dec. 1967): 67.

55. Geneviève Guillaume-Grimauld, *Le Cinéma du Front Populaire*, 112.

56. Ibid., 110.

57. Quoted in Jacques Lorcey, *Marcel Achard* (Paris: France-Empire, 1977), 173.

58. In a venal attack, Henri Jeanson accused Renoir of holding his public in disdain, and merely using democratic sentimentality for his own profit. See my extended treatment of this film, "Revolution and the Ordinary: Renoir's *La Marseillaise*," *Yale Journal of Criticism*, Autumn 1990, 53–84. Jeanson's strongest attack can be read in translation in *French Film Theory and Criticism*, ed. Abel, 2:247–49.

59. Julian Jackson eloquently summarizes both the Popular Front ideology and the congruent attitudes of Renoir in *The Popular Front in France*, 138–47.

60. Jean Renoir, *My Life and My Films*, 127.

61. See Edward Baron Turk, *Child of Paradise: Marcel Carné and the Golden Age of French Cinema*, 127.

62. Faulkner, *The Social Cinema of Jean Renoir*, 101.

63. Roger Leenhardt, *Chroniques de cinéma*, 83. The original essay was called "Jean Renoir et la tradition française," *Intermède* 1 (July 1946).

64. Once again, Faulkner makes the strongest case for taking this antiauteurist position throughout his *Social Cinema of Jean Renoir*.

65. See Daniel Serceau, *"La Règle du jeu": Jean Renoir*, 30–32.

66. *Boudu sauvé des eaux* is not only an adaptation from a play, it is also prefaced by a farce actually staged to look like a farce.

67. My views on the relation of theater to cinema have been indelibly marked by André Bazin's now famous metaphor in *What Is Cinema?* (Berkeley and Los Angeles: University of California Press, 1967), 107. Citing Baudelaire, he likens dramatic art to the crystal chandeliers that adorn better theaters (brilliant, artificial, they refract light onto the crowd that sits in wonderment beneath it). In contrast, the usherette's penlight leads the lonely film spectator forward in the darkness to meet his or her "waking dream."

68. This quotation, dated 1969, appears in Leo Braudy, *Jean Renoir: The World of His Films*, 65.

69. Ibid., 73.

70. Ibid., 72.

71. Leenhardt, *Chroniques de cinéma*, 83.

72. André Bazin in *Jean Renoir*, 80, described the productive interplay of actor and role as analogous to the tension a painter may engender between the design and the colors that bleed over its edges. Terrence Rafferty makes this point over and over in "The Essence of the Landscape," *New Yorker*, 25 June 1990, 80–92.

73. Renoir, *My Life and My Films*, 169.

74. Leenhardt, *Chroniques de cinéma*, 83–84, here prophetically lays out ideas that will be developed shortly by Claude-Edmonde Magny in her *L'Age du roman américain* (Paris: Seuil, 1948).

75. Renoir, "Jean Renoir et le réalisme au cinéma," *Ciné-Revue*, 2 Dec. 1955, 12.

76. Leo Braudy, "Zola on Film: The Ambiguities of Naturalism," *Yale French Studies* 42 (1969): 68. Earlier scholars took up this topic, some in relation to Renoir's film. See especially Pietro Paulo Thompeo, "Zola e Renoir," *Bianco e Nero* 5, no. 8 (Aug. 1941): 6–14.

77. Emile Zola, "Naturalism and the Theater," in *The Experimental Novel and Other Essays* (New York: Haskell House, 1964).

78. Renoir interview in *Positif* 173 (Sept. 1975): 17.

79. Leenhardt, *Chroniques de cinéma*, 84.

80. Shooting took place in the last two months of summer 1938, according to Faulkner, *Jean Renoir*, 113. Sesonske, however, notes that Renoir himself had been working on the project since April (private letter to the author, 5 Nov. 1987). In any case, this film moved along much more rapidly than had any of the three surrounding it. Lourié speaks of the "urgency" and speed of production. See his *My Work in Films*, 42–43.

81. See among others, François Poulle, *Renoir 1938 ou Jean Renoir pour rien*, 24–26.

82. Renoir, "*La Bête humaine*," *Cahiers de la jeunesse* 17 (15 Dec. 1938), reprinted in *Image et son* 315 (Mar. 1977): 28.

83. Renoir in *Positif* 173 (Sept. 1975): 17.

84. Roger Martin du Gard, Catalogue Exposition, section 5, Bibliothèque de l'Arsenal.

85. Claude Sicard, "Martin du Gard et *La Bête humaine*," in *Hommage à Marcel Tariol*, *Annales de l'Université de Toulouse* 16 (1980): 75–92.

86. Denise Tual, *Au coeur du temps*, 189.

87. Lourié, *My Work in Films*, 46.

88. The mediocrity of this scene was noted by Oswald Ducrot in his excellent essay on the film appearing in *Raccords*, no. 7 (Spring 1951): 16–18.

89. Denise Tual, *Le Temps dévoré*.

90. Renoir agreed with Michel Ciment that this setting might be thought of as the entry-way to the château in *La Règle du jeu*. See interview in *Positif* 173 (Sept. 1975).

91. Jean Renoir, cited in Durgnat, *Jean Renoir*, 179.

92. Lourié, *My Work in Films*, 49.

93. Graham Greene, *Graham Greene on Film: Collected Film Criticism 1935–1940*, 220.

94. See especially Poulle, *Renoir 1938*, 39–46.

95. Durgnat, *Jean Renoir*, 181.

96. Sicard, "Martin du Gard et *La Bête humaine*," 84–88.

97. This is how, according to Faulkner, François Poulle characterizes the film. See Faulkner, *Jean Renoir*, 228.

CHAPTER 10
THE MYTH OF POETIC REALISM

1. A good example was the poll conducted by the French Academy of Cinema Arts and Techniques taken in 1979 to mark the fiftieth anniversary of sound cinema. Following *Les Enfants du paradis* was *La Grande Illusion*, *Casque d'or*, *La Règle du jeu*, and *La Kermesse héroïque*. *Le Quai des brumes* placed ninth. This poll was reported in *Variety*, 14 Feb. 1979, 56.

2. Edward Baron Turk, *Child of Paradise: Marcel Carné and the Golden Age of French Cinema*, 219.

3. Jean-Pierre Jeancolas, *15 Ans d'années trente: le cinéma des français 1929–1944*, 330.

4. André Bazin, "Carné et la désincarnation," *Esprit* 19, no. 9 (Sept. 1951). This essay is translated as "The Disincarnation of Carné," trans. John Shepley, in *Rediscovering French Film*, ed. Mary Lea Bandy, 132.

5. Bazin's remarks about Carné's evolution were written with the 1951 *Juliette ou la clef des songes* in mind; still his belief in the mismatch of Carné's themes to the social mentality applies to the Vichy period as well. He would certainly be suspicious when Jeancolas, *15 Ans d'années trente*, 8, claims that "the cinema of Vichy, if it exists at all, resembles more that which preceded it than that which followed it in its form and in its rapport with audiences."

6. Walter Jackson Bate, Introduction to Schiller's essay "On Naive and Sentimental Poetry," collected in Bate's anthology, *Criticism: The Major Texts* (New York: Harcourt Brace, 1952), 407. Schiller's essay originally appeared in 1795.

7. Bazin, "The Disincarnation of Carné," 131–35.

8. My conception of melodrama is beholden to Peter Brooks's classic study, *The Melodramatic Imagination* (New Haven: Yale University Press, 1976).

9. The many studies of these two actors are summarized by Turk in *Child of Paradise*, chap. 11.

10. Brooks, *The Melodramatic Imagination*, chap. 3.

11. Marcel Oms, "*Les Enfants du paradis*: la mutation cinématographique du mélodrame," *Les Cahiers de la cinémathèque* 28 (1978): 143.

12. Brooks, *The Melodramatic Imagination*, 28.

13. For example, Oms concludes his essay, "*Les Enfants du paradis*," by stating that Carné "perpetuates a Hugoesque vision of spectacle" (146).

14. Turk disputes this view to some extent by demonstrating the "incompleteness" of the film's plots as well as the relative autonomy of most of its sequences. See his *Child of Paradise*, 230–33.

15. Brooks, *The Melodramatic Imagination*, 8.

16. Oms, "*Les Enfants du paradis*," 146.

17. Turk, *Child of Paradise*, 220.

18. For a discussion of this process in relation to the musical, see Jane Feuer, *The Hollywood Musical* (Bloomington: Indiana University Press, 1982).

19. Brooks explicitly opposes melodrama to allegory and to naturalism. The latter genres expose the hidden structures (religious or scientific) that determine their tales, while melodrama unfolds in mystery, the narrator, characters, and audience groping for glimpses of significance. See his *Melodramatic Imagination*, chap. 1, especially 12, 22.

20. *Les Enfants du paradis* stages this in its final scene wherein all of Paris dresses as Pierrot.

21. Turk, *Child of Paradise*, 357.

22. Ibid., 360.

23. This apt characterization comes from ibid., 357.

24. James Agee, *The Nation*, 12 Apr. 1947, reprinted in *Agee on Film* (Boston: Beacon Press, 1964), 246.

25. Longing in each case is embodied in the figure of a woman. Not surprisingly, these women share key characteristics. Garance, child of Ménilmontant, orphaned young, is as gay as the flower she was named for. Françoise, likewise an orphan, likewise poor, is introduced bearing the flowers she is associated with throughout. And Michèle Morgan as

Nelly in *Le Quai des brumes* is also an orphan and is abused like the other heroines by her delinquent guardian.

26. Bazin, "The Destiny of Jean Gabin," in *What Is Cinema?* (Berkeley and Los Angeles: University of California Press, 1971), 2:178.

27. Marie-Claire Ropars developed an analysis of the film's credits in a presentation at Le Centre Americain du Cinéma in Paris, Dec. 1980.

28. Paul Ricoeur, *Soi-même comme un autre* (Paris: Seuil, 1990). This formulation begs the question of gender, too complex to be addressed here.

29. Turk, *Child of Paradise*, 343.

30. Paul Ricoeur, *Time and Narrative* (Chicago: University of Chicago Press, 1988), 3:158.

31. Bazin, "The Disincarnation of Carné," 132.

32. Ibid., 135.

CHAPTER 11

EPILOGUE: *LE TEMPS DES CERISES* AND THE FRUIT OF REGRET

1. Maureen Turim argues that poetic realism repeats the melodramatic core of the classics of French film of the twenties, in her essay "French Melodrama: Theory of a Specific History," *Theater Journal*, Oct. 1987, 327. The titles of the books by François Garçon (*De Blum à Pétain*) and Jean-Pierre Jeancolas (*15 Ans d'années trente*) give away their belief that French cinema continued on its settled paths, even after the fall of the Third Republic. We should also recall that Ginette Vincendeau's thesis calculates poetic realism as merely another genre concerned with "nostalgia."

2. Lionel Trilling, *Sincerity and Authenticity* (New York: Harcourt Brace, 1974).

3. See chap. 10 above. Michael Baxandall offers a variant of this hypothesis, applied directly to questions of art history, in his *Patterns of Intention* (New Haven: Yale University Press, 1985).

4. Trilling, *Sincerity and Authenticity*, 5–6.

5. This was François Truffaut's judgment in his famous 1954 article translated as "A Certain Tendency of the French Cinema," in *Movies and Methods*, ed. Bill Nichols (Berkeley and Los Angeles: University of California Press, 1976), 224–35. I repeat the judgment at the end of chap. 10 above.

6. *Godard on Godard*, ed. Tom Milne (New York: De Capo, 1986), 121.

7. See my Introduction to Jean-Luc Godard, *Breathless* (New Brunswick, N.J.: Rutgers University Press, 1987). There I cite, for example, a review in which Godard demolished Marcel Camus's *Orfeu negro* (1958) by using the Sartrean term "inauthenticity."

8. *Casque d'or*, we have already noted, placed third in a competition selecting the greatest French films of all time. It followed *Les Enfants du paradis* and *La Grande Illusion*. See n. 1 to chap. 10.

9. Jacques Rivette and François Truffaut, "Entretien avec Jacques Becker," *Cahiers du cinéma* 32 (6 Feb. 1954): 12.

10. Jean Couturier, *Fiche filmographique*, no. 113 (Paris: IDHEC, 1957), 10. See also the interview with Becker conducted by Rivette and Truffaut, "Entretien avec Jacques Becker," 13.

11. Truffaut, "A Certain Tendency of the French Cinema."

12. Simone Signoret, *Nostalgia Isn't What It Used to Be* (New York: Harper and Row, 1978), 107–10.

13. André Bazin confessed that he should have known better and that it was Lindsay Anderson who had pointed to the film's brilliance. See his *What Is Cinema?* (Berkeley and Los Angeles: University of California Press 1971), 2:91.

14. The opening of *Casque d'or* in fact recalls a half dozen Renoir canvases, including *Le Moulin de la Gallette* (1878), *The Girl in a Boat* (1877), *The Rowers' Lunch* (1879), *The Dance in the Country* (1883), *Le Bal à Bougival* (1883). Rowboats, dancers, drinking boatmen, trellised dance floors, and a riverside setting certify the reference to the great painter.

15. See Louis Chevalier, *Montmartre du plaisir et du crime* (Paris: Laffont, 1978).

16. The casquette of *Casque d'or* is a pertinent connotation expanding a title whose prime reference is to Marie's magnificent golden tresses.

17. The original script explicitly makes Manda an orphan. The film simply puts him in jail with Raymond for a number of years.

18. Raymond Bussières has pursued this vocation from the 1920s into our own era, appearing most recently in another film evoking the Popular Front ethos, Alain Tanner's *Jonas qui aura 25 ans en l'an 2000*, a film we shall have occasion to return to in this chapter.

19. Jonathan Buchsbaum, *Cinema Engagé: Film in the Popular Front*, 234.

20. Clément became a member of the Paris commune (Belleville district) and was exiled to England and Belgium for a decade after that. A celebrated socialist, he stands alongside Eugène Pottier who wrote the "Internationale" at just this time. Clément and Pottier are often linked. In 1924 their songs were published together in a German translation, *Französische Revolutionslieder* (Berlin: Malik Verlag). After his death, but in harmony with his life, this tune would sport radical new lyrics and a small but radical shift in title, "Le Temps des Crises." See M. Berbier, "Vers la Belle Epoque," in *Histoire de France par les chansons* (Paris: Gallimard, 1959), 3:80.

21. On the notion of "partial utopia" conveyed by music in film, see Caryl Flinn, *Strains of Utopia: Gender, Nostalgia, and Hollywood Film Music* (Princeton: Princeton University Press, 1992).

22. Jean Queval, *Jacques Becker*, 46.

23. Screenplay by John Berger and Alain Tanner, *Jonah Who Will Be 25 in the Year 2000*, trans. Michael Palmer (Berkeley: North Atlantic Books, 1983), 106.

24. I am certainly not the first to recognize Alain Tanner as a disciple of Renoir. See Andrew Horton, "Alain Tanner's *Jonah* . . . : Echoes of Renoir's *M. Lange*," *Film Criticism* 4, no. 3 (Fall 1979): 25–36.

25. "Equilibrium" is the term Jean-Louis Comolli employs in his article on *La Marseillaise* in *Cahiers du cinéma* 196 (Dec. 1967): 24–26.

26. The noted art critic and writer John Berger is responsible for the film's screenplay.

27. Berger and Tanner, *Jonah Who Will Be 25 in the Year 2000*, 38–40.

28. See Christopher Faulkner, *Jean Renoir: A Guide to References and Resources*, 110.

Bibliography

THIS BIBLIOGRAPHY gathers together the principal books, catalogs, and full issues of journals that I consulted. Journal articles, including key reconsiderations of French film, can be gleaned from the notes. The notes also indicate the journals of the period that I systematically examined.

Abel, Richard. *French Cinema: The First Wave, 1915–1929*. Princeton: Princeton University Press, 1984.

————, ed. *French Film Theory and Criticism: A History/Anthology 1907–1939*. 2 vols. Princeton: Princeton University Press, 1988.

Agel, Henri. *Jean Grémillon*. Paris: Seghers, 1969. 2d ed. Paris: Lherminier, 1984.

A la rencontre de Jacques Prévert. St. Paul de Vence: Fondation Maeght, 1987.

Albrecht, Donald. *Designing Dreams: Modern Architecture in the Movies*. New York: Harper, 1986.

Amengual, Barthélemy. *René Clair*. Paris: Seghers, 1969.

Andrew, Dudley. *Film in the Aura of Art*. Princeton: Princeton University Press, 1984.

Anthologie du cinéma. Vol. 2. Paris: L'Avant-Scène, 1967. Chapters on Becker, Cocteau, Epstein, Feuillade, Feyder, Grémillon, Guitry, Vigo.

Aranda, Francisco. *Luis Buñuel: A Critical Biography*. Translated and edited by David Robinson. New York: Da Capo, 1976. Originally published as *Luis Buñuel: biografía crítica*. Barcelona: Lumen, 1969.

Armes, Roy. *French Cinema*. New York: Oxford University Press, 1985.

Artaud, Antonin. *A propos du cinéma*. Paris: Gallimard, 1961.

Aumont, Jean-Pierre. *Sun and Shadow*. Translated by Bruce Benderson. New York: Norton, 1977. Originally published as *Le Soleil et les ombres*. Paris: Opera Mundi, 1976.

Auric, Georges. *Quand j'étais là*. Paris: Grasset, 1979.

Autant-Lara, Claude. *Les Fourgons du malheur: mes années avec Jacques Prévert*. Paris: Carrere, 1987.

————. *La Rage dans le coeur*. Paris: Veyrier, 1984.

Bachy, Victor. *Jacques Feyder: artisan du cinéma, 1885–1948*. Louvain, Belgium: Librairie Universitaire de Louvain, 1968.

Baker, William E. *Jacques Prévert*. Boston: Twayne, 1967.

Bandy, Mary Lea, ed. *Rediscovering French Film*. New York: Museum of Modern Art, 1983.

Bardèche, Maurice, and Robert Brasillach. *The History of Motion Pictures*. Translated by Iris Barry. New York: Museum of Modern Art, 1938. The updated and final French version is *Histoire du cinéma*. 2 vols. Givors: A. Martel, 1953–1954.

Barrault, Jean-Louis. *Souvenirs pour demain*. Paris: Seuil, 1972.

Barrot, Olivier. *René Clair, ou le temps mesuré*. Paris: Hatier, 1985.

Barsacq, Léon. *Caligari's Cabinet and Other Grand Illusions*. Translated by Michael Bullock. Boston: New York Graphic Society, 1976. Originally published as *Le Décor de film*. Paris: Seghers, 1970.

Baudry, Pierre, and Enzo Ungari, eds. *I film di Marcel Pagnol.* Venice: La Biennale di Venezia, 1979.

Bazin, André. *Jean Renoir.* Translated by W. W. Halsey II and William H. Simon. New York: Simon, 1973. Originally published as *Jean Renoir.* Paris: Champ Libre, 1971.

Bertin, Célia. *Jean Renoir: A Life in Pictures.* Baltimore: Johns Hopkins University Press, 1991. Originally published as *Jean Renoir.* Paris: Librairie Académique Perrin, 1986.

Bessy, Maurice. *Les Passagers du souvenir.* Paris: Albin Michel, 1977.

Beylie, Claude. *Marcel Pagnol, ou le cinéma en liberté.* 2d ed., Paris: Lherminier, 1986.

Blakeway, Claire. *Jacques Prévert: Popular French Theatre and Cinema.* Cranbury, N.J.: Associated University Presses, 1990.

Brasseur, Pierre. *Ma vie en vrac.* Paris: Calmann-Lévy, 1972.

Braudy, Leo. *Jean Renoir: The World of His Films.* Garden City, N.Y.: Doubleday, 1972.

Braunberger, Pierre. *Cinémamémoire.* Edited by Jacques Gerber. Paris: Editions du Centre Pompidou et Centre National de la Cinématographie, 1987.

Brownlow, Kevin. *"Napoleon": Abel Gance's Classic Film.* New York: Knopf, 1983.

Brunius, Jacques. *En marge du cinéma français.* Paris: Arcanes, 1954.

Buache, Freddy. *Claude Autant-Lara.* Lausanne: L'Age d'Homme, 1982.

Buchsbaum, Jonathan. *Cinema Engagé: Film in the Popular Front.* Urbana: University of Illinois Press, 1988.

Buñuel, Luis. *My Last Sigh.* Translated by Abigail Israel. New York: Vintage, 1984. Originally published as *Mon dernier soupir.* Paris: Robert Laffont, 1982.

Burch, Noël. *Marcel L'Herbier.* Paris: Seghers, 1973.

Butzel, Marcia. *Illuminating Movements: The Choreographic Aspect of Cinema.* Champaigne-Urbana: University of Illinois Press, 1995.

Caldicott, C.E.J. *Marcel Pagnol.* Boston: G. K. Hall, 1977.

Carné, Marcel. *La Vie à belles dents.* Paris: Jean-Pierre Ollivier, 1975.

Castans, Raymond. *Fernandel m'a raconté.* Paris: La Table Ronde, 1976.

———. *Les Films de Marcel Pagnol.* Paris: Juillard, 1982.

Cathala, Josée. *Louis Jouvet.* Paris: Veyrier, 1989.

Chardère, Bernard, ed. *Jean Renoir.* Premier Plan 22–24. Lyon: SERDOC, May 1962.

Chazal, Robert. *Marcel Carné.* Paris: Seghers, 1965.

Chenal, Pierre. *Souvenirs du cinéaste.* Paris: Dujarric, 1987.

Chirat, Raymond. *Catalogue des films français de long métrage: films sonores de fiction 1929–1939.* 2d ed. Brussels: Cinémathèque Royale de Belgique, 1981.

———. *Catalogue des films français de long métrage: films de fiction 1940–1950.* Luxembourg: Imprimerie Saint-Paul, 1981.

———. *Le Cinéma français des années 30.* Paris: Hatier, 1983.

———. *Julien Duvivier.* Premier Plan 50. Lyon: SERDOC, Dec. 1968.

Chirat, Raymond, and Roger Icart. *Catalogue des films français de long métrage: films de fiction 1919–1929.* Toulouse: Cinémathèque de Toulouse, 1984.

Clair, René. *Cinema Yesterday and Today.* Edited by R. C. Dale. Translated by Stanley Appelbaum. New York: Dover, 1972. Originally published as *Cinéma d'hier, cinéma d'aujourd'hui.* Paris: Gallimard, 1970.

Colette. *Colette at the Movies.* Edited by Alain Virmaux and Odette Virmaux. Translated by Sarah W. R. Smith. New York: Frederick Ungar, 1980. Originally published as *Colette au cinéma.* Paris: Flammarion, 1975.

Courtade, Francis. *Les Malédictions du cinéma français.* Paris: Alain Moreau, 1978.

Crisp, Colin. *The Classic French Cinema, 1930–1960*. Bloomington: Indiana University Press, 1993.

Dalio, Marcel. *Mes années folles*. Edited by Jean-Pierre de Lucovich. Paris: Ramsay, 1986.

de Comes, Philippe, and Michel Marmin, eds. *Le Cinéma français 1930–1960*. Paris: Atlas, 1984.

Delluc, Louis. *Photogénie*. Paris: Grasset, 1920.

Desanti, Dominique. *Sacha Guitry, cinquante ans de spectacle*. Paris: Grasset, 1982.

Diamant-Berger, Henri. *Il était une fois le cinéma*. Paris: Editions Jean-Claude Simoën, 1977.

Dogliani, Patrizia, et al., eds. *Francia anni '30: cinema, cultura, storia*. Venice: Marsilio, 1982.

Dumont, Hervé. *Robert Siodmak, le maître du film noir*. Lausanne: L'Age d'Homme, 1981.

Durgnat, Raymond. *Jean Renoir*. Berkeley and Los Angeles: University of California Press, 1974.

Ehrlich, Evelyn. *Cinema of Paradox: French Filmmaking under the German Occupation*. New York: Columbia University Press, 1985.

Escobar, Roberto, and Vittorio Giacci. *Il cinema del Fronte Populare: Francia 1934–37*. Rome: Bulzone, 1990.

Esslin, Martin. *Antonin Artaud*. London: Penguin, 1977.

Faulkner, Christopher. *Jean Renoir: A Guide to References and Resources*. Boston: G. K. Hall, 1979.

————. *The Social Cinema of Jean Renoir*. Princeton: Princeton University Press, 1986.

Fauré, Michel. *Le Groupe Octobre*. Paris: Christian Bourgois, 1977.

Fescourt, Henri. *La Foi et les montagnes, ou le septième art au passé*. Paris: Paul Montel, 1959. Reprint. Plan de la Tour: Editions d'Aujourd'hui, 1980.

Flitterman-Lewis, Sandy. *To Desire Differently: Feminism and the French Cinema*. Urbana: University of Illinois Press, 1990.

Fondane, Benjamin. *Ecrits pour le cinéma*. Edited by Michel Carassou. Paris: Plasma, 1984.

Ford, Charles. *Jacques Feyder*. Paris: Seghers, 1973.

Frank, Nino. *Petit Cinéma sentimental*. Paris: La Nouvelle Edition, 1950.

Garçon, François. *De Blum à Pétain: cinéma et société française (1936–1944)*. Paris: Cerf, 1984.

Gauteur, Claude. *Jean Renoir: la double méprise (1925–1939)*. Paris: Français Réunis, 1980.

Gauteur, Claude, and Ginette Vincendeau. *Jean Gabin: anatomie d'un mythe*. Paris: Nathan, 1993.

Gilliatt, Penelope. *Jean Renoir: Essays, Conversations, Reviews*. New York: McGraw, 1975.

Gilson, René. *Des Mots et merveilles, Jacques Prévert*. Paris: Pierre Belfond, 1990.

Giroud, Françoise. *Si je mens . . . .* Paris: Stock, 1972.

Gomes, P. E. Salles. *Jean Vigo*. Berkeley and Los Angeles: University of California Press, 1971.

Grangier, Gilles. *Flash-Back*. Paris: Presses de la Cité, 1977.

Greene, Graham. *Graham Greene on Film: Collected Film Criticism 1935–1940*. Edited by John Russell Taylor. New York: Simon and Schuster, 1972.

Guillaume-Grimaud, Geneviève. *Le Cinéma du Front Populaire*. Paris: Lherminier, 1986.

Guillot, Gerard. *Les Prévert*. Paris: Seghers, 1966.

Guitry, Sacha. *Le Cinéma et moi*. 2d ed. Paris: Ramsay, 1984.

Guth, Paul. *Michel Simon*. Paris: Calmann-Lévy, 1951.

Hammond, Paul, ed. *The Shadow and Its Shadow: Surrealist Writings on Cinema*. London: British Film Institute, 1978.

Hanoteau, Guillaume. *L'Age d'or de St. Germain de Près*. Paris: Denoël, 1965.

Hayward, Susan. *French National Cinema*. London: Routledge, 1993.

Hayward, Susan, and Ginette Vincendeau, eds. *French Film: Texts and Contexts*. London: Routledge, 1990.

Icart, Roger. *Abel Gance ou le Prométhée foudroyé*. Lausanne: L'Age d'Homme, 1983.

Jackson, Julian. *The Popular Front in France*. Cambridge: Cambridge University Press, 1988.

Jacob, Guy. *Jacques Prévert*. Premier Plan 14. Lyon: SERDOC, Nov. 1960.

Jeancolas, Jean-Pierre. *15 Ans d'années trente: le cinéma des français 1929–1944*. Paris: Stock, 1983.

Jeanne, René, and Charles Ford. *Abel Gance*. Paris: Seghers, 1963.

King, Norman. *Abel Gance: A Politics of Spectacle*. London: British Film Institute, 1984.

Knapp, Bettina. *Louis Jouvet: Man of the Theater*. New York: Columbia University Press, 1957.

Kramer, Steven Philip, and James Michael Welsh. *Abel Gance*. Boston: G. K. Hall, 1978.

Kuenzli, Rudolf E., ed. *Dada and Surrealist Film*. New York: Willis, Locker and Owens, 1987.

Kyrou, Ado. *Le Surréalisme au cinéma*. Paris: Arcanes, 1953.

Lacassin, Francis. *Louis Feuillade*. Paris: Seghers, 1964.

———. *Pour une contre-histoire du cinéma*. Paris: Union Générale d'Editions, 1972.

Lagnan, Pierre, ed. *Les Années Pagnol*. Renens: 5 Continents; Paris: Hatier, 1989.

Lagny, Michèle, Marie-Claire Ropars, and Pierre Sorlin. *Générique des années 30*. Paris: Presses Universitaires de Vincennes, 1986.

Lang, André. *Tiers de siècle*. Paris: Plon, 1936.

Langlois, Georges P., and Glenn Myrent. *Henri Langlois: premier citoyen du cinéma*. Paris: Denoël, 1986.

Lapierre, Marcel. *Les Cent Visages du cinéma*. Paris: Grasset, 1948.

Leenhardt, Roger. *Chroniques de cinéma*. Paris: L'Etoile, 1986.

———. *Les Yeux ouverts: entretiens avec Jean Lacouture*. Paris: Seuil, 1979.

Leglise, Paul. *Histoire de la politique du cinéma français: le Cinéma et la Troisième République*. Paris: Librairie Générale de Droit et de Jurisprudence, 1970.

———. *Histoire de la politique du cinéma français 2: le Cinéma entre deux républiques (1940–1946)*. Paris: Lherminier, 1977.

L'Herbier, Marcel. *Intelligence du cinématographe*. Paris: Corrêa, 1946.

———. *La Tête qui tourne*. Paris: Belfond, 1979.

Lherminier, Pierre. *Jean Vigo*. Paris: Lherminier, 1984.

Lourié Eugène. *My Work in Films*. San Diego: Harcourt, Brace, Jovanovich, 1985.

Mac Orlan, Pierre. *Mac Orlan et le cinéma*. Reims: Maison de la Culture André Malraux, 1982.

———. *Masques sur mésure, essais*. Paris: Gallimard, 1965.

Magazine littéraire, no. 155. Dec. 1979 (issue devoted to Jacques Prévert).

Martin, John W. *The Golden Age of French Cinema 1929–1939*. Boston: Twayne, 1983.

Matthews, J. H. *Surrealism and Film*. Ann Arbor: University of Michigan Press, 1971.

Mény, Jacques. *Jean Giono et le cinéma*. Paris: Jean-Claude Simoën, 1978.

Michalczyk, John J. *The French Literary Filmmakers*. Cranbury, N.J.: Associated University Presses, 1980.

Milhaud, Darius. *Ma Vie heureuse*. Paris: Belfond, 1987.

Mirande, Yves. *Souvenirs*. Paris: Librarie Arthème Fayard, 1952.

Mitry, Jean. *Histoire du cinéma*. Vol. 3, *1923–1930*. Paris: Editions Universitaires, 1973.

———. *Histoire du cinéma*. Vol. 4, *1930–1940*. Paris: Jean-Pierre Delarge, 1980.

Moussinac, Léon. *L'Age ingrat du cinéma*. Paris: Français Réunis, 1967.

―――. *Naissance du cinéma*. Paris: J. Povolozky, 1925.

Pagliano, Jean-Pierre. *Brunius*. Lausanne: L'Age d'Homme, 1987.

Pathé, Théophile. *Le Cinéma*. Paris: Corrêa, 1942.

Perrin, Michel. *Arletty*. Paris: Calmann-Lévy, 1952.

Philippe, Jean-Claude. *Le Roman du cinéma 1928–1938*. Paris: Arthème Fayard, 1984.

Pilard, Philippe. *Henri-Georges Clouzot*. Paris: Seghers, 1969.

Pinel, Vincent, and Frédérique Moreau. *Filmographie des longs métrages sonores du cinéma français*. Paris: Cinémathèque Française, 1985.

Porcile, François. *Maurice Jaubert, musicien populaire ou maudit?* Paris: Français Réunis, 1971.

Poulle, François. *Renoir 1938 ou Jean Renoir pour rien*. Paris: Cerf, 1969.

Prédal, René. *La Société française (1914–1945) à travers le cinéma*. Paris: Armand Colin, 1972.

Préjean, Albert. *The Sky and the Stars*. Translated by Virginia Graham. London: Harvill, 1956.

Préjean, Patrick. *Albert Préjean . . . .* Paris: Candeau, 1979.

Queval, Jean. *Jacques Becker*. Paris: Seghers, 1962.

Rachline, Michel. *Jacques Prévert: drôle de vie*. Paris: Ramsay, 1981.

Renaitour, Jean-Michel, ed. *Où va le cinéma français?* Paris: Bandinière, 1938.

Renoir, Jean. *Ecrits 1926–1971*. Edited by Claude Gauteur. Paris: Belfond, 1974.

―――. *My Life and My Films*. Translated by Norman Denny. New York: Atheneum, 1974. Originally published as *Ma vie et mes films*. Paris: Flammarion, 1974.

Rentschler, Eric, ed. *The Films of G. W. Pabst: An Extraterritorial Cinema*. New Brunswick, N.J.: Rutgers University Press, 1990.

Richebé, Roger. *Au-delà de l'écran: 70 ans de la vie d'un cinéaste*. Monte Carlo: Pastorelly, 1977.

Rosay, Françoise. *La Traversée d'une vie: souvenirs recueillis par Colette Mars*. Paris: Robert Laffont, 1974.

Roud, Richard. *A Passion for Films: Henri Langlois and the Cinémathèque Française*. New York: Viking, 1983.

Sadoul, Georges. *Chroniques du cinéma français*. Vol. 1. Paris: Union Générale d'Editions, 1979.

―――. *Le Cinéma français*. Paris: Flammarion, 1962.

―――. *French Film*. London: Falcon, 1953.

―――. *Histoire du cinéma mondial des origines à nos jours*. Paris: Flammarion, 1963.

―――. *Rencontres 1: chroniques et entretiens*. Edited by Bernard Eisenschitz. Paris: Denoël, 1984.

Sandro, Paul. *Diversions of Pleasure: Luis Buñuel and the Crisis of Desire*. Columbus: Ohio State University Press, 1987.

Sellier, Geneviève. *Les Enfants du paradis*. Paris: Nathan, 1993.

―――. *Jean Grémillon: le cinéma est à vous*. Paris: Klincksieck, 1989.

Serceau, Daniel. *Jean Renoir*. Paris: Edilig, 1985.

―――. *Jean Renoir: la sagesse du plaisir*. Paris: Cerf, 1985.

―――. *Jean Renoir, l'insurgé*. Paris: Le Sycomore, 1981.

―――. *"La Règle du jeu": Jean Renoir*. Limonest: L'Interdisciplinaire, 1989.

Sesonske, Alexander. *Jean Renoir: The French Films, 1924–1939*. Cambridge: Harvard University Press, 1980.

Simon, William G. *The Films of Jean Vigo*. Ann Arbor: University of Michigan Research Press, 1981.

Simsolo, Noël. *Sacha Guitry*. Paris: Cahiers du cinéma, 1988.

Smith, John M. *Jean Vigo*. New York: Praeger, 1972.

Soupault, Philippe. *Ecrits de cinéma, 1918–1931*. Edited by Odette Virmaux and Alain Virmaux. Paris: Plon, 1979.

Spaak, Janine. *Charles Spaak, mon mari*. Paris: France-Empire, 1977.

Strebel, Elizabeth Grottle. *French Social Cinema of the Nineteen Thirties: A Cinematographic Expression of Popular Front Consciousness*. New York: Arno, 1980.

Taves, Brian. *Robert Florey: The French Expressionist*. Metuchen, N.J.: Scarecrow, 1987.

Thiher, Allen. *The Cinematic Muse: Critical Studies in the History of French Cinema*. Columbia: University of Missouri Press, 1979.

Thirion, André. *Revolutionaries without Revolution*. New York: Macmillan, 1975. Originally published as *Révolution sans révolutionaires*. Paris: Robert Laffont, 1973.

Trauner, Alexandre. *Cinquante Ans de cinéma*. Paris: Jade, 1986.

Tual, Denise. *Au coeur du temps*. Paris: Carrere, 1987.

———. *Le Temps dévoré*. Paris: Arthème Fayard, 1980.

Turk, Edward Baron. *Child of Paradise: Marcel Carné and the Golden Age of French Cinema*. Cambridge: Harvard University Press, 1989.

Vincendeau, Ginette. "French Cinema in the 1930s: Social Text and Context of a Popular Entertainment Medium." Ph.D. diss., University of East Anglia, 1985.

Vincendeau, Ginette, and Keith Reader, eds. *La Vie est à Nous*. London: British Film Institute, 1986.

Virmaux, Alain, and Odette Virmaux. *Les Surréalists et le cinéma*. Paris: Seghers, 1976.

Viry-Babel, Roger. *Jean Renoir, films, textes, références*. Nancy: Presses Universitaires de Nancy, 1989.

Volk, Carol, trans. *Renoir on Renoir: Interviews, Essays, and Remarks*. Cambridge: Cambridge University Press, 1989. Originally published as *Jean Renoir: entretiens et propos*. Paris: L'Etoile, 1979.

Wakhevitch, Georges. *L'Envers des décors*. Paris: Robert Laffont, 1977.

Williams, Alan. *Republic of Images: A History of French Filmmaking*. Cambridge: Harvard University Press, 1992.

Williams, Linda. *Figures of Desire: A Theory and Analysis of Surrealist Film*. Urbana: University of Illinois Press, 1981.

Index of Film Titles

General Index